Best Practices in Adolescent Literacy Instruction

Solving Problems in the Teaching of Literacy

Cathy Collins Block, *Series Editor*

Best Practices in Adolescent Literacy Instruction

Edited by **Kathleen A. Hinchman**
and **Heather K. Sheridan-Thomas**

Foreword by
Donna E. Alvermann

THE GUILFORD PRESS
New York   London

© 2008 The Guilford Press
A Division of Guilford Publications, Inc.
72 Spring Street, New York, NY 10012
www.guilford.com

Printed in the United States of America

This book is printed on acid-free paper.

Last digit is print number: 9 8 7 6 5 4 3 2 1

Library of Congress Cataloging-in-Publication Data

Best practices in adolescent literacy instruction / edited by Kathleen A.
Hinchman, Heather K. Sheridan-Thomas.
    p. cm.–(Solving problems in the teaching of literacy)
  Includes bibliographical references and index.
  ISBN 978-1-59385-692-2 (pbk. : alk. paper)
  ISBN 978-1-59385-693-9 (cloth : alk. paper)
    1. Language arts (Secondary)–United States. 2. Language arts (Middle school)–
United States. 3. Language experience approach in education–United
States. I. Hinchman, Kathleen A. II. Sheridan-Thomas, Heather K.
  LB1631.B44 2008
  428.4071′2–dc22

                                                        2007052767

About the Editors

Kathleen A. Hinchman, PhD, is Professor and Chair of the Reading and Language Arts Center at Syracuse University. A former middle school teacher, she has published her work in many journals and books, and is coauthor of *Teaching Adolescents Who Struggle with Reading.* Her current work is concerned with literacy-related middle school reform.

Heather K. Sheridan-Thomas, EdD, is Assistant Superintendent for Curriculum, Assessment, and Instruction for the Tompkins–Seneca–Tioga Board of Cooperative Educational Services, in Ithaca, New York. Formerly a teacher education professor, public school administrator, and secondary teacher, her research focuses on adolescents' multiple literacies and addressing achievement gaps for underserved students.

Contributors

Donna E. Alvermann, PhD, is University of Georgia Appointed Distinguished Research Professor of Language and Literacy Education. She teaches courses in adolescent literacy and young people's interests in popular culture. A former classroom teacher in Texas and New York, she is currently conducting research on high school students' online literate practices.

Patricia L. Anders, PhD, is Department Head and a Professor in the Department of Language, Reading and Culture at the College of Education, University of Arizona. Her scholarship focuses on adolescent literacy and teacher education.

Fenice B. Boyd, PhD, is an Associate Professor of Literacy Education at the University at Buffalo, State University of New York. She is a former music and reading teacher at the middle school level. Her research interests include adolescents' literacy learning and practices in and out of school, issues of diversity, and use of multiple text types to enhance conceptual understandings.

Karen Bromley, PhD, is a Distinguished Teaching Professor in the School of Education at Binghamton University, State University of New York, where she teaches courses in literacy instruction and assessment, children's literature, and writing. She was a third-grade teacher and a K–8 reading specialist in New York and Maryland.

Rachel Brown, PhD, a former middle school learning specialist, is an Assistant Professor and Director of the Literacy Education Master's Programs in the Reading and Language Arts Center at Syracuse University. She conducts research and publishes in the area of comprehension strategies instruction, self-regulated learning, and literacy and technology.

Kelly Chandler-Olcott, EdD, is an Associate Professor in the Reading and Language Arts Center at Syracuse University, where she directs the English Education Program. A former secondary English and social studies teacher, she has conducted research on content-area literacy, teachers' classroom-based inquiry, and adolescents' technology-mediated literacy practices.

Mark W. Conley, PhD, coordinates the undergraduate and graduate literacy programs in the Department of Teacher Education at Michigan State University. His research is in literacy assessment, content-area literacy, and literacy policy. He is author of *Connecting Standards and Assessment through Literacy* and *Content Area Literacy: Learners in Context.*

Deborah R. Dillon, PhD, is a Professor of Literacy Education at the University of Minnesota. Her research focuses on the literacy practices of teachers and learners, including the role of motivation in engaged reading. Her work has been published in major educational journals and funded by the National Science Foundation and the U.S. Department of Education.

Douglas Fisher, PhD, is a Professor of Language and Literacy Education at San Diego State University. A former staff development specialist, he has published in many journals and books, including *Creating Literacy-Rich Schools for Adolescents* and *Checking for Understanding: Formative Assessments for Your Classroom.* His current work is focused on instructional frameworks and schoolwide initiatives.

Nancy Frey, PhD, is an Associate Professor of Teacher Education at San Diego State University. A former teacher from Broward County, Florida, she focuses her work on struggling readers and writers in secondary schools. She is the coauthor of *Better Learning through Structured Teaching* and *Language Learners in the English Classroom.*

Cynthia Greenleaf, PhD, codirects the Strategic Literacy Initiative at WestEd, where she leads the initiative's research and development efforts focused on promoting higher-level literacy for diverse youth. Her research has been integral to the development of the Reading Apprenticeship framework, the central organizing principle of the Strategic Literacy Initiative.

Kathleen A. Hinchman, PhD (see "About the Editors").

Gay Ivey, PhD, a former middle school reading specialist, is an Associate Professor of Reading Education at James Madison University, Harrisonburg, Virginia. Her scholarship reconceptualizes classrooms to make them more responsive to the needs of inexperienced readers and writers. She has published numerous articles on adolescent literacy and is coauthor of *Creating Literacy-Rich Schools for Adolescents.*

Janelle Johnson, MA, is currently a doctoral student in the Department of Language, Reading, and Culture at the University of Arizona.

Cindy Litman, MS, is a Senior Research Associate with WestEd's Strategic Literacy Initiative. She has performed multiple research and development roles for elementary, secondary, and after-school literacy initiatives for over 15 years, with a special focus on the relationship between social, emotional, and intellectual/literacy development.

Elizabeth Birr Moje, PhD, is an Arthur F. Thurnau Professor of Literacy, Language, and Culture in Educational Studies at the University of Michigan, Ann Arbor, and a Faculty Associate in the Institute for Social Research and in Latino/a Studies. Her research focuses on academic and youth literacy skills, practices, and texts.

David W. Moore, PhD, is a Professor of Education at Arizona State University, where he teaches secondary school teacher-education courses. His vita shows a 25-year publication record that balances research reports, professional articles, and books. He cochaired the International Reading Association Commission on Adolescent Literacy from 2000 to 2004.

David G. O'Brien, PhD, is a Professor of Literacy Education at the University of Minnesota. His areas of research include adolescent literacy, secondary reading, reading in the disciplines, and motivation and engagement in reading. He is the author of numerous publications, and his research has been funded by the U.S. Department of Education.

Eliane Rubinstein-Ávila, PhD, an Assistant Professor at the University of Arizona, was formerly a bilingual teacher in California. Her research focuses on immigrant youths' literacy practices in and out of school contexts, and she has published articles across a range of academic journals.

Cynthia Hynd Shanahan, PhD, is a Professor of Literacy, Language, and Culture and Executive Director of the Council on Teacher Education at the University of Illinois at Chicago. She is currently working on a Carnegie-funded project to create strategies derived from the approaches of disciplinary experts.

Heather K. Sheridan-Thomas, EdD (see "About the Editors").

Jennifer Speyer, BA, is a first-year teacher, having recently graduated from the University of Michigan with a BA in history and a secondary teaching certificate.

Alfred W. Tatum, PhD, is an Associate Professor in the Curriculum and Instruction Department at the University of Illinois at Chicago. His research foci are the literacy development of African American adolescent males, adolescent literacy, and teacher professional development in urban middle schools and high schools. He authored *Teaching Reading to Black Adolescent Males: Closing the Achievement Gap.*

Codruta Temple, MA, a finishing doctoral student at Syracuse University, is Visiting Assistant Professor at the State University of New York at Cortland, where she teaches courses in foreign language methods and bilingual and multicultural education. Her research focuses primarily on adolescents' acquisition of subject-specific discourses.

Mary K. Thompson, PhD, is an Assistant Professor of Literacy Education at the University at Buffalo, State University of New York. As a former middle and high school teacher, her research examines youth popular culture and its place inside the classroom. Her current work explores multimodality as a pedagogical tool for content-area teachers.

Dana J. Wilber, EdD, is an Assistant Professor of Literacy at Montclair State University. A former seventh-grade balanced literacy teacher, she has published in several journals and books, including the *Handbook of Literacy and Technology* and *Theoretical Models and Processes of Reading.* Her research concerns new literacies and adolescents.

Shelley Hong Xu, EdD, is a Professor of Teacher Education at California State University, Long Beach, where she teaches in the doctoral, master's, and teaching credential programs. Her research includes integrating multimedia texts into literacy curriculum. She coauthored *Trading Cards to Comic Strips: Popular Culture Texts and Literacy Learning in Grades K–8.*

Foreword

Books on adolescent literacy are in greater abundance today than ever before. Books that offer "straight talk" about the most enduring issues in adolescent literacy instruction are still rare, however, and *Best Practices in Adolescent Literacy Instruction* is among the rarest. Why this claim, and what evidence supports it?

Rarely does one find, in a single edited volume, the array of expertise displayed here. The chapter authors, each of whom I know and hold in high regard, provide workable and well-researched approaches to understanding and acting on the curricular and programmatic issues that need attention if adolescent literacy instruction is to serve youth well. Rising above the rhetoric that is prevalent in the current era of high-stakes testing and teacher accountability, the ideas expressed here are refreshing for the new and practical insights they bring to bear on topics that are high on the list of priorities among most classroom teachers, teacher educators, literacy coaches, curriculum supervisors, and administrators responsible for adolescent literacy instruction.

Beyond its potential for reaching targeted audiences that can make a difference in young people's lives, *Best Practices in Adolescent Literacy Instruction* promises to be a book that won't easily find its way into the used text market. This book is a keeper. Its contents are accessible and flexibly retrieved. As I read prepublication copies of the chapters, I found that I could dip into information at will and on at least two levels: by following the logical sequencing of the chapters or by choosing a topic (e.g., motivation) and then tracing it through the various "dressings" that authors writing from different perspectives and contexts gave it. And it was those dressings that made the topic real—for adolescent literacy instruction is neither monolithic nor lacking in nuance.

Perhaps what is most unique about this edited volume is the way in which the authors' voices enliven the printed text. No vanilla-like pronouncements here. Instead, authoritative statements are tinged with passion, empathy, humor, and, most important, a sense that these authors have all walked the walk before talking the talk. Voices relatively new to the field mingle with those of earlier times to communicate the urgency of responding in culturally relevant ways to young people's literacy needs in academic settings and beyond. In some ways, I sense that the editors of *Best Practices in Adolescent Literacy Instruction* knew that the window of opportunity for communicating this message might be narrow.

If this supposition on my part is accurate—if policies governing how teachers will teach in the middle grades and above are the next wrinkle in education reform—then *Best Practices* may well become the authoritative source to which advocates of adolescent literacy instruction and support staff for policymakers turn when in need of guidance. In the interim, *Best Practices* is certain to advance the education field's understanding of, and respect for, the incredibly rich and complex set of experiences that the authors of this text bring to the table. Encouragement is its watchword; commitment to young people, its ultimate goal.

DONNA E. ALVERMANN, PhD
University of Georgia

Preface

As public school and university educators with many years of adolescent literacy experience, we continue to be surprised and excited by recent interest in the topic. Frankly, we remember conference sessions when we were the only attendees, but this no longer happens. A host of private foundations and federal initiatives now emphasize the need to attend to the literacy development of students beyond third grade—especially addressing the needs of those who struggle to develop the skills and strategies they need for successful adulthood or who disengage with school entirely. Consequently, more and more educators are addressing the literacy needs of grades 5 to 12 students. This book is a comprehensive edited volume that is designed to support these efforts.

The full title of this text, *Best Practices in Adolescent Literacy Instruction*, is intended to suggest its comprehensive contents. We note, with some irony, that the phrase *best practices* can be contentious in the adolescent literacy literature because it hints of instructional practices suited to all youth, despite the fact that our youths are most concerned with individuality and show a wide array of differences in backgrounds, needs, and interests. Even so, research on literacy instruction does, indeed, either directly support or suggest a variety of tools that can be used selectively by responsive teachers to scaffold youths' development of self-regulated reading, writing, and alternative communication. We refer to *best practices* to signal the presence of such tools, not to suggest that standardized practices be used with every youth.

Much research into the social nature of adolescence helps us understand how we construct identity as we move through adolescence—including constructions of self as competent in some, but not other, settings. Another part of our title, *adolescent literacy*, is meant to suggest the importance of such social aspects of youths' widely varying daily literacy practices in and out of school. Considering the social world helps us to shape

xiii

best practice that acknowledges and builds upon youths' expertise in realistic, useful, and engaging ways.

However, we also use the term *adolescent literacy* with caution. We empathize with those who dislike the term *adolescent* because it implies individuals who are not yet adult and are, instead, bubbling, conflicted masses of hormones (Lesko, 2001). The term *adolescent literacy* can carry an especially pejorative connotation of a not-yet-fully-formed ability to read and write. At the same time, we realize that the label can also focus educators' gaze on individuals' full complement of in-school and out-of-school literacy practices instead of on the narrower concerns suggested by such descriptions as secondary school reading or content-area literacy. We wish to align ourselves with efforts to help youths develop a full array of literacy practices.

Part I, Perspectives toward Adolescent Literacy Instruction, introduces a sampling of youths' complex enactments of adolescent literacy. This collection of chapters helps us to understand the literacies of youths whose identity constructions are aligned with quite varied social purposes, including those tied to race, age, language, location, and interest. In "Discussing Texts with Adolescents in Culturally Responsive Ways," Alfred W. Tatum leads off the volume by explaining the value of developing culturally grounded text lineages. Eliane Rubinstein-Ávila and Janelle Johnson suggest the importance of instruction that begins with adolescents' existing linguistic strengths in "Meaningful Content for Middle School Students for Whom English Is an *Additional* Language." What the research says about designing instruction at the intersection of youths' personal and academic lives is addressed in Shelley Hong Xu's chapter, "Rethinking Literacy Learning and Teaching: Intersections of Adolescents' In-School and Out-of-School Literacy Practices." That the lives of many youths are constructed from a tapestry woven on the World Wide Web is Dana J. Wilber's important topic in "iLife: Understanding and Connecting to the Digital Literacies of Adolescents." David G. O'Brien and Deborah R. Dillon's chapter, "The Role of Motivation in Engaged Reading of Adolescents," answers many teachers' most important questions about their work with older, seemingly unmotivated, youth.

Part II, Developing Reading and Writing Strategies for Multiple Contexts, contains recommendations for developing print literacies across and within social contexts. In "Actively Engaging Middle School Students with Words," Karen Bromley focuses on vocabulary development strategies that encourage student independence. Rachel Brown reminds us that our evolving insights about media and meaning construction necessitate strategic reading comprehension instruction in "Strategy Matters: Comprehension Instruction for Older Youth." Cynthia Hynd Shanahan leads us to consider strategies for "Reading and Writing across Multiple Texts." Fenice B. Boyd and Mary K. Thompson delineate methods for integrating multimodal texts in discipline-specific study in "Multimodality and Literacy Learning: Using Multiple Texts to Enhance Content-Area Learning." Heather K. Sheridan-Thomas adds "Assisting Struggling Readers with Textbook Comprehension," a reminder that those who struggle with academic literacies require guidance to access a continuing mainstay of content-area instruction: the textbook. Elizabeth Birr Moje and Jennifer Speyer show us how to deal with "The Reality of Challenging Texts in High School Science and Social Studies: How Teachers Can Mediate Comprehension." Kelly Chandler-Olcott explains literacy instructional opportunities available in "Humanities Instruction for Adolescent Literacy Learners." In the concluding chapter in this section, "Fostering Acquisition of Official Mathematics Language," Codruta Temple and Kathleen A. Hinchman help us to invite youths to learn the nuances of subject-specific language, such as that involved in mathematics study.

Part III, Adolescent Literacy Program Issues, explains how to deal with programmatic aspects of orchestrating literacy instruction for our older youths. Gay Ivey explains what to do in "Intervening When Older Youth Struggle with Reading." In "Instructional Moves That Support Adolescent Learners Who Have Histories of Failure," Douglas Fisher and Nancy Frey advise us of ways to include all students in our literacy instructional support. Cindy Litman and Cynthia Greenleaf show us how such supports yield success in one high school science class, in "Traveling Together over Difficult Ground: Negotiating Success with a Profoundly Inexperienced Reader in an Introduction to Chemistry Class." Mark W. Conley challenges us to consider carefully the role of assessment in our literacy and program development in "Literacy Assessment for Adolescents: What's Fair about It?," and David W. Moore advises us of ways to organize schoolwide programs in "Program Development." Finally, in "Multiple Dimensions of Adolescent Literacy Teacher Education," Patricia L. Anders helps us to consider organizing teacher education to foster implementation of the principles represented in this book.

We began this text by inviting contributing authors to share ideas for literacy instruction that cognitive and sociocultural research suggests is engaging and effective for youth in grades 5-12. We are most pleased with the resulting contributions, which represent very important ideas for adolescent literacy instruction and program development. Some of this work may seem more applicable to discipline-specific study, and some to academic literacy classes. Some of the suggestions may seem more appropriate to upper elementary and middle schools, and some may seem more suitable to high schools. We urge you to consider the principles and practices presented, and to design alternative literacy instruction suited to the needs and inclinations of youths with whom you work—extrapolating new applications to engage, challenge, and embrace them as they prepare for life in these quickly changing times. Do please join us in applying these exciting ideas to your work.

ACKNOWLEDGMENTS

With special thanks to Chris Jennison, Natalie Graham, and Craig Thomas at The Guilford Press, this book is dedicated to colleagues and friends for their thoughtful contributions, feedback, and encouragement—especially to Bill and Sloan, for their ongoing patience and support.

REFERENCES

Lesko, N. (2001). *Act your age: A cultural construction of adolescence.* New York: Routledge Falmer.

KATHLEEN A. HINCHMAN
HEATHER K. SHERIDAN-THOMAS

Contents

PART III. Adolescent Literacy Program Issues

Best Practices in Adolescent Literacy Instruction

PART I

Perspectives toward Adolescent Literacy Instruction

CHAPTER 1

Discussing Texts with Adolescents in Culturally Responsive Ways

Alfred W. Tatum

The tenets of this chapter are:

- Examining students' textual lineages provides valuable insights on discussing texts in culturally responsive ways.
- Understanding texts, students, and contexts is central to discussing texts in culturally responsive ways.
- Structuring pedagogy and curricula in relationship to students' lived experiences and histories is central to discussing texts in culturally responsive ways.

Discussing texts with adolescents in culturally responsive ways is the focus of this chapter. This topic is warranted because engaging adolescents in the reading of texts, particularly African American and Latino males who struggle with reading, is one of the most pressing challenges educators face. However, we must be careful not to overlook adolescent girls, many of whom are also not moved to become fully engaged with texts. Students generally participate in superficial discussions of characters and content in classrooms without gaining a deeper understanding of the text's meaning as it relates to who they are and what they can become. Or, students are disengaged from texts because they assess the texts as being irrelevant, teacher-driven selections mandated by school curricula that are more exclusive than inclusive to students with varying cultural and linguistic histories and experiences.

Classroom environments and curricula are not often structured to shape students' lives by engaging them with texts that they find meaningful and significant. This absence of meaningful texts is problematic because middle and high school students are striving to find their place in the world as they bump against academic, cultural, emotional, gender, historical, linguistic, and social forces that inform their existence. I am especially concerned that students are being deprived of textual lineages; that is, texts that they will remember years into the future as being meaningful and central to their human development. The deprivation of textual lineages is occurring, in part, because of an overbearing focus at the national, state, and local levels in the United States to focus more on *reading scores* than *scoring with reading.* Scoring with reading provides far-lasting academic, cultural, emotional, and social benefits as students mature into adulthood.

Several major issues impede students' meaningful engagement with texts in schools:

1. Age-old curriculum traditions in high schools and packaged curriculum in middle schools
2. Low levels of reading achievement among a large percentage of adolescents
3. Public policy and school district mandates in response to low levels of reading achievement
4. The absence of rigorous research on the types and characteristics of texts that students find engaging and meaningful, not simply preferential
5. The absence of classroom practices such as providing choice, exposing students to a wide range of texts, and connecting instruction to students' out-of-school lives, as suggested by the research on effective literacy instruction for adolescents
6. The absence of a clear definition of the role of literacy instruction for adolescents

In sum, classroom environments and the teaching occurring within these environments are not responding adequately to students' multiple literacy needs, but are, instead, anchored by an achievement-driven focus that is based on state standards and that lacks any serious regard to the content of texts used for meeting the standards. As a result, the meaningful encounters that adolescents could experience with books, poems, and essays in schools during an optimal period of their development are severely comprised in middle and high school classrooms.

Teachers need to foster students' partnership with texts. Many students, particularly struggling readers, simply do not know what's out there for them to read. Classrooms are ideal settings in which to introduce and engage adolescents with texts connected to some larger ideological focus of literacy instruction (e.g., functioning in a global society, improving the human condition). Also, classrooms are also ideal settings in which educators can use texts to broker positive relationships with adolescents. Middle and high school students want to be acknowledged and understood; they want to know that their existence matters while they work to define that existence. This acknowledgment and understanding can be heightened as teachers and student discuss texts together. I am reminded of a fictional character, Sipho, in Beverly Naidoo's (1995) novel of South Africa, *No Turning Back*. Sipho stated, "Even people who wanted to help him didn't know how he felt" (p. 141). He was suggesting that adults are not ready for adolescents when they appear before them seeking help.

Similar to other scholars and researchers who have given attention to culturally responsive approaches to literacy teaching (Galda & Beach, 2004; Gay, 2000; Hemphill, 1999; Moje & Hinchman, 2004; Rueda, August, & Goldenberg, 2006), I draw from a sociocultural perspective in this chapter to identify effective approaches for discussing texts with adolescents. This chapter is also grounded in the work of other researchers who have explored how gender and social class influence students' discussion of texts (Clark, 2006; Sprague & Keeling, 2007; Smith & Wilhelm, 2006) and the potential of text to be transformative for students (Lalik & Oliver, 2007; Mosenthal, 1998; Tatum, 2005). Instead of defining cultural responsiveness here, I have decided to use the voices of 15 eighth- and ninth-grade students to help shape a definition of cultural responsiveness. These students are part of a larger data pool of students who completed textual lineages and explained why they will always remember certain texts. Their textual lineages will serve as a blueprint for defining cultural responsiveness.

EXAMINING TEXTUAL LINEAGES

Concerned about engaging African American adolescent males with texts, I began examining why, from a historical perspective, African American males engaged with texts. As a data collection tool, I began to construct textual lineages (see Figure 1.1.) I was aiming to use the historical relationship African American males had with text to identify implications for engaging young men with text in today's classrooms. The examination yielded a rich history between African American males and texts. Historically, texts have been central in their literacy development, with the connection among reading, writing, speaking, and action eminently clear. African American males gravitated toward texts connected to larger ideals such as cultural uplift, economic advancement, resistance to oppression, and intellectual development. Characteristically, these texts were "enabling" texts. An enabling text is one that moves beyond a sole

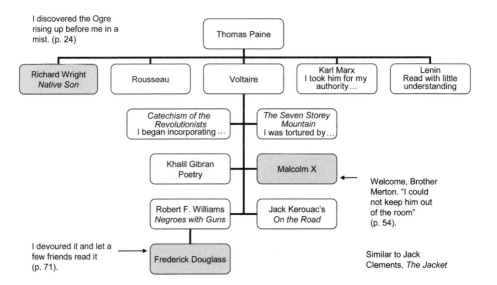

FIGURE 1.1. Eldridge Cleaver's textual lineage, constructed from reading *Soul on Ice* (1968).

cognitive focus—such as skill and strategy development—to include an social, cultural, political, spiritual, or economic focus (Tatum, 2006).

Eldridge Cleaver (1968), for example, explains how reading *Native Son* helped him discover the ogre within him, and how he accepted Karl Marx as his authority for living. He also wrote, "The library does have a selection of very solid material . . . but it is unsatisfactory to a stud who is trying to function in the last half of the twentieth century" (p. 70). Cleaver offered that although a wealth of materials existed in the prison library, very few, he assessed, provided a roadmap for African American males trying to function in the society in which he lived. I determined that African American males gravitated toward texts for four reasons:

1. The texts contributed to a healthy psyche.
2. The texts provided modern-day awareness of the real world.
3. The texts focused on a collective struggle.
4. The texts provided a roadmap.

Subsequent to my historical analysis of African American males' interaction with texts, I began to collect the textual lineages of middle and high school students in schools where I provide professional development for teachers. The goal was to use students' textual lineages, along with their voices, to shape how teachers and administrators select reading materials that speak to, inform, shape, and contribute to the intellectual and emotional development of adolescents, as well as how teachers plan instruction for adolescents (see Figure 1.2).

During the academic school year of 2006–2007, I collected more than 3,000 textual lineages from middle and high school students. They were asked to identify texts (i.e., books, essays, or poems) that they thought that they would always remember and explain why the texts were meaningful to them. Although the analysis of all the textual lineages is not complete, I have selected 15 textual lineages from eighth- and ninth-grade students as the basis for this chapter. The textual lineages were selected across ethnic and gender lines. I have formatted the students' lineages into Table 1.1. The table includes students' ethnicity, gender, and grade level, the texts they identified as ones they will always remember, their written explanations, and their ethnic and gender relationships to the central figures of the fiction and nonfiction texts.

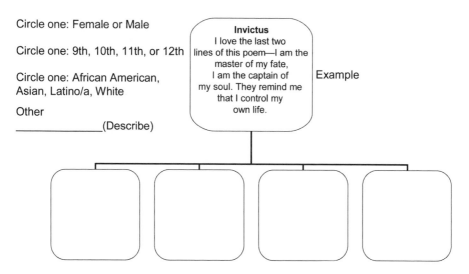

Directions: In each box below, place the title of a text (i.e., book, essay, or poem) that you think you will always remember. Place only one title in a box. Explain why you think you will always remember the text or explain why the text was meaningful to you. Look at the example.

Circle one: Female or Male

Circle one: 9th, 10th, 11th, or 12th

Circle one: African American, Asian, Latino/a, White

Other

_____(Describe)

Invictus
I love the last two lines of this poem—I am the master of my fate, I am the captain of my soul. They remind me that I control my own life.

Example

FIGURE 1.2. Textual lineage chart students completed.

TABLE 1.1. Texts Students Identified as Ones They Will Always Remember and Explanations of Why

Students	Text	Students' explanations	Connections
African American ninth-grade female	*My Skin Is My Skin* (Dejon, 2007)	Teaches me that I am beautiful. The inner beauty is what shows.	Within gender Within ethnicity
African American ninth-grade female	*Angela's Ashes* (McCourt, 1999)	So interesting that it made your life look narrow.	Within gender Across ethnicity
African American ninth-grade female	*I Know Why the Caged Bird Sings* (Angelou, 1983)	Maya Angelou inspires me in so many ways, especially in embracing life.	Within gender Within ethnicity
African American eighth-grade male	*Bang* (Flake, 2005)	It has been influential because boys do drugs in here, and I could see how it affects you so I will be strong and smarter. It's a memory for life because I love my cousin and he used to do drugs but he fighted it.	Within gender Within ethnicity
African American eighth-grade male	*No Turning Back* (Naidoo, 1995)	Because this book is about slavery and they telling how they how to go to school and be back in time to work, but it's telling they ran away and didn't look back cause black people did it.	Within gender Within ethnicity
African American eighth-grade male	*Forged by Fire* (Draper, 1998)	I like this book because I need this book. I feel it.	Within gender Within ethnicity
Asian American ninth-grade female	*Naruto* (Kishimoto, 2003)	I love this book because this book teaches you to be strong, and always believe in yourself.	Within gender Within ethnicity
Asian American ninth-grade female	*The Body* (Kureishi, 2004)	"The most important things are the hardest things to say. They are the things you get ashamed of, because words diminish them—words shrink that seem limitless when they were in your head to no more that a living size when they are brought out." I love this quote because it is very honest. There are a million things that I want to say to people, but I am always afraid to do so.	Within gender Across ethnicity
Asian American ninth-grade female	*Among the Hidden* (Haddix, 2006)	It was one of the first books I ever read that made me realize that my life wasn't as bad as I thought it was.	Across gender Across ethnicity

(continued)

TABLE 1.1. *(continued)*

Students	Text	Students' explanations	Connections
Latino ninth-grade male	*My Bloody Life* (Sanchez, 2000)	It's the only book I've actually read the whole way. It shows what I've been through.	Within gender Within ethnicity
Latino ninth-grade male	*The Contender* (Lipsyte, 1996)	The book shows me that I can make something of my life from nothing.	Within gender Across ethnicity
Latino ninth-grade male	*A Child Called It* (Pelzer, 1993)	I love books based on real life especially if it is on childhood, and how dangerous/cause it was.	Within gender Across ethnicity
Latina American ninth-grade female	*Just Juice* (Hesse, 1999)	Because I loved the book I had to read. It resembled a part of my life.	Within gender Across ethnicity
Latina American ninth-grade female	*Where the Heart Is?* (Letts, 2000)	It tell me that I shouldn't let a kid or my kid abanded on the street even if they tell me that it will mess up my life.	Within gender Across ethnicity
Latina American ninth-grade female	*My Bloody Life* (Sanchez, 2000)	I will always remember this book because it taught me that being in gangs can mess up your life. It was important because it helped me change my life.	Across gender Within ethnicity
White ninth-grade female	*Tuesdays with Morrie* (Albom, 1997)	It had lots of life lessons in it and it said things straight out; it was intense.	Across gender Within ethnicity
White ninth-grade female	*The Scarlet Letter* (Hawthorne, 1850/2000)	Reading about how a woman was outcast from her society because of a decision really made me think about my choices.	Within gender Within ethnicity
White ninth-grade female	*The Glass Castle* (Walls, 2005)	Well written and reminds me of how lucky I am.	Within gender Within ethnicity
White ninth-grade male	*Success*–author unknown	I learned this poem during tennis camp. I recite it whenever I have to overcome some sort of adversity. I enjoy it because it talks about how losing or winning is all in your head.	Not clear
White ninth-grade male	*The Zombie Survival Guide* (Brooks, 2004)	I can't afford to forget one word in this book. But honestly, it's a great self-help book.	Not clear
White ninth-grade male	*An Inconvenient Truth* (Gore, 2006)	I loved this book because it was extremely straightforward about the issue of global warming and what we can do about it.	Not clear

IDENTIFIED TEXTS

The students identified a wide range of texts that they believe they will always remember. Among the texts are classic literature (e.g., *The Scarlet Letter* [Hawthorne, 1850/2000]), young adult literature (e.g., *Bang* [Flake, 2005], *Forged by Fire* [Draper, 1998], *No Turning Back [Naidoo, 1995], The Contender* [Lipsyte, 1996]), nonfiction and memoirs (e.g., *A Child Called It* [Pelzer, 1993], *Angela's Ashes* [McCourt, 1999], *I Know Why the Caged Bird Sings* [Angelou, 1983], *An Inconvenient Truth* [Gore, 2006], *My Bloody Life* [Sanchez, 2000], *Tuesdays with Morrie* [Albom, 1997]), and adult fiction (e.g., *My Skin Is My Skin* [Dejon, 2007], *The Body* [Kureishi, 2004]). However, if the aim is discussing texts in culturally responsive ways, then the explanations the students provide are far more important than the titles and genres, because the explanations provide implications for teaching and curricula.

The students' comments suggest that texts that move them to feel differently about themselves, affect their views of themselves, or move them to some action in their current time and space are the ones they remember or find meaningful. The following explanations illustrate this point:

1. "*The text teaches me* that I am beautiful."
2. "*The text inspires me* in some many ways, especially in embracing life."
3. "*The text made me realize* that my life was not as bad as I thought."
4. "*The text shows me* that I can make something out of my life."
5. "[The text] was important because *it helped me change my life.*"

In addition to the "enabling qualities" of the texts (Tatum, 2006), the students identified texts that led them to become reflective and introspective. They mentioned:

1. "It made my life look narrow."
2. "It is based on real-life experiences."
3. "It resembled a part of my life."
4. "Reminds me how lucky I am."
5. " . . . I shouldn't let . . . my kid be abanded on the street even if [others] tell me that it will mess up my life."

The texts the students identified and the explanations they provided mesh with other research that found that readers interrogate texts for their authenticity in terms of cultural representations of students' local contexts in school and larger cultural contexts outside of school (Clark, 2006; Galda & Beach, 2004). The students also made varying connections to the texts.

ETHNIC AND GENDER CONNECTIONS

Some of the students' comments make it clear that ethnic and gender connections are paramount to their remembering of texts or the texts being meaningful. For example, one African American eighth-grade male, commenting on *No Turning Back* (Naidoo, 1995), stated, "Cause Black people did it," as part of his explanation for remembering the text. A white ninth-grade female student shared, "Reading about how a woman was outcast from her society because a decision really made me think about my choices." Another eighth-grade African American male makes a similar gender connection to the text *Bang* (Flake, 2005). He wrote, "It has been influential because *boys* do drugs in here, and I can see how it affects you so I will be strong and smart." He had the option of making the connection to the main character's African American identity; instead, he chose to focus on the gender identity.

PERSONAL CONNECTIONS

Several students made personal connections without mentioning ethnicity or gender. In explaining Kuriesh's (2004) novel, a ninth-grade Asian American female offered:

> " 'The most important things are the hardest things to say. They are the things you get ashamed of, because words diminish them—words shrink that seem limitless when they were in your head to no more than a living size when they are brought out.' I love this quote because it is very honest. There are a million things that I want to say to people, but I am always afraid to do so."

This student used the text to think about a personal goal of wanting to use her voice to communicate with people, but she was reticent because of an internal fear. In this case, the text resonated with the student as she thought about her personal identity, not necessarily related to ethnicity or gender. Other personal connections emerge from several other students. An eighth-grade African American male shared that "I like this book because I need this book. I feel it." This is similar to a ninth-grade white male, who offered, "I can't afford to forget one word in the book. But honestly, it's a great self-help book." In the case of both students, they are suggesting that they favor texts that are personally significant to them. This position is also captured by the a ninth-grade white female who found life lessons in *Tuesdays with Morrie*, and the ninth-grade Asian American student who found strength to believe in herself after reading *Naruto*, a book that is part of the Manga series.

ADOLESCENT CONNECTIONS

Ten of the fifteen adolescents identified books that had central characters in the same age range for a significant part of the text. They were able to relate to, or peep into, the experience of an age-peer who impacted their views or emotions in some way. For example, a ninth-grade Latino male, sharing his thoughts on *A Child Called It* (Pelzer, 1993), stated, "I love books based on real life especially if it is on childhood. . . . " He suggested that books about adolescents resonated with him. An Asian American girl reflected on her life through a male character, similar in age, in the text *Among the Hidden.* She shared, "It was one of the first books that made me realize that my life wasn't as bad as I thought it was." In *Among the Hidden* (Haddix, 2006), Luke, the main character, has to spend 12 years in hiding because his family had him illegally during a period of government-enforced legislation that prevented parents from having more than two children. Luke eventually comes out from hiding to find that he must suppress his personal opinions because they are considered dangerous and threatening to the government. The young man in the story has to determine what he is willing to sacrifice to live. The whole notion of suppression of freedoms resonates with adolescents, and I am assuming this to be the case with this student.

The adolescent connections cross ethnic lines, as illustrated by a ninth-grade Latino male who finds instruction from the 17-year-old African American main character from Harlem in the novel *The Contender* (Lipsyte, 1996). The student shared, "This book shows me that I can make something out of my life from nothing." He is referring to the main character, who learns how to become a man after dropping out of high school. The main character overcomes his personal fears and triumphs in the end. This student does not refer to the main character's ethnicity or gender, but suggests that he can learn from someone in his peer group.

BEING CULTURALLY RESPONSIVE

Although more research is needed to ensure that the topic of culturally responsive literacy teaching does not suffer from intellectual sterility, the 15 students who constructed textual lineages suggest that there are multiple dimensions of being culturally responsive. They suggest that being culturally responsive:

1. Encourages adolescents to reflect on and become introspective about their own lived experiences and histories.
2. Encourages adolescent to make connections across their multiple identities—adolescent, ethnic, gender, and personal.

3. Encourages adolescents to become enabled in some way to be, do, or think differently as a result of the texts.
4. Avoids pigeonholing adolescents by selecting texts based solely on ethnicity or gender; students find value in texts across ethnic and gender lines.
5. Recognizes the need to identify a wide range of texts that are more aligned to the needs of adolescents, and not limiting text selection to standards-driven or achievement-driven imperatives shaped by potentially stifling public policy and school mandates.
6. Honors the voices of adolescents, who can provide valuable insights on the types of text they find meaningful and significant.
7. Includes a wide variety of texts to expand what is generally allowed in stagnant, age-old traditions of high school English curriculum or packaged curricula in middle schools.

The suggestions emerging from the students' voices align neatly with Gay (2000), who suggests that "culturally responsive teaching has many different shapes, forms, and effects" (p. 2). She too recognizes the multidimensionality of culturally responsive teaching. This form of teaching encompasses curriculum content, learning context, classroom climate, student–teacher relationships, instructional techniques, and assessments. Gay also warns against the absence of caring in a culturally responsive approach to literacy teaching. She states, "Caring teachers are distinguished by their high performance expectations, advocacy, and empowerment of students as well as by their use of pedagogical practices that facilitate school success" (p. 62).

CULTURALLY RESPONSIVE PEDAGOGY AND CURRICULA

Texts that provide knowledge about historical and modern-day contexts can be powerful for adolescents. Commenting on Gore's (2006) *An Inconvenient Truth*, a ninth-grade white male wrote, "I loved this book because it was extremely straightforward about the issue of global warming and what we can do about it." Other adolescents, whose textual lineages I did not share here, identified Weisel's (2006) *Night* as a book that they found meaningful because of the new knowledge they gained about the Holocaust. This text also provides a straightforward, gripping account of a major historical event.

Both nonfiction and fiction texts can be used to give students knowledge about historical modern-day contexts. This is true of Iweala's (2007) *Beasts of No Nation*. This debut novel is a gripping account of a young boy who becomes a guerilla fighter in his nation's civil war. The content is quite disturbing; there is murder and man-on-boy rape. In his description of a disturbing rape of a young boy by the commandant, the author writes:

> . . . but me I was not struggling because I know that he will be killing me if I am struggling and since I am wanting to vomit and die. (p. 83)

This text is eerily similar to Jack London's (1903/2003) *Call of the Wild*, in which he describes the transformation of a civilized dog into a beast of the wild with no moral consideration. He writes:

> He must be master or mastered; while to show mercy was a weakness. Mercy did not exist in the primordial life. It was misunderstood for fear, and such misunderstandings made for death. Kill or be killed, eat or be eaten, was the law; and this mandate, down out of the depths of Time, he obeyed. (p. 54)

By page 47 of *Beast of No Nation*, the young boy becomes a ruthless killer. The author writes:

> Under the bed there is a woman and her daughter just hiding. She is looking at us and worrying so much it is looking like somebody is cutting her face with a knife. She is smelling like goat and we are wanting to kill her so we are dragging her out, all of us soldier, but she is holding her daughter. They are holding each other and shaking like they are having fever. They are so thin more than us and the skin is hanging down like elephant skin so I am know she is fat before the war is coming and making rich and fat like poor and thin. The girl is so shrinking, she is almost like unborn baby—I am knowing because I have been taking them from their mother's belly to be seeing who is girl and who is boy. Are you my mother, I am saying. Are you my sister? But they are only screaming like Devil is coming for them. I am not Devil. I am not bad boy. I am not bad boy. Devil is not blessing me and I am not going to hell. But still I am thinking maybe Devil born me and that is why I am doing all of this. . . . But it is not Devil that is borning me. I am having father and mother and I am coming from them. (pp. 47–48)

This text will lead students to question, why is this atrocity allowed to happen in our world? Some students may even ask if the content is true. These types of thought-provoking texts must be selected with care. I used the examples above to illustrate the types of controversial texts that adolescents favor, but that are often not part of the curricula. The costs and benefits of text selections should be weighed carefully to avoid alienating teachers, students, or parents.

Texts can be selected that lead students to discuss the conditions that create humans' inhumanity toward humans or humans' ways of dealing with inhumane conditioning. Jane Yolen's (1988) *The Devil's Arithmetic*, Lois Lowry's (1989) *Number the Stars*, and Julius Lester's (1968) *To Be a Slave* come to mind. Lester offers testimonies of the enslaved and their "ability to retain humanity under the most inhuman conditions" (p. 111). I am struck by the words during each reading, particularly when a slave owner, who professed Christianity, told an enslaved man, "If I catch you here servin' God, I'll beat you. You ain't got no time to serve God, We bought you to serve us" (p. 105). Or when, a son recalls, "They whipped my father 'cause he looked at a slave they killed and cried" (p. 33). He also writes, "Yet it is all the more remarkable that even two hundred years of slavery are looked upon matter-of-factly and not as a time of unrelieved horror" (p. 74). Lester's novel, as well as the others, if mediated effectively, will stand the reader in his or her tracks.

The goal is not to depress adolescents with "heavy" texts but to structure curricula by "considering what issues are worth exploring and understanding when composing essential questions" to engage adolescents (Smith & Wilhelm, 2006, p. 62). Unfortunately, we live in a country that does not have a clear definition of the role of literacy instruction for adolescents. Therefore, little discussion during curriculum conversations focuses on essential questions that young adolescents should or want to address. The discussions of 21st-century literacy skills in public policy documents and the exploration of new literacies primarily in colleges and universities have not influenced the widespread selection and discussion of texts in middle and high school classrooms. I think again to the words of Eldridge Cleaver (1968), who intimated that there are some texts that are difficult to block out; no matter what you try, they penetrate your thinking. Yet, it is easy for many adolescents to block out texts in schools because most do not allow students to navigate cultural communities, or they do not reflect cultural expectations (Galda & Beach, 2004; Moje & Hinchman, 2004) connected to essential questions that are cognitively challenging for students (Smith & Wilhelm, 2006).

Responsive teaching and curricula focus on powerful and authentic texts for adolescents that help them bridge in-school and out-of-school discontinuities that exist for many students across ethnicity, gender, and language. Walter Mosley's (2005) *47* begs for consideration of a middle school audience. This text blends historical and speculative fiction. An excerpt that promotes visual imagery follows:

> It smelled bad in there and it was too hot in the summer and freezing in the winter. And every night they chained your feet to an eyebolt in the floor. The men out there were mostly angry and so they were always fighting or crying or just plain sad. But the worst thing they said about the slave quarters was that once you were there you stayed there for the rest of your life. (p. 12)

Students can use this text to wrestle with an essential question related to breaking the chains that secures one to the floor. This focus is not too different from the students who completed the textual lineages. They shared:

- "I love this book because this book teaches you to be strong, and always believe in yourself."—Ninth-grade Asian American female
- "Reading about how a woman was outcast from her society because of a decision really made me think about my choices."—Ninth-grade white female
- "The book shows me that I can make something of my life from nothing."—Ninth-grade Latino male
- "I will always remember this book because it taught me that being in gangs can mess up your life. It was important because it helped me change my life."—Ninth-grade Latina female

Figuratively speaking, all of the students expressed an interest in breaking chains by either becoming strong, making appropriate decisions, making something out of nothing, or avoiding circumstances that shape a negative life outcome trajectory. Roadmap texts explored in caring, supportive classroom environments that honor students' voices, aligned with pedagogical practices focused on academic excellence and identity development, serve adolescents well. Adolescents respond positively to powerful texts in tandem with powerful literacy instruction. Teachers must integrate the two in order to be responsive to the need of students. This may require teachers to rebuild their textual lineages with adolescents in mind, or to be willing to explore a wide range of texts with their students.

CONCLUSIONS

In this chapter I discussed the need for examining students' textual lineages; for understanding texts, students, and contexts; and for structuring pedagogy and curricula to discuss texts with students in culturally responsive ways. Students' voices were used to help define cultural responsiveness and its multiple dimensions. It was also made evident that students connect to texts in a variety of ways—adolescent connections, ethnic connections, gender connections, and personal connections. These student voices helped provide a dynamic blueprint for discussing texts with adolescents in culturally responsive ways.

However, there is still a divide between what we know and what happens in classrooms. Several factors contributing to this divide were offered: structural and curricular handicaps influenced by tradition, public policy, low levels of reading achievement, lack of research on discussing texts with adolescents in culturally responsive ways, and the absence of a clear definition of literacy instruction for adolescents. Fortunately, more attention is being given to adolescent literacy and best practices to address some of the challenges and demands for advancing the literacy development of students who are increasingly attending more diverse schools.

Classroom contexts are changing. Out-of-school contexts are complicated by issues of race, social class, and language. Literacy instruction cannot afford to ignore either context. I have suggested that we can begin to discuss texts with adolescents in culturally responsive ways by honoring what we learn from their growing textual lineages and by building the textual lineages of students who are without them in relation to the in-school and out-of-school contexts that impact their lived experiences and histories. Becoming culturally responsive has to be less of a cliché and more of a clarion call. I offer the following to strengthen the call. We need to:

1. Define the role of literacy instruction for adolescents in a way that honors students' multiple identities and is connected to a large ideological focus.
2. Identify texts that allow students to make connections across their multiple identities.
3. Connect texts to essential questions.
4. Build the textual lineages of all students to help ensure that they can identify texts that are meaningful and significant to them.
5. Structure pedagogy and curricula that aim to strengthens students' academic, ethnic, gender, linguistic, and personal competencies.
6. Tap into students' voices to become smarter about teaching them.

This clarion call can help us move culturally responsive literacy teaching from the sidelines, where it is marginalized, to the center of instruction. This shift in focus allows us to respond to the needs of all of students as they appear in our classrooms, each wrapped in different experiences and histories.

DISCUSSION AND ACTIVITIES

1. Discuss your own and your students' textual lineages and the insights this information provides on discussing texts in culturally responsive ways. Ask your students to identify texts that have been influential to them, and why, and compare what they say to the texts you identified.

2. What recently published texts have you encountered that might resonate in culturally responsive ways with the adolescents you teach? Do keep in mind that there may be considerable differences between the texts that younger and older adolescents, and varying communities, find engaging. How do the texts compare to the texts adolescents are assigned in schools?

3. How might classroom pedagogy and curriculum selections align with, and help to develop, students' lived experiences and histories in culturally responsive ways that they recognize and value?

REFERENCES

Albom, M. (1997). *Tuesdays with Morrie: An old man, a young man, and life's greatest lesson.* New York: Doubleday.

Angelou, M. (1983). *I know why the caged bird sings.* New York: Bantam.

Brooks, M. (2004). *The zombie survival guide.* London: Duckworth.

Clark, L. W. (2006). Power through voicing others: Girls' positioning of boys in literature circle discussion. *Journal of Literacy Research, 38,* 53–79.

Cleaver, E. (1968). *Soul on ice.* New York: Delta.

Dejon. (2007). *My skin is my skin.* Urbanbooks.net: Urban Books.

Draper, S. (1998). *Forged by fire.* New York: Aladdin.

Flake, S. (2005) *Bang.* New York: Hyperion.

Galda, L., & Beach, R. (2004). Response to literature as a cultural activity. In R. Ruddell & N. Unrau (Eds.), *Theoretical models and processes of reading* (5th ed., pp. 852–869). Newark, DE: International Reading Association.

Gay, G. (2000). *Culturally responsive teaching: Theory, research, and practice.* New York: Teachers College Press.

Gore, A. (2006). *An inconvenient truth: The planetary emergence of global warming and what we can do about it.* New York: Rodale.

Haddix, M. P. (2006). *Among the hidden.* New York: Aladdin.

Hawthorne, N. (2000). *The scarlet letter.* New York: Modern Library Edition. (Original work published 1850)

Hemphill, L. (1999). Narrative style, social class, and response to poetry. *Research in the Teaching of English, 33,* 275–302.

Hesse, K. (1999). *Just juice.* New York: Scholastic.

Iweala, U. (2007). *Beasts of no nation.* New York: HarperCollins.

Kishimoto, M. (2003). *Naruto.* San Francisco: Viz Media.

Kureishi, H. (2004). *The body.* New York: Scribner.

Lalik, R., & Oliver, K. L. (2007). Differences and tensions in implementing a pedagogy of critical literacy with adolescent girls. *Reading Research Quarterly, 42*(1), 46–70.

Lester, J. (1998). *To be a slave.* New York: Puffin.

Letts, B. (2000). *Where the heart is.* New York: Warner Books.

Lipsyte, R. (1996). *The contender.* New York: HarperCollins.

London, J. (2003). *Call of the wild.* New York: Scholastic. (Original work published 1903)

Lowry, L. (1989). *Number the stars.* New York: Bantam.

McCourt, F. (1999). *Angela's ashes.* New York: Simon & Schuster.

Moje, E., & Hinchman, K. (2004). Culturally responsive practices for youth literacy learning. In T. Jetton & J. Dole (Eds.), *Adolescent literacy research and practice* (pp. 321–350). New York: Guilford Press.

Mosenthal, P. (1998). Reframing the problem of adolescence and adolescent literacy: A dilemma-management perspective. In D. E. Alvermann, K. A. Hinchman, D. W. Moore, S. F. Phelps, & D. R. Waff (Eds.), *Reconceptualizing the literacies in adolescents' lives* (pp. 325–352). Mahwah, NJ: Erlbaum.

Mosley, W. (2005). *47.* New York: Little, Brown.

Naidoo, B. (1995). *No turning back: A novel of South Africa:* New York: HarperTrophy.

Pelzer, D. (1993). *A child called "it": One child's courage to survive.* Omaha, NE: Omaha Press.

Rueda, R. S., August, D., & Goldenberg, C. (2006). The sociocultural context in which children acquire literacy. In D. August & T. Shanahan (Ed.), *Developing literacy in second language learners: Report of the National Literacy Panel on Language-Minority Children and Youth* (pp. 319–347). Mahwah, NJ: Erlbaum.

Sanchez, R. (2000). *My bloody life: The making of a Latin King.* Chicago: Chicago Review Press.

Smith, M., & Wilhelm, J. (2006). *Going with the flow: How to engage boys (and girls) in their literacy learning.* Portsmouth, NH: Heinemann.

Sprague, M., & Keeling, K. (2007). *Discovering their voices: Engaging adolescent girls with young adult literature.* Newark, DE: International Reading Association.

Tatum, A. W. (2005). Teaching reading to black adolescent males: Closing the achievement gap. Portsmouth, ME: Stenhouse.

Tatum, A. W. (2006). Engaging African American males in reading. *Educational Leadership, 63*(5), 44–49.

Walls, J. (2005). *The glass castle: A memoir.* New York: Scribner.

Weisel, E. (2005). *Night.* New York: Hill & Wang.

Wright, R. (1966). *Native son.* New York: Harper & Row.

Yolen, J. (1990). *The devil's arithmetic.* New York: Puffin.

CHAPTER 2

Meaningful Content for Middle School Students for Whom English Is an *Additional* Language

Eliane Rubinstein-Ávila
Janelle Johnson

This chapter:

- Explains the increase in the number of EAL students across U.S. schools within the past few decades.

- Compares the educational needs of contemporary ELLs with those of immigrant youth in the past and provides an overview of the educational settings designed for secondary ELLs.

- Explains the nonlinear and bidirectional nature of second language development.

- Suggests several strategies that are likely to enhance EAL students' learning across content areas, with examples of strategies in each of the four main academic subject areas (language arts, mathematics, natural sciences, and social sciences).

This chapter is intended for general secondary educators—content-area teachers and school administrators who may have had limited academic preparation in English language acquisition or the development of bilingualism. Most bilingual students in U.S. schools who are developing English as a second language, are still likely to be enrolled in English-immersion classes (Fitzgerald, 1995); this is especially the case for English language learners (ELLs) in secondary schools. Therefore, this chapter focuses on several issues relevant to secondary content-area teaching in classes where many of the students are likely to be developing English as an additional language (EAL).

We use EAL and ELL interchangeably throughout the chapter. We prefer the term "English as an additional language," used more commonly across the European Union, because it is more accurate and it acknowledges that students are already competent speakers of at least one home language. We may use the term ELL more often, because it is commonly used across the United States. We hope, however, to underscore that many students who are acquiring English competencies may be already proficient in more than one home language or dialect.

Children in many parts of the world grow up multilingual (e.g., Switzerland, India). Many immigrant students to the United States may already be bilingual before they develop English proficiency. A Mexican child who is born and raised in one of the many indigenous villages surrounding the city of Oaxaca, for example, is likely to speak one of several varieties of Zapotec as the main home and community language before he/she develops Spanish competencies at school.

Because Spanish speakers are currently the largest language minority group in U.S. schools, in this chapter we focus our attention on Latino/a students (also referred to as Hispanic). However, we would like to remind readers that Latinos/as are a highly heterogeneous student population. First, slightly different varieties of Spanish are spoken in more than 20 countries. Also, although most Latin Americans are officially Roman Catholic, Latino/a students in the United States may have been socialized in a variety of religious beliefs and cultural practices. Therefore, it is important to keep in mind that, even if students from Puerto Rico, the Dominican Republic, and Mexico are likely to share Spanish as a common language, they do not share the same history and are unlikely to share cultural practices or immigration experiences. For example, although Puerto Rican students may experience language barriers and culture shock, they are not immigrants. It is therefore not surprising that Latino/a students are likely to develop very different national and ethnic identities in the United States.

Latino/a students also vary widely in their familial socioeconomic status (SES). As is generally the case for most students, parents' SES is closely related to children's formal educational experiences. This range of educational experiences may be vast. Some may have attended rural, multigrade, one-room schools taught by a teacher who had barely completed the 8th grade; others may have attended exclusive private bilingual (Spanish/English) schools with highly educated teachers. Another point to keep in mind is that parents who may have been certified nurses and doctors in Latin America may be employed in the service sector (as janitors, kitchen staff, etc.) in the United States as a result of language barriers and the lack of reciprocity in professional certification.

Many teachers across the country, especially at the secondary level, are realizing that they are not prepared to provide challenging and meaningful content instruction to the ELLs enrolled in their classrooms. Unfortunately, some may still be under the impression that English language development ought to be the sole responsibility of ESL (English as a second language) teachers. However, the reality is that teaching ELLs is the responsibility of *all* educators, from preschool through graduate school.

ENGLISH LANGUAGE LEARNERS IN THE 21ST CENTURY: WHAT HAS CHANGED AND WHY?

Unfortunately, even with the nationwide popularity of a bumper sticker reminding us that: "Denial is NOT a river in Egypt," many, if not most, teacher-preparation programs and school districts across the country are likely to be steeped in denial about the dynamic shift that has occurred in the K–12 student population. In fact, most teachers-to-be are currently being trained to teach middle-class, English monolingual students—the type of student who is unlikely to be enrolled in their classrooms (Rubinstein-Ávila, 2003). Newly credentialed teachers across the United States may be unaware that immigrant families today are no longer only concentrated in historically immigrant enclaves in cities such as New York, Chicago, Boston, and Los Angeles, and that no matter where they teach, they will likely have several ELL students in their classes.

For example, the bustling poultry and carpet industries in states such as North Carolina, Alabama, and Georgia have attracted many immigrant laborers and their families. Although the economies of many small towns have been revived as a result, but school districts across these states have experienced a surge in the number of Latino/a students for whom they may not have been prepared (Rubinstein-Ávila, 2003, 2006).

The scope of this chapter does not allow us to elaborate on the ways in which U.S. political interventions, foreign policies such as the North America Free Trade Agreement (NAFTA), and recent changes in U.S. immigration law have contributed to the shift in student population across U.S schools. However, we believe that it is very important for teachers and administrators to become more aware of the broader issues that affect the shift in student population their school districts may be experiencing. As I (ERA) have elaborated on elsewhere (Rubinstein-Ávila, 2003), it may be tempting to compare the plight of today's young immigrants with that of immigrant youth a century ago. But such comparisons no longer hold, for too much in the world has changed.

Today's dynamic postindustrial global economy cannot be compared to a time in which industry was booming—a time in which immigrant youth, even if underage, found employment in mills and factories in spite of their limited educational background and/or English competencies. The 21st century economy calls for a skilled and educated workforce that is literate in multiple modalities. Clearly, single-subject teachers across secondary schools cannot wait for the ELLs enrolled in their classes to develop English competencies before they can engage with content (Campbell, Adams, & Davis, 2007). Unfortunately, however, the percentage of ELLs who are not graduating from high school or who are ineligible to continue their education at 4-year institutions, is on the rise. As a result, a growing number of Latino/a students' "American dreams" are unlikely to be realized. Given the current and projected growth in the population of underserved Latino/a youth, and the projected mass retirement of baby boomers, the future economic stability of the entire United States is at stake if this situation continues unchecked (Rubinstein-Ávila, 2006).

PROGRAMS FOR STUDENTS FOR WHOM ENGLISH IS AN ADDITIONAL LANGUAGE

We find that many preservice and even inservice secondary teachers are dumbfounded by the litany of terms that exist to describe the pedagogical environments designed for ELLs. Content-area teachers may find their role in developing students' second language and literacy unclear and, at times, even overwhelming. We believe that conversations about second language development, which entail reading and writing across disciplinary boundaries, will serve to disrupt the isolated educational experiences of ELLs and help them piece together their fragmented learning, as several scholars have described (Rubinstein-Ávila, 2007; Valdés, 2001).

Programs for EAL students, especially at the secondary level, vary widely from district to district across the United States. The main reasons for this variation are political ideologies (Combs et al., 2006) and the lack of trained teachers who are certified in specially designed academic instruction in English (SDAIE). State and school districts also vary in their commitment to the education of ELLs. In fact, in many secondary schools around the country ELLs are isolated not only by curricula but often also physically—relegated to self-contained classes, sometimes in basements and portable classrooms (Rubinstein-Ávila, 2003; Valdés, 2001).

With the near-demise of bilingual programs across English-only states, many secondary EAL students are either being placed in ESL programs or "transferred" into the regular programs after being in English immersion classes for 1 academic year. But because the development of academic language is likely to span several years, secondary ELLs need language support across all subject matters in order to graduate from high school. In fact, many scholars claim that the academic English register is best developed through the continuous integration of "language work" (Creese, 2006) across content, and that the two should not be viewed separately (Schleppegrell & de Oliveira, 2006).

The integration of language and content has taken slightly different forms and acronyms across continents. Approaches to the integration of language and content include sheltered instruction (SI), also known as sheltered content instruction (SCI), scaffolded reading experiences (SRE), content-based English language teaching (CELT), content-based language teaching (CBLT), and content-based instruction (CBI). Whereas some are complementary, others overlap. However, they all share the view that language and content learning should not be separated.

Developed in the 1970s, SI helps ELLs develop competencies in English while they engage meaningfully with content knowledge (Echevarria & Graves, 2007). Although *all* students can certainly gain from the SI format, it is more than "good teaching," because SI tailors the content to the students' level of English competencies. The sheltered instruction observational protocol (SIOP), developed in the mid-1990s, has been used as a guide for implementing SI instruction. The protocol, widely known as the SIOP model, provides 30 strategies for SCI organized around eight components (for more details, see Echevarria & Graves, 2007).

STUDENTS' USE OF THEIR FULL LINGUISTIC REPERTOIRES HELP—NOT HINDER—LEARNING

Monolingual English-speaking content teachers may find it perplexing that their bilingual students revert to Spanish when discussing a text or when problem solving with other bilingual peers. Others may find it perplexing that some of their ELL students, many of whom sound like fluent English speakers, are being pulled out for ESL classes. This confusion underscores the need for certain basic concepts about second language development and bilingualism to become common knowledge among all teachers. First, a second language does not develop in a vacuum. Contrary to what some monolingual English-speaking teachers may believe, secondary ELLs do not learn English "from scratch" (Rubinstein-Ávila, 2007); they build on their expanding metalinguistic knowledge. Also, a second language does not develop in a neat, organized, and linear manner, and is not independent from one's first language competencies. In fact, several scholars argue that the development of linguistic competencies in an additional language ought to be understood from a broader, bilingual/multilingual perspective—not a monolingual one (Moll & Dworin, 1996; Dworin, 2003; Valdés, 2004).

It is common knowledge that it is important to elicit and build upon all students' prior knowledge about any given topic. This may entail having students converse on a particular topic in their home language. Older ELL students, especially those who have not experienced lags in their formal schooling, are more likely to use what they already know—about language, reading, studying strategies, and content—to make meaning of new content in English. In fact, the work of Jimenez, Garcia, and Pearson (1996) reveals that strong reading comprehension in students' home language is often transferred to reading in English. It is essential for secondary teachers to understand the important role that students' home languages play in their meaningful engagement with content and in the development of higher-order reasoning competencies (McGraw & Rubinstein-Ávila, in press). In classrooms where biliteracy is not simply encouraged but also is one of the main goals, the relationship between L1 and L2 (first and second languages) is bidirectional. Students are likely to rely on both their dominant language as well as on their developing English competencies to make sense of the content they learn (Dworin, 2003; Moll & Dworin, 1996). Thus, rather than curtailing students from using their home language or code-switching between Spanish and English, and vice versa, secondary teachers ought to understand that ELLs use their existing linguistic competencies to expand their English competencies and content knowledge. English language development is fluid, nonlinear process.

THE ADVANTAGES OF INTERDISCIPLINARY UNITS: LEARNING IN CONTEXT

Longer class time spent in block scheduling facilitates the building of the background knowledge ELL students need to fully comprehend the issues surrounding a particular topic that is likely to be unfamiliar (e.g., the American Civil War). However, integrating language arts, social studies, and even mathematics is one possible way to structure learning around a historical topic. Reading and hearing related texts, viewing related films, and engaging with a variety of websites helps scaffold ELLs' comprehensive input around a particular topic. Group discussions also relate the newly acquired historical knowledge by contextualizing it through poems, diaries, original documents, (graphic) novels, picture books, maps, documentaries, and films.

In addition to the academic benefits of interdisciplinary study, ELLs are more likely to participate in inquiry-based projects that generate greater engagement with the content and with classmates. Integrated lessons are also more reflective of real-life tasks and prepare students to handle authentic challenges. Inquiry- and theme-based approaches encourage ELLs to engage with scientific, technological, and social issues while engaging in critical thinking and problem solving—all while developing language competencies (Ovando, Collier, & Combs, 2003). In fact, the use of WebQuests across content areas classes provides ELLs a range of opportunities to integrate most of these competencies and develop technological competencies (Sox & Rubinstein-Ávila, 2007). In some middle schools with a high number of EALs, content-area teachers collaborate with the ESL specialist to plan units of instructions around a particular theme. This approach provides teachers with an opportunity to share knowledge and resources, thereby generating more ideas for collaborative inquiry projects, guest speakers, and field trips.

STRATEGIES FOR MAKING CONTENT MORE COMPREHENSIBLE ACROSS CONTENT-AREA CLASSES

There are several ways in which single-subject teachers can make the content they teach more comprehensible and more meaningful for ELLs. The most important point to keep in mind is transparency; it is essential to be explicit. Rather than assume that students already know how to approach a research paper or write an essay because they are in middle school, teachers ought to provide guidelines for assignments in which the expectations are clearly stated. Academic writing that is considered acceptable in the United States is not universally practiced. For example, what teachers in the United States view as a concise, well-written essay, in which concepts are stated, supported, and then restated in the summary, may be viewed as simplistic and even redundant across Latin America. In China, and perhaps in other parts of the world, appropriating words of wisdom from others into one's own writing, without citation, is not considered plagiarism. Thus rather than assume that students already know *how* to employ particular registers and forms, teachers ought to model the expected process and outcome.

Modeling and demonstrating what is expected within a particular discipline is extremely important. Dong (2005), for example, suggests that teachers use sentence starters in order to provide ELLs with the expected use of language structures in a particular subject matter. Also, introducing discipline-specific vocabulary before and during lessons and keeping an updated Word Wall that includes transitional words and connectors (e.g., *first, then, afterward, moreover, in addition,* and *finally*) creates a context-rich academic environment for language development (Dong, 2005).

SI across the content areas also entails the use of manipulatives, realia, group discussions, the use of visuals (e.g., graphic organizers, timelines, graphs, charts, tables, diagrams), and student engagement with multimedia (technology). It is important for teachers to understand that EALs, like most students, will likely engage with content more meaningfully when a variety of modalities is presented. Thus watching a documentary or movie about a particular time in history, a place, or an event, for example, is likely to provide a shared experience from which to embark on other prereading activities such as brainstorming, predicting, and using concept maps. Listening to music that was popular at that particular time, viewing historical pictures, and reading diaries *before* reading the textbook are all ways in which teachers across content areas can build knowledge on a topic with which ELLs may not be familiar.

The idea that ELLs should first become proficient English speakers *before* they can read grade-level text or complete written assignments is erroneous. The relationship between reading, writing, and understanding is important for *all* students (ELLs included). Jacobs (2002) suggests several ways to engage secondary students in "writing-to-learn" activities, such as free writing, narrative writing, dialogue writing (i.e., communicating with an author, a peer, or the teacher), clozes (i.e., students fill in the missing words in a text using context clues), and looping (i.e., writing about a topic or an idea from a variety of perspectives). Indeed, "secondary reading and writing provides a means by which students can move from understanding to demonstrating understanding" (Jacobs, 2002, p. 61).

Instructional techniques such as modeling and demonstrations, for example, are essential across all content areas. Secondary teachers in today's middle and high schools ought not to assume that all students are familiar with genres such as essay answer, research paper, tables, graphs, or bibliographies. Manipulatives and hands-on experiments, especially in mathematics and science, are not to be considered only across the elementary grades, but are essential across middle and high school classes with ELLs. Visual aids, such as diagrams, graphs, tables, and timelines, are also crucial for assisting ELL students to make the necessary connections between their developing linguistic proficiencies and their developing content knowledge. The use of overheads, documentaries, the World Wide Web, and community-based projects and field trips helps to elicit multiple ways of engaging, communicating, and learning across all content areas.

Reducing the linguistic load across disciplines may be simple to implement, but it does not mean less substantive content learning. For example, enunciating words clearly and a little more slowly, while at the same time projecting graphic organizers on an overhead, are extremely helpful, as is exposing ELLs to as many modalities as possible (e.g., visual, audio, tactile). Also, by assigning problem-based group projects, single-subject teachers can make content knowledge not only a great deal more comprehensible for ELLs, but also more engaging and meaningful for all students. Previewing and highlighting key vocabulary words for each lesson is also essential for ELLs. Teachers trained in the SIOP model often wear one or two vocabulary words during the lesson—fastening the word to their clothing—throughout a particular class. This human Word Wall should not be limited to content-related words, phrases, and concepts, such as *linear equations* or *civil unrest*. Words and phrases such as *estimate, compare and contrast*, or *argue your point* ought to be explained and their usage modeled.

Where it is important to link all students' background knowledge and prior experiences to new concepts being developed, it is *essential* for ELLs. We all learn new information by linking it to what we already know or have experienced. Linking a new language—one with which we are less familiar to one with which we are familiar—is essential to the learning process. Although the U.S. Civil War may not be common knowledge among secondary ELLs, who are newcomers, most students are likely to be familiar with other instances of social, political, or economic unrest in their countries of origin. Therefore, eliciting ELLs' experiences and knowledge in a social studies or world geography class not only assists them in making meaningful connections to the content but also enriches native English speakers' understanding of world events in a broader context.

Other general instructional techniques such as the use of literature circles with both fictional and nonfictional texts are likely to help ELLs develop second language competencies, while increasing the likelihood that they would to contribute meaningfully to the discussion about the readings (Stien & Beed, 2004). The formation of literature circle groups of four to five students and collaborative assignments maximize students' participation; also, peer-led group discussions provide a chance for students to help each other construct shared knowledge and push each other to justify their views (Brabham & Villaume, 2000; Stien & Beed, 2004). Although literature circles are more commonly used in language arts classes, they can be ideal for collaborative reading and discussion of expository texts as well as for inquiry-based problem solving across social studies, mathematics, and science. Literature can integrate the use of technology and a host of modalities to achieve the meaningful participation of all group members.

Comprehensible input and meaning making are likely to occur on various levels when multiple strategies are employed. Scaffolding ELLs' comprehension and providing opportunities to expand their language competencies encourage students to question the authority of texts and to develop a discerning critical perspective of the complex world in which they live. Learning logs can become tools with which ELLs take notes, draw diagrams, produce charts, and jot down new vocabulary (Alvermann, Phelps, & Ridgeway, 2007). They can also become tools with which teachers encourage ELLs to reflect on their learning. The prompts in Table 2.1, suggested by Alvermann et al. (2007, p. 308), encourage students to reflect on the content and monitor their own learning.

Although it is important for teachers to respond to the learning logs, because answering students' questions provide qualitative insights about their progress, teachers can also encourage students to respond to each

TABLE 2.1. Learning Log Prompts

Process entries	Reaction entries
• What did I understand about the work we did in class today? • What didn't I understand? What was confusing? • What problems did I have with a text assignment? • How did I solve a problem with understanding, vocabulary, text, etc.? • At what point did I get confused? • What did I like or dislike today? • What questions do I have about what we did today? • Notes, lists, or jottings relevant to my upcoming assignments. • My reflections on cooperative-learning group processes—what did or didn't work and why, my role, the role of other participants. • My predictions and expectations about a new topic. • What was the most difficult homework problem? What made it so difficult? • "Unsent letters" to people, living or dead, historical or mythical, about topic of study. • Doodles; words and pictures that reflect feelings or thoughts on a topic.	• If I were the teacher, what questions would I ask about this assignment, chapter, etc.? • Explain a theory, concept, vocabulary term, etc., to another person. • Free-writing: Simply write for 5–10 minutes about a specific topic, whatever comes into the writer's mind. • Summarize, analyze, synthesize, compare and contrast, evaluate an idea, topic, event, person, etc. • Make a connection with prior knowledge or experience. • Response to higher-order questions posed by the teacher. • Reread a log entry from last week . . . write a reaction to what was written.

From Alvermann, Donna E., Stephen Phelps, & Victoria Ridgeway *Content Area Reading and Literacy, 5th Ed.* Published by Allyn and Bacon, Boston, MA. Copyright © 2007 by Pearson Education. Reprinted by permission of the publisher.

others' learning logs. Some teachers leave it up to the students to use their full linguistic repertoires (in English and/or Spanish) to make meaning of their content learning. ELLs should be especially encouraged to conduct frequent self-checks and to rely on their developing linguistic competencies as a resource.

Assessment of students' understanding is also important across all content areas at various phases of instruction, not only in the final formal assessment. For example, SIOP-trained content-area teachers are likely to have students demonstrate their level of understanding throughout the lesson by asking a group of students who work together point to a symbol that represents their collective level of comprehension. Working in pairs or in small, heterogeneous groups encourages ELLs to discuss content (using their first and second languages) and supports oral academic language development.

EXAMPLES OF CONTENT-AREA LITERACY STRATEGIES WITHIN FOUR MAJOR DISCIPLINES

Science Instruction

A hands-on science class that includes systematic observations and experiments and small-group activities is an ideal learning environment for EAL students. In middle school, science classes that rely primarily on the textbooks are especially challenging. In addition to the specialized vocabulary, the interpretation and theorizing that are likely to accompany classroom experiments often require abstract language to describe concrete situations (Fang, 2006): "For many students the greatest barrier to learning science lies in learning its language" (p. 507). Although the sciences include many words with Latin roots that may be familiar to many Spanish-speaking students, such as *volume*, students may be familiar with the words vernacular meaning, which may differ from its use in the sciences. Both the topical and process languages of science, and of mathematics, must be explicitly taught to students to help make the content accessible. One activity suggested by Fang (2006) is to create a definition table that transforms technical terms into everyday language, making disciplinary language more comprehensible and transparent for ELLs.

Even ELLs with developed oral competencies in English may find the discourse of school science textbooks daunting. But essential vocabulary words and phrases found in science textbooks can be adapted; for example, "poor soil management" can become "soil [that] is washed away slowly" (Fang, 2006, p. 501). Similarly, "desertification" can be explained as what happens when "land dries out and becomes a desert" (p. 501) and incineration as "when the waste is burn[t] down into its components" (p. 501). Moreover, even monolingual English-speaking treachers can point out to Spanish-speaking students that many, if not most, scientific vocabulary words are cognate pairs with words in Spanish (e.g., incineration/*incineración*). Although the student may not know the definition of the term in Spanish either, it may still be helpful to make such associations.

Occasionally, heterogeneous groups of students with mixed competencies in English can be given the collaborative task of translating a particular important paragraph in their textbooks into day-to-day language. The task can be accompanied by a drawing, sketch, or other type of visual representation to convey the content.

Although overreliance on textbooks is not recommended, it is important for ELLs that teachers do not do away with them altogether; negotiating the scientific discourse students are likely to encounter in textbooks is essential for their future schooling experiences. Keeping an updated class chart or a word wall of scientific definitions can help ELLs and non-ELLs alike.

Visual aids such as graphic organizers help ELL and other students connect the vocabulary and content. Even students with very limited Eng-

Day	Hypothesis: We will see	Observation: We saw	Result: Height	Result: Picture
1				
2				
3				

FIGURE 2.1. Simplified observation chart.

lish proficiency can organize information during a science experiment or activity with an observation chart. Such a chart can be used later to facilitate oral presentations of their results to the entire class. The observation chart in Figure 2.1 is an example of how both scientific and vernacular language can be included to facilitate comprehension.

Mathematics

It is not uncommon for mathematics teachers to view math as an easier subject for ELLs because it relies more heavily on "universal" numbers and symbols, rather than on words. But ELLs, like all other students, ought to engage in an array of aspects of mathematics, beyond computation. Conceptual learning in mathematics cannot be divorced from language. Campbell et al. (2007) point out that interpreting complex mathematical phrases and making strategic decisions require chunking, linking, sorting, and organizing information from text. These same authors underscore several potential linguistic challenges for ELLs; in the illustrative word problem they present, the word "*it* is used to refer to an unstated noun" (such as the cost of operating a washing machine to do laundry), not the Laundromat itself—therefore, the meaning of *it* "has to be inferred from the context" (p. 10).

Moreover, several other linguistic factors are likely to increase cognitive demands for ELLs, such as compound sentences and words that have multiple meanings; for example words such as *load* and *expression* (Campbell et al., 2007). Therefore, even if students understand the mathematical concepts, their level of English competence can impact the assessment of their knowledge of mathematics (Campbell et al., 2007). Another point to consider is that students in other countries may have learned basic operations with different algorithms than they learn in the United States. Commas and periods vary as place-value holders in different parts of the world, and most countries use a metric system of measurement. Mathematics teachers ought to encourage ELLs to share their problem-solving methods; this is a chance to affirm students' funds of knowledge and generate cross-cultural understanding. Furthermore, integrating math, language (written and/or oral), and reflection is essential for both ELLs and native speakers. Terms such as *equation* versus *expression* and *divided by* versus *divided into* can be confusing even for native speakers of English (Furner, Yahya, & Duffy, 2005). All students learn content through language; therefore, language development and content learning are inextricable.

Students' developing English proficiency should not be confused with diminished ability to reason mathematically. Too often ELLs are expected to perform only procedural mathematics. Although the precise language of mathematics can be demanding for ELLs, mathematics teachers can employ an array of second language supports (Moschkovich, 1999). McGraw and Rubinstein-Ávila (in press) report on the advanced reasoning strategies that one group of seventh- and eighth-grade ELLs demonstrated while solving a nonroutine problem. Although the problem was presented to them in English, students were encouraged to use their full linguistic repertoire to solve the problem collectively. Students relied on their stronger language (Spanish) to discuss and reason, then switched into English to explain their strategy to solving the problem to the entire class. This process allowed ELLs to employ higher-order reasoning skills (in Spanish) and, at the same time gave them the opportunity to develop oral fluency in English. Scholars are encouraging all educators to gain greater awareness about code switching and the role of two, or more, languages, when students learn mathematics (Moschkovich, 2005).

Social Studies

Social studies class may seem disconnected or incomprehensible for ELLs because the curriculum is so rooted in the U.S. context. If the curriculum relies primarily on grade-level textbook reading, it is likely to be at least twice as challenging for ELLs. But a social studies class also has the potential to unite EAL students and native speakers as a community when they reflect on their own lived experiences and identities (Ovando et al., 2003). Teachers can develop a safe and engaging environment in which students can participate and acquire social studies knowledge through carefully selected instructional techniques.

However, a safe and culturally sensitive environment alone is not enough. ELLs need teachers to explicitly demonstrate what is expected of them. Frequent demonstration (e.g., on an overhead) and a variety of supplemental materials (e.g., picture books, films, documentaries) are likely to elicit both content and language development. Szpara and Ahmad (2007) contend that social studies teachers can maintain high cognitive demands while lowering the linguistic load and affective filter among secondary ELLs with role playing and dramatization. They remind educators to move beyond simple, literal questions and elicit students' higher-order thinking by encouraging students to answer questions such as, "What would happen if . . . ?" (Szpara & Ahmad, 2007, p. 195). Other helpful graphic organizers include timelines, flow charts, Venn diagrams, charts, and tables. The graphic organizer in Figure 2.2, for example, visually reinforces the various aspects of Athenian democracy. Teachers can extend ELLs' understanding and meaning making by encouraging students in small groups to compare Athenian democracy to U.S. democracy. The chart shown in Figure 2.2 may also be springboard for a critical discussion about what a democracy entails.

Language Arts

Most of the strategies suggested to promote English language proficiency across the other content areas are appropriate for the language arts class. However, beyond story maps language arts may provide the most creative

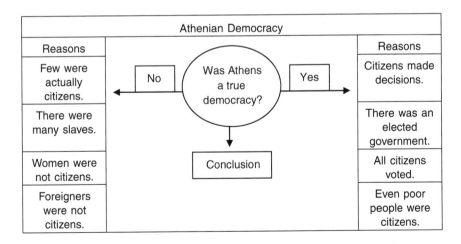

FIGURE 2.2. Sample organizer chart. From Alvermann, Donna E., Stephen Phelps, & Victoria Ridgeway *Content Area Reading and Literacy, 5th Ed.* Published by Allyn and Bacon, Boston, MA. Copyright © 2007 by Pearson Education. Reprinted by permission of the publisher.

outlets to integrate listening, speaking, reading, writing, and the visual and performing aspects of language. It is important that oral interactions between students in their small groups are directly related to the reading and writing assignments that are expected from them (Ovando et al., 2003). It is especially important for language arts teachers to supplement their "reading lists" with a wide variety of genres, which means being open to the inclusion of popular fiction and popular culture. Making deeper personal connections in language arts classes is likely to lower ELLs' anxieties (i.e., diminish the affective filter) and create greater opportunities for students to construct meaning as they develop English language competencies.

Because we all tend to view our own day-to-day cultural practices as "normal"—with the common counterpart view that others' cultural practices are somewhat abnormal—an awareness of other perspectives should be encouraged and consciously developed among students, ELLs included. Through literature circles, ELLs can receive the linguistic scaffold they need to engage with texts that are beyond their literacy comfort zone while learning to question their own assumptions and explore the embedded ideologies across texts. Short stories may be more manageable than full-fledged novels, and many recently published authors are immigrants or children of immigrants; their fictional tales are often highly autobiographical. Students can be encouraged to discuss why characters respond as they do in particular situations and infer alternate outcomes. One way to make a classical novel come to life is to have small groups perform a particular version of the text from the perspective of certain characters. Such an activity is likely not only to develop language and peer relationships but also encourage negotiation of divergent views.

All students must have access to content and higher-level abstraction; thus, academic language should be explicitly taught and used in an array of genres. Language arts teachers should teach and model the use of cohesive ties, which ELLs will be expected to include in their own writing. Teachers and students can point out cohesive ties in class readings, so that

Time/Order	Additive	Cause/Effect	Conclusive	Changing
soon	in addition	as a result	consequently	nonetheless
when	moreover	because	in summary	despite
finally	also	since	therefore	However

FIGURE 2.3. A chart showing cohesive ties. From Suzanne Peregoy and Owen Boyle. *Reading, Writing, and Learning in ESL: A Resource Book for K–12 Teachers, 4th Ed.* Published by Allyn and Bacon, Boston, MA. Copyright © 1992 by Pearson Education. Reprinted by permission of the publisher.

particular phrases can be read and interpreted in context. A chart such as Figure 2.3 can be displayed in classrooms, so that students can make use of it as needed; students can be encouraged to continue adding to the chart as they find more examples across texts.

CONCLUSION

In this chapter we focused on the increase in the number of EAL students in secondary schools, the various programs designed for ELLs, and strategies that are likely to be helpful across the four core content areas. It has become clear that the "one size fits all" approach to the standards-based teacher-education programs "do[es] not reflect effective pedagogy or methods necessary to address the needs of the majority of the growing immigrant, and non-English speaking student populations" (Balderama, 2001, p. 259).

We hope that we clarified that the English language register ELL students use for socializing is not the same as the register used in textbooks (Rubinstein-Ávila, 2006). Thus ELLs who sound orally fluent in English may be struggling with reading comprehension or disciplinary writing. Students' full linguistic repertoires (i.e., their home language(s) competencies and their expanding English competencies) should not be viewed as a threat or a detractor to developing academic English language competencies. Also, ELLs' formal schooling experiences can vary a great deal; for immigrant students who have experienced gaps in formal education, the lack of background knowledge may be an additional challenge to their developing English proficiencies. In fact, Short and Echevarria (2005) underscore that struggles with schoolwork are more likely to be a result of students' lack of background knowledge than an indicator of their intellectual abilities.

As Orellana and Gutierrez (2006) point out, ELLs are not "the problem." The problem continues to be the lack of relevance across teacher-education programs and underresourced school districts. In fact, Short and Echevarria (2005) have made an excellent point: Although No Child Left Behind called for "highly qualified teachers in every core academic classroom by 2006" (p. 10), few states require content-area teachers to obtain basic preparation in second language acquisition and cross-cultural understanding. It is time for teachers across the United State to understand that a student's home language is not a threat to English language development, and that the use of the first language to discuss the content may be crucial to meaning making. Providing EAL students with an array of learning opportunities, experiences, and modalities is likely to ensure that learning will become more relevant for many more students.

Last, it is essential to understand that a student's limited English proficiency or foreign accent is *not* a sign of a diminished ability to think and to reason at advanced levels. Whereas the linguistic load across content areas may need to be simplified, concepts and ideas do not. ELL students, like all other students, should be encouraged to engage rigorously and critically with the content they are studying in order to become critical consumers and producers of knowledge.

DISCUSSION AND ACTIVITIES

1. What are your beliefs or opinions about second language acquisition and development? Are they based on your personal experiences with learning a foreign language, living abroad, the media? Is your view compatible with those outlined in this chapter? Your views and the views of your colleagues on this topic, impact the instructional environment for ELLs in the classroom. Teachers who automatically assume ELLs are saying (bad) things about them in their first language when students are likely to be discussing the content are less likely to encourage students to use their full linguistic repertoires to their advantage.

2. Of the strategies you have just read about, which ones could you adapt and apply in your particular content area?

3. Seek out a certified ESL teacher in your school and invite her or him to plan several units with you to ensure that ELLs will have opportunities to engage with the material while they develop their English language competencies.

4. Knowing your students matters! How well do you know the students who are classified as ELLs in your class? Do you know where they are from, how many years of formal schooling they completed in their home country?

5. Do you know if the ELLs in your classes read regularly in their home language (e.g., Internet, the Bible, comic books, magazines)? If they do, they are more likely to understand the uses of cognate pairs and transfer other literacy practices to content-area literacy.

6. Consider suggesting that your principal arrange for SIOP training at your school.

ACKNOWLEDGMENTS

We would like to thank Dr. Mary Carol Combs (University of Arizona), who coordinates the undergraduate structured English immersion course, for her contribution to this chapter.

REFERENCES

Alvermann, D. E., Phelps, S. F., & Ridgeway, V. G. (2007). *Content area reading andliteracy: Succeeding in today's diverse classrooms*. Boston: Pearson.

Balderama, M. V. (2001). The (mis)preparation of teachers in the Proposition 227 era: Humanizing teacher roles and their practice. *Urban Review, 33*(3), 255–267.

Brabham, E. G., & Villaume, S. K. (2000). Continuing conversations about literature circles. *Reading Teacher, 54*(3), 278–280.

Campbell, A. E., Adams, V. M., & Davis, G. E. (2007). Cognitive demands and second-language learners: A framework for analyzing mathematics instructional contexts. *Mathematical Thinking and Learning, 9*(1), 3–30.

Combs, M. C., Evans, C., Fletcher, T., Parra, E., & Jimenez, A. (2005). Bilingualism for the children: Implementing a dual-language program in an English only state. *Educational Policy, 19*(5), 701–728.

Creese, A. (2006). Is this content-based language teaching? *Linguistics and Education, 16*, 188–204.

Dong, Y. R. (2005). Getting at the content. *Educational Leadership, 62*(4), 14–19.

Dworin, J. E. (2003). Insights into biliteracy development: Toward a bidirectional theory of bilingual pedagogy. *Journal of Hispanic Higher Education, 2*(2), 171–186.

Echevarria, J., & Graves, A. (2007). *Sheltered content instruction: Teaching English language learners with diverse abilities* (3rd ed.). Boston: Pearson.

Echevarria, J., Vogt, M., & Short, D. J. (2004). *Making content comprehensible for English learners: The SIOP model* (2nd ed.). Boston: Pearson.

Fang, Z. (2006). The language demands of science reading in middle school. *International Journal of Science Education, 28*, 491–520.

Fitzgerald, J. (1995). English-as-a-second-language reading instruction in the United States: A research review. *Journal of Reading Behavior, 27*(2), 115–153.

Furner, J. M., Yahya, N., & Duffy, M. L. (2005). 20 ways to teach mathematics: Strategies to reach all students. *Intervention in School and Clinic, 41*, 16–23.

Garcia, G. E., & Godina, H. (2004). Addressing the literacy needs of adolescent English language learners. In T. L. Jetton & J. A. Dole (Eds.), *Adolescent literacy research and practice* (pp. 304–320). New York: Guilford Press.

Jacobs, V. A. (2002). Reading, writing and understanding. *Educational Leadership, 60*(2), 58–61.

Jimenez, R. T., Garcia, G. E., & Pearson, P. D. (1996). The reading strategies of bilingual Latino/a students who are successful English readers: Opportunities and obstacles. *Reading Research Quarterly, 31*(1), 2–25.

McGraw, R., & Rubinstein-Ávila, E. (in press). Developing middle-school mathematical reasoning in a dual-language classroom. *Bilingual Research Journal.*

Moll, L. C., & Dworin, J. E. (1996). Biliteracy development in classrooms: Social dynamics and cultural possibilities. In D. Hicks (Ed.), *Discourse, learning and schooling: An interdisciplinary perspective* (pp. 221–246). Cambridge, UK: Cambridge University Press.

Moschkovich, J. (1999). Supporting the participating of English language learners in mathematical discussions. *For the Learning of Mathematics, 19*(1), 11–19.

Moschkovich, J. (2005). Using two languages when learning mathematics. *Educational Studies in Mathematics, 64*, 121–144.

Orellana, M. J., & Gutierrez, K. (2006). AT LAST: What's the problem? Constructing different genres for the study of English learners. *Research in the Teaching of English, 41*(1), 118–123.

Ovando, C. J., Collier, V. P., & Combs, M. C. (2003). *Bilingual and ESL classrooms: Teaching in multicultural contexts.* Boston: McGraw-Hill.

Peregoy, S. F., & Boyle, O. F. (2005). *Reading, writing, and learning in ESL: A resource book for K–12 teachers.* Boston: Pearson.

Rubinstein-Ávila, E. (2003). Facing reality: English language learners in middle school English. *English Education, 35*(2), 122–136.

Rubinstein-Ávila, E. (2006). Connecting with Latino learners. *Educational Leadership, 63*(5), 38–43.

Rubinstein-Ávila, E. (2007). What counts as literacy for Yanira Lara: From the Dominican Republic to Drew High. *Reading Research Quarterly, 42*(4), 568–589.

Schleppegrell, M., & de Oliveira, L. C. (2006). An integrated language and content approach for history teachers. *Journal of English for Academic Purposes, 5*(4), 254–268.

Short, D., & Echevarria, J. (2005). Teacher skills to support English language learners. *Educational Leadership, 62*(4), 9–13.

Sox, A., & Rubinstein-Ávila, E. (2007). Content area WebQuests for English language learners: Essential elements for design. Unpublished manuscript.

Stien, D., & Beed, P. L. (2004). Bridging the gap between fiction and non-fiction in the literature circle setting. *Journal of Adolescent and Adult Literacy, 57*(6), 510–518.

Szpara, M. Y., & Ahmad, I. (2007). Supporting English-language learners in the social studies class. *Social Studies, 98*(5), 189–195.

Valdés, G. (2001). *Learning and not learning English: Latino students in American schools.* New York: Teachers College Press.

Valdés, G. (2004). Between support and marginalization: The development of academic language in linguistic minority children. *Bilingual Education and Bilingualism, 7*(2&3), 102–132.

CHAPTER 3

Rethinking Literacy Learning and Teaching
INTERSECTIONS OF ADOLESCENTS' IN-SCHOOL AND OUT-OF-SCHOOL LITERACY PRACTICES

Shelley Hong Xu

In this chapter:

- Discuss the essential premises in the new literacy studies (NLS) perspective (literacy practices, context, text, and Discourse community).

- Based on these premises of NLS, explore how adolescents' in-school and out-of-school literacy practices share commonalities and differences to various degrees.

- Introduce promising possibilities for intersection of in-school and out-of-school literacy practices.

- Share an example of how a high school teacher mediated between out-of-school texts and school text in motivating struggling 12th graders in a *"remedial"* English class (the term used by the school, with which I disagree).

- Discuss main points in relation to the illustrated example of the high school teacher and some activities for readers to do.

My 10-year-old son and his friends often have a good time trading Pokémon and Yu-Gi-Oh! cards, playing online games, sending e-mails to other friends, discussing and sharing mangas, and singing pop songs. Every time I express some interest in learning about what he and his friends are "doing," he or one of his friends always say something like this: "You will not understand, OK? We are not doing school stuff, so leave us alone. And please do not spoil our fun." They would often push me out of the room when I asked them a question such as "What's all this about?" And my son would respond, "Are you going to ask me about a main idea or theme of this game?" I confess that at times, I cannot take off a teacher hat while interacting with my son and his friends. I sense that the boys dislike being questioned in a way that is similar to how their teachers have questioned them at school. To them, my questioning threatens to spoil the pleasure they have derived from what they are doing. They view what they are doing at my house as an enjoyable activity, only for insiders who are knowledgeable about the activity and who are in a community of their own interest.

Although the boys are only on their way to becoming adolescents, their view is similar to the one held by adolescents portrayed in literature that focuses on adolescents' outside school literacy experiences. For example, in an introduction to *Reconceptualizing the Literacies in Adolescents' Lives* (Alvermann, Hinchman, Moore, Phelps, & Waff, 2006), Alvermann, Jonas, Steele, and Washington (2006) shared data from interviews with a 6th grader (Eric) and 10th grader (Ariel) about their experiences with school learning and out-of-school literacy practices. Specifically, in an outside school setting, the students were engaged in reading various genres of texts (e.g., literature, comic books, and biographies), text messaging, and writing. They found school reading and writing interesting and engaging when they were allowed to select books to read and topics to write. In particular, the importance of relevance was crucial to engagement. Eric, for example, thought that "his science textbook had nothing in it that kids can relate to, nothing to do with the 'street' " (p. xxxvii). However, he did enjoy a science class during which the students made a volcano and then wrote a short paragraph about the experience. Both Eric and Ariel expressed their wish that teachers would allow them to do instant messaging. Their wish suggests a need for teachers to create a hybrid space in classrooms that allows for an intersection of out-of-school and in-school literacy practices.

This chapter focuses on the possibility of factoring adolescents' out-of-school literacy practices into school teaching and learning approaches for adolescents. My discussion of the intersection of two types of literacy practices is based on an NLS perspective.

A PERSPECTIVE OF NEW LITERACY STUDIES

Four components are central to the NLS perspective (Gee, 1996, 2003; Lankshear & Knobel, 2003; New London Group, 1996; Street, 1995): literacy practices, context, text, and discourse community. Although I discuss each component separately, these four components are closely interwoven.

Literacy Practices

First, the NSL perspective reconceptualizes what literacy is. Whereas literacy has been often associated with an ability to read and write, and in particular, an ability to read and write print-based texts, the NLS perspective recognizes different types of literacy practices in which people are engaged in various social settings (e.g., community, home, shopping mall) (e.g., Hull & Schultz, 2002; Lankshear & Knobel, 2003; Street, 1995). Thus reading a menu and drawing a comic strip, among others, are considered literacy practices in the same way that reading an assigned school book and writing in a journal are. Based on this premise, students' interaction with print, visual, aural, or digital texts (e.g., playing a video game, watching a movie) can be viewed as various types of literacy practices during which they apply their literacy knowledge and skills to "reading" a text. Given that, the term *literacy practices* is used in a broader sense (than what has been referred to—school literacy-related tasks) throughout this chapter.

Context

Closely related to the premise of different types of literacy practices is the notion of context. Literacy practices always occur in situated, specific contexts (Gee, 1996, 2003; Street, 1984, 1995); they are social practices "involving socially recognized ways of doing things" (Lankshear & Knobel, 2007, p. 4). It is a common experience for many adolescents to communicate with their peers via a device or technology (e.g., cell phone, e-mail, instant messaging) in the context of their life outside of school. However, they often do not have permission to use phone or instant messaging in a school setting. Similarly, at school, discussing a classic novel is likely to be a shared literacy experience for many adolescents, but a parent is less likely to ask an adolescent child to perform a similar task at home. Only within a specific context does a literacy practice become meaningful to the participants. As Lankshear and Knobel (2007) argued, "Within contexts of human practice, language (words, literacy, texts) gives meaning to contexts and, dialectically, contexts give meaning to language. Hence, there is no reading or writing in any meaningful sense of each term outside social practices" (p. 2).

Text

A third premise of the NSL perspective recognizes a wide range of texts as being involved in literacy practices. This recognition expands what we generally categorize as reading and writing from print-based books to print, nonprint, and multimedia texts. Scholars such as Gee (2003), Kress

(2003), and the New London Group (1996) have pointed out that besides linguistic units in a text, other modes of meanings exist. In particular, as the New London Group stated, there are modes for "visual meanings (images, page layouts, screen formats); audio meanings (music, sound effects); gestural meanings (body language, sensuality); spatial meanings (the meaning of environmental spaces, architectural spaces); and multimodal meanings" (p. 80). Multiple modes of meanings, for example, are embedded in an Internet text. In addition to linguistic units (i.e., words), the page layout of the text also communicates meanings. A heading centered in the middle of a page on a screen, and the color and font unique to this heading, often signal the importance of this heading. Images in the text also help convey the meaning.

Discourse Community

People are engaged in different types of literacy practices in different social settings, and those who share the same literacy practice form a particular community (or a group), a Discourse community (Gee, 1996). *Discourse*, with a capital *D*, is different from *discourse*, with a lowercase *d* (which refers to linguistic units). *Discourse* refers to shared "ways of behaving, interacting, valuing, thinking, believing, speaking, and often reading and writing that are accepted by instantiations of particular roles (or 'types of people') by specific *groups of people*" (Gee, 1996, p. viii). For example, in a Discourse community of teachers, each member shares an interest in teaching and student learning and communicates with one another using a set of vocabulary familiar to members (e.g., *reading, writing, genre, standardized tests, PTA, reading difficulties*). In a similar way, students interested in YouTube (*www.youtube.com*) are in a Discourse community of YouTube. (YouTube is an online service that allows members to upload and share their own videos, and view, rate, and comment on videos submitted by other members.) Each member of this community has a good knowledge and skill of uploading their videos, as well as rating and reviewing others' videos. A certain set of vocabulary (e.g., *video embeds* [an HTML element, embedded media], *APIs* [Application Program Interface], *playlist* [a list of audio and/or video files], and *tag* [a syntax in HTML]) is shared by the community members.

Each member of a Discourse community has his or her *identity* associated with the community. For example, in a school community, a person who teaches is a teacher. Teachers at the same grade level or across grade levels share, in addition to their teaching credentials, a similar set of knowledge about curriculum, standards, and pedagogy. A person also can have multiple identities. Outside a teacher Discourse community, a teacher can be a mother or father, a son or daughter, a baseball coach, or neighbor, depending on the Discourse community with which she or he is associated. Communicating among members from different Discourse communities can be less effective or virtually impossible if members of one Discourse community are not familiar with the words and symbols that members of another Discourse community use. People who have never visited the YouTube website would have a difficult time carrying on a conversation, using the same lingo, with the members of the YouTube community. These people can be *positioned* by the YouTube community as outsiders or less knowledgeable others (or less capable others, from a deficit perspective).

SIMILARITIES AND DIFFERENCES OF IN-SCHOOL AND OUT-OF-SCHOOL LITERACY PRACTICES

I have presented the four premises central to the NLS perspective. In this section, guided by each premise, I explore the similarities and differences between in-school and out-of-school literacy practices.

Literacy Practices

A wide range of literacy practices, many of them similar, exists in both in-school and out-of-school social settings. For example, adolescents *read* at school and outside school, even though the text genres may differ. At school, they read classic and contemporary literature and content-area textbooks; outside school, it is more likely that adolescents read texts of their own interests or hobbies (e.g., magazines on beauty, cars, and games; comic books; entries on MySpace; sports news online). Another layer of similarity in literacy practices across both settings is a shared set of literacy knowledge and skills required for adolescents to participate in these practices. To comprehend a text, we need to be able to do at least the following: activate prior knowledge related to the topic; make a connection between the topic and prior knowledge; predict; infer; notice important details; organize details; modify existing schemas with newly acquired information; and self-monitor comprehension. Scholars (e.g., Alvermann, Huddleston, & Hagood, 2004; Gee, 2003; Xu, Perkins, & Zunich, 2005) have identified many sets of literacy knowledge and skills that are useful for literacy practices in various social settings.

Differences in literacy practices do exist across both in-school and out-of-school settings. Discussing and demonstrating strategies needed to win a sports game on Wii among a group of adolescents is definitely not a literacy practice that will occur in a classroom (although a conversation about the strategies may occur during recess or lunch time). A certain group of literacy knowledge and skills is specific to particular literacy practices. While navigating a website, the traditional English concepts of print (e.g., reading from left to right, page by page) often do not apply. A skillful Internet surfer needs to modify a way of reading used for a print text to fit into this reading of an online text. The surfer, for example, must know how to click a specific link to get the needed information and to get back to the main page of a website without page numbers as a reference (as in a print text); and how to make sense of a text with visual, aural, and linguistic input (Coiro & Dobler, 2007).

Context

By comparison, the differences in context between in-school and out-of-school literacy practices are greater than the differences in literacy practices. At the macro-level, *in school* and *out of school* are two distinctively different settings. At the micro-level, the differences are associated with purpose and meaning, initiative, and negotiation.

Purpose and Meaning

At school, most, if not all, literacy tasks have a purpose and meaning (e.g., addressing English curricular standards). However, when a teacher fails to communicate the purpose and meaning to students, it is hard for them to associate purpose and meaning with the assigned literacy task. To many struggling and reluctant adolescents, literacy tasks often seem purposeless and meaningless. They often ask, "Why do I have to learn about Shakespeare's work?" "What does it have to do with my life or future job?" By contrast, in an outside school setting, literacy practices with various types of texts (print, visual, aural, and digital) possess purpose and meaning (which may often not be understood by adults or teachers). Adolescents, for example, use instant messaging (IM) to solicit opinions to help solve a problem; play a PS2 game to satisfy a curiosity about the tricks on a next-level game; and use Google to locate the cheapest calculus textbook.

Initiative

Due to the way that literacy curriculum and instruction are structured at school, students are not the ones who initiate literacy tasks. They are *told* or *asked* to participate in certain literacy activities in order for them to pass a class or to graduate from high school. Lack of an opportunity to initiate a literacy activity is another factor contributing to some level of purposelessness and meaninglessness in some school activities (in students' experiences). Outside school, adolescents are often in control of which literacy practices they would like to "do." No parents or guardians would tell adolescents to go ahead to play a game on Xbox360; adolescents *want* to play a game to have some enjoyment. They sing a pop song not because they have been told to do so, but because they want to have a good time with friends and music.

Negotiation

Closely related to the initiative involved in literacy practices is negotiation. In many literacy practices at school, negotiation does not exist. For example, to respond to a novel, adolescents in many schools must write in an essay format. Other genres (e.g., photo essay, collage, and slide shows) are not offered as a choice. Additionally, for assignments that require completion by individuals, adolescents do not always have opportunities to negotiate with others in constructing meaning. In outside school settings, adolescents are often engaged in literacy practices in groups, and negotiation becomes a norm among members of a particular group. For example, in a karaoke, teens can select their singing partners after reviewing and agreeing on the song lyrics and identifying partners' strengths in singing (e.g., being able to handle high pitch, having a good sense of rhythm).

Text

There is a greater variability in types of text genres and nature of text used by adolescents outside of school than in school. The texts used in secondary schools continue to be dominated by print-based literature anthologies and content-area textbooks. The content presented in these texts tends to be fixed, mostly accurate, and at times out of date (e.g., the information related to the solar system has now become inaccurate with the new scientific discovery about planet Pluto as a dwarf planet). We, however, are happy to see an increased presence of online texts and media texts (e.g., movie/DVD) in teaching and in adolescents' school-work. By comparison, adolescents have been engaged in reading a mixture of print and nonprint texts outside of school. It is fair to say that their exposure to nonprint texts is greater due to our media- and technology-oriented society (e.g., Alvermann, 2004). The content presented in these texts is often fluid and current (though not always accurate [e.g., Dan Rather's inaccurate report on President Bush's military service]). For example, at the American Idol site (*www.americanidol.com/*), one can read news related to the latest contest, interviews with the contestants, blogs, or message boards. The information in such sites is updated frequently.

Discourse Community

A classroom is a place where adolescents and teachers from their respective Discourse communities communicate with one another. As discussed earlier, communication can be less effective due to one community's lack of knowledge of the other's ways of "behaving, interacting, valuing, thinking, believing, speaking, and often reading and writing that are accepted by instantiations of particular roles (or 'types of people') by specific *groups of people*" (Gee, 1996, p. viii). Teachers often comment that they do not understand much about their students. Students may feel equally puzzled by why their teachers cannot understand them.

Particularly interesting to the relationship between teachers and students are the identities students assume or the ways they are positioned by their teachers, and vice versa. Traditionally speaking, teachers hold an identity of a knowledgeable authority who imparts knowledge to students, provides guidance in learning, and has the power to offer students choices and to discipline them. By contrast, students assume an identity of learners who lack knowledge of certain content that they would learn from the teachers and instructional sources and who are expected to follow school rules and teachers' directions and requests. Furthermore, some students are positioned by certain literacy tasks as incapable learners. For example, when an ELL newcomer is required to participate in a class debate in the same way as other non-ELLs, the ELL is positioned, by virtue of the literacy task (and by the teacher), as an incapable learner. The student may have an ability to speak eloquently in a debate, but he or she cannot do so in English, an unfamiliar language that the student is still learning.

A HYBRID SPACE
IN A 12TH-GRADE REMEDIAL ENGLISH CLASS

I have used the four central premises of NLS to analyze the similarities and differences between in-school and out-of-school literacy practices. In this section, I present an example of a 12th-grade teacher who created a hybrid space in her remedial English classroom by building her teaching of literature on students' prior experience with a popular culture text, a reality show, *Survivor: Africa*. I have written about Jana in my other work (Xu, 2004), where I focused on how teachers used the different approaches developed by Alvermann, Moon, and Hagood (1999) in their integration of popular culture texts. Here I present a more detailed account of Jana's teaching with her students.

Jana was a 2nd-year English teacher at the time of this example. Like many new teachers, Jana was assigned to teach one of the most difficult classes on her campus—a remedial English class for seniors who had failed the state-mandated high school exit exam. Most of her students were African Americans from several poor neighborhoods in the city who had struggled with reading/language arts and other content subjects. Jana was not given any curriculum for her class, as she was told that no curriculum had worked for her students. Blessed with this freedom, Jana, who loved literature, decided to teach her class with literature units. Jana chose novels dealing with issues that her students faced in their life. One novel unit included *Speak* (Anderson, 1999) and dealt with the theme of survival.

Speak is about a high school freshman, Melinda, who was raped by a peer and was then labeled by her peers as an outcast. Her peers alienated and harassed her, and even her best friend abandoned her. Through her art class and the compassionate art teacher, Melinda finally broke her silence and spoke of the sorrow and pain she had been holding for so long.

Marching into her class with the excitement of wanting to enjoy and discuss with her students a good piece of literature that she thought related to students' life, Jana was greeted by moans and puzzlement. Jana then thought that her students might better understand and enjoy the book if they could make intertextual connections to something familiar. In choosing *Survivor: Africa* (filmed in Kenya, Africa) as another text, Jana considered leveling out "the authoritative power structure between myself and the students. . . . The opportunities for exploration and discovery [of the show were] spontaneous and equal [for me and my students]" (Xu, 2005, p. 10). Furthermore, Jana noted that "her students often had a direct ancestral connection with the African people and wanted to study Kenya" (Xu, 2004, p. 427). Although Jana was not familiar with the show, she did spend some time watching it. Table 3.1 lists a set of activities in which Jana and her students engaged while reading/viewing and discussing *Survivor: Africa* and *Speak*. Following is a more detailed description of each activity.

TABLE 3.1. Activities with *Survivor: Africa* and *Speak*

Activity	Survivor: Africa	Speak
1		Saying something and asking a question about the text
2		Journal writing (describing and predicting)
3		Relating Maslow's theory about human needs to the character
4		Discussing characterization
5	Reviewing background information about the show	
6	Listing 10 needs for the contestants to survive	
7		Listing 10 needs for Melinda to survive
8	Comparing and contrasting the 10 needs	
9	Constructing a media collage on survival	
10	Creating a performance art kit on an event from *Speak*	

Saying Something and Asking a Question about the Text

After reading each chapter of *Speak*, students shared responses to the reading with their peers at their respective table groups, and asked a question about it. They had an opportunity to answer others' questions and to learn from each others' perspectives about the readings. During the discussion, Jana managed to sit with each group for a few minutes so that she could share her response, ask her questions, comment on her students' responses, and answer their questions.

Journal Writing (Describing and Predicting)

Before reading each chapter, students wrote a one-page journal entry predicting and describing the reason for what had happened in the previous chapter. Students then shared their predictions and provided evidence from the text to support them.

Relating Maslow's Theory about Human Needs to the Character

After students had read several chapters, Jana felt it was necessary to introduce her students to Maslow's (1954) theory of five levels of human needs (i.e., physiological, safety, social, esteem, and self-actualization). While discussing each level of Maslow's needs, Jana guided her students to connect the material to Melinda's situation. Specifically, Jana asked her students to identify in a journal entry Melinda's needs and to give "Melinda advice on how she could better satisfy those needs that were not getting met" (Xu, 2005, p. 12).

Discussing Characterization

Once the class had discovered (through contextual clues) the reason for Melinda's silence (i.e., she was raped by a popular senior at a summer party), Jana posed a question to start a discussion about Melinda (e.g., "Do you feel that Melinda had the right to feel bitter and negative toward her peers, given this new information about her past?"). This discussion led students to a deeper understanding of the severity of Melinda's situation—she was unable to sleep, look at herself in the mirror, and function as a normal teenager; she was struggling for survival.

Reviewing Background Information about the Show

Before reading more about Melinda in the book, Jana thought that it was a good time to bring *Survivor: Africa* into a discussion, offering students an opportunity for intertextual connections. Jana and her students discussed major concepts of the show: the tribes, days in the camp, physical challenges, immunity and its effects on tribes, and the prize for a winner. Jana also read to the class a clip from a TV guide discussing the dangers of animal attacks, disease, and dehydration that contestants would face. Lastly, Jana and the class read and discussed information downloaded from the *World Book Encyclopedia Online*. The discussion focused on the geographical location for the contestants—National Reserve (climate and wildlife).

Listing 10 Needs for the Contestants to Survive

After viewing one episode of the show, students worked in groups, generating a list of 10 needs the contestants must meet to survive the 39 days of harsh conditions on a reserve and strive for the grand prize. The list included such needs as water and food supplies, shelter, protection from natural disasters (e.g., fire, animal attacks), teamwork, leadership, locating and managing resources, and forming alliances. After each group had shared their list, Jana compiled a class list of needs by contestants. Later, Jana had students categorize the needs based on Maslow's (1954) five levels. For example, one group wrote: " 'Physiological—they need food and water. Safety—to keep endangered animals out (fenced). Social—they have to win social games/events' " (Xu, 2005, p. 14).

Listing 10 Needs for Melinda to Survive

Similarly, each group of students made a list of needs that Melinda must meet in order to survive. Her needs included: to stop hiding in the closet, to seek counseling, to release guilt and anger, to tell others who had raped her, and to get involved in extracurricular activities, among other things. Again, after the class had compiled a list of needs for Melinda, students related Melinda's needs to Maslow's different levels. One group wrote: " 'Safety—she needs to be protected from being bullied by others. Social—she needs to make friends, tell others how she feels and what she experiences. Esteem—she needs to raise her low self-esteem. Self-actualization—she needs to tell the cops who raped her' " (Xu, 2005, p. 15).

Comparing and Contrasting the 10 Needs

In a follow-up activity related to the list of needs for the *Survivor: Africa* contestants and for Melinda, each group completed a Venn diagram (see Figure 3.1) and presented it to the class. Throughout the presentation, Jana seized many teachable moments to facilitate a discussion leading to students' better understanding of the book. In her own words:

The social issues among the tribes were more apparent as contestants struggled to form alliances. I asked them if they had noticed a social structure similar to this occurring in *Speak*. They responded by discussing how the students at Melinda's school had forced her to be an outcast. They also discussed how Melinda struggled to make alliances with her old friends. Several students also brought up the distant relationships Melinda has with her parents. We also discussed social clicks [*sic*] within our high school. I am proud to say that most of these students interact like a large family. (Xu, 2005, p. 17)

Constructing a Media Collage on Survival

In order for her students to gain more knowledge of the concept of survival in relation to their own lives and society, in general, Jana had her students construct a media collage. Jana explained:

On a large piece of paper, I had the students draw and label Maslow's Hierarchy of Needs. Then the students were asked to find visual images, such as words and pictures, from a variety of magazines that represented how they fulfilled their personal hierarchy of needs. After the students had finished we shared our collages. We had a great conversation on why many Americans got hung up on the lower levels of the hierarchy such as love needs and self-esteem needs. We also discussed how the needs of people in modern Amer-

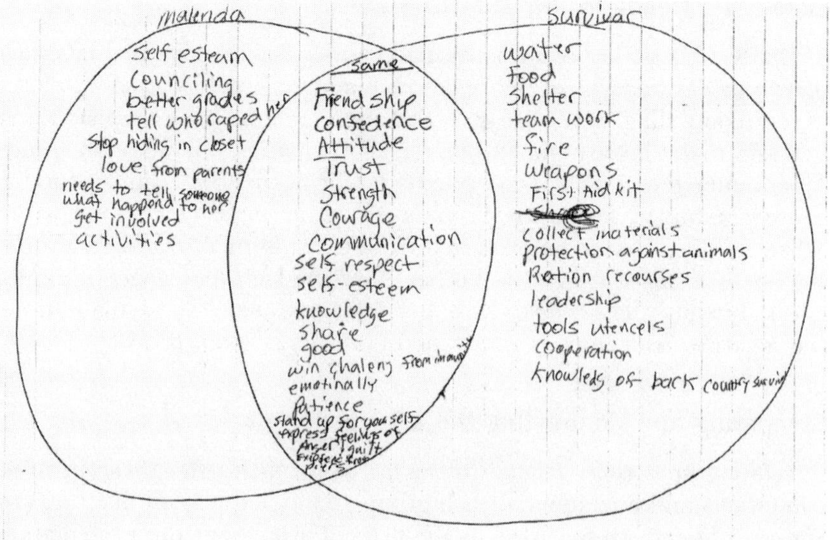

FIGURE 3.1. Venn diagram on needs for contestants and Melinda.

ica differ from the needs of people in the rural communities of Kenya, Africa. (Xu, 2005, p. 18)

Creating a Performance Art Kit on an Event from *Speak*

To conclude this unit with *Speak*, Jana had her students work in groups to create a performance art skit about an event from the book. One requirement was for students to use "symbolic animals' masks to represent the characters from *Speak*." Some examples of animal representations for the characters included (1) "Melinda was a helpless antelope," (2) "The rapist in the novel was a stalking lion" and (3) "Many of Melinda's rejecting peers were represented by laughing hyenas" (Xu, 2005, p. 19).

DISCUSSION OF THE HYBRID SPACE IN JANA'S CLASS

In this section, using the four premises of the NLS perspectives regarding literacy practices, context, text, and Discourse community, I analyze the activities in Jana's *Speak* unit to show how her teaching offered a different way for her struggling 12th-graders to become engaged in learning and to practice and strengthen literacy knowledge and skills.

Literacy Practices

In this unit students were engaged in many different types of literacy practices, some of which did not often occur in classrooms:

- Reading and discussing a novel
- Viewing and discussing a TV show
- Obtaining and comprehending information from online resources
- Journal writing
- Applying Maslow's theory to a novel and a TV show
- Analyzing similarities and differences in experiences of the characters in a TV show and a novel
- Demonstrating an understanding of the concept of survival through a media collage
- Writing a performance skit and performing it

Jana's and her students' experience with this *Speak* unit, which integrated a popular culture text, *Survivor: Africa*, showed that it is possible for a teacher to create a hybrid space in a classroom where teaching is built on students' prior experience with out-of-school literacy practices. It is also important to note that during these practices, students had multiple opportunities to apply or strengthen literacy knowledge and skills required by the state standards.

Context

Given the integration of students' everyday text and some literacy practices resembling daily practices, the context of Jana's classroom became more student-friendly and students took charge of their own learning.

- *Purpose and Meaning*. Although Jana did not set a purpose for the *Speak* unit, she did strive for communicating the purpose with students through *Survivor: Africa*. Meaningfulness of this unit then became visible to students.
- *Initiative*. Jana's students did not initiate all the activities in the unit. During each activity, each student, however, did have a choice as to how to participate. A student, for example, could choose how to relate Maslow's five levels of human needs to the needs of the contestants on *Survivor: Africa* and of Melinda in *Speak*.
- *Negotiation*. Jana presented multiple opportunities for students to negotiate in meaning construction. A good example was the group work involved in many activities. Students were also able to negotiate with Jana as to how to demonstrate their understanding (e.g., in creating a media collage, students could choose any form of artifacts).

Jana observed the effect of the context that she cultivated in her teaching and found it conducive to various types of literacy practices:

> The class discussions and group work were very insightful and beneficial to us all. The students' individual journals and reader response activities helped me to accurately assess each student's understanding of the text. The creative responses to the texts allowed students to interpret and represent their understandings of the text imaginatively and risk-free. (Xu, 2005, p. 20)

Text

Jana integrated various text genres in this unit. A mixture of text genres provided various degrees of support for students to construct meanings and make intertextual connections:

- Print (e.g., *Speak*)
- Aural (e.g., discussion, presentation, dialogues among contestants in *Survivor: Africa*)

- Visual (e.g., *Survivor: Africa*, a media collage)
- Digital (e.g., *World Book Encyclopedia Online*)

Jana explained the effect of these texts on students' learning: "Highly interesting texts that students can relate to reap the most benefits. I honestly feel like the students enjoyed themselves with this unit" (Xu, 2005, p. 20).

Discourse Community

Two Discourse communities were blended nicely to form a new Discourse community within a hybrid space in Jana's classroom. Jana belonged to a *teacher* Discourse community whose members had a good body of knowledge regarding literacy instruction pedagogy and curriculum, a developing knowledge of their students, and whose responsibility was to teach students. Jana's students were from a *student* Discourse community whose members had their own interests in, and experiences with, texts other than the ones they were reading at school, and whose responsibility was to learn from teachers, instructional resources, and peers. The newly formed Discourse community, resulting from an infusion of various text genres, a blend of literacy practices, and Jana's skillful scaffolding, changed the roles she and her students played during this unit.

In addition to continuing to function as a teacher, Jana became

- A student who learned from her students about *Survivor: Africa* and, from her adolescent students' perspective, about how Melinda felt.
- A co-participant who became a member of her students' discussion groups.
- A facilitator who posed questions for discussion and who suggested activities for the unit.
- A monitor who oversaw students' participation in activities and who documented students' learning outcomes.

Each student in Jana's class was positioned by Jana, by literacy practices, by context, and by texts as

- A teacher who taught Jana about *Survivor: Africa* and about how a student felt about school learning when his or her life experience was part of school learning.
- A participant who was engaged in different types of purposeful and meaningful activities.
- A critical thinker who was able to analyze a text (e.g., contestants'

needs and Melinda's needs) and relate Maslow's theory to both contestants' needs and Melinda's needs.

- A producer who created a media collage and a performance skit to demonstrate an understanding of the character's experience and the concept of survival.
- A capable learner who actively participated in literacy practices and produced texts to demonstrate his or her reading and writing ability.

To sum up, Jana's students' experiences taught us several lessons. One lesson was that multimodal texts challenge "schooled literacy" (O'Brien, 1998) and the institution of old learning (O'Brien & Bauer, 2005), which focuses on "book culture" (Luke, 2000). Jana's experiences also show how teachers can become knowledgeable about various types of texts familiar to their students and integrate those texts into school teaching.

In addition, the students' experience of engaging in unit activities raised a question regarding their supposed limited literacy competence. The question is not whether struggling students lack an ability to make sense out of a text, but whether multiple opportunities for engagement in purposeful and meaningful literacy practices are available to them. The importance of the question of student engagement in relation to improving literacy achievements of reluctant and struggling students echoes what Alexander (2003) argued: "Reading is an emotional domain, not a coldly cognitive enterprise. Reader motivation and affect are powerful forces in this journey toward competence" (p. 61). The value of engagement in the process of students becoming competent readers and writers (Wigfield, 2004) was further illustrated in Jana's reflection on this unit:

> We all learned much more than we would have by simply reading a novel and answering questions. One of the unit assignments was for the students to create a representation of any scene from the novel using symbolic animal masks to represent the characters from *Speak* and perform this scene. The students were extremely excited about this assignment. A few of my male students wanted to group up and write their own survivor series instead of participating in the performance art. . . . Once we began [the unit], the possibilities and opportunities to explore different concepts and ideas became almost endless. In particular, mini-lessons on reading, writing, and organizational strategies were easily integrated. All of these would have been hard for my students to accomplish in a period of one month if I had just focused on reading the novel, *Speak*. . . . My students were more motivated to learn about things that they considered "not school" items. However, they were benefiting from a multitude of educational objectives. There is absolutely no reason why students must be forced to read the same dry and boring [state standard-related] passages when you can use interesting articles from an endless amount of sources and still achieve the standards. (Xu, 2005, pp. 22, 27)

DISCUSSION AND ACTIVITIES

1. Survey students to learn about their experiences with everyday texts (print, aural, visual, and digital) and literacy practices in out-of-school settings.

2. Select and experience (e.g., listen to, view) one piece of students' everyday text, document the literacy knowledge and skills you have used in your experience, and identify similarities and differences between the knowledge and skills used in your experience and those you teach at school.

3. With your students, select and experience (e.g., listen to, view) one piece of students' everyday text, and identify similarities and differences in your experience and your students' experience.

4. Try infusing one piece of students' everyday text into your literacy teaching, document your experience and your students', analyze the infusion using the NLS perspective (the four premises regarding literacy practices, context, text, and Discourse community), and reflect on how the integration has changed your students' motivation and engagement.

REFERENCES

Alexander, P. A. (2003). Profiling the developing reader: The interplay of knowledge, interest, and strategic processing. In C. M. Fairbanks, J. Worthy, B. Maloch, J. V. Hoffman, & D. L. Schallert (Eds.), *52nd yearbook of the National Reading Conference* (pp. 47–65). Oak Creek, WI: National Reading Conference.

Alvermann, D. E. (Ed.). (2004). *Adolescents and literacies in a digital world*. New York: Lang.

Alvermann, D. E., Hinchman, K. A., Moore, D. W., Phelps, S. F., & Waff, D. R. (Eds.). (2006). *Reconceptualizing the literacies in adolescents' lives* (2nd ed.). Mahwah, NJ: Erlbaum.

Alvermann, D. E., Huddleston, A., & Hagood, M. C. (2004). What could professional wrestling and school literacy practices possibly have in common? *Journal of Adolescent and Adult Literacy, 47,* 532–540.

Alvermann, D. E., Jonas, S., Steele, A., & Washington, E. (2006). Introduction. In D. E. Alvermann, K. A. Hinchman, D. W. Moore, S. F. Phelps., & D. R. Waff (Eds.), *Reconceptualizing the literacies in adolescents' lives* (2nd ed., pp. xxi–xxxii). Mahwah, NJ: Erlbaum.

Alvermann, D. E., Moon, J. S., & Hagood, M. C. (1999). *Popular culture in the classroom: Teaching and researching critical media literacy.* Newark, DE: International Reading Association.

Anderson, L. H. (1999). *Speak.* New York: Farrar, Straus & Giroux.

Coiro, J., & Dobler, J. (2007). Exploring the online reading comprehension strategies used by sixth-grade skilled readers to search for and locate information on the Internet. *Reading Research Quarterly, 42,* 214–257.

Gee, J. P. (1996). *Social linguistics and literacies: Ideology in discourses* (2nd ed.). London: Falmer.

Gee, J. P. (2003). *What video games have to teach us about learning and literacy.* New York: Palgrave Macmillan.

Hull, G., & Schultz, K. (2002). Connecting schools with out-of-school worlds: Insights from recent research on literacy in non-school settings. In G. Hull & K. Schultz (Eds.), *School's out: Bringing out-of-school literacies with classroom practices* (pp. 32–57). New York: Teachers College Press.

Kress, G. (2003). *Literacy in the new media age.* New York: Routledge.

Lankshear, C., & Knobel, M. (2003). *New literacies: Changing knowledge and classroom teaching.* Philadelphia: Open University Press.

Lankshear, C., & Knobel, M. (2007). Sampling "the New" in new literacies. In C. Lankshear & M. Knobel (Eds.), *A new literacy sampler* (pp. 1–24). New York: Lang.

Luke, C. (2000). New literacies in teacher education. *Journal of Adolescent and Adult Literacy, 43,* 424–435.

Maslow, A. (1954). *Motivation and personality.* New York: Harper.

New London Group. (1996). A pedagogy of multiliteracies: Designing social futures. *Harvard Educational Review, 66,* 60–92.

O'Brien, D. (1998). Multiple literacies in a high-school program for "at-risk" adolescents. In D. Alvermann, K. A. Hinchman, D. Moore, S. Phelps, & D. Waff (Eds.), *Reconceptualizing the literacies in adolescents' lives* (pp. 27–49). Mahwah, NJ: Erlbaum.

O'Brien, D. G., & Bauer, E. B. (2005). New literacies and the institution of old learning. *Reading Research Quarterly, 40,* 120–131.

Street, B. V. (1984). *Literacy in theory and practice.* New York: Cambridge University Press.

Street, B. V. (1995). *Social literacies: Critical approaches to literacy in development, ethnography and education.* London: Longman.

Wigfield, A. (2004). Motivation for reading during the early adolescent and adolescent years. In D. S. Strickland & D. E. Alvermann (Eds.), *Bridging the literacy achievement gap grades 4–12* (pp. 56–69). New York: Teachers College Press.

Xu, S. H. (2004). Teachers' reading of students' popular culture texts: The interplay of students' interests, teacher knowledge, and literacy curriculum. In C. M. Fairbanks, J. Worthy, B. Maloch, J. V. Hoffman, & D. L. Schallert (Eds.), *53rd yearbook of the National Reading Conference* (pp. 417–431). Oak Creek, WI: National Reading Conference.

Xu, S. H. (2005). *Do TV shows have anything to do with literacy teaching and learning?* Unpublished manuscript.

Xu, S. H., Perkins, R. S., & Zunich, L. O. (2005). *Trading cards to comic strips: Popular culture texts and literacy learning in grades K–8.* Newark, DE: International Reading Association.

CHAPTER 4

iLife

UNDERSTANDING AND CONNECTING
TO THE DIGITAL LITERACIES OF ADOLESCENTS

Dana J. Wilber

This chapter introduces readers to the digital literacies of adolescents by:

- Describing their practices, including social networking sites such as MySpace and Facebook; blogging and wikis; podcasting, videocasting and YouTube, gaming and learning through video games; manga, anime, and fan fiction.
- Demonstrating the shift from Web 1.0 to Web 2.0.
- Explaining how and why digital practices are important to think about in terms of literacies and not just new technologies.
- Situating these literacies in the theoretical frame of new literacies, drawing on the work of Lankshear and Knobel (2007), Gee (2003), and others.
- Connecting the digital literacies of teenagers with potential and actual practices in classrooms, including blogging, podcasting, visual text creation, and comics/manga.
- Challenging teachers to think differently about the potentials and of new literacies for teaching and learning both inside and outside the classroom.

The worlds of adolescents are vastly different today compared to just 15 years ago—both in kind and in reach. Thanks to technology, teenagers can connect, read, write, think, create, film, record, and represent themselves through a variety of media formerly unthinkable. Schools, however, have stayed very similar in many ways through the past decades—implementing new technologies in mostly cursory ways (Oppenheimer, 2003). This discrepancy between the development of digital literacies by many teens and the traditional nature of much of school-based literacies continues to this day and threatens the authenticity of adolescent education. In other words, there is a vast difference between the ways in which teens read, write, create, and think online and the ways in which they are required to do so in schools. With some important exceptions, most schools do not build on the digital literacies of students in the ways they could through using student expertise and capitalizing on motivation. The purpose of this chapter is to build bridges between the kinds of things adolescents are doing digitally outside of schools and those practices we want them to develop through their education in order to prepare them for a rapidly changing world.

WHAT ARE DIGITAL LITERACIES?
AND WHY IS MYSPACE SO SCARY?

The place to begin building connections from digital to academic literacies is through a deeper understanding of the digital literacies[1] of teenagers today. (Throughout this chapter, the term *digital literacies* is used to describe the literacy practices of students that use newly developed tools, including the Internet, digital music players, digital video and still cameras, and video games.)

One point to understand in learning about these practices is that, for teenagers, digital literacies are not strange, surreal, or even all that noteworthy. Adolescents' lives are so mediated by new technologies—from cell phones to the ubiquity of the Internet—that things that may seem new to teachers, researchers, and scholars are just a part of the worlds in which adolescents live (Johnson, 2005; Green & Hannon, 2007). In fact, the distinctions we make in education and research between being on- and offline, or in and out of school are often viewed differently by our students, who see friendships and activities spanning multiple contexts at the same time (Lohnes, 2005; Leander, 2003).

The fact that our students do not perceive a gap between their lives online and offline is important to keep in mind in order to understand what our students do as *immersed users* whose expertise can be incorporated into the classroom. Digital literacies are also new literacies in that

---

[1]*Literacies*, as a plural term, is used in this chapter to recognize literacy as a complex set of practices, larger than just component skills such as comprehension or decoding. This idea of the use of literacies builds on the work of Street (1994) and others in new literacy studies, and helps focus an understanding of literacy as skills *plus* contexts and tools—that we read, and write, and use language differently in different settings and according to the tools to which we have access.

they represent new ways of using reading and writing through new media and technologies. With the advent of e-mail and instant messaging, new and different forms of language have developed—emoticons, abbreviations—that are central to the meaning making teens do with their lives (Crystal, 2006). Although these new forms of language are not useful for academic writing, it is crucial for teachers to understand, for example, how emoticons work and what abbreviations are used by their students in order to create a bridge from one type of literacy to another.

In part, then, digital literacies are:

- *Multimodal*—texts are built from linguistic, aural, visual, and kinesthetic elements (e.g., video games that allow a player to move throughout a terrain).
- *Networked and collaborative*—teenagers learn how to use new technologies by consulting each other or through trial and error, rather than going through detailed tutorials or asking an expert.
- *Simultaneous*—most teenagers use several new technologies at the same time and therefore engage in new literacies literally on top of one another, stacking open windows for Instant Messenger, e-mail, iTunes, Web browsing, and word processing.
- *Communicative*—many of the new literacies involve communicating with others in media that can be asynchronous or synchronous.
- *New*—some of the things that students can do with reading and writing online are different from what can be done with older media such as pencil and paper.

New technologies are often adopted first by teenagers and children, who may have more flexible mindsets. Adults, on the other hand, often approach new technologies with a mindset of distance, unfamiliarity, and possibly trepidation; these are different from the technologies we know, and they may seem harder to learn. Prensky (2001) calls this division between many teens and adults one of "digital nativity": Teenagers, who may have grown up with new technologies and are not unsure about using or even modifying them, are considered "digital natives," whereas adults, who are more leery of new technologies and their implications, are "digital immigrants"—those who need to learn the languages and practices for new contexts. One of the ways digital immigrants can begin to understand the practices of the digital natives is to learn more about them, followed by creating ways in which these new literacies can be used to teach students in and beyond the classroom.

First, this chapter outlines the concept of "new literacies" in relation to digital literacies. The following sections describe four types of technologies most often chosen by teens—communicative, social networking, content creation, and gaming—by providing an explanation of how they work and who uses them. Potential connections to classroom practices are noted, along with ideas about how these digital literacies can be used to inform more traditional academic literacies. As well, each section raises questions to think about in terms of each type of technology and its developing use in students' lives.

THINKING ABOUT DIGITAL LITERACIES: WHAT DO TEENS DO WITH ALL THESE NEW TECHNOLOGIES?

One way to think about teenagers and digital technologies is to understand the need students have to communicate and connect with each other. Adolescence has always been marked by an increased need in communicating with, and connecting to, peers. Comic strips and sitcom jokes have often focused on the teen with a phone permanently attached to the ear, or the nerdy geek whose lifelong desire is to be part of the in-crowd. These desires haven't changed over time—but the means by which they may be communicated has. Now teenagers can choose from a wide variety of media through which to connect and communicate. These choices run the gamut from e-mail to instant messaging to text messaging as well as the more traditional methods of phone and face-to-face communication. Students have even been known to engage in more than one form simultaneously—such as talking on the phone while instant messaging, or sending text messages while also chatting with friends face to face (Cammack, 2002).

This range of media means that adolescents have to make decisions in terms of the communication tools they choose, between options that are synchronous (meaning that their communication partner is simultaneously communicating with them), such as instant messaging; asynchronous (not simultaneous), such as e-mail; or somewhere in between, such as text messaging. Students can and do change their language to fit the medium as well, as seen in the development of abbreviations for use with instant messaging and text messaging (Jacobs, 2004). These abbreviations sometimes find their way into schoolwork and other inappropriate places, causing questions of message and medium. Although students can and do make many choices about what they want to say, to whom, and most importantly how—those choices aren't always the wisest ones or the most effective. Students need to learn critical faculties with which to approach these media and the messages they create, so as to communicate the best message possible while always remembering that anything put into a written (or visual) format (as is discussed in the section on content creation) can be saved and revisited.

The phenomenon of online and multiple communication is widespread. According to a Pew Internet and American Life Project report

(Lenhart & Madden, 2005), nearly 9 out of 10 teens spend time online and more than 80% state that "most" of the people they know are online too. Online forms of communication have supplanted other forms in many cases. Students will, most times, choose instant messaging to communicate to one another rather than e-mail—and text messaging is a close second, with nearly half of teens owning a cell phone, according to the Pew project. Teens who go online are more likely to text message, so knowing one communication medium seems to translate into others.

Interestingly, teens choose online means to talk to people they know more often than those they don't know (Fox & Madden, 2006), contrary to early and sustained fears that most of the people on a teen's "buddy list" (used in instant messaging) were strangers and that strangers present the danger of predation. Although the threat of online predators is very real, most of the people listed on a teenager's buddy list are people he or she knows face to face or through mutual and physically contacted friends (a best friend's "cute cousin," e.g.).

Perhaps most importantly, teens interviewed by the Pew Project stated that e-mail should be used to communicate with "old people, institutions, and to send complex messages, rather than casual written communication" (Lenhart & Madden, 2005, p. ii). Teachers and institutions that do not understand the workings of instant messaging or text messaging are at a disadvantage in their students' worlds, where communication is everything and the medium is often the message. The shift in the world around new technologies means that literacy is also changing, and that new literacies are developing that have a direct impact on the ways teenagers read, write, and think.

UNDERSTANDING DIGITAL LITERACIES AS NEW LITERACIES: WHAT ARE THE IMPLICATIONS?

Technologies and digital literacy practices are integral to understanding literacy for two reasons. First, new technologies are changing the ways we read and get information, create and send communications, and view the world. Second, digital technologies are so pervasive in our students' lives that many of them need to develop the critical ability to be able to step back and evaluate by thinking about the effects that using certain technologies have on their lives. Many students do not necessarily know how to evaluate research sources or conduct effective searches online, but the problem is larger than that. In having such a buffet of media available to them, students must make choices in terms of genre, language, audience, and intent. Ideally, these will be conscious choices, made after weighing the affordability of different media and understanding how the media work. That is the purview of "new literacies"—researching and understanding how digital technologies interact with literacy practices to create different possibilities.

Consider the communication examples mentioned above. Teenagers have a wide array of choices with which to communicate: speech, telephone, e-mail, chat, video, audio podcast. Each of these choices interacts with language somewhat differently and, in some cases, in ways that are also "new." The abbreviated language associated with Instant Messenger is a good example of this new aspect, as the language changed to fit the medium, and the message reflects the quick nature of synchronous online communication.

A web page is another good example. As you will read, many adolescents create online profile pages in sites such as MySpace. What does it mean to write these pages? It is different from writing a school paper or even a letter in that images can be easily incorporated, as can sound and hyperlinks to other pages. In that sense, the literacies associated with creating these pages are new: Prior to the development of these technologies, students were not able to create multimodal representations of themselves linked to an online community. What does creating these kinds of texts do for teenagers' conceptions of literacy, as compared to more traditional academic literacies? Many of these practices use copying and pasting functions; students find layouts they like or quotes and copy and paste them into their own texts. What kinds of issues does this raise in terms of authorship? And, most importantly, how do adolescents bring these kinds of conceptions into their academic literacy practices?

Leu, Kinzer, Coiro, and Cammack (2004) state that new literacies "include the skills, strategies, and dispositions necessary to successfully use and adapt to the rapidly changing information and communication technologies and contexts that continuously emerge in our world and influence all areas of our personal and professional lives" (p. 1572). Like the development of the printing press, new technologies have allowed us to create and use new forms of text for a wide variety of purposes, which bleed across school and nonschool contexts. The ways in which our students are using reading, writing, and language more generally are shifting into new areas and forms, and we, as teachers, need to be able to understand these shifts as they impact what constitutes literacy in our world today.

These literacy practices are new in a couple of ways, according to Lankshear and Knobel's (2007) work in defining and "unpacking" new literacies. First, these literacies are *ontologically* new because they allow for new forms of text (e.g., those that incorporate images and sound along with written language) that could not be created previously. Second, they are *paradigmatically* new, in that these new literacies help us think about literacy in new ways—as social practices that involve not only contexts and skills but specific tools used in specific ways. The literacies described in this chapter are dependent on new technologies in order to be successful—such as membership on MySpace, writing a blog, podcasting, posting fan fiction stories to an online site, or gaming. These are very social and technological practices that take us far from the traditional notion of literacy as involving a student, alone with a book, focusing specifically on decoding and comprehension in a private space.

This chapter therefore uses examples of students' new literacies to demonstrate these shifts in practices. The following sections outline specific technologies and literacy practices in which our students engage, as well as why those practices are important to think about in terms of school literacies. Some of these new literacies may seem divorced from teaching and learning in a more traditional sense, so it is important to keep in mind that our students do not necessarily see the distinctions that their teachers and parents do. In describing students' practices, this chapter approaches literacy and learning from their perspective and takes the position that knowing what our students do with literacy is important to teaching them.

COMMUNICATING AND CONNECTION: MYSPACE AND SOCIAL NETWORKING 101

One of the most publicized innovations in recent memory has been MySpace and other social networking sites, which dominate news items about teenagers' activities online and particularly the threat of online predators. These sites, including MySpace and Facebook, claim a majority of teens as members—with some estimates putting more than 80% of college students on Facebook and more than half of all teens with at least one online profile (Lenhart & Fox, 2006). Nearly 50% of teens visit these MySpace, Facebook, and other social networking sites at least once each day. Older teenage girls between the ages of 15 and 17 are the most likely to have created a profile and to spend significant amounts of time online each day. But what are these sites? How do they work, and why are they so enthralling for teens?

Social networking began in two different ways, with two very different senses of what it means to connect to others online. Simply put, social networking sites allow users to create representations of themselves, or "profiles," and then to connect those profiles to those of other users—some of whom they may know, whereas others will be completely new to the initial user. By connecting profiles in this way, a tangible social network is constructed whereby connections between individuals can be built and traced. The number of "friends" a teen has is thus measured and can be compared between friends, as another factor in defining of popularity. Having few "friends" on MySpace or Facebook can have repercussions online but also face to face, as can trusting someone to be a "friend" who then uses your profile information to make negative comments on your page or his or her own. The use of quotations around *friend* is intentional, because friendship in a social networking sense is not the same as more traditional notions of friendship. danah boyd (2004), in her piece on the nature of friendship on Friendster, comments that friends can become notches on a post for the reputation of the user, rather than meaningful connections both on- and offline. Whereas some friendships deepen and mature, as a more traditional definition of friendship might expect, others never go beyond listing that person's picture in your "Friend Space" or section of the page devoted to marking friendships. Certainly profile pages are used for dating and other sexual connections, as seen in the pictures posted by users (mostly female) that are lit by low light, focused on the breasts or legs of the user—all intentionally designed to show the teen in the best light possible. For many teens, there is no excuse to have an ugly online photo and lots of opportunities to represent yourself as sexy, mature, fun-loving, and popular. The combination of photos, comments from friends, and lists of interests that make up most profile pages creates a concrete representation of self that teens can constantly improve and re-create. To "be" online is an ongoing process, and it is central to most teenagers who get online today. How did this online social phenomenon come about?

The first site that used the idea of social networking was called Friendster, and it was created to facilitate connections and communication between people. Friendster was, and is, a social networking site overall—the point being to create a representation of yourself and connect up to the friends you already have as well as making new ones. The majority of users of Friendster were older teens and college-age students, who made connections for possible dating as much as anything else. Interestingly, boyd (2004) reports that the designers of Friendster intended it to be used only between those who already knew one another—they didn't expect or foresee the ways in which the site might be used to create cyberconnections across wide physical spaces, through looking up old college friends or past neighbors, as well as connecting to other people who had similar interests. Before long, the name of the game became *collection* (boyd, 2004)—or how many friends you could collect from various corners of the site. As collectors added more and more friends, the site slowed down and searching became all but impossible.

On the other hand, another site, called LiveJournal, came to prominence not as a social networking site, but as a blog (discussed more below). Early users (also known as *early adopters*) maintained personal weblogs or diaries updated in reverse chronological order (newest posts first). Users' LiveJournals are linked to each other, creating the social networking component by notifying those listed as friends when new posts arrive. Friend's lists became the beginnings of social networks, as users carefully maintained and updated their lists regularly, keeping all of their friends abreast of recent developments through ongoing posts.

The ability to keep an online accounting of whom you considered to be a friend and, by omission, whom you did not gave birth to the connections of MySpace and Facebook. These sites' strengths lie in their ability to keep a user constantly updated about his or her friends' activities and to mark social connections in a way tangible to this generation. Friends are listed as just that, marked as friends in particular networks on Facebook and as "Friend Space" on MySpace. Both sites post the total number of friends a user has (Facebook also breaks this category down by college or geographic network—friends are clustered by university, for example, although it is quite easy and common to have friends at multiple schools). Both sites "preview" your friends by posting just a couple of pictures—and in the case of MySpace, which posts those listed in your "top 8," or those eight pictures that show on your main profile page, the practice is a matter of serious concern. To have a boyfriend or girlfriend and not post him or her as your "top" friend, in the first slot of the Friend Space, is a social taboo for many couples, and changing rotations of friends are noted by those who visit your pages regularly.

Perhaps what is most interesting is how these pages do the work of friendships when the user is not logged in or active on the site. While you step away from your computer, your profile page is still being visited by friends and potential friends who post comments on your wall, "poke" you (leave a message that you have been "poked"—another feature of Facebook that makes little sense at times), comment on your pictures, and leave other signs of their presence.

The roles that these pages play in the ongoing lives of students cannot be underestimated. In the recent shooting tragedy at Virginia Tech (VT), within 24 hours Facebook groups were created both by students at the school and at other colleges across the country. Students from all over the United States—in fact, all over the globe—joined groups such as "Praying for Virginia Tech" and "Today We Are All Hokies." Students created images combining the VT logo with a black ribbon and their own college logos, including universities in New York, Oklahoma, California, Florida, Georgia, and Colorado. While the media posted constant updates on the ongoing story, students at VT used these Facebook groups to track each other down in the ensuing chaos and, sadly, to verify the victims (Heffernan, 2007). As the names of the dead were released, their Facebook and MySpace profiles were turned into online memorials, visited by friends and family and mourners from all over cyberspace. In ways that were not true for Columbine and previous shootings, the online world of social networking sites has extended the connections between students and served as an important source of emotional support.

Being a member of Facebook and MySpace provides new literacies primarily because of the offerings of each site. A successful page communicates specific messages about its creator, standing in for him or her in interactions with other users of the sites. Students work hard to shape and maintain their identities on these sites, and in order to do this they become proficient at learning how to "write" these pages. Most students learn to copy and paste HTML code in order to modify their MySpace page, and they think carefully about the interaction of a variety of elements: photos, color, sound, hyperlinks, linguistic descriptions of self, and others. Writing, then, is a multimodal art that involves linking to other texts and making use of all of these modes. Adolescents also use their profiles to communicate with teachers and other adults associated with their schools and communities (Wilber, 2007).

Teenagers learn to read and decode these texts in specific ways, incorporating visual, linguistic, and aural information into their interpretations. Teens can quickly decipher and interpret the relation of photos to the author of a page, or determine what the inclusion of certain quotes means about a person. Expertise is valued, and modified pages with an interesting layout on MySpace mean something more than a user who just leaves the default layout on his or her page. Connections to others are read in a certain way as well, and who is in your top Friend Space trumps whoever is on the rest of the list. Reading and writing on social network sites are very detailed endeavors in which every little bit counts against the whole, and attention to detail pays off in the end. However, students need to learn to think critically about issues of privacy and publicity in terms of the decisions they make in authoring a page, as well as the permanence of comments and photos that can be printed and saved. Overall, the technological aspects of being connected to others online have advanced far more quickly than our thinking about the repercussions. As literacy teaching is all about helping students understand the messages they get and create through a variety of texts, literacy teachers can create ways for students to develop the critical faculties they need.

UNDERSTANDING THE SHIFT TO WEB 2.0:
WE ALL WRITE THE WEB TOGETHER?

In the last year, descriptions of the World Wide Web have begun referring to the idea of Web 2.0, even as many users had no idea what was meant by Web 1.0. This section explains how Web 2.0 is defined, and how the practices associated with this shift are important in thinking about adolescents' new literacies.

Web 2.0 is a term that represents the ways in which the World Wide Web (still used as a term interchangeably with the Internet and the Web) has matured and shifted since its introduction to the public around 1995. Initially, most of the reasons people spent time online had to do with information seeking and gathering, along with using the new communication medium: e-mail. Today, the reasons people spend time online are much more complex, and more often those reasons involve creating something: a web page, blog, or personal profile; a video or audio file to upload to sites such as YouTube; tags or bookmarks for use through sites such as del.icio.us, which allow users to "tag" or label sites in which they are interested and then organize those tags. Web 2.0 is less about receiving information than it is about creating and re-creating it. Many teenagers today have a blog or personal journal online (Fox & Madden, 2005) and the majority access sites such as Facebook and MySpace, discussed above.

Web 2.0 is also marked by a shift in the ways that information is posted and accessed, most notably through sites based on the open and shared content of Wikipedia, a free encyclopedia that can be updated by any of its members. Wikipedia was begun in 2001 as a complement to the now-defunct Nupedia, which was a more traditional encyclopedia written by experts. Wikipedia as an idea and in its own version took off, and now there are more than 7 million articles available in more than 250 languages (*www.en.wikipedia.org/wiki/Wikipedia*). The idea behind Wikipedia is a simple one: Allow users to edit the content. Anyone who signs up for a free membership to Wikipedia can write, edit, or add to an existing article on the site, as well as create new ones. Because of this open collaboration, many have questioned the veracity of information found on the site. Articles and information are verified by senior members of Wikipedia, who tend to favor consensus of opinions over the credentials of the writers, which may lead to systemic bias throughout the site. Some schools have limited the use of the site for research, whereas others allow it as long as the information found on the cite can be verified independently of Wikipedia (Read, 2007).

The term *wiki* has now become shorthand for any site that allows users to add or change content, and wikis are beginning to be used in education for students and teachers to create information sites collaboratively. Although most of their use thus far has taken place in the context of online education, wikis can and are being used in face-to-face educational settings as a shared, coauthored space. Students who contribute information must be reflective about its veracity and usefulness, because the information will be used by others; this reflective process, in turn, encourages students to think about the nature of information as well as publishing material on the Web.

And, of course, wikis aren't the only examples of user-created content in Web 2.0. Others include photo-posting sites such as Flickr, music downloading sites such as Napster and iTunes, podcasting and other audio recordings that are posted and shared online, and now video-based sites such as YouTube and Vimeo, as well as TeacherTube, specifically for teachers. All of these kinds of sites have one main element in common: They allow users to upload content as well as view it, and therefore are created collaboratively by members. Take Flickr, for example, as a site that is created collaboratively. Users sign up for a free membership, after which they can upload their digital photos (within a certain amount each month—more access costs money). Once the photos are uploaded, users can choose to make them public or accessible only to selected friends. Public photos are open to any other member of the site; the public photos also become a part of an ever-changing array of new photos posted and searchable on Flickr, which is visited by millions each day. As more users add content, the nature of the site changes—there may be lots of photos posted about current events, or of flowers in the spring—and the overall nature of Flickr, too, changes. This is a very different situation from earlier iterations of the Web, in which content was a much more static entity, created by a main author who had knowledge of HTML and access to a server. Now everyone is a creator.

This ability to create is directly related to the new literacies defined above. For the most part, texts constructed and posted through Web 2.0 are multimodal and hypertextual. These works are as visual as they are linguistic, and they are produced not only by a main author but by those readers who comment on the work itself (such as commenting threads for photos on Flickr or videos on YouTube) and therefore contribute to the body of matter that the text becomes. As readers read and comment on Web 2.0 texts, or even create their own works in relation to the first text, the boundaries of what text is or can mean are extended. Even an article in the *New York Times* online becomes an example of this multimodality, as an electronic article can be commented on, blogged about, e-mailed as a part of an e-mail text to another person, cut and pasted, incorporated into a video, and so on. The possibilities are endless, certainly much wider than typed papers comprised solely of words printed out and handed to a single reader. The world potentially becomes both reader and author, and the text can live on, jumping around the Web and taking many formats. The potential is seemingly limitless, and teenagers must think through the texts that they believe and those they create in terms of how those potentials might play out.

GAMING AND LEARNING:
VIDEO GAMES AS COMPLEX TEXTS

Video gaming, compared to many of the technologies mentioned above, is positively "old school." The first video game console was produced in

1972, and many of us can think fondly back to the days of Pong. But that's not the world of video games anymore. As technologies develop, games have become much more sophisticated and realistic, and entire genres of video games have developed, including first-person shooters, massively multiplayer online games, puzzle games, simulations, and historical games. Teens can choose, through games, to navigate through a close approximation of Miami (*Grand Theft Auto: New Vice City*) or interact with thousands of others through society building and warfare (*World of Warcraft*). The single largest sales event in the United States thus far was the release of *Halo 2*, the second in the first-person shooter *Halo* trilogy. Sales on the premiere day exceeded $125 million (Morris, 2004). Games are big business and now, big ideas, for learning and teaching. But why?

The question most of us ask when presented with the complex, detailed games popular today is what possible connection they might have to learning. Since the early days of *Doom* in the 1990s, video games have been marked by increasing violence as well as stereotypical behavior and images of women and minorities. But video games as a group are a much wider field than this; they include "PC" games such as solitaire or *Free Cell*, the version of *Tetris* on your cell phone, learning games from *Leap-Frog* and other companies marketing to small children, and games around physical movement such as *Dance Dance Revolution*. Any technological device that plays a game you can see is technically a video game, and given the sheer number of tech devices that populate our lives today, that represents a fair number of gaming devices and opportunities. So even though *Half Life* and first-person shooter games may have garnered most of the press, all of these games are only part of the larger story of video gaming and the role games play in the lives of teens.

Countless teenagers play video games regularly; recent studies have found that more than 70% of college students play, more than half regularly (Jones, 2003). Although the perception of who plays is often centered on teenage boys, more and more girls are playing a wide variety of games, and the market is also expanding into preteens with online games and interactions such as Webkinz and Club Penguin. Club Penguin, for example, launched in October of 2005 and by January 2007 had 4 million visitors, many under the age of 12 (Braiker, 2007).

One element all games have in common is their focus on learning in order to reach goals within the game. All games build in levels of difficulty that continue to challenge the player, who then must either refine strategies or learn new ones in order to complete levels. With the increasing technological offerings, the world of games has become much more complex. *World of Warcraft*, for example, is a massively multiplayer online role-player game that can be played by many users simultaneously. The game challenges users to create systems and networks, build structures, interact with each other (both violently and not), and gain attributes to their avatars, or representations of self. There are hierarchies of players, and duels and battles may be planned and then fought between warring factions across the game world. Players can go on quests or build and manipulate the game world through programming modifications; players' avatars or representations are rewarded by gaining money and characteristics. *World of Warcraft* is a persistent draw for millions of people, who figure out ways to interact through the space and play out countless scenarios. The amount and complexity of learning required to play the game, let alone manipulate the very game structure, is staggering, and yet literally millions of people spend hours weekly learning and playing games such as this one.

In *Civilization 3*, a strategy game, users created Apolypton University online to help develop other players' skills. *Civilization*, as a series of games, is devoted to "building an empire that would withstand the test of time," according to the game description. The game challenges players to take on the role of the ruler of a society and see that society through wars and exploration, city building, diplomacy, epidemics, and more. Some researchers contend that the kind of learning required to succeed at a video game is different from the learning traditionally used in classrooms and more like the flexible collaboration required in today's work situations (Gee, 2003). In order to "beat" a video game, particularly if it is one of the more complex role-playing or strategy games, a player must try a variety of solutions, work through frustration, and in many cases collaborate with someone else to come up with potential solutions. Video games are getting longer and more challenging, and although that might seem a barrier to playing, complex games sell millions of copies each year. The interaction that is built into the games gives players immediate feedback on their learning and keeps teenagers coming back for more.

But what about *Grand Theft Auto* and other violent games? There is no doubt that many games are extremely violent—and becoming more instead of less so. For every game designed for young children, there seem to be two or more for teens and young adults that involve spewing blood, bombs, and other methods of violence. As well, games such as *Grand Theft Auto*, which are placed in a semirealistic world, perpetuate stereotypes about urban settings and crime—glorifying the "thug life." The continuing question for those of us in education is whether or not gamers can distance themselves enough from these games to understand the line between fantasy and reality—that violence in a video game is very different from violence in real life. Games that glorify criminal behavior and minimize the effects of violence may very well have negative effects on students, but research shows conflicting results as to what exactly that effect looks like and how it impacts gamers. Teenagers who play games may show lower sensitivity to violence and lower empathy, but a direct correlation to violent acts has not been established (see Funk, Baldacci,

Pasold, & Baumgardner, 2004; or Weber & Mathiak, 2006, for more detailed discussions of this issue).

In terms of thinking about new literacies, video games have a natural connection to the ways in which reading, writing, and thinking are changing. All games represent a type of multimodal text that users have to learn to read in terms of the information available to them. This information can be visual or linguistic, but it is also aural and kinesthetic in terms of the reactions a gamer must make to the variety of cues given. Many of the games present multiple, simultaneous information on the screen in order to track the action, map the gamer's location in the larger game world, show a score, give feedback on health and strength, and communicate with other players. Gamers read and make use of all of this information at the same time, a difficult cognitive task particularly at the beginning of a game. Understanding and evaluating all of this information are key parts of the new literacies involved in gaming, then, and have direct similarities to understanding information online that may be presented in a variety of formats and media.

READING, WRITING, AND REMIXING: MANGA, ANIME, COMICS, AND FAN FICTION

Part of understanding new literacies in relation to teenagers is understanding the degree to which these practices are influenced by a variety of popular cultures (Chandler-Olcott & Mahar, 2003, e.g.). An excellent example is the popularity of manga, or Japanese comics, with American teenagers. Millions of teens (and preteens) follow *Naruto* and Pokémon, reading books and strips that are confusing to adults schooled in traditional "story grammar." These texts are highly multimodal—like other comics, pictures interact with words to suggest action or develop backstory. It is impossible to read these texts without understanding how the visual and linguistic interact, often in very complex ways (McCloud, 1994). Traditionally, manga are read right to left, in contrast with the Western left-to-right orientation taught in schools, and information from the bottom of the page may need to be understood before the top. Manga authors and artists intentionally take license with text conventions, making these sophisticated texts difficult to comprehend, particularly for those unfamiliar with them. Manga texts are also appealing to both genders, for although there are many adventure and fantasy stories, there is also a strong subgenre of love stories written with a female audience in mind.

The interest in manga has spurred a connected interest in anime, Japanese animation, often based on manga characters and storylines. Anime moves very quickly, filling and then clearing the screen with visual information in the blink of an eye. The animation and illustration used in manga and anime are unique, and artistic students may choose to copy the style in creating their own comics, and even films, using still illustrations they have drawn. The growing interest in manga has spurred a type of renaissance in American comics, which are now available in a wider range of styles and stories than ever before. Along with comics, authors have further developed the genre of graphic novels, stories that are illustrated, as with comics, but book-length (this distinction doesn't hold with manga, because almost all are books initially). Famous comic artists such as Art Spiegelman have taken graphic novels to a new high, producing books such as *Maus*, about the Holocaust, and *In the Shadow of No Towers*, about 9/11. Other authors, such as Marjane Satrapi, have taken on issues of growing up in Iran under an increasingly restrictive regime. The *Bone* series, on the other hand, is a more lighthearted set of stories with lots of wordplay in the characters' names. This wide range of texts and storylines is extremely attractive to students who are visual learners and who may have difficulty with linguistic text.

Sometimes pop culture infiltrates the world of students to such a degree that students take on the characters and storylines and produce new creations that extend beyond the end of the book or movie. For example, thousands of teens fascinated by the Harry Potter story have created their own versions, stories in which Hermione and Harry fall in love or characters are added from an American version of Hogwarts. On sites such as LeakyCauldron (*www.the-leaky-cauldron.org*) and The Daily Prophet (*www.dprophet.com*), thousands of members post their own stories for others to share and, interestingly, to comment upon. Many fan fiction sites encourage peer feedback and author revision—exactly the kinds of practices we are trying to encourage in our literacy classes. These *fanfiction* sites, as they are known, are based upon not just Harry Potter but the *Lord of the Rings*, a variety of characters from various manga and anime, and many others. FanFiction.net, the largest fanfiction site online, has sections for stories based on anime/manga, books, comics, movies, television, and more. As well, the site hosts message boards for authors and editors of the stories to communicate with each other in a public forum that is useful for all.

Authors of these stories also play with genre, submitting poetry as well as stories and even plays. All of this writing is motivated simply by interest in participating in the story, creating something new that picks up where the other story left off, or re-creates the narrative trajectory by casting it in a new direction. In order to create a fanfic successfully, then, a writer needs to be intimately familiar with the original storyline, characters, and setting and be able to create a plausible text that is both based on these initial elements and goes beyond them. The other writers in these online fanfiction communities provide a tough audience, critiquing and evaluating submissions. Writers also use fanfiction as an escape from the "real world"—a way to manage stress, work through a personal issue, and communicate and connect with others (Chandler-Olcott & Mahar, 2003).

Because most fanfictions are published to communities online and exchanged via electronic means, writing fanfiction presents itself as a new literacy practice associated with those explored previously in this chapter. The motivations for writing fanfiction, combined with the publication and peer support capabilities available online, make this a particularly powerful new literacy for tens of thousands of teenagers around the world.

CONNECTING NEW LITERACIES AND BEST PRACTICES

By understanding the new literacies of students, teachers can make connections to their students' lives that are powerful and immediate. Most of the teenagers sitting before us in our classrooms live lives that are immersed in new technologies. The difference between those lives and the more traditional aspects of education grow daily, and, as a result, we lose our students just when the literacy skills of critical reading, comprehensible writing, successful research, and intentional communication are more important than ever. All is not lost, of course. We can understand and connect to the new literacies of our students through the literacy practices we enact in the classroom and beyond.

Pedagogy based on new literacies should:

- Build on the expertise of students by allowing space for practices with which they are familiar—blogging or keeping a LiveJournal, creating web pages or videos.
- Think about the components of texts differently and allow students to incorporate digital literacy elements such as sound, video, still images, or hyperlinks.
- Teach students directly about critical reading and researching online, so that they may be better able to evaluate sources and materials.
- Make use of the new technologies, such as allowing a student to download an audio version of a book or reference material, or using podcasting to record lectures and class discussions for absent students.
- Create bridges between schools and their communities through information portals, as in a classroom blog, podcast, or web page— or allowing students to have digital pen pals using e-mail.

Examples of these practices include creating and maintaining a classroom blog, such as the Reader's Study Guide to Sue Monk Kidd's (2003) *The Secret Life of Bees*, produced by the students in Mr. Richardson's class (*www.weblogs.hcrhs.k12.nj.us/bees*). In this case, the students in the class posted chapter summaries and responses for their classmates to read. Student responses to the posts were entered in the comments field, under a link that read "Discuss." The class discussions were thereby archived online. All students were required to participate, something that is much more difficult to track in oral discussions in the classroom. Others beyond the class have read and commented on the blog, thereby giving these students an authentic audience. The chapter summaries included illustrations done by the students, something much easier to do in the multimodal format of a blog. Most importantly, the author of *Bees*, Sue Monk Kidd, came on the blog and responded to questions from the students. Those are archived as a separate link on the blog and show how online formats such as a blog extend the reach of a class project far beyond the confines of a class itself.

Blogs can also be authored by individual students over the course of a semester, unit plan, or project. Students can post responses to reading, thoughts about their projects, and status reports on a piece of writing. They can also read each others' blogs and leave comments—perhaps about a piece of writing or block an author is experiencing in his or her work, or reactions to an oral presentation the student gave in class. Excellent examples can be seen on Weblogg-Ed, a blog about using technologies in classrooms (URL), and in his separate book devoted to teaching teachers about how to use blogs, wikis, and other technologies in educational settings: *Blogs, Wikis, and Podcasts in Educational Settings* (Richardson,2006). Blogs can be created for free through Blogger.com (*www.blogger.com*—owned by Google) or for education specifically at edublogs.org (*www.edublogs.org*).

Like blogs, classes can create wikis that can be used as simple repositories of information or more complex holding spaces for student projects. In one sense, a class wiki can work as a series of pages with links to essential sites online, a project timeline, instructions for assignments, and a class blog. A class wiki can also be coauthored between the teacher and students, allowing students to post finished projects, important findings and sites found through individual research, and many other things. The teacher, as main author, can set the access to the wiki from *no access*, to *limited*, to *open*—thereby controlling the opportunities students have to change the content of the wiki. Sites that offer free wiki editing software abound; one I have used for the last year is pbwiki.com, who describes their software as helping you "create a wiki as easily as a peanut butter sandwich" (available at *www.pbwiki.com*). The site allows for educational wikis, among other types, and is not laden with advertising or inappropriate links—important aspects to consider when looking for a place to host class wikis or student blogs.

Another perfect example of integrating new literacies into the traditional literacy curriculum comes in the form of podcasts, which are simply digital recordings. What is so exciting about podcasts is that they can be accessed by anyone with an Internet connection, and easily stopped, started, and replayed. Information presented in class can be reinforced by digitally recording pieces of class lectures and uploading them so students can revisit the lectures while preparing for an exam or other assessment. Student presentations can be recorded and shared with parents or the school community, or even the world at large, as with the case of Radio Willow Web, an ongoing podcast created by Willowdale Elementary School students and available through Apple's iTunes podcasts section. Past podcast topics have included light and sound, the American Revolution, learning more about Japan, and writing traits. The podcasts are available for free, and Willowdale students are a well-known group of educators working through podcasts to get information out to the world.

Podcasting can be done through the use of iLife, on Apple computers, and Audacity, a free audio program for both personal computers (PCs) and Macs. All you need to do is digitally record something: a lecture, a presentation, or a student production. Then the digital audio file needs to be compressed into a size that can be linked to a website and made available. More and more schools are using podcasts to support student learning, and it is proving to be a good way to support aural learners and difficult concepts.

Many other practices are excellent examples of using new literacies in literacy education, including creating and posting learning videos to YouTube or Google Video, allowing student writers to post to kid-friendly publication sites such as kidpub.org, creating class web pages (Scholastic.com hosts free web pages for classrooms), and many others.

CONCLUSION

As the lives of teenagers change through the introduction of new technologies, school-based literacy practices shouldn't be far behind. Not only can we build on the expertise of students and motivate them, we can teach students to approach new literacies with a critical eye and a wide variety of tools. Students should know, consciously, how to write to fit the media available to them, and how their messages may be perceived or used in different ways. The abilities of students to create multimodal texts can be bridged into new forms of text in the literacy classroom and taken into account when thinking about reading online and gathering information. Strategies students' use when gaming can also be used in the classroom, through designing narratives and learning situations that challenge students and allow them to work collaboratively as well as individually. All in all, there's no good reason why the new technologies our students use outside of the classroom shouldn't make up part of the tools and media they have access to inside the classroom as well. Too many potential connections and openings into our students' interests and lives are being dropped when we don't make use of their new literacies, as teachers and as fellow learners. There's a new digital landscape out there, and our students are our best guides.

DISCUSSION AND ACTIVITIES

1. Create a MySpace page by going to *www.myspace.com* and signing up for a free membership. In creating your profile, notice what information you feel comfortable including (your first name? your last? your hometown? your age?) and what you don't feel as comfortable about. What should kids put on their pages? Not put down? What age should membership begin?

2. Check out educational blogs available through *www.edublogs.org*. How are other teachers using blogs in their classroom? What ideas can you take from this site for your own teaching?

3. Think about all the ways in which you use technologies throughout your day—from checking your e-mail, to making calls or texting on your cell phone. How is your life different as a result of these technologies? What would it be like to go 24 hours without Internet or cell phone access?

4. Try playing a video game online (one good site is *www.freeworldgroup.com/*, which has a wide variety of free games). How do you learn how to navigate the game? To beat it? What kinds of learning do games support that are different from classroom learning? How might you build on these kinds of learning strategies with your own students?

REFERENCES

boyd, d. (2004, April). *Friendster and publicly articulated social networks.* Paper presented at the annual meeting of the Conference on Human Factors and Computing Systems (CHI 2004), Vienna, Austria.

Braiker, B. (2007). *Your igloo or mine?* msnbc.com/Newsweek Web Exclusive. February 21, 2007. Retrieved February 21, 2007 from *www.msnbc.msn.com/id/17266131/site/ newsweek.*

Cammack, D. (2002, December). *Understanding online literacy practices: Issues of access and participant observation in "electronic ethnography."* Paper presented at the annual meeting of the National Reading Conference, Miami, FL.

Chandler-Olcott, K., & Mahar, D. (2003). Adolescents' anime-inspired "fanfictions": An exploration of multiliteracies. *Journal of Adolescent and Adult Literacy, 46,* 556–566.

Crystal, D. (2006). *Language and the Internet* (2nd ed.). Oxford, UK: Cambridge University Press.

Fox, S., & Madden, M. 2006. *Generations online.* Washington, DC: Pew Internet and American Life Project. Available online at *www.pewinternet.org/PPF/r/170/report_ display.asp.*

Funk, J., Baldacci, H., Pasold, T., & Baumgardner, J. (2004). Violence exposure in real-life, videogames, television, movies, and the Internet: Is there desensitization? *Journal of Adolescence, 27,* 23–39.

Gee, J. P. (2003). *What video games have to teach us about learning and literacy.* New York: Palgrave Macmillan.

Green, H., & Hannon, C. (2007). *Their space: Education for a digital generation.* London: DEMOS Study.

Heffernan, V. (2007, April 19). The WEB: Online, students say reach out to loners. *New York Times* online. Retrieved April 19, 2007, from *www.select.nytimes.com/search/ restricted/article?res=F20F1EFB355B0C7A8DDDAD0894DF404482*

Jacobs, G. E. (2004). Complicating contexts: Issues of methodology in researching the language and literacies of instant messaging. *Reading Research Quarterly, 39,* 394–406.

Johnson, S. (2005). *Everything bad is good for you.* New York: Riverhead.

Jones, S. (2003). *Let the games begin: Gaming technology and entertainment among college students.* Retrieved July 8, 2003, from *www.pewinternet.org/reports/toc. asp?Report =93*

Lankshear, C., & Knobel, M. (2007). *New literacies: Changing knowledge and classroom learning* (2nd ed.). Philadelphia: Open University Press.

Leander, K. M. (2003). New directions in research: Writing travelers' tales on New Literacyscapes. *Reading Research Quarterly, 38,* 392–397.

Lenhart, A., & Fox, S. (2006). *Bloggers: A portrait of the Internet's new storytellers.* Washington, DC: Pew Internet and American Life Project. Retrieved December 22, 2007, from *www.pewinternet.org/PPF/r/186/report_display.asp*

Lenhart, A., & Madden, M. (2005). *Teen content creators and consumers.* Washington DC: Pew Internet and American Life Project.

Leu, D. C., Kinzer, C., Coiro, J., & Cammack, D. (2004). Toward a theory of new literacies emerging from the Internet and other information and communication technologies. In R. B. Ruddell & N. J. Unrau (Eds.), *Theoretical models and processes of reading* (pp. 1570–1613). Newark, DE: International Reading Association.

Lohnes, S. (2005, December). *Blogging within the system: Exploring undergraduate literacy practices in school-sanctioned blogs.* Paper presented at the annual meeting of the National Reading Conference, Miami, FL.

McCloud, S. (1994). *Understanding comics: The invisible art.* New York: Harper.

Morris, C. (2004, November). Halo 2 sales top GTA. *Money,* cnn.com, November 11, 2004. Retrieved March 12, 2007, from *www.money.cnn.com/2004/11/11/technology/ halosales/*

Oppenheimer, T. (2003). *The flickering mind: Saving education from the false promise of technology.* New York: Random House.

Prensky, M. (2001, October). Digital natives, digital immigrants. *On the Horizon, 9*(5).

Read, B. (2007, February 16). Middlebury College History Department limits use of Wikipedia. *Chronicle of Higher Education* online. Retrieved February 17, 2007, from *www.chronicle.com/weekly/v53/i24/24a03901.htm*

Weber, R., & Mathiak, K. (2006). Does playing violent video games induce aggression? Empirical evidence of a functional magnetic resonance imaging study. *Media Psychology, 8,* 39–60.

CHAPTER 5

The Role of Motivation
in Engaged Reading of Adolescents

David G. O'Brien
Deborah R. Dillon

This chapter:

- Discusses the role of motivation in engaged reading by exploring how general motivation constructs can inform better practices.
- Explores why motivation can play a particularly crucial role in adolescents' literacy learning and practices.
- Shows how specific motivation constructs can be used to guide "best practices" for normally achieving students and struggling adolescents.

What is motivation? What are some common conceptions and misconceptions about the importance and role of motivation in adolescents' reading? Before we explore the complex topic of motivation and consider instructional possibilities for improving motivation related to adolescent reading, we examine some common misconceptions and oversimplifications of the term.

When we initially started to explore the construct of motivation in instructional settings about a decade ago, we created an organizer to characterize the way educators talk about it. We believe that the following statements, gleaned from anecdotal records, classes, and professional development sessions, exemplify common but inaccurate perceptions about motivation. After each statement, in italics, we explain how the characterization in the statement shapes the misconceptions many educators have constructed about motivation.

- "I wish my students were more <u>motivated</u>." *Motivation is just something kids have or develop. Some kids are motivated and some are not.*
- "My students last year were more <u>self-motivated</u>." *Motivation reflects a sort of self-discipline some students have to persevere or work harder than others. Regardless of tasks and instructional factors, some kids are just more determined and self-directed.*
- "I just don't know what I can do to <u>motivate</u> these students." *Motivation is perceived by students as some kind of immediate encouragement that suddenly sparks their interest and activity.*
- "I think my class is losing some of its <u>motivation</u>." *Motivation is a diminishing, nonrenewable resource. If you lose it with a group of kids during a given year, it may be gone for good.*

As we illustrate in this chapter, the definitions of motivation implicit in the bulleted statements above represent common but inaccurate conceptions of both the construct of motivation and the degree to which teachers can influence it in the arena of literacy practices and learning. In fact, the statements are antithetical to research on best practices for facilitating motivation and engaged reading because they construct motivation as something that is magically present or that mysteriously disappears in some students regardless of the instructional environment, quality of teaching, or specific strategies that good teachers employ. Some statements also portray motivation as something that is elusive—beyond teachers' control. However, these perceptions do not adequately capture what motivation is or how it is developed or sustained.

The research literature on motivation yields a range of perspectives and definitions. For example, the terms *interest*, *attitude*, and *motivation* sometimes mean the same thing in the literature (e.g., Mazzoni & Gambrell, 1999). *Interest* might refer to preferences for certain topics, genres, or reading tasks. If readers are interested, they may be more *intrinsically* motivated—that is, they read because they want to and they find it enjoyable. If they choose reading over other activities, we could say that they have a positive *attitude* toward reading. As we get into some of the dimensions of motivation, the interrelation and interdependence of these dimensions is obvious. For example, persons who have generally positive perceptions about their abilities feel self-efficacious; that is, they believe that they have the ability and specific strategies to succeed at specific tasks. If they are working toward goals that they believe are important, they place high value on reading and related tasks (Wigfield & Eccles, 2001). So the best way to understand the research base for best practices in promoting motivation in reading is to know enough about the various dimensions that make up the concept of motivation to understand how they intersect.

WHY MOTIVATION IS IMPORTANT FOR ADOLESCENTS

Before we start the central discussion about motivation and adolescents, we acknowledge that the term *adolescence* has many definitions and that individual students' identities are much more complex and significant than membership in a community, developmental stage, or age group (see Dillon & Moje, 1998; Moje & Dillon, 2006). We touch on developmental issues aligned generally with chronological age in two groups of students: (1) typically progressing, competent readers, and (2) so-called "struggling" readers. For the first group, we look at learners who have traversed the excitement of the earliest stage of learning how to read, the engaging experience of accessing new worlds through texts, the identification with characters in stories who are like friends, and the association of reading with community and enjoyable time with peers and teachers.

We want to start the discussion with readers 10 or 11 years old. At this juncture many youth have learned to read narrative texts, take an interest in series books, and have favorite authors and genres. But many of these same students start to feel emerging reservations about reading as a school subject. They start to dislike reading textbooks in school subjects and form some soon-to-be deeply engrained notions of reading tasks related to schoolwork that may mitigate against their future motivation to read a range of texts for a variety of purposes.

The latter group, the struggling readers, by age 7 or 8, have started to see themselves as less competent than their peers. At this relatively early age they are becoming painfully aware of the difference between ability and effort. They are starting to disengage from reading and other literate practices to preserve self-esteem, realizing that getting better seems beyond their control. Overall, they read much less than more competent peers; they develop coping strategies to negotiate school tasks without reading; and they fall further and further behind. Next, we present frameworks for thinking about how to motivate and engage readers—with some distinctions between competent and struggling or disengaged readers.

MOTIVATION FRAMEWORKS
FOR GUIDING BEST PRACTICES

Why hasn't the topic of motivation found its way into discussions about reading and literacy learning until relatively recently? First, much of the current discussion about adolescent literacy concerns struggling readers, particularly how to bring these readers "up to grade level." The predominant model for "not leaving anyone behind" embraces the most technically efficient solution for equipping these youth with strategies and skills that will help them read more proficiently; that is, proficient reading as defined by performance on large-scale standardized assessments (Dillon, 2003). Using motivation to engage readers, although currently a popular topic, has been theoretically elusive, and the intersecting frameworks that define the field have been difficult to incorporate into either instructional frameworks or assessment plans.

Nevertheless, for practitioners who want to delve into the rich theoretical traditions in achievement motivation, the inquiry will yield some strong, time-tested practices. For example, researchers have revisited the constructs of intrinsic and extrinsic motivation and unearthed some common misconceptions in relation to achievement. Several scholars (Sansone & Harackiewicz, 2000) have analyzed reward systems to determine which ones work and which do not in various instructional contexts. Other scholars have reviewed 30 years of research and presented current work on achievement motivation, including how instructional practices can actually contribute to increased motivation (Wigfield & Eccles, 2001). In addition, several researchers have taken great pains to translate the knowledge base on achievement motivation into specific practices for teachers (e.g., Alderman, 2004). Guthrie and his colleagues have directed their attention to motivation in literacy, particularly in the area of reading. For example, Guthrie, Wigfield, and Perencevich (2004) examined elementary school classroom contexts that promote engaged reading, focusing specifically on Concept-Oriented Reading Instruction (CORI)—a relatively new framework with potential that has yet to be realized, especially with adolescent learners, through ongoing development.

But one of the most significant early discussions of how motivation frameworks relate to specific practices in reading, particularly as reading actually occurs in classroom contexts, is Guthrie and Wigfield's edited book (1997), *Reading Engagement: Motivating Readers through Integrated Instruction*. In this text they present a framework in the form of a graphic that guides discussions, showing the intersection of factors that support individual engagement with those that contribute to coherent classroom contexts. *Motivation* and *engagement* are not sets of isolated cognitive constructs but the result of complex factors that play out in situated practices. Similarly, Wigfield and Eccles (2001) organize motivation frameworks as responses to three questions learners might ask: *Can I do this activity? Do I want to do this activity and why? What do I need to do to succeed?* We think this question framework is particularly effective because it allows practitioners to ponder how their students might answer each question and the reasons they may give for answering affirmatively or negatively (based in the frameworks), and then the specific interventions that teachers might offer to change students' answers from negative to positive responses. Wigfield and Eccles note that these complex intersecting frameworks deviate considerably from older models in which researchers focused on processes such as reinforcement or constructs such as internal drives, with a shift toward a focus on the development of beliefs, values, and goals. They also emphasize the importance of looking at the developmental trajectory of motivation, not only in how children and youth change over time, but how their *perceptions* of the constructs—at least at an intuitive or self-reflective level—change, and, in turn change their beliefs, values, and goals. In Table 5.1, we use Wigfield and Eccles's three questions to organize, albeit at a very general level, a way of thinking about key motivation constructs in terms of struggling and normally achieving adolescent readers.

INTEGRATING MOTIVATION INTO EXISTING INSTRUCTIONAL FRAMEWORKS

We have developed sets of practices based on many motivation frameworks, including the ones highlighted in Table 5.1. Because the frameworks overlap, one set of practices based on a particular foundation might engender other sets of practices based on complementary research. For example, there are motivating ways of presenting books and other reading material to children and youth; there are motivating ways to engage adolescents who have become disengaged with reading in school; and there are ways to design and present tasks related to reading that learners find more engaging than typical school tasks.

Also, when looking more at the panorama of a classroom rather than at the microcosm of a particular reader transacting with a text, it is apparent that there are motivating ways of engaging students in an academically and socioculturally important manner. There are also discourses that cause readers to feel more confident and competent as readers—ways of respecting individual meaning constructions and opinions, as well as discursive practices, including feedback, that encourage students to tackle difficult texts and to sort out strategies that they can continue to use effectively. Overall, in the best of all possible classroom scenarios, one might see practices that tap various intersecting frameworks in creating supportive classroom environments populated by engaged readers who are motivated to critically understand texts. These students persevere to meet goals and feel in control of a repertoire of strategies. In theory, this sounds great. But how might we set up our classrooms and design instruction for all adolescent readers—especially with the range of competence and perceptions of competence in a typical classroom?

We revisit the frameworks and implications outlined in Table 5.1 in the following sections of this chapter. We realize that the dichotomy presented in the table is somewhat contrived, and that the criteria for assigning persons to the respective groups are often ambiguous and range greatly from setting to setting. Nevertheless, we use the classifications as one way to make several generalizations that we believe are important in thinking about adolescents. Specifically, we examine why adolescents are much more than simply older readers, and why some did not develop the reading skills and strategies typically associated with a given developmental stage, grade level, or chronological age.

PRACTICES FOR NORMALLY ACHIEVING READERS

As is apparent from Table 5.1, many adolescents who *are* competent readers and *believe* they are competent readers are increasingly unlikely to want to read in school and less likely to choose reading for pleasure the longer they are in school. Reading, which had almost universal appeal when these youth were in preschool and primary grades, has been replaced with reading-as-subject. Reading, which used to be an adventure, an engaging and nurturing social experience, becomes a set of tedious tasks leading to the demonstration of narrowly defined competencies—grades on homework assignments, quizzes and tests, and meeting standards. The trust that toddlers and primary-age children gave freely to teachers who guided them to exciting encounters in stories has been replaced by a distrust of teachers who assign reading in textbooks students view as ill-structured exposition and as compendia of not-so-useful information. This disengagement and lack of motivation can be reversed, at least in some measure, by drawing from the frameworks in Table 5.1.

Can I Do This Activity?

Normally achieving adolescents would usually respond, *Yes, I believe I have the ability to read and complete most tasks related to what I read.* They would qualify this confidence by subject areas, perceiving that they are more competent as readers in some subjects than others. But there are some practices that may further motivate them to read—especially in school—because the longer they encounter reading in school, the less motivated they are. These practices include the following:

• Providing more compelling reasons to read and to practice and build fluency with a range of texts accompanied by procedural feedback; this feedback includes information on what readers understand and how they understand it—not just competition and comparative performance or reading to cover the content, but a focus on reading to learn interesting things.
• Providing more instruction in important strategies coupled with more demanding reading. For example, the reading apprenticeship framework (Schoenbach, Greenleaf, Cziko, & Hurwitz, 1999) includes a focus on academic apprenticeship and feedback that enables readers to

TABLE 5.1. The Relation of Three Key Motivation Questions to Adolescents' Literacy Learning and Instruction

The key motivation question (posed by Wigfield & Eccles, 2001)	Constructs the question taps	Implications for struggling adolescents' literacy practices and growth	Implications for normally achieving adolescents' literacy practices and growth
1. **Can I do this activity?** *Literacy examples*: • Can I read as well as I can do math? • Can I read as well as Erin or Jonathan? • Do I believe that I can read and understand this text? • Can I answer the questions at the end of a text at this level?	*Self-competence; expectancy beliefs*—expectations of success across various academic areas, and in relation to others. *Self-efficacy*—belief about one's ability to learn or perform at certain levels in connection with specific tasks (Schunk & Pajares, 2001).	Struggling adolescents develop negative perceptions about ability by second grade; early in academic careers they start to disengage from reading and define themselves as incompetent; they read less, get less practice, and fall further behind peers. Individual tasks define various facets of incompetence; although they may have a generally negative set toward school reading, they may feel more positively toward reading related to enjoyment or to an after-school job.	Normally achieving adolescents believe that they are competent; they persist longer and work harder; when presented with difficult texts and tasks, they take on the challenge. Because they work hard and use effective strategies, they get feedback that their effort and strategies pay off, and they continue to achieve. Nevertheless, even for these youth, research shows that perceptions of academic competence decline the longer they are in school due to competition, norm-referenced grading and tests, and less individual attention (e.g., Covington & Dray, 2001; Pintrich & Schunk, 1996).
2. **Do I want to do this activity and why?** *Literacy examples*: • Which book would be easier to understand? (Choice = possibility for success = easier text or a skill set I have.) • How important is it to read the biology chapter and answer the questions at the end?	*Expectancy–value model*—expectations for success and the value placed on success determine motivation to perform various tasks.	As in the first question, research shows that early in their academic careers, children distinguish competence across school subject domains. By mid-primary grades, they have sorted out what they choose to work on, based on expectations for success. Struggling readers, who start to have trouble in early grades, do not expect success and hence place little value on working at texts and tasks at which they expect to fail. However, particularly as adolescents, they may place value	Similar to the response to the first question, even normally achieving students show declining expectations for success and diminished beliefs in their competency (e.g., Dweck & Elliot, 1983; Eccles et al. 1998). In this model, adolescents are particularly interesting because they are more capable than children of distinguishing between more finely tuned components of task values; they are also better at "reading" their environments, interpreting feedback, and looking at subject task

values in relation to social environments. Adolescents could decide to work harder and more strategically at something, based on a carefully elaborated set of values.

(subject task value judgments) on texts and tasks independent of their expectations for success—for example, things they like; desire to identify with social peers, etc. Girls have higher competency beliefs than boys for reading.

Normally achieving readers can self-regulate and employ strategies; however, they lack the opportunities in school to read critically, to get feedback on the effectiveness of their strategies, and to develop personally relevant purposes and goals. In short, much or most of the reading they do does not require them to use and get feedback on the self-regulation of which they are capable. If they succeed in understanding difficult texts, they need feedback about which strategies work to meet specific goals and to feel confident that they can read difficult texts because of strategies within their control (e.g., the West Ed apprenticeship model).

It is well documented that struggling readers do not self-regulate as well as normally achieving readers (e.g., Pressley, 2006). They rely on ineffective strategies and are not adept at monitoring their understanding; they are not as facile at relating what they know to the topic at hand (they are likely to actually know less because they read less than normally achieving peers) and are not as likely as skilled readers to vary their strategies according to text types and difficulty or variations in task demands.

Self regulation—of cognition, motivation, and affect when presented with various tasks and contexts (Pintrich & Zusho, 2001).

Planning and goal setting, along with activating perceptions of the task and context in relation to self.

Monitoring various aspects of self, task, and context.

Using a repertoire to regulate self, task, context.

(Value = grades; looking competent to teacher; doing as well as peers.)
- Will reading critically in this class result in anything important? (What do I need to do to get a grade; to be perceived as competent by the teacher or a valued peer?)

3. What do I need to do to succeed?
Literacy examples:

- How should I read this history unit to do well on the exam? (What is particularly challenging about text structure and content? What are some strategies I can use to learn from this text?)
- How will I know if I am not understanding the text and not using effective strategies? (or the reverse—how will I know what is working well?)
- Based on the texts and the tasks I need to complete, and my knowledge of this subject and pertinent strategies, how can I do the best job on reading for the exam (or on reading to engage in a class discussion or to complete a project)?

attribute success to something at which they are getting better. Readers talk to one another about what they understand in reading challenging texts and which strategies they used to understand the text.

Do I Want to Do This Activity and Why?

The implications column of Table 5.1 states that even confident adolescents' perceptions about their competence as readers declines somewhat as they move up through the grades. This decline is due to increased competition, a focus on grades, difficulty of texts, and reading and task demands related to wider ranges of text genres with less assistance from teachers. The following practices are supported by motivation constructs:

- Providing more access to a range of engaging texts, particularly texts that are not like textbooks, including hybrid texts such as "pseudo-narratives" and graphic text forms such as graphic novels, manga, and web pages.
- Providing choice among texts and options on tasks related to reading. A typical activity such as reading to answer questions at the end of a section or chapter would compete with options such as reading to summarize thoughts in a blog; reading to augment a media presentation; and reading multiple texts on a topic to compare authors' perspectives and credibility (Shanahan, 2003; Shanahan, Holschuh, & Hubbard, 2004).
- Allowing students to construct purposes for reading that meet personally relevant goals or enable them to engage in useful or interesting activities (e.g., O'Brien, 2003), such as reading to find out how to organize a neighborhood project or reading to complete an inquiry project.

What Do I Need to Do to Succeed?

Ironically, many normally achieving adolescents feel successful in reading, but they have little idea about what it is that makes them successful, and they don't know how they can get even better at reading. As already noted, because they often lack goals that require critically reading difficult texts, they receive little guided practice, independent practice, and feedback regarding their efforts to read effectively. Given the underlying foundation that motivated reading is reading in which readers feel self-efficacious because they have control of their reading, here are some practices teachers can employ that are supported by the research in motivation:

- Using explicit teaching of strategies appropriate for specific disciplines and in a range of texts in those disciplines; explicit instruction must then lead to guided practice, independent practice, and the successful daily use of strategies learned.

• Providing ample opportunities (built into explicit instruction to independent reading frameworks) for students to receive feedback on their reading from teachers and peers; the feedback focuses on identifying what they are doing that can be attributed to their own knowledge and control, their self-regulation, their strategies, and their effective monitoring. This feedback is the key to the development of intrinsic motivation and feeling self-efficacious.

• Reducing the focus on competition, assessment, and grades and increasing opportunities to read strategically to meet different purposes.

• Providing multiple experiences wherein teachers and peers engage in dialogue about both the content and the process of reading a range of texts for a variety of purposes.

PRACTICES FOR STRUGGLING READERS

In oversimplified terms, struggling readers are characterized as older readers who lack the skills and strategies of their more competent peers. Unfortunately, these same terms have defined struggling adolescent readers in many major research and policy reports. The instructional complement to this insufficient deficit view is that we simply need to provide struggling adolescents with the skills and strategies instruction that will move them up the developmental ladder—up to grade level or beyond Adequate Yearly Progress (AYP) cut scores. The deficit perspective ignores or subordinates most of the "affective" dimensions of reading, which, from a contemporary perspective, include sociocognitive and sociocultural aspects of motivation.

In reality, struggling readers do lack requisite reading skills and strategies, but they also experience failure on a daily basis, develop negative self-perceptions, position themselves as incompetent (based on early self-appraisals and formal and informal appraisals from others), and develop accompanying intricate rationalizations and coping strategies that protect them from additional failure. These factors must be as systematically addressed as the teaching of skills and strategies—perhaps more so with disengaged learners. Practices based on key motivation constructs can be used by educators to revive students' confidence and self-efficacy and convince struggling readers that they can use and develop skills and strategies that result in meeting goals—goals that are attributable to factors within their control. Of course, there is some overlap in addressing the three questions above for normally achieving students, but in the case of struggling readers, the instruction may be more like a targeted intervention due to the severity of disengagement and the need to resurrect something positive within relatively few remaining years in school.

Can I Do This Activity?

The answer many struggling adolescent readers give to the question "Can I do this activity?" is "*No*" or "*I'm not so sure.*" These readers have years of evidence that convinces them that they might not succeed, and they weigh this evidence against future effort. When young people say "*I think that I lack the ability*" or "*I might not be successful,*" they often convince themselves not to try. They also believe that the factors that lead to their reading failure are beyond their control: They didn't get to pick the texts, tasks, and tests; they have relatively little power to change teachers' decisions regarding what to include in the curriculum; they have a limited repertoire of strategies to apply on various texts and tasks. The following instructional practices, based on the frameworks introduced in Table 5.1, address the motivational challenges associated with struggling adolescent readers:

- Reversing disengagement with self-efficacy. Struggling readers have already disengaged, and educators who work with adolescents can't turn back the clock to intervene in early grades or easily change some students' generally negative self-perceptions about ability. However, teachers can try to build or *re*build self-efficacy, which depends on an individual's beliefs about his or her ability to perform a particular task. A practice that could yield results is to break down tasks that seem formidable and difficult into specific tasks with very clear benchmarks for success and a focus on meeting benchmarks one by one.
- Designing specific forms of feedback that show students that their progress can be attributed to actions and abilities within their control. If students read longer and more difficult books successfully, educators can build specific feedback into the task on how these readers are traversing the text features, structure, and vocabulary by using specific reading or study strategies. Educators can also share how students' use of particular reading processes and strategies has contributed to specific outcomes, such as the ability to summarize, tell peers about a section of the text, or explain which strategies they have used to understand the text.
- Reducing the anxiety over reading as a performance or process, in and of itself, by focusing on reading as just one avenue toward activity or action. For example, reading may be one source of information students use to complete a multimedia project or reading may be just a tool to

learn about something you need to be able to do to demonstrate it for peers.

Do I Want to Do This Activity and Why?

Table 5.1 explains that struggling adolescent readers are seldom enthused and often mildly to moderately disinterested in most reading tasks in school. They have the same negative, escalating feelings about reading in school that their more competent peers have: The longer they are in school, due to the factors noted, the less they like reading and the lower their perceptions about their ability. Confound this with their realizations in about second grade that they were behind their peers, that effort did not yield results, and that they lacked strategies with which to read to learn. These negative perceptions explain in large part why struggling readers don't want to participate in reading activities and related tasks.

In addition, issues from the expectancy–value model cited in Table 5.1 impact adolescent readers' beliefs and actions. Struggling students do not expect to gain anything tangible from reading; they read to meet externally established and imposed goals (e.g., read to answer the questions and complete the unit quiz). Furthermore, based on past feedback, self-appraisals, and the way they have been positioned in the institution of school (e.g., labels, special programs), even if they did decide to meet externally imposed goals, they would not expect to be very successful. In the following section we provide several instructional practices that can begin to address this seemingly intractable problem, some of which are variations on the practices provided earlier for normally achieving readers:

• Focus on accessibility. Accessibility, dimensions of a text that make it available to a reader, is not synonymous with matching reading ability to text readability. It is more like leveling, based on a range of factors including text difficulty, but also considering how difficulty can be mediated by interest, stance toward a topic, and determination and perseverance to read something one has decided to read. If students read something they really want to read and are invested in, then they choose to read it, in spite of the perception that it is difficult. This is true as long as the text is not *too* difficult on the word recognition/decoding level. The point we wish to make is that text accessibility leads to more reading, and practice leads to more fluency and competence.

• Promoting reengagement in reading for enjoyment and excitement. This can be achieved by providing students with many choices of reading materials from among a wide range of trade books and genres.

This range would include texts that are popular among adolescents, such as graphic novels, manga, and digital texts. Reading these engaging texts should also be part of instruction in various disciplines and should supplement or supplant textbooks when possible. Use of these texts should *not* lead to typical outcomes such as writing reports or answering questions. If exciting texts lead to disengaging typical tasks, it defeats the purpose of using them.

• Providing positive, specific feedback directed at facilitating self-efficacy, personal goals, and strategy use, with a focus on successes. If students choose—even with reservations—to engage in a reading task, they are more likely to want to engage in this task in the future if they have evidence that they were successful and accomplished something. Stiggins, Arter, Chappuis, and Chappuis's (2004) ideas that focus on formative assessment directed back to learners apply here. Good vehicles for providing this kind of feedback include teacher conferences or peer-to-peer conferences. wherein students share and discuss reading and strategies.

• Focusing on more appealing reading outcomes instead of requiring only typical outcomes such as answering questions, writing reports, and writing summaries. For example, constructing a menu of variations. In previous sections of this chapter we noted several examples of outcomes that would be appealing to adolescent readers, such as writing a blog (or contributing to a wiki) or producing a multimedia project. In curriculum planning, it makes sense to list all of the typical tasks educators might assign to students in one column, and then in another column list possible options that meet the same or similar instructional objectives. We have had success with media inquiry projects in which students self-selected project partners, outlined and storyboarded self-selected project ideas, and then worked from daily contracts in which they (and we) could track how they met their daily, weekly, and project goals (O'Brien, 2006). These projects required students to use a range of media, including print; they read to do research on the topic using both print and digital sources; and they synthesized their reading into multimodal texts.

• Eliciting self-selected purposes. This is a strategy already listed for normally achieving students. Rather than giving students topics and purposes for reading, educators can construct projects in which learners select topics and outcomes. Student choice and autonomy lead to motivation and engagement. The multimedia projects discussed above are a good example of this concept.

What Do I Need to Do to Succeed?

Struggling readers often draw a blank when this question is posed to them. As noted in Table 5.1, these adolescents lack a repertoire of strategies, have difficulty selecting appropriate strategies from ones they do know, or continue to use ineffective strategies. As in the case of normally achieving readers, although less often, some struggling readers think they are improving but aren't sure why, and, across the curriculum, they receive too little instruction and practice in comprehending challenging texts. We reiterate the motivation construct stated for competent readers that underlies this question: Motivated reading is reading in which readers feel self-efficacious because they have control of their reading, and they can read with confidence and an expectation of understanding what they read. The following instructional practices tap into some of the ideas already discussed for normally achieving readers, but focus more on both the lack of typical skills and strategies among struggling readers and the effect of students' negative perceptions about their ability to succeed on various tasks during particular literacy performances:

• Providing explicit instruction leading to guided and independent practice. Most struggling readers need explicit instruction in literacy strategies appropriate for specific disciplines and in a range of texts in those disciplines, particularly in using strategies with the highest utility that meet both teachers' and students' goals. For example, summarizing, exploring question–answer relationships, inferencing, and monitoring understanding are processes that should be supported with explicit strategies instruction. Some of the lowest performing struggling readers need to work on word-level strategies and build fluency. We emphatically repeat, however, that *explicit instruction must lead to guided practice, independent practice, and the successful daily use of strategies.* For example, in recent reviews of 20 years of strategies instruction, researchers (Dole, 2003; Duffy, 2003) concluded that educators are very good at teaching instructional strategies but not as proficient at providing opportunities for learners to use them.

• Providing specific feedback. Struggling readers need more feedback about specific skills they are doing well and those on which they need additional work. Feedback helps readers know that what they are doing is both effective and attributable to something within their control. Understanding the implications of their actions will positively effect adolescent readers' perceptions about their ability and, more specifically, their self-efficacy. Written individual feedback, specific classroom feedback and praise, and feedback in teacher or peer conferences are all formats that could help struggling readers understand how well they are learning effective strategies and monitoring their understanding. Other helpful practices include reducing the focus on competition, assessment, and grades; increasing opportunities for students to read strategically to meet different purposes; and providing time for teachers and students, and students and their peers, to talk about both the content and the process of reading a range of texts for a variety of purposes.

CONCLUSION

As we have discussed in this chapter, motivation is not a fixed construct. Teachers can use their understanding of motivation and engagement to improve literacy practices, achievement, and students' perceptions of their abilities. Examining motivation constructs from the perspectives of learners and responding to the three questions in Table 5.1 provide tools with which educators can map significant research-based ideas and eloquent theoretical models onto day-to-day practices. Obviously, from both the initial discussion of the motivation frameworks and the instructional practices based on them, there is a lot of overlap and intersection of various constructs within the framework. But if educators employ most of the constructs to reframe or modify instruction, positive benefits will ensue.

DISCUSSION AND ACTIVITIES

In order to work to transform relatively complex theoretical frameworks and models of motivation into practices, we have read widely in the fields of motivation in general and achievement motivation in particular. We have also implemented many of the ideas we have gleaned in both middle and high school settings, studied what happened, and modified our approaches to reflect what we learned. The instructional practices section of the chapter, organized around several key questions, could lead to many specific activities. We want to recommend the following ideas:

1. Read the research base and work leading to key motivation constructs. An understanding of these constructs will help you comprehend why particular modifications of tasks and literacy contexts should make a difference in students' perceptions and achievement.

2. Systematically map out modifications that could be made to your current instructional plans. A planning activity that we have used successfully with our school-based colleagues is one in which they have listed current reading assignments and related activities in one column, and then have used a multiple column bridging chart to explore alternatives. Part of this activity requires the use of some existing frameworks for systematically critiquing current practices with a goal of modifying as many as possible so that they are more motivating. For example, we use the "Six C's" (*choice, challenge, control, collaboration, constructing meaning,* and *consequences*), generated by Turner and Paris (1995), to provide a way to critique existing instructional frameworks. The purpose of the Six C's is to help teachers think of open-ended tasks rather than the more

TABLE 5.2. Transforming Literacy Tasks Using the Six C's.

The Six C's (Turner & Paris, 1995)	Typical closed literacy tasks	Transformation to more open-ended, motivating literacy tasks
Choice: Provide students with authentic choices and purposes for literacy. Recast activities to emphasize the enjoyment and informational value of literacy; do not refer to daily tasks as work but instead rename them by their function (e.g., ask students to plan an event by writing . . . and reading).	In eighth-grade science class, students read an assigned portion of Chapter 3 and then work on the follow-up lab. Each lab group is responsible for writing up an oral report of their findings and the group leader, assigned by the teacher, presents it to the class.	Using the classroom library and a menu of web pages, students can choose any combination of books or other texts that they think will help them complete a lab. They collaborate on the lab and choose among several different products for presenting the results, including a presentation on a web page.
Challenge: Allow students to modify tasks so that the difficulty and interest levels are challenging. Demonstrate the many ways one can complete tasks; show concrete examples to students of successful but different approaches to tasks; teach students to assess whether tasks are too difficult or too easy for them and how to adjust goals or strategies for appropriate difficulty; point out how students have molded tasks to their interests; and assign tasks that can be modified in many ways.	In a high school reading lab designed for students who struggle the most in reading (defined as the lowest 2–3% in performance on comprehension and vocabulary subtests of the state achievement test), students can pick partners and choose among several topics focusing on the impact of violence in the media on adolescents. Each pair completes an inquiry project based on teacher guidelines.	The students in the reading lab are given the broad topic, "The impact of violence in the media on adolescents." Each pair is asked to submit a plan in which they decide on which medium (e.g., film, TV, video games) they want to use. In addition, they have to plan and storyboard the process they will use and then plan a possible outcome of their project based on their perception of the level of difficulty and challenge they think is appropriate for their abilities and time frame (e.g., design a web page or a multimedia project presentation on PowerPoint; make a mini-documentary).
Control: Show students how they can control their learning. Teach students how to evaluate what they know and how to evaluate and monitor their learning. Students are probed by teachers with such questions as: Are you focused? What's more important? Students are guided to use inner speech to self-monitor.	In a middle school language arts class, students read portions of the book *Maniac McGee* for homework, in which they have discussions or answer questions about the portion of the book assigned for each day. They often turn in answers to the questions posed by the teacher for each portion of the book.	In a middle school reading "intervention" class for the lowest-level readers in the school, students read *Tears of a Tiger.* In between whole-class discussions, the students participate in peer groups focused on metacognitive conversations (Greenleaf, Cziko, & Hurwitz, 1999). The students share their evolving understanding as well as the strategies they use to meet different goals in reading the text. Through sharing both their meaning-making and the ways they tackle the text, each learner feels more control and confidence.

(continued)

93

TABLE 5.2. (continued)

The Six C's (Turner & Paris, 1995)	Typical closed literacy tasks	Transformation to more open-ended, motivating literacy tasks
Collaboration: Emphasize the positive aspects of giving and seeking help. Provide students with opportunities to work with peers; students are taught how to teach each other by emphasizing the giving of clues, not answers; many individual tasks are recast as paired or group tasks (e.g., paired reading vs. oral round-robin reading).	The teacher engages in recitation with students in a middle school health class. The topic is how to administer first aid to someone who has accidentally consumed poison. The teacher asks a series of questions, calling on one student after another. Students respond by rapidly reciting information from the text.	Students in a high school biology class, work in self-selected peer groups. The members of each group divide up tasks, with some members using resources to find answers to study guide questions, some introducing information they have done as homework, and some writing to synthesize information that the group will turn in as a shared product.
Constructing meaning: Emphasize strategies and metacognition for constructing meaning. Provide students with a repertoire of strategies in order to respond flexibly in reading and writing situations; students need extensive applications of comprehension as well as encoding and decoding strategies to assist them in acquiring an understanding of what literacy is as well as how to use and understand it.	In a high school history class, the students read a chapter entitled "Early Americans." They are assigned to read sections of the text each night for homework and to turn in questions after reading each section. When the students read, they usually read only to find answers to the questions; a typical strategy they use is skimming to find a statement that relates to or includes information needed to answer each question.	In a high school history class studying the Civil War, the students are critically reading a portion of the text entitled "The Story Behind the Story of Pickett's Charge," using a variation of the three-level comprehension guide (Herber, 1970). In the first level students find information in the text that supports statements and explain if the information is directly stated or requires minor inferencing. In the second level they find multiple places in the text that support inferences. In the third level they reread sections to synthesize main themes that they use to construct applied-level comprehension statements.
Consequences: Use the consequences of tasks to build responsibility, ownership, and self-regulation. Acknowledge that group evaluation is a regular part of literacy instruction; encourage students to share their successes and failures; help students see that errorless learning is not learning at all; rather, real learning comes through error, because errors provide information about needed improvement; emphasize the value of effort and honing strategies because these tools equip students to attempt more and more challenging tasks.	Middle school language arts students work on a collaborative inquiry project in which teacher-assigned groups study a "famous person." To pick the person, each member puts his or her preferred name on a piece of paper and a group member draws a name out of a can. The groups are given an outline to follow in constructing the project and a fixed number of points are assigned to each section of the outline.	Students in a high school literacy lab select an inquiry topic based on interest. Then they plan the project based on available resources, the amount of time needed, and the deadline for completion (e.g., a school open house when they will present their work to parents/caregivers). For each workday they write up task goals that are reviewed first by them and then by a teacher. Based on review/conferences, they revise goals when necessary.

typical closed tasks. Table 5.2 defines each of the C's and shows possible transformations of closed tasks to open-ended tasks.

3. Videotape several classroom lessons (e.g., lessons you teach and lessons taught by peer educators). The taped lessons should include interactions between you and your students and segments where you provide feedback to students during reading instruction and related tasks. Using a framework for analyzing classroom interactions, critique your lesson interactions or a peer's interactions and list ways you or your colleagues could improve upon how you motivate students via your comments, suggestions, and feedback. To analyze classroom interactions to determine what motivates students and enhances literacy learning, we have used several frameworks, including one adapted from Alderman (2004) titled "Guidelines for Effective Praise" (p. 254). Alderman's table is based on the work of Jerry Brophy (1981) and juxtaposes effective versus ineffective praise offered by teachers to students. For each type of praise listed as ineffective, it is useful for educators to reflect upon how to modify praise, monitor what it "looks like" via videotaped lessons, and then note the effect of the modification on student motivation. Videotaping lessons, analyzing interactions, and reflecting on the acts of teaching and learning are powerful ways to study motivation constructs and set goals to enhance adolescents' literacy learning.

REFERENCES

Alderman, M. K. (2004). *Motivation for achievement: Possibilities for teaching and learning* (2nd ed.). Mahwah, NJ: Erlbaum.

Covington, M. V., & Dray, E. (2001). The development course of achievement motivation: A need-based approach. In J. S. Eccles & A. Wigfield (Eds.), *Development of achievement motivation* (pp. 33–56). San Diego: Academic Press.

Dillon, D. R. (2003). In leaving no child behind have we forsaken individual learners, teachers, schools, and communities? *Yearbook of the National Reading Conference* (pp. 1–31). Milwaukee, WI: National Reading Conference.

Dillon, D. R., & Moje, E. B. (1998). Listening to the talk of adolescent girls: Lessons about literacy, school, and life. In D. E. Alvermann (Ed.), *Reconceptualizing adolescent literacy* (pp. 193–223). Mahwah, NJ: Erlbaum.

Dole, J. A. (2003). Professional development in reading comprehension instruction. In A. P. Sweet & C. E. Snow (Eds.), *Rethinking reading comprehension* (pp. 176–191). New York: Guilford Press.

Duffy, G. (2003). *Explaining reading: A resource for teaching concepts, skills, and strategies.* New York: Guilford Press.

Dweck, C. S., & Elliott, E. S. (1983). Achievement motivation. In P. H. Mussen (Ed.), *Handbook of child psychology* (3rd ed., pp. 643–691). New York: Wiley.

Eccles, J. S., Wigfield, A., & Schiefele, U. (1998). Motivation to succeed. In N. Eisenberg (Ed.), *Handbook of child psychology* (5th ed., Vol. 3, pp. 1017–1095). New York: Wiley.

Guthrie, J. T., & Wigfield, A. (Eds.). (1997). *Reading engagement: Motivating readers through integrated instruction.* Newark, DE: International Reading Association.

Guthrie, J. T., Wigfield, A., & Perencevich, K. C. (2004). *Motivating reading comprehension: Concept-Oriented Reading Instruction.* Mahwah, NJ: Erlbaum.

Herber, H. L. (1970). *Teaching reading in content areas.* Englewood Cliffs, NJ: Prentice Hall.

Mazzoni, S. A., & Gambrell, L. B. (1999). A cross-cultural perspective of early literacy motivation. *Reading Psychology, 20*(3), 237–253.

Moje, E. B., & Dillon, D. R. (2006). Adolescent identities as mediated by science classroom discourse communities. In D. E. Alvermann, K. A. Hinchman, D. W. Moore, S. F. Phelps, & D. R. Waff (Eds.), *Reconceptualizing adolescent literacy* (2nd ed., pp. 85–106). Mahwah, NJ: Erlbaum.

O'Brien, D. G. (2003). Juxtaposing traditional and intermedial literacies to redefine the competence of struggling adolescents. *Reading Online, 6*(7). Available at *www.readingonline.org/newliteracies/lit_index.asp?HREF=obrien2*

O'Brien, D. G. (2006). "Struggling" adolescents' engagement in multimediating: Countering the institutional construction of incompetence. In D. E. Alvermann, K. A. Hinchman, D. W. Moore, S. F. Phelps, & D. R. Waff (Eds.), *Reconceptualizing the literacies in adolescents' lives* (pp. 29–46). Mahwah, NJ: Erlbaum.

Pintrich, P. R., & Schunk, D. H. (1996). *Motivation in education.* Englewood Cliffs, NJ: Merrill.

Pintrich, P. R., & Zushio, A. (2001). The development of academic self-regulation: The role of cognitive and motivational factors. In A. Wigfield & J. S. Eccles (Eds.), *Development of achievement motivation* (pp. 249–284). San Diego: Academic Press.

Pressley, M. (2006). *Reading instruction that works: The case for balanced teaching* (3rd ed.). New York: Guilford Press.

Sansone, C., & Harackiewicz, J. M. (Eds.). (2000). *Intrinsic and extrinsic motivation.* San Diego: Academic Press.

Schoenbach, R., Greenleaf, C., Cziko, C., & Hurwitz, L. (1999). *Reading for understanding.* San Francisco: Jossey-Bass.

Schunk, D. H., & Pajares, F. (2001). Self-efficacy beliefs in academic settings. *Review of Educational Research, 66*(4), 543–578.

Shanahan, C. (2003). *Using multiple texts to teach content.* Naperville, IL: Learning Point Associates.

Shanahan, C., Holschuh, J. P., & Hubbard, B. (2004). Thinking like a historian: College students' reading of multiple historical documents. *Journal of Literacy Research, 36*(2), 141–176.

Stiggins, R. J., Arter, J. A., Chappuis, J., & Chappuis, S. (2004). *Classroom assessment for student learning: Doing it right–using it well.* Portland, OR: Assessment Training Institute.

Turner, J., & Paris, S. G. (1995). How literacy tasks influence children's motivation for literacy. *The Reading Teacher, 48,* 662–673.

Wigfield, A., & Eccles, J. S. (Eds.). (2001). *Development of achievement motivation.* San Diego: Academic Press.

PART II

Developing Reading and Writing Strategies for Multiple Contexts

CHAPTER 6

Actively Engaging Middle School Students with Words

Karen Bromley

They just don't seem interested. Josh slouches in his chair and won't look at me or read the material. Candace doesn't have the vocabulary to understand what she has read, so she just doesn't read. I know Tanesha uses IM and e-mail at home, but she doesn't do her homework and could care less about schoolwork.

—MARGO, SEVENTH-GRADE SCIENCE TACHER

This chapter discusses:

- The role of vocabulary.

- How words are learned.

- Rationale for engaging adolescent learners in active word learning.

- Five strategies that promote active engagement (guess and check, vocabulary anchors, 3-D words, Greek and Latin roots, video words).

Both resistant and struggling adolescent readers often experience disengagement with reading and school. Resistant readers are those who can read but choose not to, and struggling readers are those who have trouble reading and therefore do not read (Lenters, 2006). Several factors contribute to the disengagement Margo and other middle school teachers often see, including lack of interest in topics and genres used in school, rejection of school assignments that aren't meaningful or relevant, and lack of skills to support successful reading in school. To combat disengagement with reading, resistant and struggling readers need choices in topics, texts, and assignments, and they need to receive and participate in instruction in word-learning strategies they can adopt and use independently.

THE ROLE OF VOCABULARY

Margo realizes that as a science teacher, she and her fellow content-area teachers are just as responsible for teaching vocabulary as is the language arts teacher. Margo knows that unlocking and remembering difficult words in science is key to learning science concepts. She also knows that a large vocabulary is an asset because it builds students' self-esteem and confidence. As well, a large vocabulary:

- *Boosts comprehension.* Vocabulary knowledge influences comprehension and may comprise 70–80% of what students comprehend (Davis, 1972; Nagy & Scott, 2000; Pressley, 2002). For example, understanding animal migration is easier if students know that in this context a "pod" is "a group of whales" and not "the shell in which peas grow."
- *Improves achievement.* A large vocabulary means a fund of conceptual knowledge, which makes learning easier. Students with large vocabularies score higher on achievement tests than those with small vocabularies (Stahl & Fairbanks, 1986).
- *Enhances thinking and communication.* Words are tools for analyzing, inferring, evaluating, and reasoning. A large vocabulary allows students to communicate in precise, powerful, persuasive, and interesting ways (Vacca et al., 2005).
- *Promotes fluency.* When students recognize and understand many words, they read more quickly and easily than if they know few words and also lack independent word-learning strategies (Allington, 2006; Samuels, 2002).

HOW ARE WORDS LEARNED?

Many factors affect word learning, including schemas; facility with the English language; availability of supportive models, mentors, and coaches; socioeconomic status; wide reading; and purpose and relevance of learning words (see Figure 6.1). With these and other factors affecting word learning, how do students learn new vocabulary? Some words are learned as a result of *vicarious experiences* when students encounter them in casual, ways such as in a conversation or during reading; for example, the term *soul patch* is used, and students discover that it refers to a small tuft of hair that grows below a man's lower lip. Some words are learned as a result of *direct experiences*, such as when students visit an online blog and discover it is a "weblog" or diary written by an individual. Other words are learned as a result of *direct instruction* in the meaning and orthography of a word,

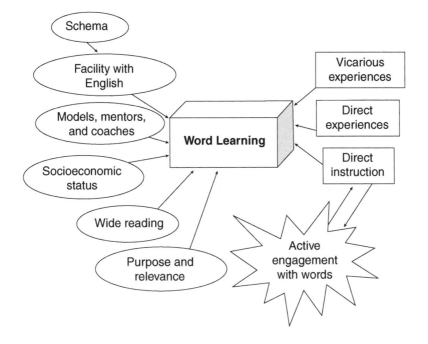

FIGURE 6.1. Elements that foster active engagement with words and support word learning.

such as when students are taught that *metamorphosis* is a noun that comes from two Greek roots, *meta* (new) and *morph* (to transform) and that describes what occurs when a caterpillar hardens into a chrysalis and then changes into a butterfly. As well, *metamorphosis* is related to other words such as *meta-analysis* and *endomorph*.

Although students may learn words as they listen, read, take part in class discussions, keep vocabulary notebooks, use Word Walls, and consult dictionaries and thesauruses, direct instruction is a key component for learning new words in school. Teachers who understand learning theory recognize that learning occurs in both linguistic and nonlinguistic ways (Paivio, 1990). They teach the linguistic elements of a word (spelling, pronunciation, graphics, meaning, and grammatical function) and reinforce them with the nonlinguistic elements of a word (a visual, auditory, or other sensory image connected to the word). Teachers who practice sound vocabulary instruction don't just assign, define, and test students on new words. They teach words in a meaningful context, associate the new words with related words, repeat new words often, and offer opportunities for active engagement with words (Stahl, 1986).

ACTIVE ENGAGEMENT

Active engagement in learning includes having students work together to teach each other and learn from each other. "Adolescents already exist in a social world, so it is easy for them to extend this natural talent to their own learning" (Santa, 2007, p. 473). Working together can help struggling or resistant learners connect with school and with other students and thereby build a classroom community of learners. When students participate in peer teaching, both observers and teachers experience learning gains (Harmon, 2002). Additionally, as a result of peer teaching, the traditional classroom context changes to create a community of learners who share in the learning process (Greenwood, Delquadri, & Hall, 1989).

Active engagement with words involves using metacognitive strategies individually and interacting with others to learn new words. By modeling the following metacognitive strategies with an unfamiliar word from text, teachers show students how to use the strategies on their own (Bromley 2002):

- Think what makes sense.
- Read it again.
- Skip it and read on.
- Think about words that look like it.
- Find a word part or "chunk."
- Sound it out.

Whether students work alone or with peers, "giving students the option (within required behavorial parameters) can improve learning for many students with both preferences" (Tomlinson & McTighe, 2006, p. 21). Interacting with other students to share the metacognitive strategies he or she uses can be an effective way for a student to learn these strategies.

Having students explore and study new vocabulary together and teach vocabulary to each other can also be an effective practice. The following sections describe five interactive strategies used by middle school teachers Margo, Dennis, and Mandy to engage students actively in independent work or working with their peers to learn new words.

Guess and Check

Margo teaches students to use Guess and Check during silent reading when they come to a word they don't know. This strategy requires students to examine context and word structure to make a guess about a new word's meaning (Bromley, 2002; Poindexter, 1994). Students search for clues and guess as they read. After Margo models the strategy for students and before they read a new chapter, she identifies five or six key words students probably don't know but need to know to comprehend the text. Then her advice is:

1. Give individual students or pairs of students a copy of the Guess and Check template (see Figure 6.2) and have them write the new words in the left-hand column under "Unknown Word."
2. During reading, have students search for context clues, look at affixes and root words, and write these under "Clues."
3. Have students use this information to guess what the words mean and write their ideas under "Guess."
4. As a class, have students share orally their clues and guesses. They can use resources (dictionary, thesaurus, encyclopedia, glossary, or you) to check their clues and guesses and write their findings under "Check."
5. Encourage students to add other new words from the selection to their charts.

Name __Stellar__   Date __5·23__

Guess and Check
• • • • •

Unknown Word	Clues	Guess	Check
myth	opposite of "truth"	makebelieve	legendary story
legacy	"monument"	statue	something that is inherited
legend	"1- fact" "2 -legal"	not fact	story from the past
Kaboodle			
orphan			

FIGURE 6.2. Using Guess and Check can help a student look for clues in text to help discern the meaning of difficult words. From Bromley (2002). Copyright 2002 by Scholastic. Reprinted by permission.

Guess and Check requires students to search for clues to meaning and pronunciation of new words. As they read difficult texts, Margo challenges students to become detectives and use bits of text information to figure out the new words. She likes the fact that students write the clues they find and keep this record as they read because it includes a physical component. She says, "The best part of the strategy is the opportunity for students to work independently or together to share orally with each other the different clues that help them figure out unknown words. This gives a typically nonparticipating student a chance to shine, and students see that they can learn from him or her and each other." Margo says the strategy also shows students that meanings for some words are not found in the text, so they must consult the dictionary or glossary for these words. She uses Guess and Check often, but not daily, until she feels that students have incorporated the idea of searching independently for clues and using them to unlock new words.

Vocabulary Anchors

Margo also uses Vocabulary Anchor sheets to help struggling students relate new words to words they already know (Bromley 2002; Winters, 2001). Like Guess and Check, this strategy is helpful for struggling readers and English language learners who have difficulty learning technical terms in science, math, and social studies. To introduce this strategy, Margo shows students a blank template and talks them through it as she fills it in (see Figure 6.3). You can also show students a picture or drawing of a boat at rest in calm water and talk about how a boat can drift away if it doesn't have an anchor. Then explain how we learn something new by "anchoring" it to what we already know. Here are Margo's instructions:

1. Draw a simple sailboat in water and write a word on it such as *patriotic*.
2. Draw an anchor below the boat, write a related word on it that students already know, for example, *pa* (father), and connect the boat to the anchor with a rope/line.
3. Discuss similarities between the two words and write this on the lines with plusses; for example, both contain *pa*, both come from the Latin *pater* meaning "father," and both are related to *patriot*.
4. Explain what *patriotic* means using the connection to "father" as you draw a picture and write the explanation on the sail of the boat.
5. Discuss the ways in which *patriotic* is different from *pa* and write these on the lines with the minuses; for example, "father's love," "love for your country," and "an adjective."

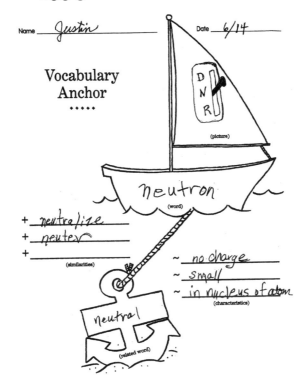

FIGURE 6.3. A Vocabulary Anchor requires students to connect a new word with a similar known word, increasing the chance that the new word will be remembered. From Bromley (2002). Copyright 2002 by Scholastic. Reprinted by permission.

6. Summarize by reviewing the drawing, what the words mean, and how they are related but not the same.
7. Have students work independently or in pairs to complete Vocabulary Anchor sheets on two or three new words they meet while reading. Then have students share their work in small groups.

Vocabulary Anchor sheets can help students connect the new to the known as they learn the important key words they don't know but need to know to understand text. As students create the boat and anchor either independently or in pairs, they are actively engaged in thinking about related words. Margo sometimes draws the picture on an overhead projector, blackboard, or whiteboard and has students copy her model, or she has pairs work together to fill in the Vocabulary Anchor sheet.

If your students keep a vocabulary notebook that includes these Vocabulary Anchor sheets, they have a record of words that are particularly hard to remember or spell. In these notebooks, students can also include their Guess and Check work or record new words with icons or pictures to help them remember the words. Vocabulary notebooks provide a written record of new words and the connections students make to learn them. You can have pairs of students review their notebook entries before reading or before a test, and the notebooks become a reference to support correct spelling when students write as well.

3-D Words

This strategy requires students to research and illustrate a word using the dictionary, glossary, and/or the Internet before teaching it to peers (Bromley, 2002; Zivcovich, 1997). Dennis, an eighth-grade social studies teacher, uses 3-D Words before or after his students read a chapter or selection because it is a way to make words concrete and interesting. First, he shows students examples and then demonstrates for them by creating a 3-D Word (see Figure 6.4). Finally, Dennis assigns words or puts them in a hat and has each student pick one to illustrate and teach it to their classmates. Here is how it works:

1. Select key words to be introduced or reinforced. If this is an end-of-unit activity, identify enough words so that each student in class has one. If it is a before-reading activity, identify a few words and form small groups, giving each member a different word and all groups the same words.
2. Give each student a piece of 8″ × 11″ tag board and have them write the word, a definition, and a sentence, draw a picture, and make the word three-dimensional with real objects.
3. Have each student teach his or her words to the small group or the class.
4. Have students record the new words with definitions, sentences, and pictures in their vocabulary notebooks, and post each 3-D Word on a Word Wall in the classroom.
5. Copy students' tag board words, make a "Team Words" book, and make copies for each student. Or, put completed 3-D Words on a class bulletin board for students to use as a reference in their reading and writing.

The 3-D Word strategy requires students to process words in several active ways, including using their creativity to compose a visual and tactile representation and teach it to their peers. Besides making a word personally meaningful, sharing with others reinforces the new word for every-

FIGURE 6.4. Creating a 3-D word requires making a visual and tactile product that students can share to support learning the word.

one. Dennis often begins 3-D Words on Friday, when he has students select words for weekend homework. On Monday, every student teaches their word, or if time doesn't allow this, a few students share words each day for the rest of the week. Dennis finds 3-D Words a good way to make every student feel part of the classroom community because each one teaches a word in his or her own unique way.

Greek and Latin Roots

The vocabulary load in science, social studies, and math in most middle school textbooks and other assigned reading is heavy. The many multi-syllabic technical terms found in this reading can make content-area learn-ing difficult. So it is important to teach students that they can infer mean-ings of 60% of the multisyllabic words they meet by analyzing word parts (Nagy & Anderson, 1984).

"Middle school students have much yet to learn about the structure of words" (Ivey & Broaddus, 2000, p. 74). Because a good portion of the English language has Greek and Latin origins, familiarizing struggling and resistant readers with the spelling and meanings of these word parts is essential (Bromley, 2007). Knowing the meaning of a prefix, suffix, or root can give clues to what a word means, especially in science. And, knowing a few roots makes it easier to figure out the meanings of other words that contain those roots. Here are some ideas for teaching Greek and Latin roots:

1. Search the Internet (or have students search) for a dictionary of "Greek and Latin roots" that includes roots, meanings, and example words. Print copies for students or have them bookmark a site such as *www.english.glendale.cc.ca.us/*, an easily accessible resource to refer to when meeting new words.

2. Teach students to analyze morphemes and determine the meanings of roots and affixes because they give clues to the meanings of words. For example, *geo* means "earth," so students can infer that *geography* means "to graph or map the earth"; *aud* means "hear," so students can infer the meanings for *audible, auditorium*, and *audience*.

3. Give students other words with the same root to extend this knowledge and figure out the meanings of related words. For example, students can infer that *geometry* means "to measure the earth," *geology* means "to study the earth," and *geomagnetic* means "the earth as a magnet." You can also challenge students to figure out the meanings of other *geo-* words, such as *geode, geomorphic, geodesic*.

4. For bell work, which is brief work in which students engage as soon as the bell rings to begin class (Moore & Hinchman, 2006), put two or three multisyllabic words on the board or on an overhead transparency. Words can be real (e.g., *photosynthesis, hypotenuse*) or nonsense words you and/or students make up (e.g., *pyrgamy, contrapent, tetrathan*). Then have students form pairs to determine each word's meaning by analyzing its morphemes.

5. Create a Word Wall in your classroom to reinforce learning roots and derivatives. List word parts alphabetically, or draw a graphic organizer such as a "word web" or a tree with bare branches (see Figure 6.5) to which you invite students to add words that contain a root such as *meta-* or words that are related to the root.

6. Have each student make a *portable dictionary* from a file folder by dividing the inside of the folder into boxes where they list words with the same word part in a square. Have students review the bulletin board words or their file folder dictionary lists with partners during bell work.

Although some roots and affixes should have been taught in elementary school, many middle school students cannot pronounce them and do not know their meanings. Some of the most often appearing roots and affixes follow (Bromley, 2007):

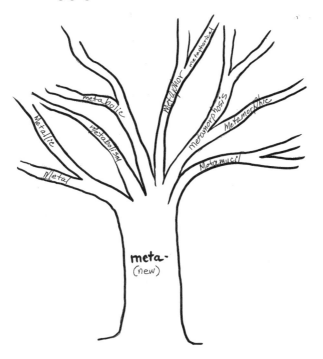

FIGURE 6.5. Inviting students to make a collection of words with common roots on a Root Tree helps broaden their vocabularies.

Common roots include:

tract	dict	rupt
spect	scrib	cred
port	vid	aud

Common prefixes include:

re-	un-	in-
en-	ex-	de-
com-	dis-	pre-
sub-		

Common suffixes include:

-ly	-er	-able/ible
-cle	-tion/sion	-less
-est	-ment	-ness
-arium	-ling	

Teaching these word parts, how to spell them, and what they mean can reap huge rewards in the number of related words that students, including struggling and resistant readers, understand independently.

Video Words

Technology often appeals to unmotivated students who are disengaged from learning (Hinchman, Alvermann, Boyd, Brozo, & Vacca, 2004). In Video Words, students work together to dramatize words by using a digital camera and creating a multimedia presentation to share with the class. "By harnessing their fascination and familiarity with multimedia, educators are striving to re-engage students—many of whom are left cold by traditional text based learning—in the learning process" (Adams, 2005, p. 1). As well, the International Reading Association's (IRA) position statement, Integrating Literacy and Technology in the Curriculum, states that full literacy in today's world includes proficiency in using technology. So there is a strong rationale for using multimedia in teaching.

Mandy, a Spanish and French teacher, uses digital video clips and multimedia presentations to teach vocabulary. Mandy knows how to use PowerPoint but had to learn to use a new digital camera before teaching her students to use it. She says, "I find it a motivating and successful way to teach not only vocabulary but also the technology savvy necessary in today's world." But Video Words is only one of many ways Mandy teaches vocabulary. She knows that overuse of one strategy can lessen students' interest and make it less effective.

Mandy first used Video Words to teach -ar verbs to her eighth-grade Spanish students. First, she shares a PowerPoint presentation that includes video clips of eight commonly used -ar verbs. She presents the verb "to cry" (*llorar*) with a clip of her son crying, and a clip of "to cook" (*cocinar*) showing her cooking, and so on (see Figure 6.6). During the week her students use these verbs in cloze passages, translation activities, and a game to practice verb conjugation. Then her advice is:

FIGURE 6.6. Inserting video clips into a PowerPoint presentation can enhance word learning and teach students to be savvy technology users.

1. Put students in small groups and give each a list of words to look up in a dictionary. Be sure that at least one person in each group knows PowerPoint or teach it to them first.
2. Circulate among students and talk to them to be sure they find and understand the definitions.
3. Have students create a plan on paper for making a slide similar to the ones demonstrated the prior week.
4. Show students how to take a video clip with a digital camera and insert it and text into a PowerPoint presentation to create slides.
5. Spend two class periods videotaping and creating multimedia presentations.
6. Have students share their multimedia presentations with the class.

Mandy believes that Video Words gives every student, even struggling and resistant readers, a chance to contribute in different ways. She often has students act out scenes from books they have read to demonstrate a timeline of events or scientific process, or students create pictures or video clips and accompany them with music or song lyrics. Mandy reports that the active engagement students experience when they work with peers to create Video Words makes learning both new vocabulary and technology skills challenging and fun for everyone.

FINAL THOUGHTS

Knowing a word well means understanding the word's meaning, pronunciation, and spelling when it is spoken and read and using the word correctly in speaking and writing. Actively engaging students with new words and with other students as they learn words can promote vocabulary development. Active engagement can also build a positive classroom environment and establish a community of learners who support each other.

Teaching students to search text and their schema for clues to a new word's meaning and teaching them to identify word parts to unlock meaning and pronunciation are important as adolescent readers encounter the heavy vocabulary load in content-area materials. Judicious use of strategies, such as those included in this chapter, is important for students such as Josh, Candace, and Tanesha in order for them to be successful readers who develop their own independent word-learning strategies.

DISCUSSION AND ACTIVITIES

1. For a strategy to be successfully adopted and used by all teachers and students across grade levels and curriculum areas, there often needs to be a schoolwide

commitment. Thinking beyond this chapter, what strategy or activity would you propose as a schoolwide initiative for improving students' vocabulary? How would you introduce it and what steps would you take to ensure its success?

2. What do you think the term *word consciousness* means? Why do you think it might be important for both teachers and students to possess word consciousness? As a teacher, how would you act if you were intent upon fostering word consciousness? (See Graves, Juel, & Graves, 2007; Graves, 2006).

3. What does a best-practice vocabulary teacher look like? What are the characteristics that set this teacher apart from a teacher who is not committed to the notion that vocabulary and comprehension go hand in hand? List five characteristics and share your ideas with someone else.

4. What does this statement by Mark Twain mean to you?: "The difference between the almost right word and the right word is really a large matter—'tis the difference between the lightning bug and the lightning" (Bainton, 1890, pp. 87, 88). Is it important to teach this concept to middle school students? How would you teach it to a seventh-grade writing class in a minilesson? How would you engage students' prior knowledge? What examples might you use? How would you have students apply the idea?

REFERENCES

Adams, L. (2005). The digitization of learning. *T.H.E. Journal*. Retrieved May 16, 2007, from *www.thejournal.com/articles/17321*

Allington, R. (2006). *What really matters for struggling readers?: Designing research-based programs* (2nd ed.). Boston: Allyn & Bacon.

Bainton, G. (1890). *The art of authorship* (pp. 87–88). Retrieved from *www.bartleby.com/73/540/html*

Bromley, K. (2002). *Stretching students' vocabularies*. New York: Scholastic.

Bromley, K. (2007). Nine things every teacher should know about words and vocabulary instruction. *Journal of Adolescent and Adult Literacy, 50*(7), 528–539.

Davis, F. B. (1972). Psychometric research on comprehension in reading. *Reading Research Quarterly, 7*, 628–678.

Greek and Latin roots. Retrieved May 24, 2007, from *www.english.glendale.cc.ca.us*

Graves, M. F. (2006). *The vocabulary book: Learning and instruction*. New York: Teachers College Press.

Graves, M. F., Juel, C., & Graves, B. B. (2007). *Teaching reading in the 21st century* (4th ed., pp. 226–230). Boston: Allyn & Bacon.

Greenwood, C. R., Delquadri, J. C., & Hall, R. V. (1989). Longitudinal effects of classwide peer tutoring. *Journal of Educational Psychology, 81*, 371–383.

Harmon, J. M. (2002). Teaching independent word learning strategies to struggling readers in facilitated peer dialogues. *Journal of Adolescent and Adult Literacy, 45*(97), 606–616.

Hinchman, K. A., Alvermann, D. E., Boyd, F. B., Brozo, W. G., & Vacca, R. T. (2004). Supporting older students' in- and out-of-school literacies. *Journal of Adolescent and Adult Literacy, 47*(4), 304–310.

International Reading Association. (2007). *Integrating literacy and technology in the curric-

ulum. Retrieved May 4, 2007, from *www.reading.org/resources/issues/positions_ technology.html.*

Ivey, G., & Broaddus, K. (2000). Tailoring the fit: Reading instruction and middle school readers. *Journal of Adolescent and Adult Literacy, 54*(1), 68–78.

Lenters, K. (2006). Resistance, struggle and the adolescent reader. *Journal of Adolescent and Adult Literacy, 52*(2), 136–146.

Moore, D. W., & Hinchman, K. A. (2006). *Teaching adolescents who struggle with reading: Practical strategies.* Boston: Allyn & Bacon-Pearson.

Nagy, W. E., & Anderson, R. C. (1984). How many words are there in printed school English? *Reading Research Quarterly, 19*(3), 304–330.

Nagy, W. E., & Scott, J. (2000). Vocabulary processes. In M. L. Kamil, P. B. Mosenthal, P. D. Pearson, & R. Barr (Eds.), *Handbook of reading research* (3rd ed., pp. 269–284). Mahwah, NJ: Erlbaum.

Paivio, A. (1990). *Mental representations: A dual coding approach.* New York: Oxford University Press.

Poindexter, C. (1994). Guessed meanings. *Journal of Reading, 37*(5), 420–422.

Pressley, M. (2002). Comprehension instruction: What makes sense now, what might make sense soon. *Reading online, 5*(2). Retrieved from *www.readingonline.org/ articles/handbook/pressley*

Samuels, S. J. (2002). Reading fluency: Its development and assessment. In A. E. Farstrup & S. J. Samuels (Eds.), *What research has to say about reading instruction* (3rd ed., pp. 166–183). Newark, DE: International Reading Association.

Santa, C. M. (2007). A vision for adolescent literacy: Ours or theirs? *Journal of Adolescent and Adult Literacy, 49*(6), 466–478.

Stahl, S. (1986). Three principles of effective vocabulary instruction. *Journal of Reading, 29*(4), 662–668.

Stahl, S., & Fairbanks, M. M. (1986). The effects of vocabulary instruction: A model-based meta-analysis. *Review of Educational Research, 56*(1), 72–110.

Tomlinson, C. A., & McTighe, J. (2006). *Integrating: Differentiated instruction and understanding by design.* Alexandria, VA: Association for Supervision and Curriculum Development.

Vacca, J. L., Vacca, R. T., Gove, M. K., Burkey, L. C., Lenhart, L. A., & McKeon, C. A. (2005). *Reading and learning to read* (6th ed.). Boston: Allyn & Bacon.

Winters, R. (2001). Vocabulary anchors: Building conceptual connections with young readers. *The Reading Teacher, 54*(7), 659–662.

Zivkovich, P. (1997). Building vocabulary with a 3-D word wall. *Teaching Pre-K-8, 28,* 58–59.

CHAPTER 7

Strategy Matters

COMPREHENSION INSTRUCTION FOR OLDER YOUTH

Rachel Brown

This chapter explains what research on cognitive and sociocultural aspects of literacy tells us that makes strategy matter to older youth and their teachers. It also reveals best practices to address strategy matters in the following sections:

- The section Why Strategy Matters explains theories that underlie comprehension instruction.
- The section Strategy Matters for Students tells what strategies students need to learn.
- Strategy Matters for Teachers explores instructional practices for teachers.
- Examples of Best Practice offers extant programs that successfully promote strategy development in older learners.

Without question, strategy matters when it comes to preparing older youth for the complex reading required of them to flourish in and beyond school. This chapter explains the ways in which strategy matters for comprehension instruction in two senses of the term. The first meaning of the term, *strategy matters*, refers to teaching students a powerful set of comprehension strategies to foster their ability to read well on their own. This capacity to self-direct reading practices has become ever more critical in our fast-paced, technologically rich world, where students increasingly interact with others from diverse backgrounds and circumstances (Leu, 2002).

In the second sense of the term, *strategy matters* refers to teachers who continually make strategic decisions while preparing students to become active, independent readers. More than simply learning about students' interests and backgrounds, and more than transmitting standards-based content to students, teaching older youth entails drawing from students' everyday lives in such a way that they can comprehend and apply the often abstract information presented to them in their high school classes (Moje & Hinchman, 2004). Strategic teaching capitalizes on the expertise of both older youth and subject-area teachers to create collaborative learning in which instruction is rich, engaging, meaningful, and potentially transformative (Greenleaf, Schoenbach, Cziko, & Mueller, 2001). It also means preparing adolescents for the manifold literacy practices (with both print and digital texts) that they will face when leaving school (Moje & Hinchman, 2004). This strategic decision making enables teachers to respond flexibly to the needs of older youth, enacting comprehension instruction that rouses minds and stirs hearts.

WHY STRATEGY MATTERS

In recent years, definitions of comprehension have changed, largely as a result of evolving theoretical perspectives toward literacy. Viewing literacy learning from various theoretical perspectives enables educators to better understand the reasons and origins for their particular instructional practices:

> The more lenses educators possess for examining the reading process and instruction, the better equipped they will be to understand, facilitate, and articulate literacy development. Knowledge of theories and models, along with their implications for practice and research, will contribute to educators becoming informed decision makers. The conceptualization of teachers as informed decision makers is consistent with exemplary literacy instruction practice. (Morrow & Tracey, 2006, p. xii)

Dimensions of Reading Comprehension

Theoretical perspectives on comprehension have addressed four intersecting dimensions to varying degrees: the reader, the text, the task, and the context (RAND Reading Study Group, 2002; Underwood & Pearson, 2004). During the reading process, the *reader* actively draws upon prior academic and nonacademic knowledge, cognitive abilities, and motivation to construct meaning from a *text*, the to-be-understood material. Another key component, the *task*, refers to the reader's ability to analyze the purpose for reading and understand the demands of the activity within which reading is nested (e.g., to take notes, prepare for a discussion, learn more about a musician or hobby).

The context can be defined both narrowly and broadly. A narrow conception of *context* denotes the immediate circumstances surrounding the reading experience, such as whether reading occurs alone or in a group, or whether it happens in or out of school. Other proximal variables include a teacher's knowledge and expectations, the quality of instruction, and the classroom climate (Gaskins, 2005). When considered more expansively, context refers to reading that occurs in a specific point in time, within a particular sociocultural milieu. In effect, linguistic, social, cultural, historical, political, and economic factors all mediate the way in which texts are understood by readers as they engage in learning tasks. Because the reader, the text, the task, and the context are so essential to meaning construction, difficulties associated with any of these components can contribute to breakdowns in the comprehension process.

As notions of reading and learning have evolved over time, so too have conceptions of the reader, text, task, and context. Such adjustments directly reflect shifts in theoretical perspectives, which, in turn, influence the conduct and outcome of comprehension research (Underwood & Pearson, 2004). Theories from approximately the 1980s onward can be positioned, for the most part, along a continuum that ranges from cognitive to sociocultural perspectives. Although researchers periodically ground their studies in other theories, these perspectives are most frequently cited in the research.

Cognitive Views of Comprehension

On the cognitive end of the spectrum, what we know about reading comprehension largely derives from the study of proficient readers (Duke & Pearson, 2002; Pressley & Afflerbach, 1995). In the late 1980s and 1990s, researchers explored the comprehension behaviors that skilled readers exhibited by asking them to think aloud, explaining their thoughts as they read (Pressley & Afflerbach, 1995). That research and other cognitively oriented comprehension research culminated in a theoretical depiction of reading expertise known as the good-strategy-user model (Almasi, 2003; Pressley, Borkowski, & Schneider, 1989). This model incorporated theoretically grounded research on prior knowledge, metacognition, motivation, and strategy use. That is, good readers apply their extensive stores of background knowledge, set goals and monitor both their understanding and progress, and put effort into reading, particularly when challenged. In addition, good readers enact various strategies to support their thinking. Strategies that have a firm research footing include (Duke & Pearson, 2002):

- Making and verifying predictions.
- Asking oneself questions.
- Constructing mental images (i.e., visualizing).
- Making connections to prior knowledge.
- Summarizing and analyzing text structure.
- Clarifying and using "fix-it" strategies to eliminate confusions.

From the cognitive perspective, reader, text, task and context all play a central role in the comprehension process. As suggested above, the various components continually impact and interact with each other. For instance, without adequate prior knowledge about a topic (reader) in a science book (text), a reader might have difficulty comprehending the text sufficiently at home (context) to take notes for an upcoming report (task).

Moreover, readers need to make constant strategic decisions while reading. They have to monitor comprehension, recognize when a problem occurs, and select an appropriate strategy to resolve any comprehension block. When experiencing other difficulties, they persist with the text and task because they know from previous experience that using strategies, even though time consuming and effortful, will compensate for their lack of prior knowledge. Thus, a cognitive perspective primarily attends to the strategic processing that occurs in the mind of a reader. However, text, task, and context also matter to the extent that older youth read texts to complete specific learning tasks within particular contexts.

Best practice in comprehension strategies instruction that reflects a cognitive perspective entails teaching students to coordinate their use of several research-based strategies, simulating the way that good readers use them. Strategies-based instruction provides students with the cognitive tools necessary to take charge of their reading both in English and other subject-area classrooms. As long as teachers want students to think deeply about what they read, it makes sense for them to actively mesh process-oriented strategies instruction with their teaching, regardless of content.

Sociocultural Views of Comprehension

Beginning with the 1990s, research saw a shift from cognitive toward sociocultural views of meaning construction. Although task and context mattered in the cognitive view, less emphasis was placed on these than on various aspects of reader–text interaction. In the sociocultural view, decreased emphasis was placed on understanding what went on inside the head of the reader. Instead, the context of literacy learning gained prominence. That is, sociocultural theories proposed that comprehension is tied to social interaction.

One of the most influential theories of meaning construction was based on the work of Lev Vygotsky, a 20th-century Russian psychologist who explored the relationship between thought and language. Vygotskian (Vygotsky, 1978) theory straddles cognitive and sociocultural perspectives. According to Vygotsky, cognitive development is contingent on social interaction and the cultural settings in which individuals share experiences. When people interact, they use tools, such as oral and written language, to mediate their activities in various contexts. Children initially use language to perform social functions and communicate needs.

With time, such tool use becomes internalized, leading to the formation of thought. In this view, the construction of meaning is mediated by the social practice and cultural context in which it is situated.

Vygotskian theory also suggests the importance of a cognitive apprenticeship, given that learning stems from participation in language-embedded activities wherein more adept individuals scaffold the socialization and learning of newcomers. In a traditional apprenticeship, a novice, the apprentice, learns a craft or trade from a master teacher, who models the to-be-learned skill for the learner in a real-life setting. The apprentice learns by engaging in joint activity with the teacher. However, with a cognitive apprenticeship, the expert teaches strategic processing to the novice. Because thinking cannot be observed, cognitive apprenticeships "are designed, among other things, to bring these tacit processes into the open, where students can observe, enact, and practice them with help from the teacher" (Collins, Brown, & Newman, 1989, p. 458).

In a cognitive apprenticeship, the expert initially explains and models what he or she is doing and thinking. The apprentice then performs the same action as the expert who provides just enough coaching for the apprentice to be successful at the task at hand. Eventually, under the master's tutelage, the apprentice learns to perform the action independently.

Vygotskian theory, and particularly its derivative notion of a cognitive apprenticeship, has led to an instructional prototype known as the gradual-release-of-responsibility model (Duke & Pearson, 2002). Whereas cognitive research identified *which* strategies to teach, Vygotskian theory provided the framework for understanding *how* best to teach them. That is, the teacher, as expert, explains, models, and coaches students until they successfully emulate the real-life strategic thinking and practices of good readers. The approach enables students to assume eventual control of their independent use of comprehension strategies.

Strategies instruction can occur in whole-class, small-group, or one-on-one instruction. At first, the teacher shoulders more responsibility for using strategies when interpreting text. The teacher explicitly explains and models the use of strategies by talking though his or her thinking processes. The purpose for these explanations and think-alouds is to increase students' awareness and control of their knowledge resources, motivations for reading, and mental processing, including when and where it makes sense to apply specific strategies.

As instruction proceeds, the teacher provides guided support and begins to transfer responsibility for strategic processing to students, asking them to use their strategies to form interpretations and address challenges. During this guided phase, the teacher scaffolds students who need additional practice. Also, more capable students begin to model their strategies use for peers. The model suggests that, over time and with sufficient support, students will internalize what they practice collaboratively with others. That is, they learn to use comprehension strategies adaptively in response to their needs, cues from the text, and the goals set for the task.

In the last few decades, other research has shifted our attention even more toward sociocultural concerns. This work, gleaned from diverse academic disciplines (e.g., anthropology, psychology, sociology, philosophy), shares the notion that learning originates in social and cultural interactions (Gee, 2000). Theories cited most frequently by literacy researchers include situated cognition and the communities of practice perspectives (Brown, Collins, & Duguid, 1989; Lave & Wenger, 1991); activity theory (Engeström & Miettinen, 1999), new literacy studies (Street, 2006), critical literacy theory (Siegel & Fernandez, 2000), discourse theory (Gee, 1996), multiliteracies (New London Group, 2000), and new information and technologies literacies (Leu, 2002).

These theories have shaped contemporary views of comprehension instruction in several ways. First and foremost, comprehension can be viewed as embedded in the specific sociocultural contexts of which it is a part, influenced by the circumstances in which printed and electronic texts are produced and consumed. In fact, "knowledge and meaning are seen as emerging from social practices or activities in which people, environments, tools, technologies, objects, words, acts and symbols are all linked to ('networked' with) each other and dynamically interact with and on each other" (Gee, 2000, p. 184). These theories also have changed thinking about the nature of prior knowledge and expert reading. Moreover, the sociocultural theories emphasize identity issues, multiple ways to represent meaning in digital and multimedia texts, and the links between ideology and language use. These changes, in turn, have reframed conceptualizations of the reader, the text, the task, and the context in comprehension and comprehension instruction.

Advocates of the sociocultural perspective reject the view that comprehension originates with the reader, disconnected from social and cultural realities. In effect, sense making is not considered a product of individual cognitive activity. Rather, the prior knowledge that contributes to how a text is understood is distributed across all readers. Consequently, the knowledge needed to construct meaning in a classroom reading event resides not in the individual teacher or student but across all the members in the "community of readers."

Prior knowledge is also conceptualized in terms of the academic resources that readers bring with them to any reading experience. That is, students interpret new texts against the backdrop of the knowledge they have accumulated about the world and texts in school from previous social interactions. Students have access to everyday "funds of knowledge" (Gonzales, Moll, & Amanti, 2005). These funds include knowledge of (1) variants and conventions of language used outside of school, (2) awareness of social and cultural everyday practices in the home or community, and (3) procedures that are valued by members of specific communities who possess common goals, shared norms, and similar values.

The difficulty for some older youth is that their funds of knowledge are not showcased in school. Teachers may communicate that students' funds of knowledge are somehow less suitable resources to tap than school-based ones for the construction and production of meaning. For instance, although making connections to prior knowledge is considered a strategy that matters, teachers may not value, or know how to help students take advantage of, their funds to help them better understand the academic texts they read in school.

According to the apprenticeship model, the more expert readers in a reading community mentor the less capable ones. In this sense, struggling readers are apprenticed to more strategic experts during participation in the meaning-construction practices of the group. However, from a sociocultural perspective, expertise is constructed and varies within the individual from one context to another. That is, just because an individual is an expert in one discipline does not mean that expertise translates to other subject areas as well.

From a sociocultural perspective, language use in its many forms shapes, and is shaped by, human identities. In effect, reading, writing, listening, and speaking embody the beliefs, values, and conventions of interaction associated with a particular social group or institution (otherwise known as a pattern of *Discourse*, spelled with an uppercase *D*; Gee, 1996). In a sense, these communicative ways of being can be conceptualized as "identity kits" in that they establish and reinforce ways of relating with objects and individuals—the norms or "rules of the game" for participants in a given context. They also serve to classify or socialize individuals into particular roles. Essentially, those who follow the tacit norms are considered normal by group members; in contrast, those who resist are viewed as deviants or outsiders. Furthermore, dominant Discourses typically are linked to those who hold power or comprise the majority.

During adolescence, older youths often try out different identities. Such experimentation can lead to new social practices and relationships with language. In effect, older youth may begin to think differently about the role of reading in their lives (Greenleaf et al., 2001). They also may use and produce texts in novel ways based on their emerging interests, beliefs, values, and goals.

In addition, a multiliteracies perspective suggests that we encounter increased cultural and linguistic diversity in our local communities due to globalization. With more heterogeneous communities, older youth need to learn to negotiate the multiple Discourses they encounter everyday—both in and out of school (New London Group, 2000). Multiliteracies (New London Group, 2000) and new literacies (Leu, 2002) perspectives claim that new information and communication technologies (ICTs) have impacted the way that meaning is represented in both print and digital texts. With the proliferation of ICTs and their implications for a networked world, older youth now have ready access to an array of multimedia and digital popular culture texts. These texts communicate information using a mix of modes (i.e., images, film, artwork, icons, print, animation, speech, gestures, and music) that creates a blended message to be comprehended by the reader (Albers, 2006). Given the increasingly prominent role of multimedia texts in our society, older youth need to learn how to communicate information using multiple symbol systems as well as to gain competence in interpreting those complex representations of meaning (Cope & Kalantzis, 2000).

Theorists on the sociocultural end of the theoretical continuum assert that spoken or written communication is not value-free. Instead, language is said to be inherently ideological, organized around usages that privilege some forms of expertise and insight over others. One goal of instruction, then, is to help older youth become more aware of the bias and power relations embodied in texts. Making students cognizant of the ways in which language encodes, shapes, and reproduces power is the first step in providing them with the tools that they will need to resist oppression.

STRATEGY MATTERS FOR STUDENTS

With time, sociocultural influences have occasioned our rethinking of dimensions that comprise the comprehension process—the context, the reader, the text, and the task. As was suggested in the preceding section, this means that the ways in which strategy matters for students has also evolved.

Sociocultural theories ascribe far greater importance to the role of context in comprehension. There is increased awareness of the various environments in which literacy is practiced both in and out of school. Social and cultural perspectives provide a lens through which to view the reading practices that occur within a variety of settings, and they hint of the strategies needed by students to excel in those environments. For instance, research topics include the shifting roles that participants assume as members of a community of readers, as well as the power relations that are embedded in classroom talk about texts. Context issues also relate to the literacy practices in which students engage outside of school, including their immersion in popular cultural texts and ICTs that saturate their everyday lives.

Furthermore, networking via the new ICTs means that contexts (such as those located in specific schools in specific states in specific countries) are not fixed. Instead, youth can access individuals and places far beyond their usual spheres of activity. They can communicate with others at opposite ends of the world and easily access distant resources and institutions.

Sociocultural theories have also redefined what constitutes reader expertise. Instead of identifying expertise as a generalized and unitary construct, expertise in this view is rooted in particular contexts. For instance, older youth may excel at literacy practices that involve new social networking and digital technologies, such as their facility with weblogs, iPods, and instant messaging, yet not exhibit similar competency with academic texts. Or, older youth may master such out-of-school literacy practices using strategies that are not recognized as valuable in school.

Also, the sociocultural perspective suggests that expertise does not reside solely with the teacher. In a community of readers, participants bring a unique constellation of knowledge, experiences, and skills that they are able to invoke during reading, enriching the experience for everyone involved. All reasonable interpretations are perceived as necessary to the task of collaborative meaning making. In addition, the teachers' interpretations are not necessarily held in higher regard than those of other group members.

Expertise is reexamined in another sense as well. From a cognitive perspective, expert readers apply a critical but small set of comprehension strategies to construct meaning (e.g., predicting, making connections, questioning, visualizing). Although these strategies are necessary, they are insufficient to support the skilled reasoning and literacy practices in which experts engage when reading texts in their area of expertise. For instance, mathematicians, scientists, and historians have learned specific strategies, conventions, and Discourses that enable them to participate centrally in the activities and practices typical for these fields.

The new technologies present extra literacy learning opportunities and challenges for older youth. Students need to learn new and expanded strategies for comprehending information that is communicated via technologies that employ multiple methods for representing meaning (e.g., speech, sound, image, gesture, etc., used in combination). Good readers not only employ foundational cognitive strategies such as predicting, making connections, asking questions, visualizing, summarizing, and clarifying confusions, they also strategically cull relevant documents from irrelevant ones during Internet searches, monitor their comprehension as they move between Web-based documents, problem-solve in complex ICT environments, synthesize information within and across websites, evaluate the usefulness of Web resources, and share information using ICTs (Coiro, 2003).

Theories grounded in a sociocultural perspective suggest that teachers need to help students recognize how text and media messages position individuals to ensure their compliance with particular ideological stances. As such, older youth need to learn new and expanded strategies for identifying hidden biases and critically evaluating the tacit messages of print, digital, and multimodal texts. These strategies are required to check the credibility and worth of authors' claims and to interrogate the embedded power relations and ways that texts shape readers' thinking.

Our understandings of text have also changed. Advocates of sociocultural perspectives agree that multimodal and popular cultural texts with which older youth interact, such as songs, fanfictions, and graphic novels, should be acknowledged as valid resources. New literacies have also arisen in response to such texts as video games, instant messaging, e-mail, discussion boards, text messaging, weblogs, webpages, and zines—just to name a few (Knobel & Lankshear, 2005). These and other digital texts have led to the identification of new and hybrid genres that provide teachers with opportunities to talk about text conventions in relation to older youths' out-of-school literacy practices (Chandler-Olcott & Mahar, 2001). Students' transactions with these texts should be seen as constituting authentic literacy engagement, and strategies developed for understanding these texts can be transformed to aid the comprehension of academic texts. Furthermore, given how pervasive such texts have become in our society, teachers need to ensure that youth are able to comprehend them effectively, use them efficiently, and evaluate them critically.

As notions of expertise have changed, so too have views on the range of tasks students might undertake in school. One notion is to prepare students to participate in the kinds of authentic activities that practitioners perform in their disciplines. Another idea is for teachers to think more strategically about the literacy practices they require for their students, altering or expanding their current repertoires to better prepare students to function as global citizens once they leave school. For example, older youth need to learn strategies to help them manage tasks more efficiently in a wide range of contexts: at home, at school, in their communities, in their workplaces. Furthermore, they will need to know how to complete tasks that require the use of both print and digital texts and how to comprehend texts that deploy various representational schemes to communicate information to readers. Finally, they will need to recognize how and why strategic, self-directed reading will help them attain important personal and social goals.

STRATEGY MATTERS FOR TEACHERS

Strategy matters not just for older youth who encounter new text types, new roles as readers, new tasks, and new contexts for reading. For teachers, rethinking the four dimensions can lead to important changes in practice. Moreover, strategy matters if teachers are interested in extending their students' ability to apply strategies to all forms of text , print or otherwise.

Teachers can begin to question their current instructional strategies as they consider the rich resources students bring to the classroom, ready to be tapped. They may move to a more flexible and collaborative instructional approach to capitalize on students' knowledge of particular literacy practices, especially those involving new digital technologies. They also may consider what it means to provide support that is calibrated just beyond students' current abilities, deciding how students, in addition to the teacher, can explain, model, and scaffold strategic reading. Reminiscent of Vygotskian theory, this tact reflects a "cognitive apprenticeship," an approach wherein the self-regulated practices of more experienced others are observed by those still honing their strategic abilities.

Teachers also have to make strategic decisions about which texts and tasks best coincide with updated notions of comprehension instruction. For example, to what extent do they want students to decipher the meaning of multimodal, multimedia texts? To what degree do teachers want students to draw upon their existing funds of knowledge, their reading of popular culture texts and interests to support engagement with academic texts and tasks? Furthermore, how can and should teachers immerse students in tasks that are steeped in the language of specific disciplines and Discourses?

Strategy also matters for teachers, given the technology-driven nature of U.S. society. Unquestionably, teachers need to think about instruction that helps students deal with new tools and rapid change. Moreover, they need to adopt new strategies for working with adolescents who, in some cases, possess more knowledge about ICTs and new literacy practices than they do. Finally, teachers need to find strategic, creative, and meaningful ways to include ICT comprehension instruction so that it melds with ongoing instruction rather than taxing already compressed schedules.

In sum, more than anything else, the sociocultural milieu calls for a finer-grained understanding of the complexities involved in teaching comprehension. As teachers plan, implement, and assess instruction, they need to consider how multiple literacies, multiple Discourses, multiple text types, multiple modalities, multiple contexts, and multiple identities all play key roles in comprehension instruction. Each one of these "multiples" signals strategic decision making regarding how best to integrate these elements into a cohesive program. Certainly, the teaching of comprehension, which has never been easy, represents an even greater challenge than before. However, this kind of comprehension instruction is possible, and it is beginning to make its way into classrooms.

EXAMPLES OF BEST PRACTICE

Given the challenges brought about by new conceptions of comprehension, how can a teacher expect to coordinate all of these elements in instruction? The purpose of this section is to explore some exemplary comprehension instruction for older youth. The vignettes of best classroom practice, included in this section, reflect the field's most current understanding of key cognitive and sociocultural theories and the research that has been based on them. These instructional frameworks enact what we currently understand about the reader, the text, the task, and the context and illustrate what excellent comprehension instruction can look like in the classroom. Although these approaches may not embody all characteristics of practices explained above, they do incorporate several key aspects of cognitive and sociocultural theories into their instructional mix.

A Reading Apprenticeship Approach

A professional development collaborative, known as the Strategic Literacy Initiative, developed a reading apprenticeship approach for adolescents that showcases the teaching of comprehension strategies (Greenleaf et al., 2001). Although promoting independent, motivated reading through the use of comprehension strategies is a key goal, the approach also emphasizes reading as social practice.

A reading apprenticeship approach requires that secondary school instruction should do more than simply transmit content to students in several disciplines. Thus math, science, social studies, and literature teachers are encouraged to become more conscious of the strategies they use to understand texts in their disciplines. As teachers become more cognizant of strategies that are associated with particular disciplines, they assist students to actively and genuinely participate in the strategic practices and Discourses of historians, mathematicians, scientists, and writers. In the process, students learn how language reflects ways of thinking and being in particular disciplines. They gain access to these Discourses—these "habits of mind" and "hidden codes" of language—when teachers in various disciplines reveal their strategic reasoning during think-alouds and when they explicitly discuss with students the knowledge, strategies, and conventions associated with specific subject areas.

This type of teaching is based on a cognitive apprenticeship model. In a reading apprenticeship classroom, students are apprenticed to the expert reader, the teacher. The approach subscribes to a gradual release of responsibility model of instruction, wherein the teacher initially plays a strong role in explaining and modeling strategy use but soon invites students to participate in "metacognitive conversations." Such conversations give them a chance to shape existing expertise to discipline-specific contexts. During these collaborative and socially supportive discussions, students explicitly talk about their application of predicting, questioning, clarifying, and summarizing strategies (among others) with different types of subject-area texts (Greenleaf et al., 2001).

In one school that adopted the reading apprenticeship model, the teaching of strategies was interwoven into three instructional units: Reading, Self, and Society; Reading Media; and Reading History. In each unit, students wrestled with inquiry questions that were intended to heighten their sense of identity as readers. To initiate metacognitive conversations, teachers asked questions such as "What is reading?" "What do successful readers do when they read?" "What strategies do I use as I read in this particular context?" "Why read—for what purposes?" "What role does reading serve in people's personal and public lives?" (For more detailed information about this model, see Greenleaf et al., 2001.)

As with many theories representing a sociocultural perspective, the reading apprenticeship stresses the importance of students' everyday life and language experiences—their funds of knowledge. For example, in one unit, students drew on their experiences with out-of-school literacy practices and multimedia texts to better understand why these texts were created and how they positioned readers to adopt certain views. They also discussed the barriers individuals face when they do not adopt the literacy practices of those in economic, political, and cultural power in a given society. When students answer questions and engage in discussions such as the ones stated above, they begin to understand the manifold ways in which strategic reading supports their identity development, knowledge building, and goal attainment.

The Literacy Lab

Another example of best practice in comprehension instruction for older youths is the multiliteracies work conducted in the literacy lab at Jefferson High School in Lafayette, Indiana (O'Brien, 2001). David O'Brien, who researched the literacy activities at this site, found that older youth, viewed as at risk when tackling academic tasks, were quite capable of reading multimodal texts and creating multimedia projects.

As an example, O'Brien (2001, 2003) introduced us to several students, deemed underperforming on traditional assessments, who were negative about reading due to their previous academic experiences. However, when these students participated in the literacy lab, they became animated when reading supported tasks of interest. They imitated comic book conventions, waded through software documentation, poured through magazines, and read information presented in visual, aural, iconic, and video formats. Furthermore, their print literacy improved as a consequence of working in the literacy lab.

O'Brien suggested that new literacy *envisionments*, such as those occurring in the literacy lab, could prompt educators to consider the ways in which printed texts and conventional academic tasks are privileged when compared to tasks involving multimodal texts and multiliteracies. He proposed that teachers, like those in the literacy lab, consider using popular culture texts in their instruction to help older youth develop life-long strategies for critically evaluating media texts. Furthermore, O'Brien conjured up a vision of a future wherein:

> We will see that socially and culturally mediated perspectives, rather than marginalizing these adolescents, can invite them to participate as capable and expert literate consultants. But we need to continue to encourage [at-risk youth] to draw on their experiences and to participate within a community of peers in exploring those experiences if they are to help us construct a relevant curriculum. (O'Brien, 2001, n.p.)

Teachers, similar to those in the literacy lab, can use digital and multimedia texts and tasks to enhance students' reading comprehension. After all, whether students read print or digital texts, reading comprehension is essential. Moreover, for students to craft a multimedia project of substance, they need to complete some preliminary, and often extensive, reading to support their research.

Older youth in the literacy lab setting need to be strategic readers. Even if students acquire new or expanded strategies to navigate their way through complex multimedia and digital projects, they still need to employ the strategies cognitive researchers identified, such as predicting, making connections, asking questions, visualizing text, clarifying confusions, and summarizing. For instance, students need to determine which information is important to highlight from their reading of both print and digital texts, to question what is confusing, and to summarize and synthesize information within and across Internet documents into a cohesive whole. In addition, students need to predict which forms of representation work best to convey content in their multimedia projects, based on their knowledge of texts authored by others. Finally, students may willingly learn and expend extra effort in using strategies when they perceive how their use will enhance the final product.

Culturally Responsive Pedagogy

Responsive pedagogy refers to instruction that takes into account students' interests and cultural backgrounds while also tapping into their funds of knowledge to create optimal environments for learning. The approach acknowledges that students' goals are influenced by their memberships in different sociocultural groups, which exist both in and out of school

(Moje & Hinchman, 2004). Thus, culturally responsive teaching takes what students already know and care about as members of these groups and extends that knowledge to new contexts, texts, and tasks. Subject-area teachers draw upon students' funds of knowledge, connecting them to the practices and texts employed in the disciplines of math, science, history, and literature, to name a few.

For culturally responsive pedagogy to work, teachers need to possess knowledge of discipline-specific Discourses as well as of their students' out-of-school interests, backgrounds, and reading practices. Only when they know both domains well can they scaffold students to make meaningful connections between the two.

Readers have specific reasons for reading, whether a teen scours the Internet for more information about weight lifting or whether a scientist seeks to expand his or her knowledge of black holes. Although cognitive strategies (e.g., predicting, self-questioning, visualizing, making connections, clarifying, summarizing) are common to all types of reading, practitioners in a given field also apply specific strategies when reading disciplinary texts in order to perform particular tasks. For instance, scientists, more than historians, literary critics, or mathematicians, make predictions for natural occurrences, verify those predictions by gathering evidence from textual or other sources, conduct and summarize the results of their experiments, and evaluate their findings in relation to others presented in the literature (Moje & Hinchman, 2004). In comparison, mathematicians, who use multiple means to represent meaning, may require more strategies for interpreting graphs, formulas, symbols, diagrams, as well as printed text than practitioners in other disciplines.

Responsive pedagogy means that teachers can find ways to help students merge out-of-school funds of knowledge and Discourses with reading in the disciplines. In one study, Moje et al. (2004) explored how a literacy bridge could be constructed in a Spanish–English immersion public high school. For instance, during discussion of an article on growing square watermelons, a student referred to an episode of *The Simpsons* that addressed the same subject. The researchers believed that talking about the popular culture text in conjunction with the academic text not only enabled students to better understand the content in the article but also helped them perceive how depictions of science in popular culture "are accurate or problematic, how they raise questions about the role of science in people's lives, and how they represent science as authority, solution, or problem" (p. 64).

Thus responsive pedagogy creates a space in the classroom where students explore and question the relationship between their everyday sources of knowledge and their academic learning (Moje et al., 2004). The hope is that older youths' interactions with popular culture print and media texts will enable them to learn the generic and more specific strategies necessary for comprehending academic texts. Moreover, it provides students with an opportunity to be critical about the power relations and ideologies encoded in diverse materials. Teachers can support students in this process by exploring how strategies used in various disciplines can complement their current and future goals.

CONCLUSION

The best practice examples above show that it is possible to restructure teaching based on what the field currently knows about strategy matters for students and teachers. In effect, exemplary practice means building on the best of what educators have learned from both cognitive and sociocultural perspectives.

Theory and research suggest that it is not sufficient for teachers to convey curriculum by requiring students to read texts without teaching them the strategies they need to do so. Given adolescents' increasing exposure to diversity in people and technologies, they, more than ever, need to learn the processes for accessing and applying strategies in varying contexts. To meet this goal, it is important to understand why strategy matters not only for older youth but also for their teachers. Effective comprehension instruction involves making strategic decisions about how best to meet the needs of adolescent readers, and in the process, drawing upon an informed and updated understanding of texts, tasks, and contexts.

DISCUSSION AND ACTIVITIES

1. How do reading comprehension strategies matter in your day-to-day life? How have the strategies that matter to you each day evolved to suit the context, expertise, texts, and tasks that you encounter, especially those involving new technologies?

2. Discuss how strategy matters are, or might be, attended to in your school's classrooms. How might such attention vary by subject area? How can students' existing expertise be recognized within such an approach?

3. What resources do teachers need in order to design the kind of responsive pedagogy described by Greenleaf, O'Brien, Moje, and their colleagues? How can acquisition of these resources be facilitated?

REFERENCES

Albers, P. (2006). Imagining the possibilities in multimodal curriculum design. *English Education, 38,* 75–100.

Almasi, J. F. (2003). *Teaching strategic processes in reading.* New York: Guilford Press.

Brown, J. S., Collins, A., & Duguid, P. (1989). Situated cognition and the culture of learning. *Educational Researcher, 18*, 32–42.

Chandler-Olcott, K., & Mahar, D. (2001). Considering genre in the digital literacy classroom. *Reading Online, 5.* Retrieved June 1, 2007, from *www.readingonline.org/electronic/elec_index.asp?HREF=hillinger/index.html.*

Coiro, J. (2003). Reading comprehension on the Internet: Expanding our understanding of reading comprehension to encompass new literacies. *The Reading Teacher, 56*, 458–464.

Collins, A., Brown, J. S., & Newman, S. E. (1989). Cognitive apprenticeship: Teaching the craft of reading, writing and mathematics. In L. B. Resnick (Ed.), *Knowing, learning and instruction: Essays in honor of Robert Glaser* (pp. 453–494). Hillsdale, NJ: Erlbaum.

Cope, B., & Kalantzis, M. (2000). *Multiliteracies: Literacy learning and the design of social futures.* London: Routledge.

Duke, N., & Pearson, P. D. (2002). Effective practices for developing reading comprehension. In A. E. Farstrup & S. J. Samuels (Eds.), *What research has to say about reading instruction* (pp. 205–242). Newark, DE: International Reading Association.

Engeström, Y., & Miettinen, R. (1999). Introduction. In Y. Engeström, R. Miettinen, & R. L. Punamäki (Eds.), *Perspectives on activity theory* (pp. 1–18). New York: Cambridge University Press.

Gaskins, I. W. (2005). *Success with struggling readers.* New York: Guilford Press.

Gee, J. P. (1996). *Social linguistics and literacies: Ideology in discourses* (2nd ed.). London: Taylor & Francis.

Gee, J. P. (2000). The new literacy studies: From "socially situated" to the work of the social. In D. Barton, M. Hamilton, & R. Ivanic (Eds.), *Situated literacies: Reading and writing in context* (pp. 180–196). London: Routledge.

Gonzalez, N., Moll, L. C., & Amanti, C. (2005). *Funds of knowledge: Theorizing practices in households and classroom.* Mahwah, NJ: Erlbaum.

Greenleaf, C. L., Schoenbach, R., Cziko, C., & Mueller, F. L. (2001). Apprenticing adolescent readers to academic literacy. *Harvard Educational Review, 71*, 79–129.

Knobel, M., & Lankshear, C. (2005). "New literacies": Research and social practice. In B. Maloch, J. V. Hoffman, D. L. Schallert, C. M. Fairbanks, & J. Worthy (Eds.), *54th yearbook of the National Reading Conference* (pp. 21–42). Oak Creek, WI: National Reading Conference.

Lave, J., & Wenger, E. (1991). *Situated learning: Legitimate peripheral participation.* Cambridge, UK: Cambridge University Press.

Leu, D. J. (2002). The new literacies: Research on reading instruction with the Internet. In A. E. Farstrup & S. J. Samuels (Eds.), *What research has to say about reading instruction* (3rd ed., pp. 310–336). Newark, DE: International Reading Association.

Moje, E., Ciechanowski, K. M., Kramer, K., Ellis, L., Carrillo, R., & Collazo, T. (2004). Working toward third space in content area literacy: An examination of everyday funds of knowledge and Discourse. *Reading Research Quarterly, 39*, 38–70.

Moje, E., & Hinchman, K. A. (2004). Developing culturally responsive pedagogy for adolescents. In J. Dole & T. Jetton (Eds.), *Adolescent literacy research and practice* (pp. 331–350). New York: Guilford Press.

Morrow, L. M., & Tracey, D. H. (2006). *Lenses on theory: An introduction to theories and models.* New York: Guilford Press.

New London Group. (2000). A pedagogy of multiliteracies: Designing social futures. In B. Cope & M. Kalantzis (Eds.), *Multiliteracies: Literacy learning and the design of social futures* (pp. 9–37). London: Routledge.

O'Brien, D. (2001). "At-risk" adolescents: Redefining competence through the multi-literacies of intermediality, visual arts, and representation. *Reading Online, 4*(11). Retrieved June 1, 2007, from *www.readingonline.org/newliteracies/lit_index.asp? HREF=/newliteracies/obrien/index.html*

O'Brien, D. (2003). Juxtaposing traditional and intermedial literacies to redefine the competence of struggling adolescents. *Reading Online, 6.* Retrieved June 1, 2007, from *www.readingonline.org/newliteracies/lit_index.asp?HREF=obrien2*

Pressley, M., & Afflerbach, P. (1995). *Verbal protocols of reading: The nature of constructively responsive reading.* Hillsdale, NJ: Erlbaum.

Pressley, M. Borkowski, J. G., & Schneider, W. (1989). Good information processing: What it is and how education can promote it. *International Journal of Educational Research, 13,* 857–867.

RAND Reading Study Group. (2002). *Reading for understanding: Toward an R&D program in reading comprehension.* Santa Monica, CA, and Washington, DC: RAND Corporation.

Siegel, M., & Fernandez, S. L. (2000). Critical approaches. In M. Kamil, P. Mosenthal, P. D. Pearson, & R. Barr (Eds.), *Handbook of reading research* (Vol. 3, pp. 141–151). Mahwah, NJ: Erlbaum.

Street, B. (2006). New literacies, new times: How do we describe and teach the forms of literacy knowledge, skills and values people need for new times? In J. V. Hoffman, D. L. Schallert, C. M. Fairbanks, J. Worthy, & B. Maloch (Eds.), *55th yearbook of the National Reading Conference* (pp. 21–42). Oak Creek, WI: National Reading Conference.

Underwood, T., & Pearson, P. D. (2004). Teaching struggling adolescent readers to comprehend what they read. In T. L. Jetton & J. A. Dole (Eds.), *Adolescent literacy research and practice* (pp. 135–151). New York: Guilford Press.

Vygotsky, L. S. (1978). *Mind in society: The development of higher psychological processes.* Cambridge, MA: Harvard University Press.

CHAPTER 8

Reading and Writing across Multiple Texts

Cynthia Hynd Shanahan

This chapter:

- Makes an argument for teaching students to understand, think about, and write multiple texts on the same topic.
- Discusses research and practice regarding multiple-text reading and writing strategies.
- Provides activities that can be used with students in English, social science, science, and mathematics classes for reading and writing multiple texts.

THE CASE FOR MULTIPLE TEXTS

We make decisions every day regarding the various aspects of our lives. Should we go on this diet or that one—or should we adopt more realistic body images? Is this candidate's plan for the budget realistic? Is what the president or Congress says about Iraq credible? What will the consequences of global warming be, and what should we be doing about it? Which brand of toothpaste should we buy? These decisions may all be quite difficult to make, because we rely on information that comes from multiple viewpoints, in multiple formats (e.g., letters, essays, reports, advertisements, lectures), through various venues (e.g., newspapers, television, podcasts, websites, billboards, books, magazines), and is often contradictory. The information changes based on who said it, when it was said, what evidence was used to support it, and on and on. There is no one, definitive answer, though many messages claim to be just that. Yet, regardless of how confusing the messages are, we are compelled as citizens to vote for the person who has garnered our trust, we actually do have to buy toothpaste, and we either do something about global warming (e.g., take public transportation, buy eco-friendly light bulbs) or do nothing—but either way, respond.

Our nation is based on informed citizenry, and that means we have an obligation to learn about the issues that affect our country and ourselves. If we don't truly inform ourselves on the issues related to global warming, for example, we end up making decisions based upon an 8-second sound bite or because a celebrity said so.

The necessary reliance on multiple messages that conflict or disagree and through which we find no right answer is also a reality in most disciplines. Think of the discipline of history, for example. Historians use evidence from multiple sources (e.g., film, newspapers, autobiographies, letters, firsthand accounts, interviews) to *construct* plausible views of historical events and make cause–effect claims or claims of significance about them. They construct those claims based not only on the evidence but also on their particular viewpoints. For example, if a historian believes that history is a story of progress (i.e., things just keep getting better and better), he or she will interpret the evidence in a different way than a historian who believes that the past is glorious and that the future is getting worse and worse. A grass-roots historian will be looking for different kinds of evidence than a biographer of presidents, even though the two may be focused on the same era and even the same events. Also, historians often argue about the meaning of events or change how they think about events based upon new evidence or a new outlook; hence the phenomenon of revisionist history. Christopher Columbus, for instance, has been lauded as a great man who discovered the New World; scorned for the way in which he took advantage of the Taino people and decimated their population; and defended as an individual acting within the constraints of his time in history—each view depending upon the era in which historians were doing the writing and who the historians were. Historians not only read multiple genres when creating historical accounts and interpretations, they also write them. Academic prestige is achieved through the writing of scholarly books, but historians also write journal articles, take elaborate notes, engage in conversations with other scholars (and sometimes the press), and so on.

Multiple texts are also the purview of science. Scientists keep reinventing the world. What we think of as scientific truth at one time is later discarded as new tools (e.g., the telescope), new theories (e.g., quantum physics, black space), new procedures for analysis, and new experiments are created. Even though scientists' views of the world are constrained by the scientific method and what they count as evidence is subject to the rigors of experimentation, scientists decide what is significant and what is accepted as scientific fact only after evaluating numerous experiments and after reading numerous documents—not all of which consider the subject matter in the same way or agree. And if we consider phenomena that are difficult to measure, such as the phenomenon of global warming, then, scientists are often divided in their views. Too, when scientists write, they do not write in only one format for one purpose. They write multiple documents: scientific reports, proposals for funding, laboratory observation notes, explanations of science for popular consumption, and so on. Bazerman (1998) discusses how important it was to incandescent lighting, as we know it, that Edison could communicate in writing via the patent application, the newspaper, technical journals, legal briefs, and so on. The transformation of information from one domain to another is perhaps the hallmark of a skilled language user.

Even in a highly constrained field such as mathematics, experts read and write multiple texts for a variety of purposes, especially when mathematical principles are applied to the real world. Mathematical principles, for example, are sometimes applied for political purposes in order to make particular claims (e.g., that a state can afford a new health plan or that a new building code will add not only to a building's safety but also be cost effective), and these claims can be refuted by a look at the same issues with different sets of figures. In summary, although the various disciplines are far from similar in the ways experts approach reading and writing and in the challenges their present to adolescent readers (see Shanahan, Shanahan, & Misischia, 2006), discipline experts all read and write multiple texts regarding the topics they study.

In today's information-rich society, adolescence, too, is awash in multiple, conflicting messages. The world's teens are channel switchers; they are constantly searching the Web for information, blogging their views, and, sadly, becoming victims of misinformation, fraud, and exploitation. A series of studies (Leu, 2007) shows that, even with all of the practice adolescents seem to be getting reading multiple documents, they are alarmingly unfamiliar with search strategies and are unaware of issues such as the credibility of information sources. Students do not know how to refine their search terms, and they overwhelmingly choose the first Google hits without examining their relevance. Once on a web page, they do not know where to find, or choose not to read, text that might tell them about the origin of the information on the page and the particular biases of the site owner. A colleague told me about a teenager who definitively announced to his teacher that the Holocaust was a hoax after having read the views of a professor at a university on a website he discovered. It seemed credible, considering the university affiliation; yet the student had not been taught that the tilde after the university URL indicated that the website he had accessed was not an official university site, and he had not noticed the affiliation of the professor with the Ku Klux Klan.

In addition, despite the writing practice they seem to be getting when they write to their peers using blogs, e-mail, and text messaging, adolescents also continue to have difficulty providing appropriate evidence for claims, engaging in more formal writing activities, and writing about the same topic from multiple viewpoints or for multiple purposes. In other words, adolescents need instruction in how to read and write multiple texts.

Yet, as important as reading and writing multiple texts are, much of our instructional effort in literacy is focused on teaching the understanding and creation of single texts on any one topic. We rarely teach students to read across various texts and to write about the same topic in multiple ways and for multiple purposes. The research that has been done on multiple-text reading and writing is synthesized in the next section.

RESEARCH AND PRACTICE
WITH MULTIPLE-TEXT STRATEGIES

We know from studies of multiple-text reading in history that students do not, on their own, use effective strategies for reading several texts on the same topic. Wineburg (1991) had high school students and historians read several documents on a particular event in history. The high school students had already learned about the event in school, so they had background information. The event was not part of the expertise of the historians; thus they lacked background information. The historians, however, engaged in a highly sophisticated read of the documents. In addition to learning the information in the texts, they engaged in three processes: sourcing, contextualization, and corroboration, as described in Figure 8.1.

In short, the historians evaluated the documents for their credibility. They thought of the documents as arguments for a particular interpretation of history, and they used the credible information to form their own interpretations. The high school students, on the other hand, treated each of the documents as a separate entity and engaged in fact collection.

- **Sourcing**: When sourcing, they looked for information about the author, they checked the sources of information the author used, they looked at the kind of document it was, and so on.
- **Contextualization**: When contextualizing, they thought about the time in which the document was written in terms of the political or socioeconomic climate; for example, and they thought about the kind of history being portrayed, among other considerations.
- **Corroboration**: When corroborating, they looked for agreements and disagreements across the texts and with their own knowledge and experiences.

FIGURE 8.1. The processes used by historians.

Wineburg's findings have been corroborated by a number of other studies (Britt, Rouet, & Perfetti, 1996; Perfetti, Britt, Rouet, Mason, & Georgi, 1993; Stahl, Hynd, Britton, McNish, & Bosquet, 1996; VanSledright & Kelly, 1998). In the Stahl et al. (1996) study, for example, students did seem to learn the information that was common across the various texts, but there was no indication that the students were utilizing corroboration—just that the information that was repeated got remembered. They did not seem to notice when information in the various texts conflicted, and with few exceptions, they did not seem to engage in sourcing or contextualization.

Could students learn to engage in the processes the historians used? Several studies confirm that the answer to that question is *yes*. Hynd-Shanahan, Holschuh, and Hubbard (2004) found that college students not only engaged in sourcing, contextualization, and corroboration but also changed the way they thought about history. In thinking about the texts as arguments for historical interpretation, they ended the study with more sophisticated strategies, more engagement in reading, and a more nuanced and critical view of what it meant to learn historical information. It is not only college students who can use those strategies, however. VanSledright (2002a, 2002b) taught fifth graders to use historical reasoning to read multiple texts, concluding that the students learned "how to make sense of historical documents as evidence, identify the nature of the documents as sources, judge the reliability and perspective of those documents, and corroborate details across accounts in order to construct evidenced-based assumptions" (VanSledright, 2002a, p. 131). Wolfe and Goldman (2005) taught low-performing middle graders to think across two texts about the fall of the Roman Empire, and found that even these struggling readers could make cross-textual connections, given easy texts. De La Paz (2005) found that instruction of middle school students in historical reasoning strategies helped them to write more accurate and persuasive historical essays than students who did not have such instruction. So, studies across grade levels provide evidence that students are capable of learning multiple-text strategies in history for both reading and writing.

In the sciences, Prain, Hand, and their colleagues engaged in a series of studies using models of writing in science and found that students benefit from instruction that involves them in writing for a variety of purposes to a variety of audiences and in a variety of genres (Hand, 1999; Hand & Prain, 2001; Hand, Prain, & Wallace, 2002; Prain & Hand, 1999). They recommend that students be given writing assignments in science that include explanation, sets of instructions, letters, reports, diagrams, and so on, for the purpose of clarifying, applying, or persuading peers, younger students, a government agency, and others. Elizabeth Moje (2007) and her team (funded by the Carnegie Foundation) have developed units that teach science by pairing a textbook passage with a popular science passage on the same topic. By using the two texts, they hope to teach students how rigorous science knowledge translates to real-world applications.

ISSUES WITH MULTIPLE TEXTS

Teachers usually want to know several things before they teach students multiple-text strategies. Some of these issues are addressed in this section.

Readability

Adolescent readers often struggle with their content-area texts for a variety of reasons. It could be that they have general reading difficulties, such as word recognition and fluency problems, that affect all of their reading. It could be that they lack adequate general vocabulary knowledge (especially true of students who are learning English) or that they struggle with the abstract, decontextualized nature of academic language. It could be that the text genre (e.g., a scientific journal article, a speech before Congress) or structure (e.g., a mixture of narrative and expository text, a text that moves back and forth across time) is one that is unfamiliar. It could be that the student lacks appropriate background information. It could be that the text itself is "inconsiderate" (e.g., Beck, McKeown, & Worthy, 1995)—it fails to provide explanation of technical vocabulary, lacks appropriate explanations and examples, uses arcane language, etc. In addition, it could be that students do not approach the reading using a particular disciplinary lens and therefore do not understand what is important to pay attention to or what questions to ask.

Whatever the reason, these struggles are still evident when there is more than one text, and may be magnified if the texts represent different genres, were written in different contexts, or have contradictory purposes and messages. Thus the difficulty level of the texts students read is an issue, but the measurement of difficulty is complex. For a single reading, any one of the conditions noted above could make the texts too difficult, and most often, more than one of the conditions interact. For example, Britton and Gulgoz (1991) found that students who lack background information are more troubled by inconsiderate texts than students who have high levels of background knowledge, especially when the text comprehension requires extensive inferential thinking. Multiple-text reading compounds the complexity. Depending upon the type of problems, different solutions are called for—and not all of them involve finding texts at lower readability levels.

One study (American College Testing, 2006) found that students' reading achievement did not improve sufficiently throughout the high school years to prepare them for the more complex reading demands of college. The study suggested that students were not receiving enough instruction and practice in reading complex academic texts. When students have difficulty reading, their teachers discard texts (so that their students can learn the information) and rely on lecture and discussion, visual displays, film, read the texts to them, or have students engage in round-robin reading with only the good readers participating. So, at the end of the year, students have not learned how to read the texts in that content area, and they enter classes in subsequent years being even less equipped to read those texts. In addition, they perform poorly on tests of content that relies on reading. Because we want to avoid these negative consequences, it may be neither realistic nor wise to ensure that all of the texts read by students are within their independent reading level (i.e., a level at which they can read on their own without help). With a high level of instructional support, students may be able to read text that approaches their frustration level when read without the support. There is some research support for that notion. For example, students who practiced fluency with texts that were at their frustration level improved in fluency and comprehension more than students who practiced fluency using texts at their independent reading levels. And, from my own experience teaching college students whose reading levels were low, providing support with background information, vocabulary instruction, and strategy instruction improved students' ability to learn from even very difficult text.

Depending upon the reasons students experience difficulty reading the texts, different solutions are needed. Some possibilities are listed in Figure 8.2.

Teachers could:

- Preteach potentially troublesome vocabulary.
- Have students read an easier text, or to provide information to build background knowledge, use an anchor text or experience before reading a more difficult text.
- Teach students to use strategies that will help them to better interpret the texts.
- Teach students about various genres and structures used in particular texts and how texts within those genres signal important information.
- Teach students information about the discipline in which they are reading—about how experts in that discipline approach and use information in text to build upon existing knowledge.
- Set up cooperative grouping structures that allow students who are weaker readers to be supported in their reading by a better reader; one of the online translation sites could be used to translate text to a student's primary language.
- Find easier texts or alter existing texts to make them easier, if the difficult texts are so challenging that students become unmotivated, even with all of the support they receive.

FIGURE 8.2. Ways teachers can deal with difficult texts.

The use of more than one text about a particular topic may actually facilitate gains in comprehension of that topic. The easier texts in the set could build the background knowledge that makes the more difficult texts easier to understand. Also, multiple readings of information that is repeated across texts may increase the likelihood that students' understanding of the information will deepen.

How Many Texts?

I've found that teachers who introduce multiple-text instruction sometimes make the mistake of assigning too many texts, too soon. The middle and high school history teachers with whom I work have had success with this beginning to multiple-text instruction: Have students read an easy and "objective" background text that sets the context and introduces key vocabulary. Next introduce a second text and study it. Then introduce a third text, studying it as well and comparing and contrasting it to the second text. With that introduction to multiple-text study, it will be easier in the future to introduce a larger text set.

What Kind of Instruction?

Students need to be taught how to think about more than one text's coverage of a topic. My research has convinced me that, without this instruction, just having students read more than one text will have minimal effect on comprehension or learning. But the answer to the question "What kind of instruction?" is somewhat dependent on the discipline one is teaching, the kinds of texts that are being introduced, and the purpose for reading. For that reason, this section discusses the application of multiple-text strategies within disciplines and for specific purposes that are, to some extent, discipline-specific.

History

As discussed previously in this chapter, historians read texts with a critical eye—they read the texts as arguments for particular interpretations of historical events. Thus, when reading multiple texts in history, the most authentic purpose for reading is to determine a credible historical interpretation of an event—what caused it, what effects it had, how significant it was. In reading any document in a set of documents, the reader has to determine the credibility of the source, evaluate the context in which the material it was written, weigh the evidence that is being offered for the interpretation, and evaluate how well that interpretation agrees or disagrees with others in order to decide what to believe.

In my teaching of multiple texts in history, I first ask students what it is that historians *do*. My research (Hynd-Shanahan et al., 2004) suggests that students begin to answer that question in a way that assumes historians to be none other than documenters. They believe that historians write down exactly what happened. In the discussion, however, they soon come to realize that that is an inadequate description. Because historians search for many different accounts of what happened, students begin to view them as synthesizers. Some subsequently start to shift their opinions to note that historians need to decide about the accuracy of accounts—thus, they believe historians act as arbiters. If they keep on discussing the issue, some will even come to recognize that historians have their own viewpoints and biases that play into their final interpretation. These emerging notions of the role of the historians in the interpretation of historical events are key. To read and write like historians, students need to understand that they are reading *arguments*, rather than truth, when they read historical text.

I then teach students about the strategies that historians use when they read: sourcing, contextualization, and corroboration. That is, I explain each strategy, model how each is used by thinking out loud as I read a text excerpt, and have the students practice using all the strategies, both as a whole group and independently or in small groups. It is only after I know that students understand the task (to determine a credible interpretation of an event) and the strategies (sourcing, contextualization, and corroboration) that I introduce the text set. As I said earlier, three texts are an optimal beginning point. The first text sets up the context and provides background information. The second and third texts are read using the strategies. To help students engage in the strategies, I ask them to create two compare-and-contrast charts. On one chart, students take notes about the *source* of each text (the author, the kind of text, the publisher, where the information came from) and the *context* of each text (when it was written, for what audience, in what political, social, economic climate). All of these variables are found outside of the body of the text itself. On a web page, for example, students might have to search for this information by clicking on various buttons, or in a book, they might have to search the jacket or read the preface and table of contents. To find out the political, social, or economic climate, students may have to search outside sources again, such as newspapers from the era or a history textbook; at this point the teacher might want to provide his or her expertise in helping students understand contextual issues or pointing them to key sources of information, such as the anchor text they read for background information. Appendix 8.1 has one version of this chart.

The second chart I have students create is a compare–contrast chart of the issues for the purposes of *corroboration*. For example, when we studied the Tonkin Gulf incident of the Vietnam conflict, students knew from the background text that historians argued about three points: (1) what happened; (2) whether or not the United States instigated it; and (3) whether or not President Johnson pushed the Tonkin Gulf resolution through Congress, knowing that the justification he used was not entirely truthful. Students wrote these points in the form of questions that could be answered "yes" or "no" (or, in some cases, "maybe") across the top of their chart, and they put the text titles down the side of their chart. That is, they wrote these three questions: (1) Did North Vietnam attack the *USS Maddox*? (2) Did the U.S. intentionally provoke North Vietnam? (3) Did President Johnson manipulate Congress? When they came to evidence in their reading that addressed one of the points, students answered the question, then paraphrased the evidence in the appropriate box and wrote down the page number on which they had found it. They could then compare the texts on those three issues. Appendix 8.2 shows a version of this chart.

Students need to discuss with a more knowledgeable other, such as the teacher, what they find using the charts. This discussion is important, because students do not have the expertise or the mature viewpoints of practicing historians. For example, my students thought that a book that was "self-published" was automatically as credible as a book published by a reputable publishing company, and that an article in a local newspaper carried the same evidentiary weight as an article published in a newspaper such as the *The Washington Post* or *The New York Times*—papers that are (or which used to be) known for their dogged pursuit of reliable information. They also held a considerable bias for authors who "were there" over historians, believing, for example, that Dean Rusk was a more credible source of information than the historian who had written his dissertation on Vietnam and who had published a three-volume set of annotated primary documents. However, when I asked questions that got them to think about these beliefs, they changed their thinking. For example, when I asked students what made them think that Dean Rusk was without bias, some students brought up the idea that he had his own reputation on the line and, in defending that reputation, might not be giving his audience the most unbiased presentation of the facts. I set up a scenario for them of an accident site and asked them who would have the more credible account—any one person who witnessed the accident or the reporter who interviewed all of the witnesses. But students were rightly quick to point out that the reporter, too, could have had biases. These discussions helped students form more nuanced interpretations of the event.

In their essays that were part of the exam about the Vietnam conflict, students were asked to take a stand on one of three questions and provide evidence for their viewpoint. Because they all had thought very deeply about their stand and the evidence to support it prior to the test, they could easily write coherent, well-supported essay. The first time I engaged students in a multiple-text project, I was surprised by the quality of their writing; as I continued to engage students in this kind of instruction, I came to expect it. I still am, however, amazed at the transformation that takes place in students' understanding of what it means to read history and how much more students are engaged in learning history when they take responsibility for their interpretation.

Other Multiple-Text Strategies for History. The strategy of questioning the author (QtA; Beck, McKeown, Hamilton, & Kucan, 1997) can be adapted for use with multiple texts, because the purposes of the strategy are to help readers understand that each text has a human, fallible author and to read texts with a reviewer's eye. The idea is that students "question" the unseen author in order to determine the meaning he or she intended. The teacher initiates the discussion ("What is the author trying to say?"), helps students focus on the author's message ("That's what the author says, but what does it mean?"), links information, in this case, to the other texts they have read ("How does this connect with what we already read?"), identifies difficulties ("Does that make sense?"), and encourages a close reading of the text ("Did the author tell us that? Where?"). For multiple-text lessons, these questions can be used with the texts as they are read to help students comprehend them and make appropriate links to the other texts.

In addition, teachers can construct other guiding questions that students can use in collaborative work to help them think critically about the various texts they are reading. Steve Stahl and I (Stahl et al., 2006) call these "procedural facilitators," in that they facilitate the use of the same procedures historians use. (See Appendices 8.1 and 8.2 for examples.)

When historians are reading the text, they look for evidence of bias in the language authors use by asking themselves questions about the connotation of particular words, by evaluating what was *not* said about the topic, and so on. All of these questions, if students learn to ask them, help them to evaluate a particular text and compare it with the others they are reading. The final result should be students who are better able to decide what kind of cross-textual evidence is credible as they learn to make their own interpretations of historical events.

Science

As noted, scientists read multiple texts on any one topic and engage in writing across multiple contexts for multiple purposes. Teachers need to invite their students into the various discourses used in science. Scientists approach reading somewhat differently than do historians, however. Shanahan et al. (2006) found that the chemists they studied engaged in two distinct kinds of reading, depending on the kind of text they read and their level of knowledge about the topic. Bazerman (1998) found that physicists engaged in those two processes, as well. That is, when their topic knowledge was low, the scientists read uncritically, for the purpose of learning. When we asked the chemists about how students should read their textbooks, they emphasized this kind of learning-focused reading. If they knew a lot about the topic or if they were reading a journal article or a piece in the popular press (e.g., a newspaper article), they would adopt a critical reading style, engaging in many of the same processes the historians used when reading (sourcing, contextualizing, and corroborating).

How should multiple texts be used in science classes? Certainly, students should read the various discourses of science, classified by Wignell (1994) as (1) procedure (to provide instruction for experiments); (2) procedural recount (to record what has already been done in an experiment); (3) science report (to organize information by setting up taxonomies, parts, or steps, or by listing properties); and (4) science explanation (describing how and why phenomena occur). Note that points 3 and 4 appear most often in science textbooks and points 1 and 2 appear most often in scientific journals. In addition to these, Prain and Hand (1999) note other genres that are appropriate for science writing, such as field notes, diagrams, brochures, or letters. Considering Bazerman's (1998) reminder that scientists have to cross genres to gain funding, secure patents, and disseminate findings to a lay audience, asking students to read and write these different types of texts in science class makes sense. For writing assignments, Prain and Hand recommend that teachers vary these four elements on any given topic: (1) the genre, (2) the purpose, (3) the audience, and (4) the method of text production. If the topic were "the urban heat island," for example, students might be asked to write a scientific explanation for the purpose of clarifying ideas for another student, using pen and paper; or write a proposal to a government agency to alter the effects of the urban heat island for the benefit of the city's inhabitants (a persuasive argument that includes how the ideas are applied), using a computer. For our purposes (teaching students to process multiple texts), students would be asked to engage in both types of writing. Because each of these genres uses distinct structures and rhetorical moves, these need to be taught.

Moje's (2007) idea of pairing a textbook-like scientific explanation with an article in a popular science magazine or other type of text showing an application of the scientific phenomenon makes sense as well. When reading the scientific explanation in the textbook, students would be in learning mode. They would engage in strategies to help them learn the information in the text, such as transforming text into diagrams (or vice versa), identifying and learning key vocabulary through activities such as concept cards, and so on. When reading the popular science text, they would engage in sourcing, contextualization, and corroboration. That is, they would find out who the author is and to what audience he or she is writing, the context of the writing, and how well the text corresponds to the science.

Another way of pairing articles to help students make sense of scientific study might be to pair an experimental article on a particular topic with a newspaper or popular science article on the same topic. In such a pairing, students could evaluate the science (how well did the scientists follow the scientific method? did their findings make sense?) and then see how those findings are translated for another audience. Alternately, an article on a particular topic written in the past paired with one on the same topic written more recently would help students understand how scientific findings change with new methodology, new measurements, and so on.

I use two popular science texts on sea turtles to help students engage in critical thinking about science information. One text is dated, and some of the information is no longer thought to be true. If students don't pay attention to the dates of the articles, they become confused. That text is written to persuade the audience to back conservation efforts of a particular government agency. The other is written to provide information about sea turtles to students. For science topics, I suggest focusing on learning the information first. Students read one of the texts, write down the information they learn, then group that information and label it. For the sea turtles topic, for example, students write down information and group it under labels such as (1) physical appearance, (2) reproduction, (3) habitat, and so on. They place this information on a chart (see Appendix 8.3 for an illustration of this chart), with the labels along the vertical axis, the two texts across the horizontal axis, and the actual information (e.g., weight = 150 pounds; large flippers) in the boxes under the first text. Then students read the second text. If the second text agrees with the first text, they place a check in the box under the Agreements column. If it is new information, they put a plus in the New Information column and add the new information, and if it disagrees with the first text, they but an X in the Disagreements column and write down the divergent information. Students can complete this task in small groups or alone.

When they are finished, the students discuss the similarities and differences across the texts. The differences provide the teacher with the opportunity to help students pay attention to the source of the information and the context in which it was written. The contextual analysis includes recognizing *when* the text was written, to *what audience*, and for *what purpose*. Students see that one of the texts is dated and are then able to evaluate the credibility of the information. The final step is to have students write a synthesis of the two texts, using only the information that appears to be credible. The activity loosely mirrors the processes used by scientists when they read several texts on the same topic.

Science inquiry projects (such as those required in science fairs) all involve the synthesis and critical evaluation of multiple texts as well as the ability to use the scientific method to answer a question. Yet, students are expected to know how to think about the information in more than one text without being taught how to do so. That assumption may be unfair to students, and as a result, they may flounder in their attempts to engage in true scientific inquiry.

Mathematics

The Shanahan et al. (2006) study found that the mathematicians they studied did not view sourcing and contextualization as key elements in reading mathematics. One of the mathematicians explained that it just doesn't matter when a mathematics text was written. Years later, it could still be the object of intense study. In the same vein, it doesn't matter who did the writing. What matters is on the page. Mathematicians engage in critical reading, but it looks different from the critical reading done by scientists and historians. Mathematicians, they told us, look for a kind of precise sense making. They want to make sure that the mathematics is without error, and that every word and term is accurately used, that a logical progression of ideas unfolds. So reading and writing multiple texts in mathematics will look different than it does in science or history. But in the application of math to everyday life, precision truly matters. For example, it is a matter of life and death that an engineer correctly calculates the weight that can be borne by a particular floor.

That a sloppy or inaccurate application can be quite important is an idea that is more easily communicated to students through multiple texts. As in the science example above, a typical textbook explanation of a mathematics principle could be paired with an applied text—such as in a magazine or journal article. The textbook passage is read in a learning mode. That is, students learn key vocabulary and the processes that are described. They write explanations of the processes in their own words, solve problems using the processes, and engage in other activities such as writing their own problems. When they are asked to read the applied text, they are told to read critically. That is, they look for errors in the text—to see if all vocabulary, formulae, explanations, and so on, are accurate, that they are appropriately applied, that there is a logical progression of ideas, and that the unit of measurement makes sense. Corroboration, too, is an important process to be used in mathematics. Mathematics teachers commonly complain that students can do the problems assigned after reading the text but have difficulty figuring out how to solve problems on a test, when they have to decide among several different processes for solving them. They say that students don't know how the problems on the test compare with the ones they learned to do in their assignments. Thus, the application text could be compared and contrasted in relation to the process that is carried out. When writing, students could write multiple texts about the same process. One might be an explanation of the process and another might be an application of the principle or process.

CONCLUSION

This chapter has made a case for using more than one text when teaching content-area subjects. I used examples from three discipline to discuss how this might be done—history, science, and mathematics. Even beyond these examples, however, we need to do more to teach students how to take into account multiple messages when they read and to write for different audiences. Students are already reading multiple texts, but they won't be able to process them critically unless they are given some instruction in how to do it. Furthermore, the context in which they read in some ways changes the kinds of processes they will use. Thus, teachers need to help students learn how to read and write multiple texts.

DISCUSSION AND ACTIVITIES

1. What difficulties do adolescents experience when they have more than one text to read about a particular topic? How can these difficulties be ameliorated?

2. Think of a topic you would teach in your subject area. What kinds of texts would be good choices for involving students in learning about that topic? Where would you find them?

3. How would you teach students to search for multiple texts they might find on the Internet regarding topics in your subject area? How would you help them evaluate those texts for credibility?

4. How would you react to students who, after evaluating the credibility of the texts they are reading, decide to believe a harmful or untenable position (e.g., racist or in some other way biased or offensive)?

5. What writing genres are used in your subject area? How could you help students write in these various genres?

REFERENCES

American College Testing. (2006). *Reading between the lines: What the ACT reveals about college readiness for reading.* Available at *www.act.org/path/policy/reports/reading.html.*

Bazerman, C. (1998). *Shaping written knowledge: The genre and activity of the experimental article in science.* Madison, WI: University of Wisconsin Press.

Beck, I., McKeown, M. G., Hamilton, R. L., & Kucan, L. (1997). *Questioning the author: An approach for enhancing student engagement with text.* Newark, DE: International Reading Association.

Beck, I., McKeown, M. G., & Worthy, J. (1995). Giving a text voice can improve students' understanding. *Reading Research Quarterly, 30,* 220–238.

Britt, M. A., Rouet, J. F., & Perfetti, C. A. (1996). Using hypertext to study and reason about historical evidence. In J. F. Rouet, J. T. Levonen, A. Dillon, & R. Spiro (Eds.), *Hypertext and cognition* (pp. 43–72). Mahwah, NJ: Erlbaum.

Britton, B., & Gulgoz, S. (1991). Using Kintsch's computational model to improve instructional text: Effects of repairing inference calls on recall and cognitive structures. *Journal of Educational Psychology, 83*(3), 329–345.

De La Paz, S. (2005). Effects of historical reasoning instruction and writing strategy mastery in culturally and academically diverse middle school classrooms. *Journal of Educational Psychology, 97*(2), 139–156.

Hand, B. (1999). A writing-in-science framework designed to enhance science literacy. *International Journal of Science Education, 21*(10), 1021–1035.

Hand, B., & Prain, V. (2001). Influences of writing tasks on students' answers to recall and higher-level test questions. *Research in Science Education, 32*(1), 19–34.

Hand, B., Prain, V., & Wallace, C. (2002). Influences of writing tasks on students' answers to recall and higher-level tests questions. *Research in Science Education, 32*(1), 19–34.

Hynd-Shanahan, C., Holschuh, J., & Hubbard, B. (2004). Thinking like a historian: College students' reading of multiple historical documents. *Journal of Literacy Research, 36*, 141–176.

Leu, D. (2007, May). *What happened when we weren't looking? How reading comprehension changed and what we need to do about it.* Paper presented at the annual research conference of the International Reading Association, Toronto, Canada.

Moje, E. (2007, May). *Adolescent literacy: The Crisis and the solutions.* Paper presented at the Summit on Adolescent Literacy, sponsored by the Wisconsin Department of Education, and the Alliance for Excellent Education with support from Carnegie Corporation of New York and the Great Lakes West Comprehensive Center, Madison, WI.

Perfetti, C. A., Britt, M. A., Rouet, J. F., Mason, R. A., & Georgi, M. C. (1993, April). *How students use texts to learn and reason about historical uncertainty.* Paper presented at annual meeting of the American Educational Research Association, Atlanta, GA.

Prain, V., & Hand, B. (1999). Students' perceptions of writing for learning in secondary school science. *Science Education, 83*(2), 151–162.

Shanahan, C., Shanahan, T., & Misischia, C. (2006, December). *Frameworks for literacy in three disciplines.* Paper presented at the annual meeting of the National Reading Conference, Los Angeles.

Stahl, S., Hynd, C., Britton, B., McNish, M., & Bosquet, D. (1996). What happens when students read multiple source documents in history? *Reading Research Quarterly, 31*, 430–457.

VanSledright, B. (2002a). Confronting history's interpretive paradox while teaching fifth graders to investigate the past. *American Educational Research Journal, 39*, 1089–1115.

VanSledright, B. (2002b). *In search of America's past: Learning to read history in elementary school.* New York: Teachers College Press.

VanSledright, B., & Kelly, C. (1998). Reading American history: The influence of multiple sources on six fifth graders. *Elementary School Journal, 98*(3), 239–265.

Wignell, P. (1994). Genre across the curriculum. *Linguistics and Education, 6*(4), 355–372.

Wineburg, S. S. (1991). On the reading of historical texts: Notes on the breach between school and academy. *American Educational Research Journal, 28*, 495–519.

Wolfe, M. B. W., & Goldman, S. R. (2005). Relationships between adolescents' text processing and reasoning. *Cognition and Instruction, 23*, 467–502.

APPENDIX 8.1. Sourcing/Contextualization in History

When historians read documents, they pay attention to the source of the information and to when the document was written in order to determine if the source is credible.

Text	Source		Context			How is credibility affected?
	What author and credentials?	What kind of text?	Who was the audience?	When was it written?	Why was it written?	
1						
2						
3						

Author: Was the author a historian? An individual writing a first-hand account? Other? What are the author's credentials for writing the document? What sources of information did the author use? Is there a reason the author could be biased?

Kind of text: Is the document a primary, secondary, or tertiary source? Is the document from a book, a newspaper, or other source? What is the reputation of the publisher?

Audience: To whom is the author writing? Why this audience?

When: In what time period was the document written? What was going on politically, economically, and socially at the time that could have influenced the author's message?

Why: What does the author want the reader to think after reading the document?

Credibility: How does the information regarding the source and context of the document affect your judgment of the document's credibility? Are you inclined to believe what it says? Why or why not?

APPENDIX 8.2. Corroboration

Historians note the agreements and disagreements across texts. Write down what each text has to say about these three issues (and include page numbers). Then compare and contrast what they say. What do you believe about the three issues? Why?

Text	Issue 1	Issue 2	Issue 3
1			
2			
3			
My View			
Reasons for my view			

Other considerations:

What kind of evidence did the author use? Was the author's interpretation supported by that evidence?

What kind of language did the author use? Did the language signal bias?

When did the author's story begin and end? Would the interpretation have been different given an earlier or later beginning or ending?

Are the events in an appropriate sequence? If not, what affect does the sequence have on the author's interpretation?

What view of the past does the author have? Does he or she glorify the past or show it negatively?

Whose voice is being left out? Who was there who is not part of the story?

APPENDIX 8.3. Science Reading

Label 1	Text 1	Text 2		
		Agreements 4	Disagreements 5	New Information 9
(Physical characteristics)	• Note 1 • Note 2 • Note 3			
Label 2 (Reproduction)	• Note 1 • Note 2 • Note 3			
Label 3 (Habitat)				

CHAPTER 9

Multimodality and Literacy Learning
USING MULTIPLE TEXTS
TO ENHANCE CONTENT-AREA LEARNING

Fenice B. Boyd
Mary K. Thompson

Our chapter portrays a multimodal approach to literacy learning demonstrated by one seventh-grade English language arts teacher and her students. In our chapter, we:

- Describe a portrait of the classroom context where a seventh-grade English teacher, Deborah, incorporated a variety of text types to help students think about the diverse perspectives toward Melba Pattillo Beals's experience as a member of the Little Rock Nine.

- Discuss how multiple text types were used to enhance students' conceptual understandings about the civil rights movement in general, and specifically, the integration of Little Rock's Central High School.

- Convey how a teacher can design a multimodal approach to teach multiple perspectives.

- Demonstrate how students can use multiple modalities to represent their conceptual understandings about past and present issues.

- Share students' multimodal connections to showcase how using a multimodal approach invites students' lifeworlds into the classroom.

Multimodality is a central aspect of millennial learners' everyday lives. The term *millennial learners* refers to youth who have never known a world without multiple modes of access to information. As teachers provide students with varied ways to "read" text—whether it is a book or image—these critical pedagogical tools help students think about issues from multiple vantage points. We ascribe to Jewitt and Kress's (2003) theory on multimodality and literacy learning: "A multimodal approach to learning requires us to take seriously and attend to the whole range of modes involved in representation and communication" (p. 1). Multiple text types, various resources, or *modes*, assist us in making meaning in our daily lives, and different modes have their own meaning-making potential (Moss, 2003). Gesture, gaze, image, movement, music, speech, and sound effects are all modes that afford us an opportunity to interpret and construct our own meanings (Jewitt & Kress, 2003) as we go about daily life. Whether we are admiring beautiful fall colors or summer flowers, or analyzing the emotions evoked from the sound effects of a movie, multimodality plays a role—connotatively—in the sense we make of these modes, individually and collectively. We rely on these modes as ways of being and knowing.

CLASSROOM PORTRAIT

Deborah begins class by directing students to the chapters read for homework.

> DEBORAH: Last night you read three chapters [from *Warriors Don't Cry*, by Melba Pattillo Beals, 1994] because I wanted you to get that whole first day and night in Melba's life where they tried to go to school and were kept out by the soldiers. We're going to be looking first at a photograph and then at real film of this event happening [to look at multiple perspectives]. And we're going to be learning how to look carefully at those photos and film and how to interpret what's really going on in those pictures and what's really going on in this film. And, so it will be taking a closer look at stuff you've already read about. The purpose of doing the reading first is to make you a bit of an expert, so that you come to the photo and the film with some knowledge. The photo we're going to be studying today is a photo you've already seen because it's in your *Warriors* book, but it is considered a very famous photo because it was a symbol of the racial hatred in our country at the time. It made the national newspapers, and the international press [see Figure 9.1]. It was shown all over the world. . . . Photos are really important in terms of how people remember history. I don't know how big this event will seem to us 50 years from now, but right now we're in the middle of the Iraqi war. What video image or photo do you think is most likely to be the one people are going to remember? Alexis?

> ALEXIS: Um, like how those people were tearing down the statue of Saddam Hussein when we took over Baghdad, or when we were fighting for Baghdad.

> TYRONE: Like the emotional things, like maybe people dying.

FIGURE 9.1. Hazel Bryan, Elizabeth Eckford, and adult protestors. Reprinted with permission from the Arkansas Democrat Gazette. Deborah used photograph while teaching point of view.

> DEBORAH: OK. We certainly have pictures . . . we've seen pictures of wounded people and they stick in our minds because it's graphic. But that video of the statue toppling to symbolize the downfall of that government is a picture that people will associate with that time in history.

This vignette conveys how Deborah used multiple texts and layered them for meaning making with her students. What we find particularly poignant in this example is how Deborah also connected a historical event to current events in her students' lives. By doing so, Deborah showed (1) how the way in which events are documented impacts the way in which we understand and think about them in a modern context, (2) how to consider the importance of events in the time period in which they occurred, and (3) what documented images might mean 50 years from now. A multimodal perspective is central to this narrative because it highlights how different pieces of the past come together with different kinds of text to enhance students' conceptual understanding. Moss (2003) argues that multimodality offers the potential to expand our understandings in different ways, based on the affordances (Kress, 2004) and resistances that any mode offers and the use that is made of multimodal resources in any given case. In this case, Deborah first called students' attention to chapters read from Beals's memoir the previous evening, a photograph, and then an image from television. Jointly, these multiple text types allowed the teacher and students to slow down and think closely about different texts to engage in "reading" and interpretations. These modes (i.e., print; still and moving images) potentially afforded the seventh graders a chance to engage in an analytic endeavor of meaning making.

CONCEPTUAL UNDERSTANDING AND MULTIMODAL TEXTS

We now turn to discuss how multimodality, as a pedagogical tool, enhances conceptual understanding inside the classroom. Teaching for conceptual understanding is emphasized in inquiry-based learning wherein students begin with a question, theme, or issue designed to focus attention on the context within which a concept is situated. In Deborah's classroom, the seventh graders had a range of reading abilities, but no students read below grade level. Most of their school reading experiences in the past had centered on more traditional texts such as novels, short stories, and textbooks. The challenge for Deborah was to teach students how to understand the Little Rock Nine event conceptually. The process of layered meaning making is central to Deborah's themed unit because students today are expected to read many different types of text that are complicated and that have a wide variety of content and information (e.g., video games, hypertext, film, material on the Internet). Teaching for conceptual understanding requires giving students critical pedagogical tools to help them make connections through a wide variety of multimodal texts.

Electronic and media texts introduce complexity that promotes conceptual understanding, because they require skills and abilities beyond those required for traditional school-based comprehension of conventional print materials. When adolescents are engaged in conversations about popular electronic media, their readings of such texts often involve sophisticated, interpretive, and analytical skills. In viewing a movie for interpretive as well as entertainment purposes, the viewer must be able to understand movement, lighting and camera angles to make reasonable interpretations about scenes, situations, and the director's message. In print text, authors use metaphors, imagery, and other symbolic meanings in language to challenge readers to delve into deeper understandings. Thus "reading" is a complex interactive process that requires readers to perform multiple tasks simultaneously. Reading any type of text entails much more than decoding words, and critically understanding multiple text types requires teachers to teach students that while reading widely, they must read interactively and critically.

MULTIMODALITY: DIVERSE PERSPECTIVES WITH MULTIPLE TEXT TYPES

Multimodality refers to the modes of representation beyond print, including such domains as the visual, auditory, gestural, and kinesthetic. Kress and Van Leeuwen (2001) developed a multimodal theory of communication that focuses on practices and resources in relation to meaning. In doing so, they considered multiple semiotic meanings derived from varied levels and modes within a culture, rather than holding to a traditional view that meaning is made once (Love, 2005). In using multiple text types Deborah encouraged the students to consider how different modes within a text represent the Little Rock Nine in vastly different ways. In their theory of multimodality Kress and Van Leeuwen discuss four domains of practice in which meanings are made: discourse, design, production, and distribution. Although each domain is arranged in a particular order, it is not viewed within any hierarchy, where one domain exists above another. In this next section we examine the concept of design and how it relates to the idea of multimodality and multiple text types for layered meaning making.

In framing key theoretical concepts from the work of Kress and Van Leeuwen, we draw upon the earlier work of the New London Group (NLG; 1996) and their concept of design as it relates to multimodal texts and conceptual understanding. The NLG broadened the view of literacy to account for a multiplicity of discourses. In this view learning occurs in a social context. The NLG conceptualize a multiliteracies pedagogy wherein design is integral, and the group emphasizes meaning making as an active and dynamic process, not something governed by static rules. In discussing design the NLG group highlighted multimodality as it relates to all the other modes and accounts for the layered complexity that fosters active design. For example, Deborah asked the students to connect the famous picture of Elizabeth Eckford and Hazel Bryan to their own lives. In this picture Bryan heckles Eckford as she walks to Central High during the height of the integration movement. Deborah paralleled two mediums—a photograph and a moving image—to invite students to think about the impact of the Eckford and Bryan photograph almost 50 years later, and what they might recall of Saddam Hussein's statue toppling in Baghdad 50 years into the future.

DESIGN AND MULTIMODALITY

Design is multifaceted and includes a conceptual and expressive side. Love (2005) writes, "Design is a way to understand discourses within a communication situation and involves deliberate choice of mode (form) for representation and how the presentation will be framed" (p. 304). To illustrate this point, we turn to another classroom portrait wherein Deborah juxtaposes multiple texts to showcase how the modes have the potential to change the meaning in significant ways. Three texts were used for analytical purposes, chosen to assist students' thinking about how an event is portrayed and how the modes influence the representation and meaning. Each text portrayed this key event differently.

The scene at Central High was of Minnijean dumping hot chili on one of the white students who had been harassing her for extended periods of time. Deborah used each text to discuss with the students why this event might be portrayed so differently across modes, and the reasons the authors of each text might have for doing so. Deborah noted that in *Warriors Don't Cry*, Minnijean's experience is told through Melba's voice. Deborah explained: "We never get to hear from Minnijean. I don't have any interviews with her, but if I sat behind you in class and just kept doing this [harassing], eventually you will throw your book at me, right? I mean, eventually you are going to lose it." In the memoir, Beals does not communicate the extent of Minnijean's frustration and harassment. This text minimizes Minnijean's experience because it was told in Melba's voice and conveys the overall experiences of the Little Rock Nine in general, and Melba's specifically.

After Deborah showed a short clip from the documentary *Eyes on the Prize, Part II* (Hampton, 1986), a discussion ensued about how the movie versus the memoir represented the chili incident. Deborah pointed out that Minnijean does not speak for herself in *Eyes on the Prize* either, but Little Rock Nine students Ernest Green and Melba Pattillo Beals report that Minnijean was constantly harassed. Again Minnijean's experience is highlighted, although not in her voice per se, nevertheless showing the significance of this event as remembered by her peers.

The goal in showing one event across texts is to show how the mode of the narrative distinguishes different points in the story. As told in Melba's memoir, the event is powerful. But when juxtaposed with the documentary, Melba's written description of the harassment of Minnijean feels static in comparison to Ernest and Melba's verbal description of the chili incident, which, as members of the Little Rock Nine, they witnessed firsthand. In the documentary we see, hear, and feel the emotion in their voices and see their gestures as they describe how Minnijean and the cafeteria staff, who were primarily African American, reacted to her throwing chili on one white student, and the consequences Minnijean faced on her impending expulsion from Central High School. These layered modes in the documentary changed the way Deborah's students thought about the chili event and its historical significance.

The third text, a docudrama titled *Crisis at Central High* (Johnson, 1980), is based on the journal of Mrs. Huckaby, an English teacher and the assistant principal at Central High in 1957. This low-budget, HBO film depicts yet another perspective of the event and the only one in which the Little Rock Nine are seen in third person. Each text shows a different perspective of Miniijean's experience. Although none of them is in her voice, the memoir highlights how this event impacted all of the Little Rock Nine. The documentary *Eyes on the Prize* emphasizes the event through two interviews and provides an additional context to the many reactions of the chili incident. The docudrama, in comparison, overly simplifies the complexity of the event and shows how a telling can mask the importance of real-life situations. Further, Deborah called to the student's attention the fact that docudramas have actors, directors, producers, and editors who decide what is portrayed in the film and how, and can silence voices and perspectives in the process. Although *Crisis at Central High* is based on a diary kept by one of the teachers, the film was biased. This point became a central part of the discussion as students became aware that what is left out of a telling is often just as important as what is told. How emotions get portrayed influences how events are perceived, remembered, and internalized.

These examples validate the significance of questioning, posing dilemmas, and wondering what is and is not in a text. It is important to teach millennial youth that asking questions about a text type is not an admission of not knowing, but rather a powerful way of "reading" across multiple text types. When students read texts without posing questions, they may not be reading critically and thinking about what the design of modes affords them in meaning making. Deborah's culminating activity required the seventh-grade students to make multimodal textual connections to the experiences of the Little Rock Nine by sharing different types of texts from their own lives that would lend support to the value of multiple perspectives of an event or issue. The students selected movie clips, hip-hop, a canonical text, a different school integration story, the Iraq War, and personal struggles (e.g., teasing in middle school) to make connections to issues studied in *Warriors Don't Cry*. Their final presentations and papers conveyed critical perspectives about obstacles faced when attempting to think analytically about events from multiple perspectives. In our next section, we examine students' multimodal connections across texts to explore how, when invited, they may bring to the classroom texts from their own lives to exhibit their conceptual understanding of critical historical events.

STUDENTS' MULTIMODAL CONNECTIONS

Perhaps what is most striking are the seventh graders' personal responses to Melba and her experience. Students expressed tremendous appreciation of her, citing her as one of the bravest people they ever read about. Being bullied and teased are not things they have to imagine; many middle school students have experienced both, albeit probably not to the degree of the Little Rock Nine. But jumping through obstacles in order to acquire an education is not within their imaginations. When they hear about daily, aggressive harassment and physical abuse going unchecked in school, and when they can visualize aspects of this type of harassment from a film or documentary, they empathize with Melba and other members of the Little Rock Nine, about how difficult it would be to take the daily unrelenting abuse without retaliating. In students' final inquiry projects, there was greater depth to their conceptual understanding of the historical event because they were allowed to layer texts multimodally from their own lives. To examine the students' writing about their multimodal artifacts, we have divided their responses into three sections: personal connections, current events, and popular culture.

Personal Connections

Lindsay's personal connection to the experiences of the Little Rock Nine is focused on teasing in middle school. She writes, "My experience was tough, but Melba's put her life in grave danger. She had to walk her halls watching her back in fear of getting jumped, hurt, or killed. Even though my middle school experience had strong effects on me, it was just boys being stupid little boys. In Melba's case she was being teased and harassed by people who could seriously hurt her." In her essay, Lindsay specifically acknowledges the difference between what she endured versus Melba's life-threatening experience.

Like Lindsay, Tyrone also made a connection to the discriminatory perceptions people hold, but discussed Melba's experience as one removed from his own. "At CHS [Central High School] she [Melba] had her humanity taken away from her and was treated as the Other by the white people, meaning they didn't consider her another human being like themselves. If you treat someone as the Other, you don't have to treat them with basic decency. Nothing in my life connects because that has never happened to me." Tyrone critically notes how people from diverse backgrounds are often "othered," as he capitalized Other in his discussion. Although not able to imagine the enormity of what Melba endured, Tyrone shows an excellent understanding of the ultimate consequence of exiling a person based on the color of his or her skin, rather than attempting to know the individual.

Popular Culture

Jamal selected an appropriate song from the hip-hop genre to bridge music from his world to that of the Little Rock Nine. He wrote:

> 2Pac also says in the beginning of his song "I see no changes." When Melba attended Central High she saw no changes in how integration was getting better, if anything it was getting worse and harder for her to survive in Central High. Melba wants integration to work out for the sake of all the black people in her city. She's trying so hard to hold on and stay in Central High, but she sees no changes in how kids are treating her, which she doesn't want. She wants them to get to know her and get to be good friends with her, which I think is reasonable and if I were in her position that's what I would do.

Grace (2004) defines "culturally conscious hip-hop as oral text with lyrics and messages that enlighten with social consciousness, engage with politicized messages, and empower by instilling cultural and self-awareness" (p. 484). Grace also cautions that some hip-hop genres are not suitable for the classroom and may present risks for teachers and students. Deborah was not familiar with rap or hip-hop but discussed with students the appropriateness of lyrics.

Mo chose to make connections to movies from which he had learned about race-related issues:

> In the movie *Remember the Titans* they tried to integrate a football team. This started because of a new coach that was black in a white school. The white players would not play for the team because they did not want to play with the black players. They finally joined together. . . . This is the same as Melba because of the white people of Central are mad that these nine kids are coming into this all white school and starting integration. Another connection is that Melba gets hurt just like some of the players in *Remember the Titans*. Melba gets hurt in the bathrooms, hallways, and in the classroom.

Current Event

Still a different kind of connection made to Melba and the Little Rock Nine was a connection to a current event. At the time Deborah implemented her unit, the United States had just invaded Iraq. Earlier in this chapter, we described Deborah's reference to the toppling down of Saddam Hussein's statue, and what that would mean 50 years in the future. Alexis expanded on the link that Deborah had opened to all students and called attention to the discrimination Muslims today might face in the United States. Alexis said, "This connection is similar to Melba's experience because the Muslims in America today are treated exactly how the blacks were treated by the whites in 1957. They are very much stereotyped because of what they look like and what they believe in. Also the Muslims in the United States today are the minority, just like the blacks were, so it is easier to pick on them." Table 9.1 summarizes the students' multimodal connections. Table 9.2 lists all multimodal texts Deborah used to teach students while studying *Warriors Don't Cry*.

CONCLUSION

What do multimodal texts contribute to students' critical understandings about a political and social event, such as the integration of Little Rock's Central High School, that a print-only text cannot? For a print-only text, finding the point of view can seem abstract, and given that Deborah's students were far removed from the era of school desegregation, the events

TABLE 9.1. Students' Multimodal Connections

Students	Text type	Themes
Mo	Movies • *Remember the Titans*	• Integrating a high school football team
Jamal	Hip-hop • "Changes" by Tupac (1998)	• Reality of being black and male in the United States
Tyrone	Book • *Catcher in the Rye* (Salinger, 1951) • *Jackie Robinson* (Dunn, 1999)	• Holden [main character] was isolated, alienated, and suffered emotionally • Integrating major league baseball • "Othering" of people who come from diverse backgrounds
Lindsay	Personal story • Teasing in middle school	• Exclusion from the "cool girls club"
Alexis	U.S. and international news events • September 11, 2001	• Discrimination against Muslims in the United States

were difficult to imagine. Deborah had noted that even though *Warriors Don't Cry* is well written, students were always left with so many questions. Because students were so bewildered by the adults' behavior in the story, Deborah believed that had she not used additional text types, the students may not have believed what they read.

When a photograph is used to teach adolescents how to think about an issue conceptually, they can literally place a finger on each individual face and shift the point of view while critiquing the picture, and take a stance from which they can understand that person's motivation. The photograph does not reveal how the people in it really feel about the situation, but from "reading" body language (e.g., angry-looking faces), students can make reasonable interpretations and create layered meaning making about the context at hand. Watching a documentary, students can "read" voice, gestures, etc., compare and contrast the memories, and add yet another layer to their meaning making. A docudrama, inspired by true events, is additional fodder for critique, and lends itself to discussions about behind-the-scenes voices (e.g., producers, directors, editors)—whose voice is added or deleted from the story. Engaging with multimodal texts allows students to develop sophisticated, complex, and yet quite concrete understandings of concepts and events that might otherwise have remained only vague abstract references. Teaching with multimodal texts also provides opportunities to introduce and practice critical analytic skills that will serve students well as they "read" today's multimodal world.

TABLE 9.2. Deborah's Curriculum Materials

Text type	Title	Synopsis	Purpose
Main book	*Warriors Don't Cry* (Beals, 1994)	A memoir written from the perspective of Melba Pattillo Beals—one of the Little Rock Nine—centered on the integration of Central High School	Used as an instructional tool to show hostile and violent incidents in the hallways and classrooms that went virtually unreported by local and national media in 1957. Also the memoir shows the complex roles that all of the people involved played in integrating the school
Supplementary books	*Leon's Story* (Tillage, 1997)	Told in regional dialect, the book is an oral history of a sharecropping family living in the Jim Crow South	Used to convey Tillage's views on the horror of Jim Crow laws and answer questions of why it was hard to fight them
	Gandhi (Demi, 2001)	A biography and picture book portraying Gandhi's life	Used to introduce Gandhi's life and the philosophy and practice of nonviolent resistance
	The Century for Young People (Jennings, Brewster, & Armstrong, 1999)	A children's version of the popular book of photographs	Contains interviews of some people involved in resistance to Central High School's integration
	A Life Is More Than a Moment (Counts, 1999)	Interviews and photographs of Central High School in 1957 and 1997, taken by a white student who attended the school	Offers varying points of view at the time and shows how views have changed (or not) over time

(continued)

TABLE 9.2. (continued)

Text type	Title	Synopsis	Purpose
Documentary	*Eyes on the Prize, Part II* (Hampton, 1986)	An award-winning documentary series of the civil rights movement from the 1950s to the 1960s	Used to show real-time footage of the mob and to hear the Little Rock protagonists telling stories
Docudrama	*Crisis at Central High* (Johnson, 1980)	A movie based on the journal of the assistant principal and English teacher	Told from the perspective of a white adult in the school, the movie makes students aware that perceptions can differ. The docudrama shows actual footage shot at Central High School so that students understand the size and scope of the building
Photographs	Water fountains in the 1950s	A visual demonstration of how separate is not equal	Still photographs "freezes" a historical moment so it can be closely examined and critiqued
	Beal's family and friends	A visual representation of a middle-class African American family with friends	
	Elizabeth Eckford, Hazel Bryan	A visual of Elizabeth Eckford walking stalwartly toward school, followed by Hazel Bryan and a mob of angry white adults	
Encyclopedia articles	*Plessy v. Ferguson*	An article describing Plessey's arrest and the court case	Makes clear how Plessey and others deliberately planned for his arrest so that he would have the opportunity to question the law's constitutionality
	Brown v. Board of Education	An article describing Linda Brown's school and the U.S. Supreme Court case	Helps students see that when people challenge a law, they benefit many people more than they benefit themselves

DISCUSSION AND ACTIVITIES

1. In what ways does using a multimodal approach allow students to bring their worlds into the classroom? How does "reading" across text types assist students in thinking about events and ideas differently? How might multimodal texts be used inside the classroom to promote critical literacy skills for millennial learners? In what ways is conceptual understanding strengthened by the use of multiple text types?

2. Brainstorm with students several critical events that have occurred within their lifetime. Talk about how these events are retold, portrayed, and narrated across several kinds of texts (modes). Discuss how they may want to remember this event, and how they would place themselves in the telling.

3. As a research project, form groups based on an event students want to research and have them find several kinds of texts that each tells one perspective of the event while leaving another perspective untold. Have each group present its findings and lead the class in a critical conversation about how the event is captured through the various types of texts.

4. Have students consider how they might retell an event to link it to their own lives and then create their own multimodal texts in the process. This project would open the classroom to critical inquiry and multimodal learning, allowing millennial students the creative freedom to design their own texts, such as an original rap song, I-movie, poem, or PowerPoint show, about an event that is significant to their lives.

REFERENCES

Beals, M. P. (1994). *Warriors don't cry.* New York: Washington Square.

Grace, C. M. (2004). Exploring the African American oral tradition: Instructional implications for literacy learning. *Language Arts, 81*(6), 481–490.

Hampton, H. (Director). (1986). *Eyes on the prize.* Washington, DC: PBS Home Video.

Jewitt, C., & Kress, G. (Eds.). (2003). *Multimodal literacy.* New York: Lang.

Johnson, L. (Director). (1980). *Crisis at Central High.* Los Angeles: HBO.

Kress, G. (2004). *Literacy in the new media age.* New York: Routledge.

Kress, G., & Van Leeuwen, T. (2001). *Multimodal discourse: The modes and media of contemporary communication.* New York: Oxford University Press.

Love, M. S. (2005). Multimodality of learning through anchored instruction. *Journal of Adolescent and Adult Literacy, 48*(4), 300–311.

Moss, G. (2003). Putting the text back into practice: Junior-age non-fiction as objects of design. In C. Jewitt & G. Kress (Eds.), *Multimodal literacy* (pp. 73–87). New York: Lang.

New London Group. (1996). A pedagogy of multiliteracies: Designing social futures. *Harvard Educational Review, 66*(1), 60–92.

CHAPTER 10

Assisting Struggling Readers with Textbook Comprehension

Heather K. Sheridan-Thomas

The purpose of this chapter is to suggest ways that middle and high school teachers can assist struggling readers to read and comprehend textbooks. Specifically, this chapter:

- Explains the importance of textbook comprehension for adolescents.

- Defines what I mean by *struggling readers*, including possible attributes of struggling readers that need to be considered when teachers plan textbook reading instruction.

- Suggests the importance of choosing considerate content-area texts.

- Suggests principles for organizing and delivering effective textbook reading instruction.

- Provides examples of instructional methods teachers can use to deliver textbook reading instruction.

WHY TEACH TEXTBOOK COMPREHENSION?

At a time when much that is written about adolescent literacy focuses on multiple literacies and popular culture, writing a chapter on supporting textbook reading seems like an anomaly. Literacy educators and research-ers recommend that content-area teachers use multiple text sources, either to replace or at least supplement textbook readings (Allington, 2002; Hinchman, Alvermann, Boyd, Brozo, & Vacca, 2003/2004). Text-books can be dense, dry, and difficult to comprehend. Adolescents themselves describe textbook reading as " just hard and really boring" (Sheridan-Thomas, Ro, & Bromley, 2004, p. 14).

Nonetheless, textbooks and textbook reading remain central to many content-area classes. Textbooks are a bastion of secondary subject area instruction and are unlikely to disappear in the foreseeable future. Content-area teachers use textbooks to convey an overview and summary of course information as well as to provide an easy reference for students working on classroom tasks and homework assignments. Textbooks are an efficient source of information and a readily available place to start in communicating main points related to a topic. They are also carefully sequenced so that each chapter provides information needed to understand the next. These features make teacher planning easier, especially as current textbooks are often correlated with national and even state standards, curriculum, and assessments. Textbooks can clearly be useful to teachers, but they are only useful to students if the students are able to read and understand them (Allington, 2002).

Students who struggle with extracting important information and making meaning from textbook reading do not have the same access to course material as competent textbook readers. Helping all students comprehend textbook reading is an equity issue. For courses in which textbooks are used, whether as the main source of course information or as a secondary reference source, all students need to be able to use the textbook with as much competence and independence as possible. It is therefore the responsibility of content-area teachers to use explicit strategy instruction, including modeling, to teach students how to read and comprehend textbooks. This approach is particularly important for students who struggle with textbook reading and other academic literacy tasks, but even otherwise competent readers often benefit from additional support with textbook reading, especially in middle school.

Despite the fact that textbooks are unlikely to be considered the kind of reading material that anyone would choose from the library shelf for pleasure reading, many are, in fact, carefully constructed to provide easy access to large amounts of information on a specific topic. Features such as headings that signal text organization, clear contextual definitions of technical vocabulary backed up with a glossary, abundant visuals, and chapter summaries that highlight the most important information, assist readers in understanding main ideas or locating specific information quickly.

WHO ARE THE READERS
WHO STRUGGLE WITH TEXTBOOKS?

This chapter focuses on assisting readers who struggle with academic literacy generally and reading textbooks in particular. The phrase *struggling readers*, has replaced terms such as "at-risk" or "below-level" students as a more respectful way of describing the situated nature of the challenging interaction between reader and text. The struggles that these readers encounter in school can be seen as socially constructed—by the ways in which schools are organized and scheduled, by assumptions that are made about home life and school abilities, by a curriculum that is often devoid of connections to students' lives, and by texts that may be too difficult for students to read (Triplett, 2007).

We all struggle with some types of reading (Alvermann, Phelps, & Ridgeway, 2007), so it is important to note that adolescents who have difficulty comprehending textbooks are often proficient with other forms of literacies. Some are competent users of technology (O'Brien, 2001), and others avidly consume high-interest literacy materials such as topical magazines (Sheridan-Thomas et al., 2004), graphic novels (Frey & Fischer, 2004) and manga comic books (Schwartz & Rubinstein-Ávila, 2006). Some boys may eschew reading as unmanly (Smith & Wilhelm, 2002) yet still engage in purposeful reading of auto repair manuals and sports-related websites. The term *struggling reader* is used in this chapter as an efficient shorthand, but with full awareness that it describes a relationship between a student and a text that is situated, variable, and unique to each student. I am clear that this label should not at any time be taken to represent the sum total of the literacy competencies of the students it designates.

When it comes to academic literacy, and reading textbooks in particular, students' difficulties can stem from a combination of factors. Some students may struggle because of cognitive processing, hearing, or vision problems. However, many more adolescent readers struggle because they are not motivated by textbook reading and do not know effective strategies for gleaning meaning from dense expository text. Much of the reading done in elementary school is of narrative text, so most students come to middle school familiar with, and competently able to read, narrative text. Even the nonfiction texts that are increasingly used in elementary school during science and social studies instruction are often written in a narrative style, with a sense of story, rather than in traditional expository text patterns. Many students come to secondary school with little experience reading the kinds of textbooks they encounter. In addition, the overall amount of reading engaged in by students declines as they move from elementary to secondary grades.

Not only do many students choose to read less in the secondary grades, but intrinsic motivation to read declines for some students as well. More competent readers maintain a degree of intrinsic motivation even while reading academic texts, but readers who struggle are more likely to require a heavily extrinsic source of motivation to read—in a trend that accelerates as students move through middle school to high school (Harter, Whitesell, & Kowalski, 1992). For many students, the only purpose for reading academic texts becomes the weak purpose of getting assignments done and getting a good grade. Strategies associated with these extrinsic goals, such as hunting for answers without actually reading the material, predominate. Adolescents who cannot see any meaningful purpose for reading textbooks become disengaged readers, passing their eyes over textbook pages without even the intention of gaining meaning. Assisting struggling readers to comprehend textbooks must begin, therefore, with attention to motivation. However, it cannot end there.

Once they are motivated to read textbooks, struggling readers need explicit instruction in how to make the most effective use of textbook features, and they need a great deal of guided practice embedded in lessons focused on understandings meaningful content-area concepts. All of this will be most effective if teachers begin by selecting "considerate" textbooks (Armbruster & Anderson, 1988)—texts that are coherent, well-structured, appropriate for students' age and grade, and designed to include a variety of text features that assist readers in comprehending and retaining the text content.

SELECTING A CONSIDERATE TEXTBOOK

Content

In selecting a textbook, starting with a focus on content not only makes sense for subject-area teachers, it is also crucial in choosing the best possible textbook for a wide range of readers. Content-area teachers should also be concerned about whether the text is current, accurate, free from inappropriate bias, and well-matched to required standards and curriculum. For increased textbook readability, it is important to note the density of concepts, the degree to which the text accurately matches students' prior knowledge, and the text's support for subject-specific vocabulary.

External Text Structure

A second selection consideration is the structure of the text. "Considerate" text features that are part of the external structure of the text can go a long way toward improving comprehension and retention for struggling readers. Chapter outlines, clear text headings, the use of color or font to signal new vocabulary and/or important points, visuals, sidebars, and chapter summaries are all features that make the information in the textbook "friendlier" (Schumm & Mangrum, 1991) and easily accessible. However, it is important to notice whether visuals, sidebars, and other features are used in a text in a way that actually assists students in understanding challenging text concepts. Pictures and other visuals that are added to increase text interest but do not directly support important text ideas may serve only to distract some readers and interfere with the coherence of the text.

Coherence and Internal Text Structure

Text coherence is a third textbook selection criterion. Initially, coherence relates to whether the text reads well and is written in a language style that is appealing to the targeted readers. Coherence is also directly related to internal text structure and the degree to which the organization of the text (cause–effect, sequence, compare–contrast) promotes understanding of important text ideas and details. Overattention to readability formulas can lead to attempts to make textbooks easier by reducing word length and sentence length. This approach can produce choppy, unreadable, incoherent text that is missing connecting words and phrases (e.g., *because, in contrast*) that might signal connecting ideas and text structure.

Selecting a considerate textbook will make the process of improving struggling students' textbook comprehension and motivation to read less challenging for a content-area teacher. Nonetheless, teachers often do not have a choice about the textbook they use. The principles described below for enhancing students' comprehension of textbooks will prove useful whether or not the required textbook is the teacher's first choice.

HOW CAN CONTENT-AREA TEACHERS IMPROVE TEXTBOOK COMPREHENSION?

Principles for textbook comprehension instruction that is effective and engaging to struggling students are listed in Figure 10.1 and described in more detail below. Instructional strategies that exemplify these principles are embedded within the explanation of each principle.

- Select a considerate textbook.
- Start with motivation and purpose setting.
- Embed literacy strategy instruction in the context of meaningful content and concepts.
- Provide explicit literacy strategy instruction, including modeling.
- Design guides and classroom opportunities for guided practice of literacy strategies.
- Build in a progression toward gradual release of responsibility.
- Reinforce strategies consistently across content areas and across classroom and special support settings.

FIGURE 10.1. Principles for effective and engaging textbook instruction.

Motivation and Purpose Setting

Because struggling readers are often disengaged readers, and textbooks are rarely inherently engaging, involving students in *prereading activities* is a crucial first step to improving comprehension. One commonly recommended prereading activity is an "anticipation guide" (Duffelmeyer, 1994; Kozen, Murray, & Windell, 2006). Students react to teacher-constructed statements about ideas that are covered by the text. This step allows students to start thinking about the content of the textbook selection and begin making connections to related prior knowledge before they start reading. Having taken a stand on such issues, they are motivated to read the textbook and see whether or not their position is supported. Another engaging prereading strategy is problem posing or "establishing problematic perspectives" (Vacca & Vacca, 2008, p. 191). The content-area teacher creates a problem scenario designed to pique students' curiosity and interest. Students discuss the problem before they read, brainstorming solutions or voicing their reactions. As students read the textbook passage, they have the immediate purpose of using the information to solve the given problem.

Because adolescents who struggle with academic reading may be avid consumers of one or more forms of popular culture texts (Alvermann, Moon & Hagood, 1999), one way to motivate struggling students to read textbooks is to provide a *popular culture bridge*. Teachers can create a "text twin" set (Camp, 2000) of a popular culture and a textbook reading on a topic. Students can be introduced to the topic through engaging with familiar media forms and popular culture materials such as songs, magazine or newspaper articles, videos/DVDs, trading cards, or video games. They can then be guided to read the textbook selection, looking for content similarities and differences between the popular culture source and the textbook. For example, Xu (2005) suggested using *Yu-Gi-Oh!* trading cards to focus on Egyptian deities and related symbols. Later students read about Egyptian religion and the origin of the symbols, completing a comparison chart with what they knew from the trading cards. Other examples might include using currently popular songs about soldiers returning from the Iraq war to help students understand a history textbook reading about returning Civil War soldiers, or focusing on the geometric transformations embedded in many video games before reading a math textbook section on translation, rotation, and reflection.

An often overlooked source of motivation for reading textbooks is *critical literacy* (Luke, 2000). Teachers know that nearly all textbooks include some erroneous information and that no textbook reflects all of the possible views and opinions on a topic (Loewen, 1996). Textbook authors write from viewpoints that privilege some voices and silence others. Rather than trying to hide this reality, it can be used to motivate adolescents, who are at a prime age for questioning authority, to read their textbooks with a critical eye. For example, students can be encouraged to look at whose point of view is represented in a history textbook and whose voices are silenced (Wolk, 2003). Adolescents also want to learn information that is relevant and useful to them. Engagement in critical literacies empowers students to read textbooks with an eye to information that might help them make real-life decisions as citizens and consumers. Problem posing (see above) can strengthen this connection by setting a real life scenario to which students can apply newly learned information.

It is obviously not helpful if struggling readers misunderstand the purpose for reading textbook material. It is rare for middle or high school teachers to expect students to construct meaning about a topic independently from reading a textbook. Yet that is the message students often get, leaving them confused and frustrated. Textbooks are poorly designed if the goal is reading for in-depth and nuanced understanding (Daniels & Zemelman, 2004); they are considerably designed as a reference source to look up specific information, as on overview of a new topic, or as a summary and review of information learned in a variety of other ways. If teachers set and explain *clear and honest purposes* for assigning a textbook reading, then students will have an easier time choosing strategies to match that purpose.

Embedded Comprehension Instruction

Although numerous strategies can be taught to support struggling readers, the best textbook comprehension lessons remain focused on the content of the reading and on making the content interesting and understandable (Hinchman et al., 2003/2004). Because motivation is one barrier to textbook comprehension, shifting instructional focus heavily toward learning textbook reading skills—not a particularly motivating endeavor—is unlikely to be a good solution. Research on engagement suggests that "classroom goals that emphasize students' understanding of meaningful materials are essential to motivation and cognitive strategy learning" (Guthrie & Davis, 2003, p. 72). Textbook reading strategy instruction is, therefore, best *embedded* in lessons designed to teach the content and concepts found in the textbook material.

Embedded strategy instruction also addresses the concerns of teachers who feel that there is too much content in their subject area to take time to focus on literacy strategies. Engaging and interactive lessons that teach literacy strategies while remaining focused on content serve to deepen student understanding of content. Although it is clearly not possible to teach literacy strategies in every lesson, it works well to integrate strategy instruction into lessons with the highest priority course content.

Embedded strategy instruction can also focus on the skills required to read a particular textbook in a specific content area. Scientific reading can be quite different from the reading of historical text, and math textbooks have their own unique format and text features. It is not content-area teachers' job to be "teachers of reading" so much as to be teachers of the kinds of texts and reading strategies most likely to be found in their subject area. Embedding textbook strategy lessons in conceptually focused units of instruction allows teachers to develop and support content-specific literacy skills.

For example, a sixth-grade math teacher may provide embedded instruction on focusing on question words during a unit on exponential notation (Kenney, Hancewicz, Heuer, Metsisto & Tuttle, 2005). As students work on answering the directive "Write $7 \times 7 \times 7 \times 8 \times 9 \times 9$ in exponential notation," the teacher suggests they look at the words in the question carefully for clues as to what kind of answer might be expected. Students who focus on the words *write, exponential*, and *notation* realize that the problem involves translation, rather than calculation, and are able to come up with a correct answer. Literacy strategy instruction may also be embedded in other content areas, such as science. During a high school biology unit on the human body, students may be introduced to structure/function text organization by being asked to make a chart of various organs and their roles in maintaining a healthy body. As students learn about human physiology, they also learn the literacy strategy of using text structure to help decide what textbook information is most important to learn and remember (Vacca & Vacca, 2008).

In order for students to become independent users of textbook reading strategies, they must know when to apply strategies and which ones to select. Embedded strategy instruction promotes independence by giving students specific models of the appropriate use of particular strategies on particular types of subject-area textbook reading. To develop struggling readers' full independence, however, teachers need to plan a sequence of explicit introduction and ongoing practice for high-utility textbook reading strategies.

Explicit Strategy Instruction

Struggling readers often rely on a small number of strategies, which they use in all situations. Successful readers not only apply a larger number of strategies flexibly, but they can also articulate which strategies are best suited for specific texts and tasks (Paris & Myers, 1981). Explicit instruction in strategies can help bridge the gap between successful and struggling readers by helping struggling readers develop the metacognitive awareness necessary for independent reading (Gersten, Fuchs, Williams, & Baker, 2001). Steps in effective strategy instruction have been clearly outlined (Vacca & Vacca, 2008, pp. 46–47):

1. Explain why a strategy, such as previewing a textbook section, is useful, when it is best employed, and review the steps in the strategy.
2. Model or demonstrate the strategy while thinking aloud about how to use each of the strategy steps.
3. Provide guided practice, preferably in pairs or cooperative groups that allow for peer modeling and think-alouds.
4. Create opportunities for students to apply strategies independently.

It may appear contradictory to suggest that strategy instruction should be both embedded and explicit. It is true that one teacher will need to introduce a strategy initially, providing direct explanation of what the strategy is, when it can best be used, and the steps for using it. Once that has been accomplished, however, content-area teachers can carry out the remaining steps in explicit instruction in short minilessons embedded in their content lessons. These minilessons focus on the tasks and texts central to the current topic of the class. One crucial literacy strategy for assisting students in comprehending textbooks is the use of text features designed to focus students on the most important text information.

Instruction in text features is one kind of explicit strategy instruction that can be implemented in a content-area class. In order to easily access textbook information and make the best use of the considerate features of well-designed textbooks, struggling readers need explicit instruction in how to utilize the features. These features can assist readers with identifying the vocabulary and comprehension demands of reading assignments and can also guide students in finding definitions or specific information.

Early in the school year, teachers can introduce students to the overall organization of their particular textbook. Middle school students may enjoy engaging in a "scavenger hunt" for various parts of the textbook, such as table of contents, glossaries, and index. Once students are familiar with the overall organization and features of their textbook, they can be shown how these features can help them with high-utility textbook reading strategies. Strategies such as understanding subject-specific vocabulary, determining importance, noting text organization, and making inferences are at the heart of comprehending texts. Figure 10.2 shows textbook features that can help struggling students engage in reading strategies.

Often content-area teachers introduce students to the textbook early in the school year but do not consistently refer them to text features throughout the year. Students who struggle with academic reading need consistent reminders and practice to get to the point where they become independent users of such features. This ongoing review and practice can be provided through teacher-guided textbook comprehension activities.

Reading strategy	Useful text feature/s	Explanation
Subject-specific vocabulary	Bold, italicized, or colored print	Different typefaces alert students that a word is important.
	Contextual definitions	In most cases, a contextual definition for highlighted words is provided in nearby text.
	Sidebars	Many textbooks, especially science, include definitions of important terms in a sidebar.
	Glossary	A handy alphabetized list of definitions is provided in the textbook glossary.
Determining importance	Overviews/ summaries/questions	Chapter overviews or outlines highlight important points at the beginning.
	Headings	Text headings call attention to important information throughout the chapter.
	Pictures/visuals/ captions	Pictures or other visuals restate and provide examples related to important information.
	Sidebars	Important details are sometimes restated in sidebars.
	Redundancy	Information that appears in two or more places is the most important.
Text structure	Headings	Text headings may signal the organizational structure of the text. Headings may include structure words such as *causes* or *effects* or signal a pattern such as compare–contrast through the use of several parallel headings (e.g., Life in Cities, Life in Small Towns, Life on Farms).

FIGURE 10.2. Reading strategies supported by considerate textbook features.

Teacher-Guided Comprehension

Once students have been introduced to a strategy through explicit strategy instruction, multiple opportunities to practice the strategy can be provided through teacher-created guides. The major focus of reading guides in a content-area class remains on the content—on helping students comprehend the most important concepts and related details in a textbook section. At the same time, students using the guides are practicing textbook reading strategies. Effective textbook reading guides model the way a good reader would use the strategy and also provide explicit reminders of strategy steps. Because struggling readers are often disengaged readers, textbook guides need to be constructed to promote engagement. Interactive reading guides (IRGs; Wood, 1988) involve students in deciding which content statements are actually reflected in the text, using textbook organization to extract important information, in making connections between textbook information and prior knowledge, and in reflecting on deeper meanings. Teachers design IRGs to focus on a particular text section, guiding students to use and practice effective literacy strategies as well as focusing them on the most important content.

These guides are interactive in two ways: They encourage individual students to interact thoughtfully with the text, and they can also serve to guide cooperative group sharing and discussion around a piece of text. The best reading guides resist student attempts to use "search and destroy" tactics for finding answers without reading or thinking about the text. IRGs can be designed to focus on one or several text reading strategies. An IRG focused on comprehension at and beyond the literal level is discussed below.

Two crucial skills for comprehending textbooks are *determining importance* and *making inferences*. One instructional method that lends itself to helping students do both of these is question–answer relationships, or QARs (Raphael, 1986; Raphael & Au, 2005). Figure 10.3 shows the reader–text relationships delineated in the QAR method.

In the book		In my head	
Right there	The answer to the question is explicitly stated in the book. Question words and the answer are found in the same sentence or adjacent sentences. Often, the reader can point to the answer.	Author and you	The answer is *not* found in the text. Information from the text must be combined with the reader's prior knowledge or information from another text to form an answer.
Think and search	The answer is found in the text but not stated explicitly. Information from more than one sentence or text section must be put together to form the answer. Text structure patterns (e.g., comparison–contrast, cause–effect) can help readers find the required pieces of information.	On my own	The answer is *not* found in the text. The answer is based entirely on the reader's prior knowledge, without reference to the text. Teachers often use "on-my-own-questions" to cue students to call up relevant prior knowledge before reading a text.

FIGURE 10.3. Question–answer relationships (QARs). Based on Raphael (1986).

QARs focus students on different levels of questions and where answers can be found. Categorizing answers as those that can be found "in the text" and "in my head" helps students understand that whereas some questions can be answered directly from the text, others require the reader to combine previously learned information and text information. The QAR terms for question–answer relationships are clear and provide direction to students as to where to look for answers to different kinds of questions. In addition, students who understand QARs can be guided to ask themselves questions beyond the relationship that is right there as they read, leading to a deeper comprehension of textbook material.

Once students have received explicit instruction in QAR, IRGs can be created that use QAR language to help students with the toughest aspects of textbook comprehension. QARs are particularly helpful for assisting students to make inferences from text, because they guide students to synthesize text information (think and search) and analyze it in light of their own prior knowledge (author and you).

Focus on text structure can also be embedded in the "think and search" section of a QAR guide. Attention to the organizational pattern or structure of text has been shown to improve readers' comprehension of textbooks (Armbruster, Anderson, & Ostertag, 1987). Struggling readers need specific help in knowing how and where to search for information that is not explicitly stated. Knowing that a textbook chapter has a compare–contrast structure can lead the student to search for similarities and differences as important chapter information to learn and remember.

A sample IRG, provided in Figure 10.4, shows how such guides can direct student attention to specific features of given textbook section, assist them in comprehending the content of the section, and also teach a transferable reading strategy, such as QAR.

Gradual Release of Responsibility

Content teachers who consistently provide their students with reading guides may become disheartened when they ask students to read independently and comprehend a textbook chapter. Elementary teachers are likely to have a clearer sense of the importance of multiple opportunities for guided practice and peer modeling in order for students to gain independence and control in relation to a reading strategy. Once a strategy has been introduced in a large, group-shared reading setting, students can practice it in smaller guided reading group discussions and while discussing reading "knee to knee" with peer partners (Cole, 2003).

Modifications of these techniques can be used to good advantage in secondary content classes. IRGs, discussed above, can be used to promote not only student interaction with the textbook but with each other as well. Guides can be completed and discussed in small groups, or students can

A Call for Freedom Guide PLUS Textbook Reading Review
The American Journey, Glencoe/McGraw Hill, 2003, pp. 473–477

Using Text Evidence to Support Inferences

Good readers look for <u>important details</u> (**Right There**), such as people, events, and dates. Good readers also need to be able to make and support <u>inferences</u>. There are different kinds of inferences. Some inferences can be supported with information that is all in the text, but may be in more than one place (**Think and Search**). Other inferences must be supported with text information AND information you already know (**Author and You**).

- One common kind of **Think and Search** inference authors may expect you to make is to compare and contrast two events, people, or ideas. Question 4 on p. 477 is a **Think and Search** question (How did Lincoln's personal stand on slavery differ from his political stand?").
- The answer to this question can be found in the reading, but it is not all in one sentence AND you cannot find it by looking for exact matches to the words in the question.
- Here are some steps you can take to answer a question like this one.

1. Decide if you are being asked to COMPARE, CONTRAST, or BOTH. This question uses the word *differ*, so you are being asked to _. When you answer this question, you will only discuss how Lincoln's two stands were _, not how they were alike.
2. Look for the section(s) of text that discuss the question topic. In this case there is no topic heading on slavery that can direct you to the answer. If you skim the first few paragraphs of this section, you'll see that Lincoln and his views on slavery are mentioned frequently on pp. 473 and 474.
3. Make a chart in your notes of the two ideas you are being asked to contrast. In this case it is Lincoln's _____ stand on slavery and his _____ stand, so your chart can look like this: _ stand _ stand
4. Look for words that have similar meanings to question words and find answers nearby, either before or after these words. Remember that the information you need to answer the question may be in more than one place and even on different pages.
   a. The words *political stand* are not used in the text on pp. 473–474. But on p. 474 the words *official position* have a similar meaning. Where on that page do you find Lincoln's "official position"? In your chart under "political stand" write what you think his official position was.
   b. Find words in a nearby sentence that you think mean the same as *personal stand*. What words are used to mean personal stand? Look near these words to see what Lincoln's personal stand was and write it in you chart.
5. Now write two or three sentences that answer the question. In this case, tell how the two stands differ. It's a good idea to start your first sentence with words from the question. One possible frame for the answer to this question is provided below, but you can write the answer in different words if you wish.

President Lincoln's personal stand on slavery differed from his political stand during the Civil War. Personally, Lincoln believed that _____ but in the beginning of the Civil War, he had a different political stand. Lincoln's political stand on slavery was that _____ .

(continued)

FIGURE 10.4. Example guide using QARs to focus on inferences and text structure.

Making Inferences: Author and You

- Remember that AUTHOR-and-YOU questions ask you to put information from the text together with information that you already know to make an inference.
- One kind of AUTHOR-and-YOU question asks you to state an opinion about an issue in the reading and provide evidence to support your opinion.
- On p. 477, your book states, "By becoming soldiers, African-Americans were taking an important step toward securing civil rights."

Decide whether you AGREE or DISAGREE with this statement and write a paragraph explaining why. Be sure to use supporting evidence from the textbook AND from other readings and your own prior knowledge.

Step 1: Choose whether you will AGREE or DISAGREE.
Step 2. Set up a chart to be sure you get the needed information.

AUTHOR	**YOU**
What information in this section supports your opinion?	What information from other readings supports your opinion?
	What information have you learned in this course or other classes that would support your opinion?
	What personal experiences or other background information supports your opinion?

Step 3. Look in the textbook for information about:
- Why African Americans joined the army
- Conditions for African Americans in the Civil War Union Army
- Reactions of different kinds of people to the African American soldiers (white and black, North and South)
- How African Americans felt about being soldiers

Step 4: Look for information in other readings and your head about:
- The definition of civil rights
- The history of the fight for civil rights for African Americans in this country
- Conditions for African Americans in the Civil War Union Army
- How African Americans felt about being soldiers
- How being a soldier in the Union Army might help or hinder an African American's progress toward gaining civil rights

Step 5: Start your paragraph by stating the quote and clearly agreeing or disagreeing.

Our textbook states that, "By becoming soldiers, African-Americans were taking an important step toward securing civil rights." I disagree/agree.

Step 6: Continue your paragraph by stating evidence from the text and from other readings or your prior knowledge to support your position. Be sure to conclude your paragraph by restating your opinion.

FIGURE 10.4. *(continued)*

complete the guides at home and meet in small groups to discuss their answers.

Beyond discussing their responses to teacher-created reading guides, small groups and partner sharing can provide opportunities for students to move toward independent use of reading strategies. Students in cooperative groups can be asked to share strategies they used to comprehend a textbook section. Struggling readers who have been learning textbook strategies in support classes can take an active role in these discussions, especially if they have prepared by reading and discussing the specific text section with a reading, special education, or English-as-a-second-language (ESL) teacher ahead of time.

Students can also be asked to "think aloud" with a partner about their strategy use. For example, students might be asked to list the five most important points in a textbook section and to defend their choices to a classmate. The discussions should focus on the use of text headings; text features such as chapter overviews, summaries, and sidebars; and the overall impact of redundancy in determining importance. Students might also be asked to think aloud about the questions they ask themselves to facilitate their own understanding of the text as they read (Davey, 1983).

Consistent Strategy Reinforcement

It is difficult for any one content-area teacher to provide enough practice opportunities for each reading strategy to allow struggling readers to become independent strategy users. However, if teachers across content areas can agree to use a small set of target strategies, students can get enough cumulative practice to make the strategies "stick." A second advantage to agreeing to a set of target strategies across a grade level or teacher team is that it allows a different teacher to introduce each strategy through explicit strategy instruction, whereas the other teachers need only commit to reinforcing the strategies through teacher-created guides, classroom tasks, and homework assignments. To best assist struggling readers who receive additional support from academic intervention services (AIS), special education, or English for speakers of other languages (ESOL) teachers, it is crucial to also engage these support specialists in reinforcing target strategies. Support specialists can provide a second dose of explicit instruction and can help students focus on target strategies as they assist in assignment completion. The vignette below provides a glimpse into a middle school where teachers have agreed to work together to support students' reading of content-area textbooks. The IRG used in this lesson is provided as Figure 10.5.

It is 15 minutes into third period and Ms. V's eighth-grade science class is studying weather. Jake has already stepped outside to record the temperature,

Weather IRG #3   Name _____

Sun's energy and wind   Date _____

Part I. Prereading: Before reading pp. 136–137b, read the following statements and fill in the prediction column. **After you have read**: Go back and complete the conclusion column. Be sure to correct the false statements.

Prediction T/F	Statement	Conclusion T/F
	The Sun is the main source of energy in the Earth's atmosphere.	
	The Earth's surface is heated relatively evenly.	
	Altitude and type of surface affect the temperature in the atmosphere.	
	Warm air is less dense than cold air, that's why it rises.	
	Air circulation, called convection, only covers 1 mile or less.	
	The sun's rays hitting the equator at close to a 90° angle make the energy more concentrated there.	
	Air rises at the poles and sinks at the equator.	
	Longitude is the distance north or south of the equator.	
	Summer vacationers enjoy sea breezes flowing inland, off the water, during the day.	

Part II. Read pp. 136–137a "Sun's Energy" and answer the following questions.

1. What is the main source of energy in the atmosphere? _____

2. What two things affect how much of the sun's energy is absorbed by the Earth's surface?

3. What happens when air is heated? Complete the chain of events below:
   Use the word bank provided. *Note*: not all words will be used.
   a. Air is _____.
   b. Heated air is _____ dense than the surrounding air.
   c. Warmer air then _____.
   d. _____ air then in to replace it.

Cooled	heated	less	more
warm	cold	rises	sinks
cooler	warmer		

4. Draw a simple graph showing the relationship between air temperature and density. Be sure the label the axes.
   a. Describe the relationship between air temperature and density.
   b. What kind of a relationship is this? _____

(continued)

FIGURE 10.5. Weather interactive reading guide created by Cathy Exantus. Reprinted by permission.

5. **Look at Figure 7-4**
   a. What would you feel if you were standing on the shore (include temperature and direction)?
   b. What do you call this type of air circulation?_____

6. **Look at Figure 7-5**
   a. Where do the Sun's rays hit at a 90° angle, perpendicular to the surface?
   b. What are two results of the Sun's rays hitting the Earth slanted at an angle?
   c. Where are the Sun's rays most slanted? _____

   Draw a simple graph showing the relationship between latitude and air temperature.
   Be sure to label the axes.
   d. Describe the relationship between latitude and air temperature.
   e. What kind of a relationship is this? _____

7. What is latitude?
8. Where does most of the United States lie (in terms of latitude)? _____
   _____
9. How do the prevailing westerlies affect the United States? _____
10. Why are these winds called the *prevailing westerlies*? _____
11. **Look at Figure 7-6**
    a. If you were on a sailboat adrift in the Caribbean, what direction are you likely to go?
       EXPLAIN. _____
    b. How do wind belts above the equator compare to those below the equator?
    c. Read p. 137b and then answer questions 46a and 46b in your packet.
    d. Flip back to Figure 7-4 on p. 136. What kind of a breeze is this?_____

Part III. After reading

1. Go back and complete the conclusions on p. 1.
2. Write a complete paragraph describing under what conditions you might really enjoy a sea breeze and then under what conditions would you not enjoy a sea breeze. Be sure to include why it was or wasn't enjoyable. Use complete sentences and neat handwriting.

FIGURE 10.5. *(continued)*

barometric pressure, and wind direction for the day and reported back to the class. Students have recorded all of this information in their daily weather journals along with their initial impressions of the day's weather as they came to school. Now students are working in small groups to discuss and complete an IRG related to the sun's energy and wind.

In one group, Brenda is explaining how "prevailing westerlies affect the United States" to her classmates. Although her English is accented, and she occasionally searches for exactly the right word, her explanations are clear: She knows what westerlies *are and how they can affect weather. Her groupmates accept her answer to question 9 of the guide, with appreciation a few small additions, and they go on talk about why these winds are called "westerlies."*

Another group is talking about how they can use a visual aid to show the slant of the sun's rays to figure out where the rays will be perpendicular to the Earth's surface. Jake points out that perpendicular *means that there will be a right angle, and he suggests that they read the title of the figure to see if it will help them figure out the location of the 90-degree angle.*

Yesterday in Ms. H's ESL class Brenda reviewed the content-related vocabulary for the section they would study today. Ms. H showed them how they could get definitions from the textbook—using context clues, sidebars, the glossary. The students also previewed the reading, with particular attention to the figures that are a major focus of Weather IRG #3 (see Figure 10.5). Ms. H reminded her ESL students that the figures in a textbook are a great way to get information visually with less reliance on their developing knowledge of the English language.

Students in Ms. C's AIS class and Ms. G's special education resource room (including Jake) received a similar kind of advance instruction, focusing on both the science content and the literacy strategies addressed by the IRG. Ms. C and Ms. G reviewed the figures in the reading and talked with their students about how to interpret the graphs, pictures, and visual organizers in the chapter. Ms. G reviewed angles with her students, so that they could interpret the figure related to the angle at which the sun's rays hit the Earth. In addition, Ms. G coteaches one section of eighth-grade science, which contains several of her learning-disabled students.

As students work in small groups on the IRG in their eighth-grade science classroom, Ms. V and coteacher Ms. G check in with each group. They are pleased to see that their collaborative work, both in and out of the class, has helped the special education, ESL, and AIS students become active participants in group discussion focused on using text features to gain content understandings about the sun and wind.

CONCLUSION

Because textbooks remain a mainstay of secondary content-area instruction, content-area teachers need to know how to assist their struggling readers with textbook comprehension. Inadequate access to, and under-standing of, textbook content will only exacerbate achievement gaps. Choosing a considerate content-area text is an important first step, but it is not sufficient. Teachers need ideas for how to motivate students to engage with textbooks and how to suggest ways in which students can motivate themselves. Embedding textbook reading strategies in lessons focused on high-priority, meaningful subject-area content enhances students' motivation and engagement, as well as helping teachers deal with the "content crunch" often associated with standards-driven curriculum and high-stakes assessment.

Teachers also need to know how to use explicit instruction to help struggling readers understand when, why, and how to use textbook reading strategies. Explicit instruction, including teacher and peer think-aloud modeling, helps struggling readers develop metacognitive strategy awareness and the independent control exhibited by competent readers. However, numerous opportunities for practice are required before students truly gain independence in the use of textbook reading strategies. These opportunities can be provided by using teacher-designed IRGs, which engage students in using textbook reading strategies as they learn content. Consistent reinforcement of textbook reading strategies across subject areas and between regular education and support specialists' classrooms takes planning, but pays off in terms of students' growing ease with use and transfer of strategies.

Thoughtful, well-planned instruction in textbook comprehension strategies can give struggling readers the kind of access to textbook information and resources taken for granted by students who are more comfortable with academic literacies. This access to textbook content is a critical piece of the puzzle of reducing academic achievement gaps, improving adolescents' content-area literacy skills, and preparing adolescents to be independent consumers of college-level textbooks.

DISCUSSION AND ACTIVITIES

1. Review a textbook that is currently used in your content area. Determine how considerate the text is. How does it measure up in terms of content, structure, and coherence? Decide how desirable this text is for use in your classroom. What weaknesses would you have to overcome through targeted lessons?

2. Design an activity that would motivate students to read a section of a textbook in your content area. You can design an anticipation guide or create a problem that can be solved using text information. You may also create a matched text set with a piece of popular culture or real-world text (widely defined to include music, film, TV, video games, websites, as well as print text) to motivate students and help them connect to related prior knowledge.

3. Choose a section of text from a textbook in your content area. Make a list of

the important content points you want students to get from their reading of the text section. Think about which reading strategies students need to effectively learn those main points. Also notice the text features that might help students choose and comprehend important text ideas. Now create an IRG that will help students use the strategies and text features to understand the most important information in the chosen textbook section.

4. Different schools have developed different ways to organize instruction in textbook and other content-area literacy strategies so that students receive both the explicit introduction and the amount of ongoing guided practice they need. Think about how teachers are organized in your school (or make up a fictitious school and organization)—whether it is into grade-level teams or cross-grade departments. What kinds of conversations would need to occur for content-area teachers in your school to agree to a plan for introducing and reinforcing textbook reading strategies? What might such a plan look like?

REFERENCES

Allington, R. L. (2002). You can't learn much from books you can't read. *Educational Leadership, 60*, 16–20.

Alvermann, D. E., Moon, J. S., & Hagood, M. C. (1999). *Popular culture in the classroom: Teaching and researching critical media.* Newark, DE: International Reading Association.

Alvermann, D. E., Phelps, S. F., & Ridgeway, V. (2007). *Content area reading and literacy: Succeeding in today's diverse classroom.* New York: Allyn & Bacon.

Armbruster, B., & Anderson, T. (1988). On selecting "considerate" content area textbooks. *Remedial and Special Education, 9*, 47–52.

Armbruster, B., Anderson, T. H., & Ostertag, J. (1987). Does text structure/summarization instruction facilitate learning from expository text? *Reading Research Quarterly, 23*, 331–346.

Camp, D. (2000). It takes two: Teaching twin texts of fact and fiction. *The Reading Teacher, 53*, 400–408.

Cole, A. D. (2003). *Knee to knee, eye to eye: Circling in on comprehension.* Portsmouth, NH: Heinemann.

Daniels, H., & Zemelman, S. (2004). *Subjects matter: Every teacher's guide to content-area reading.* Portsmouth, NH: Heinmann.

Davey, B. (1983). Think-aloud: Modeling the cognitive processes of reading comprehension. *Journal of Reading, 27*, 44–47.

Dufflemeyer, F. (1994). Effective anticipation guide statements for learning from expository texts. *Journal of Reading, 37*, 452–455.

Frey, N., & Fisher, D. (2004). Using graphic novels, anime, and the Internet in an urban high school. *English Journal, 93*, 19–25.

Gersten, R., Fuchs, L., Williams, J., & Baker, S. (2001). Teaching reading comprehension strategies to students with learning disabilities: A review of the research. *Review of Educational Research, 71*, 279–320.

Guthrie, J. T., & Davis, M. H. (2003). Motivating struggling readers in middle school through an engagement model of classroom practice. *Reading and Writing Quarterly, 19*, 59–85.

Harter, S., Whitesell, N. R., & Kowalski, P. (1992). Individual differences in the effects of educational transitions on young adolescents' perceptions of competence and motivational orientation. *American Educational Research Journal, 29*, 777–807.

Hinchman, K. A., Alvermann, D. E., Boyd, F., Brozo, W., & Vacca, R. (2003/2004). Supporting older students' in- and out-of-school literacies. *Journal of Adolescent and Adult Literacy, 47*, 304–310.

Kenney, J. M., Hancewicz, E., Heuer, L., Metsisto, D., & Tuttle, C. L. (2005). *Literacy strategies for improving mathematics instruction.* Alexandria, VA: ASCD.

Kozen, A. A., Murray, R. K., & Windell, I. (2006). Increasing all students' chance to achieve: Using and adapting anticipation guides with middle school learners. *Intervention in School and Clinic, 41*, 195–200.

Loewen, J. W. (1996). *Lies my teacher told me: Everything your American history textbook got wrong.* New York: Touchstone.

Luke, A. (2000). Critical literacy in Australia. *Journal of Adult and Adolescent Literacy, 43*, 448–461.

O'Brien, D. (2001). "At-risk" adolescents: Redefining competence through the multiliteracies of intermediality, visual arts, and representation. *Reading Online, 4*(11). Retrieved December 15, 2006, from *www.readingonline.org/newliteracies/lit_index. asp?HREF=/newliteracies/obrien/index.html*

Paris, S., & Myers, M. (1981). Comprehension monitoring, memory, and study strategies of good and poor readers. *Journal of Reading Behavior, 13*, 5–22.

Raphael, T. (1986). Teaching question–answer relationships, revisited. *The Reading Teacher, 39*, 516–522.

Raphael, T. E., & Au, K. H. (2005). QAR: Enhancing comprehension and test taking across grade levels and contents. *The Reading Teacher, 59*, 206–221.

Schumm, J. S., & Mangrum, C. T. (1991). FLIP: A framework for content area reading. *Journal of Reading, 35*, 120–124.

Schwartz, A., & Rubinstein-Ávila, E. (2006). Understanding the manga hype: Uncovering the multimodality of comic-book literacies. *Journal of Adolescent and Adult Literacy, 50*, 40–49.

Sheridan-Thomas, H. K., Ro, J. M., & Bromley, K. (2004, November). *Educating ourselves: Teacher educators and graduate students explore the in and out of school literacies of local adolescents.* Paper presented at the annual meeting of the National Reading Conference, Scottsdale, AZ.

Smith, M. W., & Wilhelm, J. D. (2002). *"Reading don't fix no Chevys": Literacy in the lives of young men.* Portsmouth, NH: Heinemann.

Triplett, C. F. (2007). The social construction of "struggle": Influences of school literacy contexts, curriculum, and relationships. *Journal of Literacy Research, 39*, 96–126.

Vacca, R. T., & Vacca, J. L. (2008). *Content area reading: Literacy and learning across the curriculum.* New York: Allyn & Bacon.

Wolk, S. (2003). Teaching for critical literacy in social studies. *Social Studies, 94*, 101–107.

Wood, K. (1988). Guiding students' reading through informational texts. *The Reading Teacher, 41*, 912–920

Xu, S. H. (2005). *Trading cards to comic strips: Popular culture texts and literacy learning in grades K–8.* Newark, DE: International Reading Association.

CHAPTER 11

The Reality of Challenging Texts in High School Science and Social Studies

HOW TEACHERS CAN MEDIATE COMPREHENSION

Elizabeth Birr Moje
Jennifer Speyer

This chapter:

- Describes the complex connections between reader purpose, engagement, and knowledge; texts of the subject areas; and the social networks within which texts are embedded.

- Uses short pieces of science and history texts to illustrate what youth need to know and be able to do to comprehend texts at the high school level.

- Summarizes what teachers need to know and be able to do to mediate these challenges.

- Presents content literacy teaching practices that can be adapted for particular youth, particular texts, and particular contexts of instruction.

INTRODUCTION: WHAT'S THE BIG DEAL WITH READING IN HIGH SCHOOL?

Imagine walking into your classroom, the teacher's lounge, or your office and being asked to read the following text:

Emergency Quota Act of 1921

AN ACT

To limit the immigration of aliens into the United States.
Be it enacted by the Senate and House of Representatives of the United
States of America in Congress assembled. . . .
Sec. 2. (a) That the number of aliens of any nationality who may be admitted
under the immigration laws to the United States in any fiscal year shall be
limited to 3 per centum of the number of foreign born persons of such
nationality resident in the United States as determined by the United States
census of 1910. (Retrieved April 9, 2007, from *tucnak.fsv.cuni.cz/~calda/Docu-
ments/1920s/QuotaAct1918.html*)

What is the first thing you would do upon being presented with this
reading task? Can you identify the main idea of the passage? What kinds
of questions would you ask the person who demanded this reading act of
you? What kinds of questions would you ask yourself? Perhaps most
important, would you do it?

Many of you reading this chapter would probably ask, "Why? What
do you want me to do with it?" if presented with this reading task. You
might ask these questions simply because you are a good reader, and as
such, you automatically seek to establish your purpose for reading. Or you
would ask these questions because you know that good readers attempt to
establish a purpose for reading when presented with a text they have not
chosen to read. When good readers have not chosen texts for themselves,
they recognize that the purpose for reading is not up to them to determine. Finally, you might ask such questions because you know you have a
choice and can refuse to read the text if the reason for reading is not to
your liking.

This note about choice is an important one. Literacy theorists argue
that choice in reading and writing tasks makes an enormous difference in
one's motivation or engagement with those tasks (Guthrie & Wigfield,
2000). A number of studies have demonstrated that many young people
do not read academic texts with proficiency or high interest (Moje, 2007;
Perie, Grigg, & Donahue, 2005). The lack of proficiency has been attributed variously to low literacy skills, to motivation and engagement, and to
text difficulty.

However, studies have also indicated that young people read many
different kinds of texts—including challenging texts—outside of school,
and they read them with fluency and reasonably high comprehension
(Alvermann, Young, Green, & Wisenbaker, 1999; Gee, 2003; Leander &
Lovvorn, 2006; Moje, 2006). Many of these same scholars have suggested
that motivation and engagement are at work in young people's abilities to
read out-of-school texts. But we believe that is it not just that youth *want* to
read these texts. Motivation matters, but what may help youth persevere

even in the face of challenging texts may be the fact that these texts are embedded in meaningful social networks of the young people's lives. As such, these social networks provide important background knowledge that helps youth establish a purpose, ask questions of text, monitor their comprehension, and synthesize ideas for each new text they read.

By contrast, the texts of high school classrooms are not embedded in the social networks of most students' daily lives. They are embedded in the social networks represented by the disciplines, which means that they draw on different kinds of knowledge and skills. In this chapter, we want to highlight the vast requirements of knowledge and skill required to read the texts of high school subject-matter areas. Understanding the text of the Emergency Quota Act excerpt requires the ability to set purposes for one's reading; to ask questions about authorship, historical context, and political attitudes and ambitions; to give meaning to words used in particular ways; to monitor comprehension and to know how to find information alluded to, but not explained in the text. These skills are often mentioned in discussing comprehension but are rarely examined in terms of what it means to, say, set a purpose for reading a primary source. Just what is it that the reader is supposed to understand about the act? What level of comprehension is demanded here? What will the reader have to do with this text?

Likewise, producing a well-written argument in science or social studies depends on an ability to set purposes for the writing. But even that one skill—purpose setting—is complicated, requiring extensive knowledge, experience, cognitive development, and engagement. It also requires that youth become part of the social networks in which these disciplinary texts are embedded. Several education researchers and curriculum developers have experimented with activities and practices that foster students' entrance into disciplinary networks, usually by focusing on typical practices or ways of doing, thinking, talking, reading, and writing. Project-based science curricula, for example, introduce young people to the practice of developing questions and carrying out scientific investigations of natural phenomena (Krajcik, Blumenfeld, Marx, Bass, & Fredricks, 1998). In history and science classroom research, scholars have developed technology scaffolds that engage students in examining primary sources (Bain & Ellenbogen, 2001). Others have experimented with bringing practicing scientists into the science inquiry process (Hall & Turow, 2006) as a way of modeling scientific thinking practices for students. In most of these cases, these useful practices are not specifically focused on text reading (Robert Bain's [2006] work in history classrooms is a notable exception). In addition, although these practices help to build necessary knowledge and skills of the subject-matter areas, they do not necessarily make explicit the knowledge and skills necessary for developing high school text reading skills among students.

What follows is an analysis of some the skills and knowledge that young people need in order to comprehend the texts of high school content areas. These skill and knowledge demands complicate secondary school reading and are unique to subject-matter texts, suggesting that what we know about comprehension and comprehension instruction at the elementary level may not be easily extrapolated to comprehension instruction at the secondary level.

The analysis emphasizes the different types of knowledge necessary for purpose setting, comprehension monitoring, and sense making, with an examination of how knowledge and development intersect with engagement in reading. To frame the analysis, we draw from our recent experience co-teaching 11th-grade social studies students in a predominantly Latino/a neighborhood of a large Midwestern city. As hinted at by the Emergency Quota Act text excerpt with which we opened the chapter, we were studying a unit on U.S. immigration issues and history. We framed the problem under study in terms of contemporary questions around who should be allowed to immigrate into the United States, and whether and how immigration should be monitored. We started with a contemporary problem and then looked back in time to our nation's founding, moving forward until we returned to the present day. Our analysis of the text challenges students faced as they read primary sources throughout U.S. history is bolstered by findings from Moje's research with young people in and out of school.

The chapter concludes with a discussion of teaching practices and specific strategies to help teachers mediate these challenges and support young people's reading comprehension and written production of the texts demanded for high school content-area learning. The suggested practices are not intended to supplant project-based practices described above, but to complement such practices, in an attempt to support text reading while conducting both natural and social science investigations.

TYPES OF KNOWLEDGE AND SKILL NECESSARY FOR PURPOSE SETTING AND COMPREHENSION

We feature the Emergency Quota Act of 1921 text because it was in the process of teaching it that we began to think about the complexity of knowledge and skill demands implicit in what is, at first glance, a seemingly straightforward piece of text. Our analysis—conducted at some level in the midst of trying to help students understand the text—revealed at least six types of knowledge or skill necessary for purpose setting and sense making of this short passage: (1) semantic, (2) mathematical, (3) historical, (4) geographical, (5) discursive, and (6) pragmatic.

Semantic Knowledge and Skill

That semantic—or word—knowledge is needed to make sense of this passage may seem rather obvious and is often the first factor considered by content teachers, literacy coaches, and reading theorists. The technical words of the passage include *immigration, aliens, Senate, House of Representatives, Congress, assembled, fiscal year, per centum, nationality,* and *census.* The everyday terms that might give adolescent readers pause, particularly in relation to the syntax in this passage, include *enacted* and *resident.* Many of these terms are ones that most youth are likely to have heard before; however, the difference between their casual use and their meaning in this passage may be critical. Readers who do not know the technical or everyday meanings of these and other words in the passage could nevertheless work to comprehend the passage, provided they possess the semantic skill not only to locate words in dictionaries, but also to discern which meaning is more appropriate in the context of the passage. Such semantic skill, however, is complicated by the other knowledge demands embedded in the passage. As we used the Emergency Quota Act and other texts in the immigration unit, we found ourselves repeatedly turning our students to the dictionary, asking students to read each of the definitions provided, and then working with them to choose the word that best fit the context in which we were reading.

Mathematical Knowledge

As mentioned above, *per centum* is a key phrase in this text that needs to be understood in order to make sense of the text. However, the knowledge required is not merely definitional (i.e., it is not enough merely to know that the Latin phrase translates as "per one hundred," it is also essential that students understand what it means mathematically when a limit is set at 3 per 100). As obvious as this may seem to the adult reader, students in our classes answered the question, "If there were 100 people from Albania in the United States in 1910, then how many Albanians could immigrate to the United States in 1921?" with responses such as, "Five?" or "Twenty?" Students' responses indicated cither a lack of skill in calculating percentages (or even a lack of conceptual knowledge of what a percentage represents) or a lack of interest in applying the mathematical concept to the historical information of the passage (in some cases, they seemed to simply call out a number without really stopping to think about the question). Both language and minimath lessons were useful here, as we discussed both the meaning of *per centum,* using the Spanish for 100 as a way into the Latin word, and how to calculate three per centum of a given number of residents. Making sense of the numbers, however, raises questions about another kind of knowledge required for making sense of this passage: knowledge of history.

Historical Knowledge

One of the most important types of knowledge for making sense of this particular historical document is knowledge of past events, data, people, and social and political issues and conflicts. Although a reader could comprehend the Emergency Quota Act's surface meaning to be that in 1921, U.S. immigration law set limits on immigration that equaled 3% of the people of a given nationality living in the United States in 1910, the significance of the text is revealed only when one either knows or examines the numbers of immigrants from different countries living in the United States in 1910. If readers know anything about U.S. immigration during the early 1900s, then they will know that the numbers of different nationalities living in the United State were vastly different. They might even know something about the nature of the differences (e.g., that the country was heavily populated by people of English and German descent, and less heavily populated by people of Italian, Romanian, or Polish descent). If, for example, readers had knowledge of the information shown in Table 11.1 then they would be able to draw inferences about the intent of the act, and they might put a different spin on the word *emergency*.

Armed with the knowledge that the number of British residents in 1910 was higher than the number of Romanian or Polish residents, the reader might infer that the law targeted 1910 as a way of limiting the numbers of Romanian and Polish residents and allowing British peoples to maintain dominance in the larger population (the same sort of argument could be made for German immigration in comparison to Italian immi-

TABLE 11.1. Foreign-Born Residents by Selected Country of Origin, 1890–1920

Country/region	1890	1910	1920
Great Britain	1,251,402	1,221,283	1,135,489
Ireland	1,871,509	1,352,251	1,037,234
Germany	2,784,894	2,311,237	1,686,108
Italy	1,887	1,343,125	1,610,113
Romania	NA	937,884	1,139,979
Poland	48,557	65,923	102,823

Note. Based on information retrieved April 9, 2007, from *www.u-s-history.com/pages/h1398.html* and April 20, 2007, from *www.census.gov/population/www/documentation/.*

gration). However, to do so, readers would then have to employ their mathematical knowledge to determine that 3% of 65,923 (the number of Polish-born residents in 1910) is smaller than 3% of 1,221,283 (the number of British-born residents in 1910). But the need to make that mathematical calculation depends on the knowledge that the groups differed in number. Without that knowledge, the words would be taken at face value and the law would appear to be equitable. With that knowledge, readers would have access to deeper and historically important interpretations of the text. Specifically, they would come to understand that the Emergency Quota Act of 1921, despite its seemingly equitable application of the same *per cent* limit to all nationalities, was established to limit the immigration of certain groups (Eastern and Southern Europeans, in particular) into the United States. To draw that conclusion, however, one would also need to know that the numbers of those groups immigrating were on the rise, as shown in Table 11.2. It could be argued that the savvy reader would ask questions of that text that would demand the answers provided via these data. However, that savvy and the accompanying critical reading practice require additional types of knowledge and skill, such as knowledge of geography and skill in making sense of geographical data.

Geographic Knowledge and Skill

A lengthy list of countries and population numbers included in the 1924 law requires either extensive knowledge of geography or well-developed geographical skills to find the countries and attempt to identify demographic characteristics of the populations therein (see list in Appendix 11.1). However, these knowledge and skill demands are even more complicated: To recognize the import of either the 1921 act or

TABLE 11.2. Immigration Statistics, 1920–1926

Year	Total entering United States	Country of origin		
		Great Britain	Eastern Europe	Italy
1920	430,001	38,471	3,913	95,145
1921	805,228	51,142	32,793	222,260
1922	309,556	25,153	12,244	40,319
1923	522,919	45,759	16,082	46,674
1924	706,896	59,490	13,173	56,246
1925	294,314	27,172	1,566	6,203
	304,488	25,528	1,596	8,253

Note. Based on information retrieved April 9, 2007, from *www.u-s-history.com/pages/h1398.html* and April 20, 2007, from *www.census.gov/population/www/documentation/*.

the 1924 law, one needs to recognize that the people of some countries were not as highly regarded as the people of other countries, at times on the basis of social class, at other times on the basis of race, ethnicity, or language. To know these differences requires deep geographical knowledge beyond simply knowing where a country is located on a map or globe.

Discursive Knowledge and Skill

One additional type of knowledge is discursive, or the knowledge that the construction of texts is tied to the domain in which, and the purposes for which, they were originally written. Understanding the Emergency Quota Act of 1921 as more than a string of words demands that the reader possess and use discursive knowledge of how and why legal documents from a particular time period were written, to what audiences they spoke, and to what issues they were addressed. Discursive knowledge is even more useful in understanding a later immigration law, the Immigration Act of 1924, wherein limits are reduced to two per centum of the foreign-born persons resident in the United States in 1890 (note both the reduction in percentage and the backward move by 20 years from 1910 to 1890), particularly in the final portion of the act, which reads:

> The immigration quotas assigned to the various countries and quota-areas should not be regarded as having any political significance whatever, or as involving recognition of new governments, or of new boundaries, or of transfers of territory except as the United States Government has already made such recognition in a formal and official manner. (Retrieved April 9, 2007, from *www.u-s-history.com/pages/h1398.html*)

This attempt to disavow political intent in the law requires an understanding of the nature of political back-room negotiations, U.S. foreign policy, and of the likely targets of this law. A skilled reader should wonder about the politics at work in the time period upon reading these words; the skilled reader should also question the intent behind the words. In the absence of such knowledge, skill with navigating discourse communities can come into play and aid in comprehension. However, the discursive skill here involves imagining reactions from various countries around the world, as well as from various national groups within the United States at the time, and analyzing how the text was constructed in attempts to minimize those reactions. Thus, the discursive skill requires knowledge of politics, rhetoric, history, and geography—a point that emphasizes the complicated, interrelated nature of bodies of knowledge and skill in making sense of texts at the high school level. No text is an island unto itself; an awareness of *intertextuality*—that is, the interconnectedness of multiple texts and ideas across texts—is especially important for both the high school reader and the teachers of high school readers.

Making sense of these texts also requires another kind of discursive knowledge or skill, one that is tied to the original question of purpose. The reader needs to recognize that one should get information, ideas, or perspectives from texts. The question, however, is which information, ideas, or perspectives are to be taken away from the text, and once one has them, what is to be done with them? Expert reader studies (Alexander, 2003; Alexander, Kulikowich, & Jetton, 1994; Pressley & Afflerbach, 1995; Wineburg, 1998) have demonstrated that expert readers either ask for, articulate, or have in their minds an explicit purpose when approaching a text. How many high-school-age readers approach texts such as the Emergency Quota Act with a specific purpose in mind? From where would this purpose come? Would the purpose come from the discipline of history? That would require discursive knowledge of historical reading practices and problem framing (Bain, 2006). How often do high school teachers help readers set such purposes for the various texts they read? And when we do set purposes for student readers, how clear and specific are they?

For example, as we taught these texts, we provided an interpretive task for our 11th-grade students to complete after reading the Emergency Quote Act of 1921. The students were asked to draw a representation of what they had read for placement on a timeline we were building as a class. We saw this task as an excellent way to translate across communicative forms (i.e., from print to drawing), and the collection of drawings placed on the timeline helped to make visual the laws and to frame them chronologically. The timeline provided a stable referent as we worked through the unit. But the question remains as to how clear we made *what* the students were supposed to take away and represent from the Emergency Quota Act text. It was in working with several small groups of students as they struggled through this text that we realized a weakness in our lesson design. Specifically, although our students could visually represent a surface-level meaning of the texts they read, they were not able to dig deeper into the texts to comprehend more nuanced meanings, and nothing in the task's purpose demanded in-depth reading. The task was a comprehension task, but comprehension to what *end*? This problem became especially clear with the Emergency Quota Act and the Immigration Law of 1924, because so much meaning lies beneath the surface of the words in those two laws. Thus the purpose we set of representing the laws visually provided one way into the laws, but it did not provide the students with the kind of purpose they really needed in order to understand the importance of the laws historically.

In effect, high school readers and their teachers must juggle different purposes for reading at all times. As Wineburg (1991, 1998) demonstrated, historians read archival material with two purposes in mind. One is the purpose involved in doing history: that of constructing accounts from the range of sources they analyze. The other purpose for which they read is to discern the purpose of the original writer, the context in which the text was written, and the probable effects of the text on other people or on historical events. Historians read with their working purposes in mind, and those purposes demand that they examine the author's purpose and context for the texts that they study. Like historians, secondary school students must approach texts, then, with multiple purposes in mind: One purpose might be to complete the school task they have been assigned. But if we want students to learn the concepts of the discipline, then students in a history class must assess an original author's purpose; analyze the historical, geographical, political, and discursive contexts; corroborate evidence and information; and read between the lines of the texts (Wineburg, 1991; VanSledright & Kelly, 1998). In other words, they need to read as historians would, not so that they can become historians, but so that they can understand the importance of the information for their lives as citizens (Wineburg & Martin, 2004). Very rarely are students taught to read like historians, and thus, very rarely are they reading history in ways that will inform present-day social issues and decisions.

Pragmatic Knowledge and Skill

One type of pragmatic knowledge is the recognition that texts can be questioned. The Emergency Quota Act and its partner, the Immigration Act of 1924, provide excellent examples of texts that convey a simple piece of information and appear to lay down equitable laws but, in fact, are replete with hidden implications—implications that are dependent on knowledge of history or, at least, on the knowledge that one should ask questions such as, "Why, in 1921, would the U.S. immigration law refer back to 1910 to calculate its immigration quotas?" And just who lived in the United States in 1910? Knowing that one can ask such questions of a text (and being motivated to do so) is something that may need to be taught. At one point in our unit, I said to one class, "So, what do you think: Is this Immigration Law [of 1924] equitable? It says that every resident ethnic/national group can have the same percentage of immigrants, right?" One young woman responded, "I would have thought so, until you showed us all of that [referring to the data tables presented previously]." In other words, this student may not have asked the question about the equity of the act unless we had modeled how to ask and how to make sense of related information. On another note, other students may not have recognized embedded inequities had we not probed this point through questioning and revisiting the ideas across multiple texts and sources of information.

The idea of making sense of related information is linked to two additional types of pragmatic knowledge or skill required for reading the seven lines of the Emergency Quota Act of 1921: search skills/knowledge and analytical skills/knowledge. Let us assume that all of our high school readers possess, at some level, many of the different kinds of skills described above. They still need to build relevant historical knowledge or information (we can assume that they do not possess it in depth, or we would not be teaching them history). Thus they either need the information handed to them (e.g., in the form of a lecture) or they require knowledge of how to access information and the skill to do so. Once they have access to the information, they must be able to determine its relevance and make sense of it.

Knowledge of and Skill to Retrieve Data or Information

This set of knowledge and skills may seem trivial and yet was central to us as teachers in preparing to teach this text. As adults with history degrees, we did not have the immigration statistics relevant to interpreting the text stored in memory; we had to search for them. In our current context, we relied heavily on the Internet, which meant that we needed not only digital search skills but also *critical* digital search skills. We checked and double-checked sources, assessing each site's provenance and checking the numbers across multiple sites. In this lesson, we supplied these materials for students, but our analysis of this text suggests that this data retrieval knowledge and skill would be an important comprehension skill to teach in future lessons.

Analytical Knowledge and Skill

Consider the data tables shown previously. Think of the many challenges in making sense of those tables, let alone in applying them to the print text they inform. First, one must know how tables work. This kind of knowledge is often assumed, but it is not clear in what grade the reading of tables is taught. To read Table 11.1, for example, the reader must know that the items in the rows of the tables do not necessarily have a relationship to one another except insofar as each item represents a country of origin from which people have emigrated to the United States. The columns, however, *do* have a relationship because the information in the columns represents trends in numbers of people from each of those countries over 10-year time periods. The time periods, which are written from least to most recent, represent the periods critical to the two pieces of immigration legislation under study.

Table 11.2, however, is arranged in exactly the opposite order and includes a total immigration column. Both of these tables are types of primary historical texts that adolescents must be able to read and then apply to their reading of the immigration laws. The irony of the process of table reading in this case is that reading the tables depends at some level on knowing what one needs to learn from them. In other words, one must have a purpose for reading the tables as well, and that purpose derives from knowing what one needs to learn from the legislation under study. But reading the legislation requires knowing the importance of the numbers in the table. Again, these texts are interconnected and are dependent on relatively high levels of background knowledge and analytical skill. We can teach such knowledge and skill simultaneously, but such teaching is challenging and takes time. Thus, as we taught this unit, we found that we needed to guide our students in making sense of these tables and that we had to make direct links back and forth from legislation to tables. Our students could engage in analysis of the numbers and the words and ideas, but only with our support and direction.

THE ROLE OF MOTIVATION AND INTEREST IN BUILDING KNOWLEDGE AND COMPREHENDING TEXTS

Thus far, we have emphasized the role of knowledge and skill in making sense of high school content-area texts. However, understanding this text may depend most on readers' interest in the topic or motivation to make sense of the text for some purpose beyond being interested (e.g., to get a school task done, to use the text as evidence in a debate). That is, people need to *want to know* what texts mean in order to spend the time asking questions, searching for information, or questioning contexts.

There are many possibilities for building on students' motivation for, and interest in, reading various texts, particularly if teachers choose topics that appeal to youths' interests. Many young people in this particular urban neighborhood read texts outside of school that address issues and topics commonly covered in social studies (Stockdill & Moje, 2008)—which suggests that they should find school social studies to be a fascinating and useful subject. In other words, young people *are* motivated to learn social and natural science concepts. The same research, however, yields data that report the opposite finding: These same students rate social studies among their least useful and enjoyable subjects, with science a close second. What explains this contradiction?

One challenge to interest and motivation may be that although adolescent students may be highly interested in a topic, they are often less engaged with academic texts about the topic because of the writing style of those texts. Several researchers have found that the lack of voice of academic texts make them difficult for students to access (Paxton, 1999;

Schleppegrell, 2004). Indeed, as we taught our unit on immigration, we noted many of the youth appeared to be highly engaged in our brainstorming discussions (K-W-L; what I *know*, what I *want* to know, what I *learned*; Ogle, 1986) about immigration, but groaned when we passed out written texts to read to help them learn what we wanted them to know.

One notable exception was the reading of "The New Colossus" (Lazarus, 1883), a poem that we read together, engaging in a close reading and analysis of each stanza. Although neither of us would claim that the students were enthralled with this text, they did appear to be more engaged than when they were asked to read texts independently, even when the activities attached to the independent reading were ostensibly engaging (e.g., drawing a political cartoon to represent the texts of immigration laws). Their interest in "The New Colossus" may have something to do with its narrative form (a hypothesis borne out by their similar interest in the 1940s journal entry of a Mexican *bracero* [worker]). However, we would also assert that working through the text with the students helped to maintain their engagement.

Thus we suggest spending a fair amount of time on whole-class thinkalouds of readings, especially early in a unit, to model for students how to set a purpose, ask questions of the text, and troubleshoot when comprehension goes awry. Even reading small portions of challenging texts can make a difference. In a study of middle school students' reading of science texts, for example, we noted that a newspaper article on HIV/AIDS confused middle-school students because the text had been edited to delete a reference explaining how an 11-year-old boy had acquired HIV/AIDS in the birth process (Cleveland, Heitzman, & Moje, 2007). The information that the virus was transmitted from mother to child in the birth process was supplied by one teacher during an in-class reading of the text, helping students focus their attention on the central ideas of the texts, rather than on questions about whether the young boy had engaged in sexual activity at a very early age. Navigating such points of confusion can make an important difference in students' motivation to keep reading.

Another important way to engage youth, and maintain their engagement even as they encounter lengthy print texts is to build units on the issues and concerns about which they care deeply. However, as we learned with the immigration unit, teachers need to be prepared to address students' well-developed beliefs about the concepts under study. Adolescent youth, more so than young children, also possess deeply entrenched views and opinions, as well as self-interested perspectives. These opinions and perspectives are useful for building interest and motivation to learn more, but they can also serve as a roadblock for learning information or ideas that may contradict those opinions or perspectives. Our students' views on immigration were shaped by important life experiences and thereby shaped what they were willing to hear, read, or discuss. Many were either immigrants themselves or knew people who had immigrated. Many of them knew stories of immigration challenges. At the same time, they appeared to lack knowledge outside of their own experiences. This lack of knowledge outside themselves, coupled with their belief that they already knew what was important to know about immigration, made deep learning of new or different ideas challenging.

Students' beliefs also played a role in their interest in, and willingness to read, the texts of U.S. immigration history. Encouraging them to use the information they had learned throughout the unit—much of which actually bolstered their perspectives—was challenging because they said that their arguments were strong without the benefit of additional historical information. However, discussion of what these texts meant for their beliefs, and explicit attention to how the students might use the texts to support or challenge particular ideas, seemed to generate interest in the texts.

For example, at the end of the unit, as we reviewed immigration laws throughout history, one student objected to the name of one law, *Operation Wetback* (Garcia, 1980), stating that the name of the law was racist. That statement inspired a different student to raise the question of when racial slurs are considered racist, and when they are not. The heated and difficult discussion that ensued was generated from word and text and pointed back to word and text, as well as to the central issue we were investigating: the role of race in immigration law. Ultimately, the texts we read and the discussion we had about racist language helped to frame an argument that many of them planned to make in their final essays. The opportunity to discuss their beliefs and values stemmed from, and supported, their readings of text.

Another excellent motivational resource in working with the youth in our classrooms was the rich vocabulary and experience they possessed, usually from interactions with previous classes, families, peer groups, and popular cultural texts. Students were familiar, for example, with a number of terms relevant to immigration, such as *alien, quota, undocumented, bracero* (worker), *green card, visa, passport,* and many others. They also knew many technical terms from their previous history courses. They were less familiar, in this case, with nontechnical vocabulary such as *per centum* (see above), *teeming* or *colossus* (both from the Lazarus poem), or *pauper* and *moral turpitude* (used in an 1891 immigration law).

We spent a great deal of time defining such terms, but we were also able to make use of students' extensive knowledge of popular culture in interesting ways as we defined vocabulary or built background knowledge. For example, when discussing the Chinese Exclusion Act of 1882, one student volunteered that he had played a computer game in which the goal was to protect Chinese workers who were building railroads in the United States during the 1800s. Other students drew on their knowledge of the African slave trade from past history courses to raise questions about whether and how Africans were counted in immigration quotas, or about the history of world wars in developing hypotheses about which immigrant groups were most accepted during different time periods of U.S. history. In another instance, while engaging in a think-aloud of a journal entry written by a Mexican *bracero* (worker), Speyer commented that the worker's mention of being fed bread and bologna as "glory" indicated how hungry he must have been. Two male students began to sing, "I'm from the ghetto, homies, I grew up on bread and bologna," an excerpt of lyrics from a popular rap song, "Move Around" (feat & Fresh, 2006). Their invoking of these lyrics led to a discussion of what bread and bologna signified in the *bracero's* text. In each of these cases, and many others, our students exhibited a wealth of knowledge—albeit not always conventional, not always deep, and not always complete or fully accurate—that could be expanded to support their sense making of these historical texts.

WHAT KNOWLEDGE AND SKILLS DOES HIGH SCHOOL COMPREHENSION INSTRUCTION REQUIRE OF TEACHERS?

Just as comprehending the complex texts of high school classrooms makes many knowledge and skill demands on adolescent students, comprehension instruction at the high school level makes comparable knowledge and skill demands on teachers.

The first type of knowledge teachers need is knowledge of students' interests, knowledge, and skills. We knew that our students would be interested in immigration because we knew that immigration was a major issue in the community, and we knew that immigration issues were a focus of national news. We were not always prepared, however, to have to push our students to think critically and objectively about immigration issues. Moreover, we were also not always prepared to help them think about how to give nuanced responses to questions about immigration. At the start of the unit, for example, we asked them to engage in a free writing activity in response to the question, "Should open immigration be allowed for any person to any country at any time?" Our students believed that they could only answer the question with a yes or a no, setting up challenges for students who believed that immigration law should be more open than it currently is, but not completely open. In some ways, the belief was an artifact of repeated practice for state writing assessments that required students to take a clear stand on issues; they believed that a nuanced perspective was unacceptable in writing school essays. This belief required us to engage in a different kind of writing instruction than we had planned, but it was important to helping the students articulate their ideas, and would support their ability to compose sophisticated responses to test prompts.

Teachers can also benefit from having deep knowledge of, and relationships with, students, families, and the community served by the school. As coteachers with investments in the community, we had built relationships with youth and parents. As a result, we knew about common immigration concerns, we knew the different perspectives represented in the community, and we knew about planned activities around immigration law and policy. We could build on these interests and issues as we tried to make connections from the past to the present-day lives of our students.

High school teachers also need special knowledge of (or talent with) how to maintain student engagement when turning to lengthy print texts. Even the youth appeared to possess reasonable reading skills expressed dismay when asked to read texts of more than a page. As mentioned previously, think-aloud strategies that provided opportunities to discuss not only what the texts meant but also what students thought of the texts, seemed motivating. In addition, Jennifer's provision of visual images to give life to texts helped a great deal. As we discussed the Emergency Quota Act of 1921 and the Immigration Law of 1924, Speyer presented carefully selected images of typical immigrants from different areas of the world in the 1920s and asked the students to make predictions about which groups might be allowed to immigrate into the United States and to discuss why. This discussion allowed students to see, read, think about, and feel their way through a history of U.S. immigration law.

A second kind of knowledge teachers need is deep disciplinary knowledge. Our previous discussion of the underlying information necessary to understand the laws we taught in this unit barely scratches the surface of the historical, geographical, political, and discursive knowledge systems on which these laws are based. Also crucial for our teaching was information on immigration statistics, the political and economic systems of both the United States and countries of origin, the political actors behind each law, and the other world events that shaped the laws. Our combined expertise in U.S. history made a vast difference in the ease with which we searched for and retrieved useful background materials. Our knowledge of history and political science also allowed us to hear students' questions or assess their confusion more readily than would a teacher from a different content background.

This point about disciplinary knowledge seems critical in a time period marked by the increased presence of literacy coaches in schools.

Literacy coaches bring valuable information about reading and writing processes and literacy teaching strategies, but content-area teachers must contribute critical information about the content of *their* disciplines— content that will shape the purpose is to be set for reading, what information is to be drawn from reading, and what background information is necessary for deep comprehension. Content teachers also contribute information about the practices of their discipline. Literacy teaching strategies can rarely be applied apart from the knowledge and particular discursive practices valued in the discipline under study.

A third kind of knowledge teachers need is knowledge of how to support adolescents of varying skill and interest levels in building relevant knowledge or in developing skills for finding and interpreting information. Teachers also need to know not only how to develop reasoned critiques of issues, but also how to teach novices to do so. For example, simply knowing that young people may rarely think to ask questions such as "Who lived in the United States in 1910 or 1890?" is central to knowing that the question must be posed initially for the students and methods for answering the question modeled. Teachers should also know that they can be explicit about *why* they are engaging in a certain practice (e.g., posing a question, walking students through a process) and still engage students in constructing the knowledge themselves. Being explicit about processes and practices is not the same thing as engaging in *explicit instruction* or a *pedagogy of telling* (Sizer, 1984). Being explicit about why members of a discipline read or write in particular ways (e.g., why scientists always make claims related back to their initial hypotheses and reason through their data in formal written reports) provides adolescent readers and writers not only with the practices they should follow to read and write proficiently, but also with a rationale for why these practices have been developed in the disciplines. Teachers may likewise need to model how to make sense of the data they find, again explaining *why* they are engaging in their sense-making practices.

Finally, teachers who seek to build on students' interests as a way of engaging them must then possess skill in how one maintains and sharpens interests while asking students to examine their own beliefs, to take dispassionate stances on passionate beliefs in order to develop strong arguments for or against issues, and to look carefully at data and assess the validity of their own beliefs. This is perhaps the most challenging skill of all: How can teachers draw from and expand on young people's passion and conviction while also teaching the dispassionate stances often valued in the social and natural sciences? Modeling how to challenge one's passionate beliefs by confronting conflicting data could be one of the most useful content literacy teaching practices teachers enact in high school classrooms.

WHAT MIGHT THIS LOOK LIKE
IN THE HIGH SCHOOL CLASSROOM?

Content-area literacy teaching strategies (e.g., K-W-L, semantic feature analysis) provide a framework for thinking and an organization for instruction and are invaluable tools for fostering literate practice. We used these teaching tools routinely during our 2-week unit, relying heavily on Buehl's (2002) excellent resource of a host of classroom strategies. However, the analysis of these history texts demonstrates that literacy teaching strategies alone may not address the greatest challenges presented by advanced content-area texts being read by a wide variety of youth (who may or may not be as interested in the content as those of us who chose to spend our lives teaching it). We need to continue to use literacy teaching strategies, but those strategies appear to work best if embedded in content teaching *practices* that make working with texts central to the work of content learning (Greenleaf, Schoenbach, Cziko, & Mueller, 2001; Sutherland, Moje, Cleveland, & Heitzman, 2006).

The difference between *strategies* and *practices* is analogous to the difference between tools and habits, or what Deshler and colleagues refer to as *routines* (Deshler & Schumaker, 2005). When Moje teaches preservice teacher education courses, for example, she uses a variety of tools or strategies—such as preview guides or concept maps—to support undergraduate students' reading of education research. Those literacy teaching strategies serve as tools for the practice of trying to build knowledge, set purposes, and guide students' reading and thinking as they grapple with a text. In other words, the strategies themselves are not the teaching practice; they simply support it.

As one uses various teaching strategies, then, it is important to consider the overarching practices the strategies support. We have chosen to highlight five overarching practices we think high school content-area teachers should try to enact in routine ways: (1) whole-group knowledge building, (2) scaffolded reading, (3) questioning, (4) visualizing, and (5) summarizing. A variety of daily practices and strategies can be embedded within these overarching practices, as described in the following material.

Whole-Group Knowledge-Building Activities

Setting Purpose, Framing Problems

At the beginning of a unit, set a purpose for the entire unit by framing a problem for study. Project-based science curricula, for example, always begin by posing driving questions for students to investigate throughout the course of the unit. Similarly, history and other social studies units could begin with the kind of problem framing we posed in our immigration unit, with a focus on a contemporary problem that requires knowledge of how the issue has evolved throughout history. We set a purpose by asking students to free-write to the problem of whether the United States should allow immigration by any person from any country at any time. We posed a new aspect of U.S. immigration issues each day for free writing. Free writing is a useful tool because it also serves to focus students' attention at the start of the class, but there are many other literacy teaching strategies that could be employed to frame problems and set purpose.

Preview Concepts and Texts

Before reading, whether whole class or independently, preview texts with strategies such as K-W-L, anticipation guides, preview guides, and advanced organizers. When previewing, keep in mind the two levels of purpose—purpose of the reading task and purpose of the text in the discipline—discussed previously. Make explicit what you expect your students to do with the text (whether to ask questions, to use it in an essay, to link it to another text, and/or to critique or question its purpose in history). Second, discuss with students the purpose of the text for the context in which it was written. Who was its author? What did the author intend? To whom was the author writing? Although these are questions that historians routinely ask of texts in their work (Wineburg, 1991; Bain, 2006), these questions are relevant for students reading texts in any content area, because no matter what the text is, they are reading it outside of the context in which it was written. Often mathematics and science teachers will argue that context does not matter for the texts of mathematics and science, but all texts are produced in and for particular contexts and purposes, and students benefit from knowing what those are or knowing how to ask what they are and how to find out and assess those contexts and purpose

Scaffolded Reading

Talk about the Texts

In addition to brief lectures or mini-lessons as knowledge-building activities, engage in text reading and discussion strategies such as close reading, dictionary searches, concept mapping of ideas in texts, and text–self/community/world connections. As you talk about texts, define words and interpret nuances in meaning. Model for students how to ask questions even at the word level. While defining the word *quota* with our group of 11th-grade students, for example, we read several different definitions and then talked about which definition best fit our text and historical context.

Make Texts Visible

Project sections of text on overhead screen so that students can see and hear words read and so that you can point to words as you read. Look up important words together in the dictionary while also pointing to them on a common text. Look carefully at words, phrases, and syntax of sentences. Point out how headings signal what is coming up in the text. Refer readers to images that accompany the text.

Read Charts and Tables

Try not simply to refer readers to these images or to present charts and tables, but *work through them* with students. Chart/table/graph reading is a skill that is often not explicitly taught. Reading images is an important skill and often dramatically supports the reading of print (see later section). These skills are useful whether reading social studies, science, literary, or mathematics texts. As we worked through the charts we used in our immigration unit, we blocked out certain bits of information in the chart, in part to encourage students to focus on certain statistics before encountering other statistics, but in part to reveal a kind of logical progression in looking at the information. We walked the students through the chart, rather than simply offering it to them *in toto*. In this way, reading the chart was a kind of puzzle, as students tried to figure out how to interpret the numbers they saw. The important information was not contained in the numbers alone, but in what the trends or patterns in numbers over years and by immigrant groups meant for immigration history and law.

Questioning or Pressing for Understanding

One observation Moje made after a day in the classroom is that our students did not appear to have much experience answering *why* questions. For example, while brainstorming *want-to-know* items in our K-W-L activity, one young woman stated that she wanted to know why there were fences and guards at the U.S. border with Mexico but not at the U.S. border with Canada. Moje wrote her question on the board and then said, "That's an interesting one. Anyone have any ideas why that might be?" Another student said, "Because they were ordered to go there." Not taking up the validity of that statement, Moje simply asked, "Oh? Why would that be?"

"Because they were sent there," responded the student.

"OK, but why do you think guards were sent to the Mexican border and not the Canadian border?" Moje asked.

The student appeared to be perplexed by the question, and none of the other students seemed able or inclined to help support or refute the claim. Eventually, the student said, "Because they think more Mexicans [than Canadians] want to come to the United States"—but getting this idea out took approximately 5 minutes of probing around a single statement. We maintained this pattern of probing for reasons throughout the unit, and the students did shift to engaging the *why* questions, but it took some time and required us to make a trade-off between teaching youth how to ask questions of texts and themselves—even when their ideas may have been inaccurate or partial—and covering content.

In related work in science classrooms, a number of researchers have found that teachers often resist what some researchers refer to as *pressing for understanding*, in part because they fear alienating or threatening students (Blumenfeld, Marx, & Harris, 2006; Blumenfeld, Kempler, & Krajcik, 2006). Many of the science teachers with whom we work also argue that they need to maintain a fast pace in order to cover curriculum content, engage in science investigations, and keep students' attention. This rapid movement pushes them through the curriculum and keeps students' attention focused on the points at hand, but does not necessarily engage students in the kind of questioning they need to develop for deep comprehension of advanced subject-matter texts or for taking inquiry to new levels.

Images and Visualization

The students we taught needed help visualizing what these texts meant in terms of actual people. When we presented them with visual images of different groups represented by the numbers in the tables we presented, our students appeared to make connections to the implicit goals of the laws, underscoring the idea that literate practice, although focused on making sense of encoded symbols, is also about more than just print codes or other symbols (Moje, 2000). Images can help readers interpret texts (Eisner, 1994; Kress, 2003; Kress & van Leeuwen, 1996), and visual images can prove to be important tools in supporting students' comprehension.

That said, it is important to note that visual images should not *replace* print, especially for struggling readers. Some adolescent literacy researchers have noted a tendency to offer struggling adolescent readers ways to opt out of reading print in an effort to make content information accessible; these scholars have also noted that such options may make content accessible, but do not help adolescents improve their literacy skills (Dressman et al., 2005). Thus, the point of using visualization and images is that they should be used to support print reading and writing (and vice versa). One form of representation should not simply replace the other. Moreover, teachers can work with students to draw upon past visual images to support their comprehension of print and other symbolic texts. New images do not need to be offered with each reading; rather, readers can be encouraged to visualize without the aid of actual images, but only if they are introduced to relevant images when they first encounter new material or concepts outside their experience.

Summarization

A final overarching practice is that of summarizing. Central to this practice is the idea that teachers must teach students *how* to summarize, rather than summarizing key points or ideas for the students. This practice involves repeatedly coming back around to ideas covered in previous lessons. The practice can be aided by literacy teaching strategies. For example, keeping a K-W-L chart visible in the classroom can allow a teacher to revisit ideas the students claimed to know at the outset of a unit, suggesting modifications, additions, or corrections to the original ideas. Having the chart as a visual prompt is an excellent management device for the teacher and students, as days or weeks into a unit, they may not recall the exact content of their initial brainstorming. Similarly, the *want-to-know* items can be ticked off as they are covered, and those that are never or partially addressed can be listed in a *want-to-learn* column at the end of the unit (Blachowicz & Ogle, 2001). For secondary school teachers who will be likely to have several different sections of students producing several different K-W-L charts (or other artifacts of student thinking), keeping a permanent record might seem to pose a problem. We found it useful to make notes on the students' ideas at the end of each class period and then to type and distribute them at the next class session for students to keep as references (for underresourced schools, teachers could make a single chart or overhead transparency for each class). Whatever the method, the permanent—but changeable—K-W-L (or other strategy) artifact serves as a tool that facilitates the practice of coming back around and summarizing ideas throughout the unit.

Similarly, as our students in the social studies class prepared to write essays that expanded on their free writing from the first day of the unit, we reviewed with them the different laws they had learned (referring to our visual timeline), the different texts they had read, and the different approaches they might take toward making an argument, incorporating an *if–then* writing strategy (see Buehl, 2002). In every case, our summarization work always referred back to the texts that we had read in class. In many cases, we read excerpts of those texts again for the students, both as a way of taking them back to the text and as a way of synthesizing ideas across texts. For example, when discussing a 1903 immigration statute, which prohibited *paupers* (among others) from entering the United States, we reread *The New Colossus* (after looking up the word *pauper* in the dictionary). In our read-aloud of *The New Colossus*, we emphasized the line, "Give me your tired, your poor, your huddled masses, yearning to breathe free," comparing it the text of the statute, which reads:

> The following classes shall be excluded from admission to the United States ... all idiots, insane persons, epileptics, and persons who have been insane within five years previously; paupers; persons likely to become a public charge; professional beggars; persons afflicted with a loathsome or with a dangerous contagious disease; persons who have been convicted of a felony or other crime or misdemeanor involving moral turpitude. (32 Stat. 1214, sec. 2 of 1903 U.S. Statutes at Large)

We asked the students to evaluate whether the law excluding paupers and sick people lived up to the sentiment expressed in Lazarus's poem. Through this process, we were teaching vocabulary; summarizing ideas within texts; synthesizing ideas across texts; modeling critical reading, questioning, and thinking; and, most important, teaching concepts, events, and actions central to the study of history and the social sciences. In short, we were engaging these youth in comprehension instruction in the service of social studies learning, not apart from it.

CONCLUSIONS: BUILDING DISCIPLINARY LITERACY BY TEACHING WITH TEXTS

We believe that all subject-matter teachers can engage in similar kinds of teaching, setting up routines, habits, and practices that turn students to the texts of their content areas, whether textbooks, related real-world texts (e.g., newspaper articles), or primary sources. We also believe that these turns to subject-matter texts can be engaging for young people if couched in meaningful purposes for reading the texts. Too often, text reading in high school subject matters such as social studies and science is relegated to the background. Bringing text reading to the foreground and modeling for young people how texts of history and science can inform their everyday lives will not only improve their literacy skills, but also enhance their content learning and their possibilities for future participation as educated citizens.

DISCUSSION AND ACTIVITIES

1. Consider your own students. What do you know about them? What topics in social studies or science seem to interest them most? How could you connect their interests to the central concepts of your subject matter? And what might you have to watch out for as you do make those connections? Specifically:

- What you can say about the range of literacy skills your students demonstrate? How might those skills play a role in their understanding of different texts in your content area?
- How might students' interests and passions for a topic help you get them interested in subject-matter texts?
- How might students' interests and passions challenge them in conducting careful, objective inquiry into these topics?

2. What are the major concepts of your subject area? How might you frame a problem for students to study or on which they could take a stand, using text resources from your area. What texts would be useful for helping them investigate the problem or take a stand?

3. Now, considering those texts, what would your students need to know and be able to do to understand the big ideas and apply them to the problem or issue under study? As an experiment, take a piece of text from your subject area and analyze the necessary language skills, content knowledge, and discipline-based thinking skills needed to construct deep meaning from the text. You might want to use the six types of knowledge/skill discussed in the chapter as a guide for your analysis.

4. Once you've conducted the text analysis, construct a lesson or unit around the central problem or issue you've chosen, and then use the text or texts you analyzed. Try building in some of the teaching practices and strategies outlined in the chapter.

REFERENCES

Alexander, P. A. (2003). Profiling the adolescent reader: The interplay of knowledge, interest, and strategic processing. In C. Fairbanks, J. Worthy, B. Maloch, J. V. Hoffman, & D. Schallert (Eds.), *53rd yearbook of the National Reading Conference* (pp. 47–65). Milwaukee, WI: National Reading Conference.

Alexander, P. A., Kulikowich, J. M., & Jetton, T. L. (1994). The role of subject-matter knowledge and interest in the processing of linear and nonlinear and nonlinear texts. *Review of Educational Research, 64,* 201–252.

Alvermann, D. E., Young, J. P., Green, C., & Wisenbaker, J. M. (1999). Adolescents' perceptions and negotiations of literacy practices in after-school read and talk clubs. *American Educational Research Journal, 36,* 221–264.

Bain, R. B. (2006). Rounding up unusual suspects: Facing the authority hidden in the history classroom. *Teachers College Record, 108,* 2080–2114.

Bain, R. B., & Ellenbogen, K. M. (2001). Placing objects within disciplinary perspectives: Examples from history and science. In S. Paris (Ed.), *Perspectives on object-centered learning in museums* (pp. 153–170). Hillsdale, NJ: Erlbaum.

Blachowicz, C., & Ogle, D. (2001). *Reading comprehension: Strategies for independent learners.* New York: Guilford Press.

Blumenfeld, P. C., Kempler, T. M., & Krajcik, J. S. (2006). Motivation and cognitive engagement in learning environments. In K. Sawyer (Ed.), *The Cambridge handbook of the learning sciences* (pp. 475–488). New York: Cambridge University Press.

Blumenfeld, P. C., Marx, R. W., & Harris, C. (2006). Learning environments. In I. Siegel & A. Renninger (Eds.), *Handbook of child psychology* (Vol. 4, pp. 297–342). Hoboken, NJ: Wiley.

Buehl, D. (2002). *Classroom strategies for interactive learning*. Newark, DE: International Reading Association.

Cleveland, T., Heitzman, M., & Moje, E. B. (2007, April). *When is a detail seductive? On the challenges of constructing and teaching from engaging science texts*. Paper presented at the Institute on Science Education Research: Science Education as a Pathway to Learning Literacy, Chicago.

Deshler, D. D., & Schumaker, J. B. (2005). *High school students with disabilities: Strategies for accessing the curriculum*. New York: Corwin Press.

Dressman, M., O'Brien, D. G., Rogers, T., Ivey, G., Wilder, P., & Alvermann, D. E. (2005). Problematizing adolescent literacies: Four instances, multiple perspectives. In J. V. Hoffman, D. L. Shallert, C. M. Fairbanks, J. Worthy, & B. Maloch (Eds.), *55th yearbook of the National Reading Conference* (pp. 141–154). Oak Creek, WI: National Reading Conference.

Eisner, E. W. (1994). *Cognition and curriculum reconsidered* (2nd ed.). New York: Teachers College Press.

feat, B. G., & Fresh, M. (2006). *Move around: The heart of tha streetz: Vol. 2–i am what i am* [song]. Koch Records.

Garcia, J. R. (1980). *Operation wetback: The mass deportation of Mexican undocumented workers in 1954*. Westport, CT: Greenwood Press.

Gee, J. P. (2003). *What video games have to teach us about learning and literacy*. New York: Palgrave Macmillan.

Greenleaf, C., Schoenbach, R., Cziko, C., & Mueller, F. L. (2001). Apprenticing adolescent readers to academic literacy. *Harvard Educational Review, 71*, 79–129.

Guthrie, J. T., & Wigfield, A. (2000). Engagement and motivation in reading. In P. B. Mosenthal, M. L. Kamil, P. D. Pearson, & R. Barr (Ed.), *Handbook of reading research* (Vol. III, pp. 403–419). Mahwah, NJ: Erlbaum.

Hall, R., & Turow, S. (2006, April). *Hybrid interactional practices: Expanding the disciplinary expertise of a middle school mathematics classroom*. Paper presented at the American Educational Research Association, San Francisco.

Krajcik, J., Blumenfeld, P. C., Marx, R. W., Bass, K. M., & Fredricks, J. (1998). Inquiry in project-based science classrooms: Initial attempts by middle school students. *Journal of the Learning Sciences, 7*, 313–350.

Kress, G. (2003). *Literacy in the new media age*. New York: Routledge.

Kress, G., & van Leeuwen, T. (1996). *Reading images: The grammar of visual design*. London: Routledge.

Lazarus, E. (1883). *The poems of Emma Lazarus* (Vol. 1). New York: Houghton Mifflin.

Leander, K. M., & Lovvorn, J. F. (2006). Literacy networks: Following the circulation of texts, bodies, and objects in the schooling and online gaming of one youth. *Cognition and Instruction, 24*, 291–340.

Moje, E. B. (2000). To be part of the story: The literacy practices of gangsta adolescents. *Teachers College Record, 102*, 652–690.

Moje, E. B. (2006). Motivating texts, motivating contexts, motivating adolescents: An examination of the role of motivation in adolescent literacy practices and development. *Perspectives, 32*, 10–14.

Moje, E. B. (2007, April). *Social and cultural influences on adolescent literacy development*. Paper presented at the American Educational Research Association, Chicago.

Ogle, D. M. (1986). K-W-L: A teaching model that develops active reading of expository text. *The Reading Teacher, 39,* 564–570.

Paxton, R. J. (1999). A deafening silence: History textbooks and the students who read them. *Review of Educational Research, 69,* 315–339.

Perie, M., Grigg, W. S., & Donahue, P. L. (2005). *The nation's report card: Reading 2005* (No. NCES 2006-451). Washington, DC: U.S. Government Printing Office.

Pressley, M., & Afflerbach, P. (1995). Verbal protocols of reading: The nature of constructively responsive reading.

Schleppegrell, M. J. (2004). *The language of schooling: A functional linguistics perspective.* Mahwah, NJ: Erlbaum.

Sizer, T. R. (1984). *Horace's compromise: The dilemma of the American high school.* Boston: Houghton Mifflin.

Stockdill, D., & Moje, E. B. (2008, March). *Adolescents as readers of culture, history, economics, and civics: The disconnect between student interest in their world and social studies schooling.* Paper presented at the annual meeting of the American Educational Research Association, New York, NY.

Sutherland, L. M., Moje, E. B., Cleveland, T. E., & Heitzman, M. (2006). *Incorporating literacy learning strategies in an urban middle school chemistry curriculum: Teachers' successes and dilemmas.* Paper presented at the American Educational Research Association, San Francisco.

VanSledright, B. A., & Kelly, C. (1998). Reading American history: The influence of multiple sources on six fifth graders. *Elementary School Journal, 98,* 239–265.

Wineburg, S. S. (1991). On the reading of historical texts: Notes on the breach between school and the academy. *American Educational Research Journal, 28,* 495–519.

Wineburg, S. S. (1998). Reading Abraham Lincoln: An expert/expert study in the interpretation of historical texts. *Cognitive Science, 22,* 319–346.

Wineburg, S. S., & Martin, D. (2004). Reading and rewriting history. *Educational Leadership 62,* 42–45.

APPENDIX 11.1. Country or Area of Birth Quota, 1924–1925

Note. Retrieved from *http://www.u-s-history.com/pages/h1398.html.*

- Afghanistan—100
- Albania—100
- Andorra—100
- Arabian peninsula (1, 2)—100
- Armenia—124
- Australia, including Papua, Tasmania, and all islands appertaining to Australia (3, 4)—121
- Austria—785
- Belgium (5)—512
- Bhutan—100
- Bulgaria—100
- Cameroon (proposed British mandate)—100
- Cameroon (French mandate)—100
- China—100
- Czechoslovakia—3,073
- Danzig, Free City of—228
- Denmark (5, 6)—2,789
- Egypt—100
- Estonia—124
- Ethiopia (Abyssinia)—100
- Finland—170
- France (1, 5, 6)—3,954
- Germany—51,227
- Great Britain and Northern Ireland (1, 3, 5, 6)—34,007
- Greece—100
- Hungary—473

- Iceland—100
- India (3)—100
- Iraq (Mesopotamia)—100
- Irish Free State (3)—28,567
- Italy, including Rhodes, Dodecanesia, and Castellorizzo (5)—3,845
- Japan—100
- Latvia—142
- Liberia—100
- Liechtenstein—100
- Lithuania—344
- Luxemburg—100
- Monaco—100
- Morocco (French and Spanish Zones and Tangier)—100
- Muscat (Oman)—100
- Nauru (proposed British mandate) (4)—100
- Nepal—100
- Netherlands (1, 5, 6)—1648
- New Zealand (including appertaining islands (3, 4)—100
- Norway (5)—6,453
- New Guinea, and other Pacific Islands under proposed Australian mandate (4)—100
- Palestine (with Trans-

- Jordan, proposed British mandate)—100
- Persia (1)—100
- Poland—5,982
- Portugal (1, 5)—503
- Ruanda and Urundi (Belgium mandate)—100
- Rumania—603
- Russia, European and Asiatic (1)—2,248
- Samoa, Western (4) (proposed mandate of New Zealand)—100
- San Marino—100
- Siam—100
- South Africa, Union of (3)—100
- South West Africa (proposed mandate of Union of South Africa)—100
- Spain (5)—131
- Sweden—9,561
- Switzerland—2,081
- Syria and The Lebanon (French mandate)—100
- Tanganyika (proposed British mandate)—100
- Togoland (proposed British mandate)—100
- Togoland (French mandate)—100
- Turkey—100
- Yap and other Pacific islands (under Japanese mandate) (4)—100
- Yugoslavia—67

CHAPTER 12

Humanities Instruction for Adolescent Literacy Learners

Kelly Chandler-Olcott

Goals of this chapter include the following:

- To provide several definitions of the term *humanities* to demonstrate what various conceptions have in common, as well as how they differ.
- To describe the characteristics of various models of humanities instruction and explain the benefits of these approaches for adolescent literacy learners.
- To describe a set of best practices in adolescent literacy for humanities classrooms.
- To propose several avenues for further research related to literacy instruction for adolescents in humanities classes.

Tuesday afternoons were special at Fenway Middle College High School during the 1992–1993 school year. Classes ended an hour early, and students with backpacks and Walkman boarded the subway to go home while their teachers remained for an hour or more of collaborative planning in interdisciplinary teams. Teachers were in the midst of constructing a brand-new curriculum for year 3 of humanities, the class taken instead of traditional English or social studies by sophomores, juniors, and seniors in this alternative school within the Boston public system. Focused around the question "What does it mean to be human?", the curriculum considered such diverse topics as the nature of good and evil, colonialism in Africa, the founding of the American Constitution, capital punishment, and the Salem witch trials. In keeping with Fenway's membership in the

Coalition of Essential Schools, a reform network for secondary schools (Sizer, 1992), each of the five units ended with an exhibition, a time when students shared the results of individually chosen inquiries through presentations, papers, art, music, or drama.

I was fortunate enough to be a part of Fenway's intellectual richness because I was assigned an internship there during my master's program. Over 9 months I participated in humanities team meetings; taught three sections of humanities classes in collaboration with my mentor, Eileen Shakespear; and, at the invitation of the school's headmaster, Larry Myatt, documented the new curriculum so the team could use and revise it in subsequent years. When I sought secondary teaching positions at the end of my experience, I chose a school that placed a similar premium on integrated curriculum and teacher collaboration.

I begin this chapter with my personal narrative for two purposes: (1) to situate myself as its author (those early experiences with Fenway continue to influence how I view curriculum development, interdisciplinary collaboration, and the need to thread literacy instruction through adolescents' schooling experience), and (2) to illustrate the possibilities of humanities planning and instruction in real, not merely hypothetical, contexts. Whereas literacy instruction for most adolescents remains organized within traditional disciplinary lines, Fenway (which continues to offer humanities to urban adolescents in a new building and with a slightly different name) is but one of numerous schools and programs where these boundaries are blurring.

DEFINING HUMANITIES INSTRUCTION

The term *humanities* means different things to different people. For example, the National Endowment for the Humanities (NEH; 2007), an independent agency of the United States government devoted to research, education, and public programming, uses the following definition:

> The term "humanities" includes, but is not limited to, the study of the following: language, both modern and classical; linguistics; literature; history; jurisprudence; philosophy; archaeology; comparative religion; ethics; the history, criticism and theory of the arts; those aspects of social sciences which have humanistic content and employ humanistic methods; and the study and application of the humanities to the human environment with particular attention to reflecting our diverse heritage, traditions, and history and to the relevance of the humanities to the current conditions of national life. (n. p.)

The Massachusetts Foundation for the Humanities (2007), an NEH state affiliate, argues, and I concur, that it may be more useful to think about what the humanities offer us than it is to list the academic disciplines that term might subsume. The leaders of this organization see the humanities

> as a way of thinking about and responding to the world—as tools we use to examine and make sense of the human experience in general and our individual experiences in particular. The humanities enable us to reflect upon our lives and ask fundamental questions of value, purpose, and meaning in a rigorous and systematic way. (n. p.)

In most secondary school settings, the term *humanities* is used to indicate an approach to instruction that unites content and processes from two or more of the traditional school subjects—most often English language arts and social studies, but sometimes including art, music, religion, philosophy, and so on (Wineburg & Grossman, 2000). Students read, write, listen, speak, and view in different ways, depending on which disciplines and which issues are emphasized. Their instruction can take different configurations, as Table 12.1 illustrates.

TABLE 12.1. Definitions and Examples of Possible Configurations for Humanities Instruction

Possible configurations	Examples
One teacher integrates more than one disciplinary perspective into a course designated with one subject label	A teacher weaves a range of historical fiction and nonfiction picture books into the study of the Civil War and Reconstruction (Sandmann & Ahern, 1997) in middle school social studies
One teacher addresses various disciplines in a course designated as integrated	A teacher with dual certification in English and social studies addresses literature, history, and philosophy in an elective for juniors and seniors titled "The Holocaust and Human Rights"
Two or more teachers representing different certification areas collaborate to plan an interdisciplinary curriculum that is carried out in separate courses	Teachers of separate eighth-grade English and social studies classes co-construct their yearlong curricula together and collaborate on a culminating project of student-designed interdisciplinary museum exhibits (Smith, 2000)
Two or more teachers representing different certification areas plan and team-teach an integrated course	An art teacher, music teacher, and English teacher collaborate to plan and instruct an arts seminar, a project-based class enrolling 50–75 juniors and seniors at a time (Kist, 2005)

BENEFITS OF HUMANITIES INSTRUCTION

Advocates argue for numerous benefits of humanities instruction. Most commonly, they claim that a humanities approach helps learners make connections among ideas in ways that the fragmented separate-subject model does not (Jacobs, 1989; Sizer, 1984). According to Sandmann and Ahern (1997), "integration honors the connections students need in order to remember" (p. 26). Not only do students remember more under such conditions, but they're also better able to apply what they've learned to the world beyond school, where most problems can't be neatly classified within one traditional academic discipline or another.

Humanities-focused courses can also increase academic rigor for adolescents, including those who have traditionally been excluded from challenging instruction. One of the key findings of the Humanitas program, a thematic and team-based interdisciplinary program implemented in numerous Los Angeles high schools, is that students from a variety of profiles benefit from the opportunity to approach their learning conceptually, rather than around basic skills (Aschbacher, 1991). Similarly, Suzanne Miller and her colleagues (Cliff & Miller, 1997; Miller, 1996) found that participation in integrated literature–history classes helped high school students learn to be critical thinkers who could reflect on their own and others' values in ways central to participation in a pluralistic society.

Finally, humanities instruction offers a way to address some of the persistent criticisms of typical instruction in some of the single subjects that can be integrated underneath that umbrella. For instance, art classes in K–12 settings are sometimes critiqued for their overemphasis on art making (Anstead, 1993); humanities classes that integrate art tend to include more attention to other branches of the discipline, including aesthetics and art history. Social studies has been censured for its overreliance on textbooks that are inconsiderate of student readers (Armbruster, 1984); humanities classes usually involve students in reading a range of texts, including literature, which may spark students' interest, and visually oriented texts, which may be more accessible to struggling readers.

BEST PRACTICES IN LITERACY
FOR HUMANITIES CLASSROOMS

In this section I review a series of best practices recommendations for literacy in humanities classrooms for middle and high school students, including the following: Consider Essential Questions, read and view multiple texts, compose in multiple genres from multiple perspectives, and engage in collaborative peer talk. Some of these practices are well supported by research on adolescent literacy, whereas others, despite being commonly espoused in practical resources for and by teachers, have yet to be rigorously tested by empirical study. My own experience as a humanities teacher, fieldwork in secondary classrooms, and knowledge of the literature give me confidence that teachers who adopt this set of practices with care and reflection will likely see increases in adolescent literacy learners' engagement and achievement. In naming and describing them, though, I hope to suggest a framework for future research as much as a blueprint for future instruction.

Consider Essential Questions

Many educators associate the term Essential Question (EQ) with the Coalition of Essential Schools, the reform network to which I alluded earlier (Cushman, 1989). In my mind, however, the idea of units being driven by an overarching question or series of questions predates the 1984 founding of the coalition, hearkening back to the inquiry-focused curriculum espoused by progressives such as John Dewey and Lucy Sprague Mitchell in the 1920s and 1930s. EQs can guide discrete inquiry within disciplines, and they also can be applied to science and mathematics. Think, for instance, about how a question such as "How can linear relationships be used to make decisions?" might structure a unit in an algebra class. Many questions with the most resonance for everyday life—"What does it mean to be human?" "Whose America is it?" "Is justice blind?"— require a humanities lens to be answered fully.

According to Wiggins and McTighe (2005), EQs have the following characteristics in common:

- They cause genuine and relevant inquiry into big ideas and core content.
- They provoke deep thought, lively discussion, sustained inquiry, and new understanding as well as new questions.
- They require students to consider alternatives, weigh evidence, support their ideas, and justify their answers.
- They stimulate vital, ongoing rethinking of big ideas, assumptions, and prior lessons.
- They spark meaningful connections with prior learning and personal experiences.
- They recur naturally, creating opportunities for transfer to other situations and subjects. (p. 110)

Figure 12.1 includes a sampling of EQs from humanities-focused classes for middle and high school students.

- In what ways does art reflect, as well as shape, culture?
- How much diversity can any nation tolerate?
- To what extent do we need checks and balances on government power?
- How have American teenagers' lives changed over time?
- What constitutes a just war?
- What are the roots of prejudice?
- How is a family like a community?
- What is the price of progress?
- How does the law help us live together?
- How does South Africa's past shape its present?
- What kinds of harm can be done by fame and fortune?
- What is the best way to balance the need for resource development with protection of the environment?

FIGURE 12.1. Sample essential questions from humanities classrooms. Questions adapted from Jorgensen (1998), McKenzie (2005), and Wiggins and McTighe (2005).

New York City teachers Sue Schaller and John Wenk (1997) described the possibilities for intellectual connections and inquiry when they organized a 10th-grade humanities class around a series of EQs related to Western civilization. For example, their unit on ancient Greece focused on this question: "How did the Greeks succeed and fail in their search for *arete* (excellence)?" Although this 6-week study included reading and discussion of a number of traditional print texts, including Sophocles' *Oedipus the King*, Plato's *Apology*, and Aristotle's *Nicomachean Ethics*, it also included a range of multimodal experiences. Students toured the Metropolitan Museum of Art's collection of Greek artifacts; viewed slides of other pieces of Greek architecture; and created scenes, dances, and songs based on Edith Hamilton's *Mythology*. The carefully crafted EQ for the unit helped both teachers and students integrate this wide-ranging series of experiences and come to cross-cutting conclusions about their value.

Jorgensen (1998) has further argued that EQs are a key component in unit and lesson planning for heterogeneous classrooms, including those enrolling students with disabilities. According to her, EQs are useful because they require higher-order thinking for all students but can be answered with varying degrees of sophistication, depending on learners' skill levels and background experience. She quotes one teacher on the role such questions played in a unit she planned for an inclusive class of 10th graders:

> When I did a unit on slavery and the Civil War, we used the question "Can you be free if you aren't treated equally?" Some students in my class could answer that question using information from their Civil War reading and by thinking about the progress of civil rights in the United States. One or two students in my class had to approach this question first from their own personal perspectives. Amro knew that he was treated differently from his brothers because of his disability, and he has a strong opinion about that. If we start with his personal experience, it's a little bit easier for him to make a connection with the Civil War. (p. 78)

In terms of literacy, EQs offer a number of benefits. First, they help students set a purpose for reading before they even begin to interact with a text. Research suggests that proficient readers engage in purpose setting on their own and that these purposes help them construct and monitor their own understandings (Sweet & Snow, 2003). Too often in school, however, adolescents' purpose for reading is to get enough gist from a text to complete a low-level task such as answering factual questions. EQs that are posted in the classroom, used as prompts for journal writing, and considered again and again during text-based discussions help to keep a different kind of purpose—a longer-term and more intellectually rigorous one—front and center over an extended instructional sequence.

EQs also aid students in synthesizing information from disparate sources because they place in the foreground particular aspects of a topic, making it easier for students to determine what is important as they read and try to remember it. To enhance these skills, students might be taught to use an adapted version of the I-chart, a tool originated by Hoffman (1992) to keep track of information from reading and viewing related to an EQ. Although the empirical study of this tool has focused on its usefulness in recording data from student research, it can easily be adapted to document emerging answers to an overarching question (see Figure 12.2 for an example focused on the question "What does it mean to be human?", documenting insights from texts with connections to psychology, literature, and disability studies). These charts could be used as the springboard for student-led group discussions, wherein individuals compare their notes from each of the common sources they have read, or the charts could serve as the starting point for a more formal written essay explicitly addressing the EQ(s) for the unit.

Read and View Multiple Texts

Literary texts are among the most commonly used reading material in humanities classes. Advocates point to literature's potential to create empathy and interest for adolescents, whether the texts are plays such as *A Doll's House* in a unit on women's rights (Schaller & Wenk, 1997) or

Name: Lucy   Essential question: What does it mean to be human?

Source	Ideas related to the EQ
Article on Maslow's hierarchy of needs	• When people's deficiency needs, especially those related to the body and physical safety, are not met, it is really hard for them to focus on positive interactions with other people. • The need for belonging can cause people to treat others negatively (e.g., peer pressure).
Lord of the Flies	• When adult civilization is far away, children construct new hierarchies. • People pick on others' differences to gain power for themselves. • The need to belong can lead individuals to dehumanize others.
Viewing of *Million Dollar Baby*	• People differ in terms of the physical limitations they will tolerate. • Disabilities can be construed by others as dehumanizing.

Key words:
• Self-actualization
• Hierarchy
• Civilization
• Humanity
• Euthanasia

New questions to consider:
• How are humans and animals the same? Different?

FIGURE 12.2. Sample adapted I-chart tracking an essential question.

nonfiction trade books in a unit on the Civil War and Reconstruction (Sandmann & Ahern, 1997). In some cases, classic literary texts such as *The Odyssey* are juxtaposed with media texts such as the movie *Superman* to provide students with different vantage points on such themes as the heroic journey (Jorgensen, 1998).

In addition to literary texts, humanities classes benefit from the inclusion of a wide range of primary source material. Social studies teachers have been in the forefront of recent trends toward engaging students with primary sources such as speeches, cartoons, maps, posters, photographs, letters, and diaries. This makes sense, of course, because contemporary social studies instruction has as a primary goal that students learn to "do" history, constructing historical understandings for themselves with the raw materials of the discipline, rather than parroting received facts and truths (Stahl & Shanahan, 2004). But social studies is not the only subject area involving students in work with original documents. Art teachers such as Dawn Hartigan, one of my current students, might ask middle school learners exploring the early Expressionist movement to read excerpts from *Dear Theo* (Stone & Stone, 1995), a collection of letters from Vincent van Gogh to his brother. A high school English teacher assigning *A Tale of Two Cities* by Charles Dickens might launch her unit (as did another of my students, Nakia Gray) by organizing small-group discussions around an 18th-century engraving of a guillotine and a Romantic poem, among other sources, to enhance students' knowledge about the time period surrounding the French Revolution. These trends within single-subject classes suggest that work with primary source documents can be even more essential to integrated humanities instruction that draws on perspectives from these various disciplines.

It is important to recognize, however, that simply assigning multiple sources in humanities classes will not, by itself, lead to increases in literacy achievement. A line of research by Steven Stahl, Cynthia Hynd Shanahan, and their colleagues (Hynd, 1999; Stahl & Shanahan, 2004) suggests that adolescents are unlikely to engage in processes such as sourcing (considering who authored the text) or contextualization (considering the time period of a source) without modeling and mediation of those processes by their teacher. Being presented with multiple, even conflicting, texts on a topic—or, perhaps more powerfully, around an EQ—can create seeds of understanding that texts are constructed to represent different perspectives, some of which may be less immediately obvious than others, but deliberate instruction is likely needed for those seeds to grow.

One useful resource for humanities teachers who want to scaffold their students' interactions with multiple genres is the website of the National Archives (*www.archives.gov/education/lessons/index.html*). In addition to lesson plans tied to key epochs in American history and linked to online documents from the collection, the site includes reproducible templates to guide student analysis of eight different kinds of texts, including written documents, cartoons, sound recordings, and others. Questions from the guide for photograph analysis appear in Figure 12.3.

Compose in Multiple Genres from Multiple Perspectives

As Miller (1996) points out, humanities instruction is often about taking perspectives on complicated issues that affect various constituencies differently. One way to support adolescents' development of these habits of mind is to engage them in reading and discussion of multiple sources, as I argued in the previous section. Another way is to ask them to compose in multiple genres from multiple perspectives, sometimes by taking on personas other than their own.

1. Study the photograph for 2 minutes. Form an overall impression of the photograph and then examine individual items. Next, divide the photo into quadrants and study each section to see what new details become visible.
2. Use the chart below to make notes about the photograph:

People	Objects	Activities

3. Based on what you have observed, list three things you might infer from this photograph.

4. What questions does this photograph raise in your mind?

5. Where could you find answers to them?

FIGURE 12.3. Template for analyzing photographs from the National Archives.

Among the best-known—and from my perspective, most useful—instructional approaches to support the latter is the RAFT assignment, popularized by Carol Santa and her colleagues (Santa, Havens, & Maycumber, 1996) as part of the CRISS (creating independence through student-owned strategies) approach to content literacy. RAFT is an acronym for

R: role of the writer (who are you?)
A: audience for the writer (to whom are you writing?)
F: format of the writing (what form will your writing assume?)
T: topic to be addressed in the writing (what are you writing about?)
   (Buehl, 2001)

When teachers design a RAFT assignment—perhaps as the culminating project for a unit—they can narrow student choices within one or two categories while allowing considerable student freedom for the others. For example, when one middle school teacher collaborated with her reading specialist (Topping & McManus, 2002) to design a RAFT about Edward Jenner, the developer of the smallpox vaccine, they required all students to write on the same topic (the first successful vaccination in 1796), but offered them a choice of five roles and an even wider range of formats and audiences. The combination allowed the teachers to ensure that students had access to relevant readings while encouraging them to find their own vantage point on that material.

Topping and McManus (2002) cite choice and ownership as two elements crucial to the success of RAFT writing for students. I would add "the potential for differentiation" to their list, as the possibilities teachers generate for any of the four categories can, and should, be tailored with students' specific needs in mind. For instance, a teacher who assigns a RAFT in a unit devoted to antebellum America may steer a struggling reader to the *role* of Frederick Douglass, the former slave and abolitionist about whom much has been written at various reading levels, rather than to a figure such as George Fitzhugh, a Southern planter and apologist for slavery whose life is described in more difficult sources. Similarly, a less skilled adolescent writer might find more success with an informal *format* such as the personal letter than with the more structured newspaper editorial. Teachers can improve students' writing considerably by ensuring a range of difficulty for the items within each RAFT category and then by helping learners to make appropriate choices through whole-class planning sessions and individual conferences.

Another approach that can promote perspective taking and multigenre composition is the WebQuest, initially developed by San Diego State University professor Bernie Dodge, who defined it as a "inquiry-oriented activity in which most or all of the information used by learners is drawn from the Web" (Dodge, 2007, n.p.). Although the term *WebQuest* is sometimes used generically to refer to any activity requiring students to collect information online (including some glorified worksheets!), I see the most potential for humanities classes in WebQuests that require students to collaborate with each other in some way and that include all six of the following components Dodge recommends:

- *Introduction*, which creates student interest and provides some background knowledge
- *Task*, which describes what students will produce by the end of the experience
- *Process*, which explains how students will go about completing the task
- *Resources*, which includes links to the websites (and, in some cases, references to the print sources) that students will need to complete the task
- *Evaluation*, which explains the criteria against which performance will be measured, often in the form of a student-friendly scoring rubric
- *Conclusion*, which encourages students to reflect on their experience (and, in some cases, to consider further inquiry they might pursue on the topic)

Figure 12.4 includes a description of sample WebQuests with a humanities focus.

Title	Author	Grade Level	Subject Areas
Things Fall Apart: Understanding Context through Expert Interviews	Cherisse Jackson	High school	Social studies, English language arts
Flight to Freedom: A WebQuest about the Underground Railroad	Deborah Harmon & Toni Stokes Jones	Middle school	Social studies, art, music, English language arts
Gallery of Art-i-Facts	Peggy Walker	High school	Art, social studies, social sciences, English language arts
Searching for China	Tom March	Middle school	Social studies, English language arts
Hello Dolly: A WebQuest on Human Cloning	Keith Nuthall	High school	Science, social studies, English language arts
Egyptian Mummy Quest	Joanne Loring	Middle school	Social studies, English language arts

FIGURE 12.4. Sample WebQuests with a humanities orientation. As of this writing, all of these WebQuests could be found by searching Google using the author's name and the title.

Some WebQuests require students to compose from their own perspective in genres largely associated with school, such as a learning log or journal. My favorites, however, ask students to take on a persona and create a product with usefulness in the world outside the classroom. For example, *Weather Watch: Searching for Home Insurance*, by Katisha Von Lintel (*www.questgarden.com/46/32/5/070206083643/index.htm*), asks pairs of middle school students to imagine that they are co-owners of an insurance company who have decided to create a brochure for prospective clients on what kinds of insurance to purchase, based on the natural disasters occurring in different regions of the United States. The task requires learners to explore important content related to geography, economics, science, and language arts as they interact with Web-based information from sources such as the Federal Emergency Management Association (FEMA) and the U.S. Geological Survey. Because they must filter this information through the lens of an insurance agent, they have to analyze and synthesize it—a simple recording of the facts will not be enough to accomplish the task. Composing a brochure with the aid of computer software requires them to consider the new literacies—visual, technological, and critical—that are key in today's society (Kist, 2005), along with more traditional literacy skills, such as providing supporting details in their writing and editing their text for technical errors.

Composing from multiple perspectives and within multiple genres helps adolescents to think about how literacy varies within different discourse communities. They can practice adjusting their tone and focus to meet others' needs, and they can try out stances on issues and questions different from their own in a low-risk environment. Composing in traditional print and multimedia forms thus supports their own meaning making while it simultaneously makes their thinking available to other students and their teachers.

Engage in Collaborative Peer Talk

Successful humanities classes and programs thread various kinds of print literacy through daily activity, but they also emphasize oral language, particularly collaborative talk with peers. This pattern is evident, I think, for two reasons: (1) engaging in such talk is part of what is required by the real-world problems that the humanities can illuminate; and (2) such talk, like composing, helps students learn and reflect on new content more deeply.

One model of collaborative talk employed frequently in humanities classrooms is the dialogical discussion, sometimes in a small-group format, other times with an entire class (Cliff & Miller, 1997; Schaller & Wenk, 1997). Often focused on one or more of the EQs for a unit, discussions of this kind deliberately position the teacher as the facilitator of student talk, rather than the conduit through which the conversation must flow. These discussions encourage students to share tentative thinking, to try on alternative perspectives (however briefly), and to see themselves, in Miller's (1996) words, as participants in a "multivocal community space" (p. 26).

One specialized kind of classroom discourse that has found popularity in humanities classrooms is the Socratic seminar (Tredway, 1995). Most seminars are text-based, meaning that participants prepare for them by reviewing a common source or sources related to the unit's central focus or question. Although these texts are often print sources such as essays, poems, or articles, they do not have to be. Pieces of artwork, musical compositions, or film excerpts can also launch a rich, multilayered conversation among participants. Most Socratic seminars last between 20 and 40 minutes, though they can sometimes be sustained for longer periods. Ground rules such as the following are typically made explicit to students before beginning:

- Refer to the text(s) to make your points.
- Take turns speaking and don't interrupt each other.

- Talk to each other, not just to the teacher.
- Respect each others' perspectives, focusing on ideas instead of personalities.
- Take notes on the discussion so you can reflect on it later.
- Stay on the topic as much as possible.

In addition to text-based discussions, humanities classes also frequently require students to talk with one another as they collaborate on a culminating project. In the team-taught arts seminar researched by Kist (2005), for example, small groups of students were assigned to "create a three-dimensional abstract model of a monument commemorating a person, event, or phenomenon" (p. 33). Students used informal oral language to brainstorm three possible designs, select one of the three to build as a group, and translate their plan into a finished model. At the end of the unit, each group made a formal presentation to the class that included some background information about their subject and explained the significance of their design choices. Although Kist's data suggest that students weren't always successful in negotiating their differences or dividing labor evenly in these small groups, the projects gave them valuable communication practice nonetheless. Other kinds of projects requiring problem-solving peer talk in humanities classes include museum exhibits, mock trials, and video productions (Cliff & Miller, 1997; Jorgensen, 1998; Kist, 2005; Smith, 2000).

CONCLUSION

In focusing on these four components of effective literacy instruction within humanities classrooms, I have inevitably omitted numerous other components that are important. Because my list includes only practices in which adolescents themselves would engage, I have excluded discussion of the key role of teacher collaboration, both in planning and instruction, that both my experience and the literature (Aschbacher, 1991; Schaller & Wenk, 1997; Smith, 2000) suggest is key to success with this approach. Similarly, my decision to abstract my themes primarily from the existing humanities literature means that I have paid less attention to explicit instruction in comprehension strategies or genre conventions than adolescents in these interdisciplinary classrooms will likely need from their teachers to perform at high levels (fortunately, Chapters 7, 8, and 10, this volume, attend to those latter issues more directly than I have done here).

Despite these omissions, the practices that emerged from my analysis seem extremely promising. If more adolescents experienced instruction organized with *them* at the core, it seems likely that they would read, write, view, and talk more extensively than they currently do in school, and that they would be more invested in the ideas they construct and represent through those activities.

I make these assertions tentatively, however, as I am aware that the field has too little empirical data about the effects of most of these practices on adolescents' literacy development. A Google search, for example, with the phrase "Socratic seminar" turns up nearly 41,000 websites, with those listed first appearing to be aimed almost exclusively at practicing teachers. In contrast, the Education Resources Information Center, known more familiarly as ERIC, yields just nine hits for the same term, only one of which is data-driven. Even in those areas where more research has been conducted, such as the role of open-ended classroom discourse in learning, we know very little about how such dialogue influences other aspects of literacy learning—say, how students' ability to discuss complex ideas transfers to their writing or whether such discussion promotes better comprehension of subsequent texts on similar topics.

Consequently, I've come to believe that literacy researchers need to take an integrated stance to our work that parallels the integrated stance that humanities teachers take to curriculum development and pedagogy. We need to look carefully, with both wide and narrow lenses, at how literacy is embedded in various humanities-focused programs that integrate most or all of these components, not just one or two. And we need to listen carefully to adolescents in those programs, as well as their teachers, about how they are making sense of those practices, even when it seems that we can describe them for our own perspectives as researchers.

DISCUSSION AND ACTIVITIES

1. Choose two related concepts (e.g., diversity, tolerance) taught at your grade level in your discipline or others and frame an EQ that connects them (e.g., "How much diversity can one nation tolerate?").

2. Brainstorm a range of texts with varying degrees of complexity that students might read or view to explore that EQ from multiple perspectives (e.g., excerpts from Robert Putnam's *Bowling Alone* [2001], U.S. census data, an essay by Anne Coulter, excerpts from Alexis de Tocqueville's *Democracy in America* [1831/2003], Spike Lee's *Do the Right Thing* [1989]).

3. Brainstorm genres in which students could compose, either independently or in small groups, various answers to that EQ (e.g., position paper from political candidate, speech by community activist, training pamphlet for immigration officials, letter to the editor from a small business owner).

4. Choose one of the texts related to that EQ and frame an opening question for a Socratic seminar focused on it (e.g., "What kinds of social interactions make us more tolerant of others' differences?").

REFERENCES

Anstead, N. (1993). Hooking kids with humanities. *Educational Leadership, 51*(1), 84–86.

Armbruster, B. (1984). The problem of "inconsiderate text." In G. Duffy, L. Roehler, & J. Mason (Eds.), *Comprehension instruction: Perspectives and suggestions* (pp. 202–217). New York: Longman.

Aschbacher, P. (1991). Humanitas: A thematic curriculum. *Educational Leadership, 49*(2), 16–19.

Buehl, D. (2001). *Classroom strategies for interactive learning* (2nd ed.). Newark, DE: International Reading Association.

Cliff, C., & Miller, S. (1997). *Multicultural dialogue in literature–history classes* (Report No. 7.9). Albany, NY: National Research Center on English Learning and Achievement.

Cushman, K. (1989). Asking the essential questions: Curriculum development. *Horace.* Retrieved May 21, 2007, from *www.essentialschools.org/cs/resources/view/ces_res/137#figure1.*

de Tocqueville, A. (2003). *Democracy in America.* New York: Penguin Classics. (Original work published 1831)

Dodge, B. (2007). *The WebQuest page.* Retrieved May 21, 2007, from *www.webquest.sdsu.edu*

Hoffman, J. (1992). Critical reading/thinking across the curriculum. *Language Arts, 62*(2), 121–127.

Hynd, C. (1999). Teaching students to think critically using multiple texts in history. *Journal of Adolescent and Adult Literacy, 42*(6), 428–436.

Jacobs, H. (1989). *Interdisciplinary curriculum: Design and implementation.* Alexandria, VA: Association for Supervision and Curriculum Development.

Jorgensen, C. (1998). *Restructuring high schools for all students: Taking inclusion to the next level.* Baltimore: Brookes.

Kist, W. (2005). *New literacies in action: Teaching and learning in multiple media.* New York: Teachers College Press.

Lee, S. (Director.) (1989). *Do the right thing [film].* Los Angeles: Universal Studios.

Massachusetts Foundation for the Humanities. (2007). *What are the humanities?* Retrieved May 21, 2007, from *www.mfh.org/foundation/human.htm*

McKenzie, J. (2005). *Learning to question to wonder to learn.* Seattle: FNO Press.

Miller, S. (1996). *Making the paths: Constructing multicultural texts and critical narrative discourse in literature–history classes* (Report No. 7.8). Albany, NY: National Research Center on English Learning and Achievement.

National Endowment for the Humanities. (2007). *Who we are.* Retrieved May 21, 2007, from *www.neh.gov/whoweare/overview.html*

Putnam, R. D. (2001). *Bowling alone: The collapse and revival of American community.* New York: Simon & Schuster.

Sandmann, A., & Ahern, J. (1997). Using literature to study the Civil War and Reconstruction. *Middle School Journal, 99*(8), 25–33.

Santa, C., Havens, L., & Maycumber, E. (1996). *Project CRISS: Creating independence through student-owned strategies* (2nd ed.). Dubuque, IA: Kendall Hunt.

Schaller, S., & Wenk, J. (1997). A humanities class for the twenty-first century. *English Journal, 86*(7), 75–78.

Sizer, T. (1984). *Horace's compromise: The dilemma of the American high school.* Boston: Houghton Mifflin.

Sizer, T. (1992). *Horace's school: Redesigning the American high school.* Boston: Houghton Mifflin.

Smith, H. (2000). A world of ideas: Creating an interdisciplinary museum of history. *Middle School Journal, 31*(4), 5–12,

Stahl, S., & Shanahan, C. (2004). Learning to think like a historian: Disciplinary knowledge through critical analysis of multiple documents. In T. Jetton & J. Dole (Eds.), *Adolescent literacy research and practice* (pp. 94–115). New York: Guilford Press.

Stone, I., & Stone, J. (1995). *Dear Theo: The autobiography of Vincent Van Gogh.* New York: Plume.

Sweet, A., & Snow, C. (2003). *Rethinking reading comprehension.* New York: Guilford Press.

Topping, D., & McManus, R. (2002). *Real reading, real writing: Content-area strategies.* Portsmouth, NH: Heinemann.

Tredway, L. (1995). Socratic seminars: Engaging students in intellectual discourse. *Educational Leadership, 53*(1), 26–29.

Wiggins, G., & McTighe, J. (2005). *Understanding by design* (2nd ed.). Alexandria, VA: Association for Supervision and Curriculum Development.

Wineburg, S., & Grossman, P. (2000). *Interdisciplinary curriculum: Challenges to implementation.* New York: Teachers College Press.

CHAPTER 13

Fostering Acquisition of Official Mathematics Language

Codruta Temple
Kathleen A. Hinchman

STUDENT: Miss, do I have to explain all that?

TEACHER: You sure do! What did you start with? Start with that.

STUDENT: I doubled one dimension.

TEACHER: OK, what dimension did you double?

STUDENT: This one right here. And I increased the other dimension by 7.

TEACHER: So what'd you get for the expanded form?

STUDENT: x squared plus x squared plus $7x$ plus $7x$.

TEACHER: Is there someone who had a different answer for that? Michael, what did you have?

STUDENT: I got $2x$ squared plus $14x$.

TEACHER: All right . . . Michael, what did you do different than Charlene?

STUDENT: I collected the like terms.

The purpose of our chapter is to explain best practice for fostering mathematics literacy. It includes:

- Background explanation of research on literacy development in mathematics class, ending with explanation of why helping students develop official mathematics language is best practice.

- Additional principles of classroom practice, drawing on snippets of observations in one teacher's classroom to illustrate our points.

- Implications for mathematics instruction and points for discussion.

We share this snippet from a much longer interchange in an eighth-grade urban mathematics classroom because we think it is notable in several ways. First, the students, not the teacher, are explaining various ways they solved a problem. Second, all seem to assume that there is more than one way to solve this problem. Third, the students seem not only willing to explain their solutions to a whole class, but also to accept the teacher's help with technical vocabulary and syntax to yield more precise explanations.

WHAT THE RESEARCH SAYS ABOUT LITERACY DEVELOPMENT IN MATHEMATICS CLASS

Supporting Reading in Mathematics Class

With the advent of Herber's (1970) *Teaching Reading in Content Areas*, many recommendations encouraged subject-area teachers to support students' reading development with research-based before-, during-, and after-reading activities, such as anticipation guides, graphic organizers, and various kinds of study guides. Such activities structure students' textbook reading, with a focus on building prior knowledge, on drawing inferences, attending to text structure, and developing technical vocabulary. Growing out of burgeoning cognitive theory of the 1960s and 1970s, the approach provided teachers with easy-to-implement tools to support students' reading of subject-area materials. Tools for speaking, listening, and writing were later added to the repertoire, and *content-area reading* was extended to the term *content-area literacy*.

Even as preservice and inservice requirements for learning such methods of teaching multiplied, so too did research explaining why most teachers did not use them. Assessment-driven curriculum was thought best explained through lecture–discussion, with textbooks reduced to a backup role. Support for reading—textbooks or other primary sources—was thought to divert needed attention from explaining content (O'Brien, Stewart, & Moje, 1995). Secondary school mathematics classes typically concentrated only on the syntax of the numerical symbol system, limiting literacy work to vocabulary and word problem support. Indeed, the 1980s yielded mathematics textbooks with brief written explanations and many sample solutions and problem sets (Ernest, 1987).

Conceptualizing Mathematics Discourse

At the same time, researchers were developing a more complex argument regarding the need to know mathematics discourse as grounding for mathematics knowledge. At the 1974 UNESCO Symposium on Linguistics and Mathematics Education, Halliday introduced the notion of *mathematical register*. He defined it as "a set of meanings that is appropriate to a particular function of language, together with the words and structures which express these meanings" (cited in Pimm, 1987, p. 75) for social purposes. Pimm (1987) described this register as including specialized terms—everyday words with specialized meanings (e.g., *any* to mean *every*), specialized expressions (e.g., "if and only if"), and sentence constructions less common in everyday speech.

With research into sociocultural aspects of education and discourse, mathematics came to be seen as social practice carried out in different social contexts (National Council of Teachers of Mathematics, 1998). Steinbring (1998) explained that this social practice involved discipline-specific mathematics discourse constituted by social conventions and socially shared understandings that remained "invariant over different social practices" (p. 116). Halliday and Martin (1993) suggested a similar idea when they described science language as varying across practices while being "by and large . . . a recognizable category, [which] any speaker of English for whom it falls within the domain of experience knows . . . when he sees it or hears it" (p. 54).

Rittenhouse (1998) identified three communities of practice, each with its own distinct mathematics discourse: the theoretical mathematics discourse community, the applied mathematics discourse community, and the school mathematics discourse community. The major characteristic of the school mathematics community is its heavy emphasis on getting a "right answer" and on algorithms as basic tools for deriving this answer. By contrast, the discourse needed to understand theoretical and applied mathematics derives its specificity from the norms that govern language use in constructing arguments and mathematical proofs. Rittenhouse suggested that students would more likely develop this discourse knowledge if school mathematics extended beyond providing students with algorithms toward helping them "to understand how to talk, think, and act mathematically in different contexts" (p. 165), so that they could participate in each of the three mathematics discourse communities.

Bringing Mathematics Discourse to School

To help us to understand how to bring theoretical or applied mathematics discourse into school mathematics instruction, van Oers (2002) distinguished between mathematical activities and mathematical practices. He saw *activities* simply as ways of dealing with quantitative and spatial relationships of the physical environment in general. In his view, only activities that followed the values, rules, and tools specific to the mathematical community could be called mathematical practices. Mathematical *practices* contain "performative actions" with mathematical meaning and "conversational actions" that are instances of communication about mathematics. To be recognized as mathematical, conversational actions need to conform to rules of mathematics discourse, a speech genre developed for communicating in the mathematical community of practice. The "real" mathematics of theoretical and applied discourse communities can be accomplished when "one legitimately participates in a mathematical practice, either by acting mathematically in an acceptable way, or by discussing mathematical or discursive mathematical actions" (van Oers, 2002, p. 71).

Sfard (2001) suggested that mathematics discourse is one identifiable form of communication whose distinct identity is due to the presence of mediating tools and metadiscursive rules. Mediating tools are primarily linguistic but, in mathematics, also include numerical notation, graphs, tables, and algebraic formulas in addition to language. Such tools are "the shapers of the content" (p. 28). Metadiscursive rules guide the general course of mathematical communication, according to which particular interactions are deemed appropriate in a mathematical context. That is, mathematics discourse is derived from a distinct set of metarules that regulate the way in which symbolic tools should be used in mathematical communication or in the construction of mathematical genres, such as defining or proving.

Learning mathematics discourse means learning the norms and rules of language use in mathematical contexts. Thus best practice begins with developing students' ability to read mathematics texts in the manner of earlier content-area reading instruction—but does not stop here. Instead, best practice also involves fostering students' understanding of the rules and norms of mathematics discourse, and the ability to produce and respond to such discourse within appropriate social contexts.

PRINCIPLES TO HELP STUDENTS LEARN OFFICIAL MATHEMATICS LANGUAGE

Our recent work as part of an National Science Foundation (NSF) sponsored collaborative project on mathematics literacy (Temple, Hinchman, Chandler-Olcott, Doerr, & Masingila, 2007) involved us in developing a framework, building on work by Herbel-Eisenmann (2002), that captured classroom mathematics discourse as using three registers: everyday language, official mathematics language, and bridging language. For us, everyday language is the spoken language register of everyday interactions, using nontechnical words and references to the immediate context in which the text is produced. Official mathematics language is the more abstract, written language register of the discipline of mathematics, easily recognized by its high concentration of technical vocabulary and the absence of references to context outside the text.

Bridging language capitalizes on technical vocabulary but borrows characteristics from everyday language. As such, bridging language can assist students in negotiating the meaning of texts in official mathematics language, as well as in gradually transitioning from using everyday language to official mathematics language—even though students' everyday language varies widely with background and academic experience. The instructional snippet with which we began our chapter was an example of students' use of bridging language in the classroom of a teacher who participated in our NSF project.

I (C. T.) recently spent a year gathering data in a 10th-grade Romanian mathematics classroom with a teacher whose practices also encouraged students' acquisition of bridging language, and, eventually, official mathematics language. We share this teacher's presentation of one concept in the following sections, and we segment one instructional sequence to point out principles for teaching discipline-specific discourse that can be derived from her classroom orchestrations.

Invite Students to Figure Out and Describe Concepts in Everyday Language

In the first part of this lesson, the students discussed the new concept (the slope of a line) starting from the word *slope*, which they said meant "inclination" or "steepness." Ariadna, the teacher, drew an oblique line on the board that intersected the *x*-axis of a system of Cartesian coordinates and asked the students to hypothesize how they might find the steepness of the line. In the conversation that followed, a student suggested drawing a triangle and finding the tangent of the angle formed by the line and the *x*-axis. Starting from her suggestion, the class eventually produced a definition of the slope: "the tangent of the angle formed by a line and the *x*-axis, positive direction." They continued to discuss the slopes of lines that were parallel to or perpendicular on the *x*-axis. In the episode below, Ariadna wanted to take students one step further and have them use the new concept to find, and then to define, the slope of a line determined by two points. She framed this as a problem for students to solve and then, like our chapter's introductory example, to explain their solution to the class. Figure 13.1 presents the classroom transcript of this process.

One thing that is remarkable about this episode is the sparseness of directions for how the students should go about solving problems. In this particular instance, Ariadna instructs them to "think" and be ready to share ideas. She does not tell them whether they should write or draw, or whether they should work individually or otherwise. Students seem to have different preferences and are free to pursue them. Ariadna ignores side-talk, as if it were a natural ingredient of the practice of problem solving.

Misha's explanation of his solution stops the side-talk. It is less than clear, so Ariadna adds information before she evaluates it as a possible variant for solving the problem. Raul volunteers a different solution and explains it clearly enough for Ariadna to be able to point out its fallacy,

ARIADNA: I have two points, A, of coordinates x_1 and y_1, and B, of coordinates x_2 and y_2. I would like you to determine the slope of line AB using the coordinates of the points. . . . Please think and let's see what ideas you have for determining the slope.

(*Students start talking among themselves, some in pairs, some in spontaneously formed small groups—they turn around to face the people sitting behind them. Some move their chairs to join a group at a different table. Some are writing in their notebooks, alone. Cristina is having a heated argument with Ovid. At one of the front tables, Dean and Raul are laughing heartily. June and Carmela are laughing, too, while drawing lines and angles in the air. There's much noise but they are all working on the problem. I hear Chip say to Ada, "And there goes my axiom, right down the drain." Nobody volunteers for about 5 minutes. Ariadna waits in silence.*)

MISHA (*over the noise*): If we take the projection of B on the x-axis, and we take the projection of A on the x-axis, we get two small triangles, and the slope would be the tangent of the angle between the line and the x-axis.

ARIADNA: You want to construct a parallel to AB through this projection point. It's a variant. Yes, Raul, how did you do it?

RAUL: I prolonged the line to make it intersect the x-axis and . . . we need the coordinates of the point of intersection.

ARIADNA: But do you know . . . ? I don't know what coordinates the point of intersection has.

RAUL: And y . . . and then the tangent is $y_2 - y$ over $x_2 - x$.

ARIADNA: Well, yes, except that you are introducing an x and a y in the formula that I don't need, because I want the slope to be only a function of the coordinates of A and B.

IOLANDA: If I write $y_B - y_A$ over $x_B - x_A$ . . .

ARIADNA: I know where you want to get, but I'm asking you, how do you get there? You're perfectly right, Iolanda, but what did you do to get there?

IOLANDA: I drew a parallel to the x-axis through B, I got similar triangles, corresponding angles . . . and then the angle is the same and I can write the tangent.

ARIADNA: I got you. But I want to see what Laurel understood. He will dictate the solution and I will write it on the board.

LAUREL: We draw a parallel and we will have similar triangles.

ARIADNA: So, we construct a parallel to the x-axis . . .

(*As Laurel begins his explanation, Ariadna starts drawing and writing on the board, converting his words into symbolic language. Several other students join in the explanation.*)

ARIADNA: This means that the slope of a line determined by the points of coordinates (x_1, y_1), (x_2, y_2) will be . . . ?

MARIA: The slope of a line determined by the points of coordinates x_1, y_1, x_2, y_2 will be $y_2 - y_1$ over $x_2 - x_1$.

Classroom transcript and field notes, March 2, 2006.

FIGURE 13.1. Genres. Definition and explanation.

namely, that it requires information not given in the problem. Iolanda proposes a third solution and, prompted by Ariadna's questions, she explains how she derived it.

Up to this point, Ariadna has allowed the class to explore the problem, construct hypotheses, and test them in one-on-one dialogues with her students. In these short dialogues, she expanded students' explanations, pointed out fallacies in solutions, and pushed them to provide more information, as if to clarify their thinking. What she did not do was ask them to use more precise language, although her remark ("I got you. But I want to see what Laurel understood") suggests that she was aware of the fact that the students' explanations were probably not clear enough for some of the other students. The principle here is that an important instructional move for helping students acquire official mathematics language involves inviting them to figure out the concept in question, using everyday language to describe what they have learned.

Model Use of Official Mathematics Language for More Precise Concept Descriptions

Once Iolanda has shared her solution, which Ariadna acknowledges as valid, the exploration of the problem ends and the focus of the activity shifts to constructing a clearer explanation of the steps used and of the reasoning behind them. Laurel, joined by other students, gives the explanation, and Ariadna converts their sentences into symbolic language on the board. Meanwhile, she assists them in expressing their ideas by rephrasing and completing them so that they are more precise (Laurel: "We draw a parallel and we will have similar triangles." Ariadna: "So, we construct a parallel to the x axis"), and by asking questions in words that students can use as models (Ariadna: "This means that the slope of a line determined by the points of coordinates x_1, y_1, x_2, y_2 will be . . . ?" Maria: "The slope of a line determined by the points of coordinates x_1, y_1, x_2, y_2 will be y_2 minus y_1 over x_2 minus x_1").

Maria's sentence is at once the solution to the problem and definition of a new concept (slope of a line determined by two points), demonstrating that the solving of the problem actually consisted of constructing a proof to demonstrate that the relationship expressed in the definition was true. Once the proof is constructed and the definition elicited and recorded on the board in symbolic language—$m_{AB} = \text{tg}BAC = BC/CA = (y_2 - y_1)/(x_2 - x_1)$—the students do a practice problem and are assigned four more practice problems for homework.

The principle here is that a teacher can shape her students' explanations with more precise bridging language—without hurting their feelings. Ariadna did not devalue students' explanations in anyway. Yet she also did not let them rest with unclear explanations. Instead, she shaped their language, introducing them to alternative word selection for greater precision.

Invite Students to Use Key Technical Terms to Express Concepts

At the beginning of the next lesson, Ariadna has the class return to the definition and embed it in a written 10-line summary of the lesson on slope. Her purpose is to see what they did, or did not, understand from the lesson. The task, however, serves the additional purpose of inviting students to integrate all the information they now have about the concept. To scaffold the task, Ariadna asks the class to use a list of words, which she writes on the board, to compose their summaries: *slope, number, xy plane, value, two points, the difference of the ordinates, the difference of the abscissas, ratio, increasing oblique line, decreasing oblique line, horizontal line, vertical line.*

Except for the new concept, "slope," all the other terms were part of students' mathematical vocabularies, and most of them had been used in previous lessons. Some had not, and the definition of *slope of a line determined by two points* had last been given by Maria: "The slope of a line determined by the points of coordinates x_1, y_1, x_2, y_2 will be y_2 minus y_1 over x_2 minus x_1." Ariadna's including the terms "ratio," "the difference of the abscissas," and "the difference of the ordinates" on her list of terms to be used pushed the students to rephrase Maria's definition in more general terms, which, as shown in Figure 13.3, many of them succeeded in doing.

When students finished writing and submitting their papers, Ariadna asked, "Who would like to try to formulate a text, remembering what they wrote in their paper, that includes all the words on the board?" Figure 13.2 is an excerpt of the dialogue that ensued.

Just like the written assignment, this sharing episode gave students the opportunity to practice explaining the concept of slope using the terminology of mathematics. As Misha's self-corrections demonstrate, integrating the mathematical terms in sentences was not an easy task, so Ariadna provided assistance. Instead of resorting to direct correction or negative feedback, she used communication strategies that resembled the ones native speakers of a language use when interacting with non-native speakers, or that parents use when assisting language acquisition in young children. For instance, she echoed students' statements as questions, expecting self-correction (Theo: "The slope is the angle . . . " Ariadna: "The slope is the angle?"); she recast parts of their sentences using mathematical terminology (when Theo uses the phrase "direction plus," Ariadna recasts it as "positive direction"); she relied on other "non-native speakers" to clarify the message (Maria and Alex); and she invited stu-

RADA: I said that the slope of a line represented the tangent of the angle formed by a line and the abscissa of the system in which the line is situated . . . and that the line is in the *xy* plane.

THEO: The slope is the angle made by the line and the *x*-axis, direction plus.

ARIADNA: The slope is the angle?

STUDENT: The tangent.

ARIADNA: The tangent of the angle, be careful! So, the slope is the tangent of the angle made by the line and the *x*-axis, positive direction.

DEAN: I said that the tangent was determined by the angle.

ARIADNA: It's OK if you said that it was determined by the angle and then said that it was the tangent of the angle. What else . . . ?

MISHA: The value of the slope of a line in an *xy* plane, which passes through two points, equals the difference . . . the ratio between the difference of the abscissas and . . .

MARIA: The other way around! Of the ordinates.

ALEX: Of the ordinates and of the abscissas.

MISHA: Of the ordinates and of the abscissas.

ARIADNA: And then?

Classroom transcript and field notes, March 3, 2006.

FIGURE 13.2. Student oral explanation.

dents to produce more language through questions that contained continuatives ("What else . . . ?" "And then . . . ?").

Not surprisingly, writing explanations proved to be more challenging for some students than for others. Of the 18 students who were in class that day, 10 succeeded in using eight or more of the terms correctly in their writing, and 7 students were able to use six or seven terms correctly. One student, who had been absent from the previous class and had presumably studied the lesson from the textbook (she included a drawing that appeared in the textbook and which had not been used in class), used several terms in her written summary but showed a lack of understanding of the relationships among the terms. Her summary (Sample 1) and three other samples of student writing are presented in Figure 13.3. to illustrate the students' range of success on the writing assignment. They were ranked by the teacher as low, medium, medium-high, and high based on the number of terms used correctly from a mathematical point of view.

Trying to use all the key words forced the students to make their definitions even more general and more syntactically elaborate—a rather challenging task, at which the students were differentially successful, with the high achievers succeeding, nevertheless, in integrating all the terms. Compared to Iolanda's definition, the definition in Sample 4 of Figure

13.3 ("The slope of a line that crosses two points on an *xy* plane equals the value of the ratio between the difference of the ordinates and the difference of the abscissas of the two points") shows not only better understanding of the concept, but also more fluency in using the mathematical register—both of which are likely to have developed concurrently during the multiple opportunities the students had to explain the concept.

Besides providing repeated opportunities for students to operate with the new concept and assisting them in talking about it with increasing precision, one other instructional move that Ariadna made is worth

Sample 1. (low) Although I was absent from the last math class, I know that the title of the last lesson was the slope of the line. In an *xy* plane the slope of the line is the angle formed by a line and an angle. The value that this slope takes is the ratio between the difference of the ordinates and the difference of the abscissas. To be able to realize the slope of the line, we need two points (the projections of the tips of the angle).

Sample 2. (medium) The slope is the steepness of the line that crosses an *xy* plane. It has a value equal to the ratio between the difference of the ordinates and the difference of the abscissas of the two points that it crosses. If the line is an increasing oblique line, then the value of the slope is a positive number; if it is a decreasing oblique line, then the slope has a negative number as its value. If the line is vertical, then the value of the slope is 0. The value of the slope is calculated using the function of the tangent of the angle formed by the line with the *x*-axis, positive direction.

Sample 3. (medium-high) In our last lesson we studied the slope of a line. We represented two points on an *xy* plane, thus determining a line. The slope of the respective line is the tangent of the angle formed by the line with the *x*-axis if the line intersects the *x*-axis. If it doesn't, we draw a horizontal line parallel to the *x*-axis through the first point, and a vertical line parallel to the *y*-axis, through the second point. If the line is an increasing oblique line, the angle will be acute, and if the line is a decreasing oblique line, the angle will be obtuse. To find the value of the slope, we tried to determine the tangent of the angle formed. This was equal to the ratio between the difference of the ordinates and the difference of the abscissas, and the result was a number that gave us the value of the slope.

Sample 4. (high) The slope of a line that crosses two points on an *xy* plane equals the value of the ratio between the difference of the ordinates and the difference of the abscissas of the two points. If the line is horizontal (parallel to the *x*-axis), then the slope equals 0. If it is vertical, then the slope cannot be defined (as the angle between the line and the *x*-axis has 90 degrees). If the line is an increasing oblique line, then the value of the slope is a positive number, and if it is a decreasing oblique line, then the value of the slope is a negative number. By definition, the value of the slope is equal to the tangent of the angle between the line and the *x*-axis, positive direction.

Student artifacts, March 3, 2006.

FIGURE 13.3. Student written explanations.

special attention: her scaffolding of the writing task. Contrary to the widespread belief that understanding mathematical concepts is manifested through knowledge of the technical terms that name the concepts, Ariadna's writing task seems to suggest that such understanding involves primarily the ability to express relationships among technical terms. The task does not require students to recall vocabulary items in isolation; instead, the key terms needed to explain the concept of slope are given to them, and the challenge is for students to relate the terms to one another by using them in sentences.

A similar view of the meaning of scientific terms was theorized by Lemke (1990). According to Lemke, just as a concept does not stand by itself but is always part of a conceptual system, the word that stands for the concept does not have meaning by itself; rather, it derives its meaning from the ways in which it is related to other words that stand for other concepts. Lemke calls such words "thematic items," and he calls the connections among their meanings in a particular discipline a "thematic pattern." Further, he argues that teaching disciplinary content is teaching students how to use language to construct thematic patterns to express the conceptual system of the discipline. A teacher can build bridges to the mathematics conceptual system by inviting students to express evolving understanding of key concepts and to use technical vocabulary to do so.

Provide Feedback to Foster
Official Mathematics Language Acquisition

Ariadna attempted to share additional insights with her students in the feedback that she gave them after reading their explanations. She began by emphasizing the fact that the slope of a line was not a line and not an angle, which were two conceptual confusions that had surfaced in some papers. After having the class briefly review and clarify the definition, she directed the students' attention to the precision of their written expression (see Figure 13.4).

The two phrases that some of the students had used inappropriately in their papers, "ratio between" and "positive angle," gave Ariadna the opportunity to teach a mini-lesson in mathematical literacy. Besides clarifying the meaning of the terms, she illustrated how the same technical terms had different meanings in different syntactic structures, and she emphasized the need for precision in using mathematical terminology lest the meanings made should be different from the ones intended. Her reference to the "reader who knows mathematics" also suggested that mathematical texts are read somewhat differently from other texts, in that a reader's success in making sense of them depends critically on technical terminology being used accurately.

Ariadna: Another observation: When you write "The slope is the ratio between the difference of the ordinates and the difference of the abscissas" from the point of view of a reader who knows mathematics, that means that the numerator is the difference of the ordinates and the denominator is the difference of the abscissas. That's what "the ratio between" means. If you write, "the slope is the ratio between the difference of the abscissas and the difference of the ordinates," then you are obviously saying quite the opposite. . . . "Positive angle," somebody said. "For any line, we take the positive angle." We talked about the angle between the line and the *x*-axis, positive direction. There are such things as positive angles, but we haven't studied them. They are oriented angles. So, if I go this way (*draws an angle and an arrow on the board*), it will be a positive angle, and if I go this way, it will be a negative angle.

Classroom transcript, March 9, 2006.

FIGURE 13.4. Feedback to writing (I).

Having discussed the need for precision in combining technical terms, Ariadna went on to give students feedback on the structure of their texts (see Figure 13.5). This part of the feedback was meant to raise students' awareness of three features that a text in the genre of mathematical explanation should have. One is that the explanation of a concept should begin with a definition of the concept. Another is that it should be complete, including all the information needed to fully understand the concept. The third is that the explanation should be coherent, that is, organized in a way that shows logical connections between the concept being explained and other related concepts—mirroring the internal logic of the larger conceptual system.

Such expression could also be facilitated by inviting students to read and compare others' explanations of the construct, including those found in textbooks, and to discuss strengths and weaknesses among explanations. The principle here is that a teacher can provide feedback to stu-

Ariadna: As for the construction. . . . Those of you who tried to include all the phrases that I gave you succeeded in constructing a fairly coherent text, in the sense that you started with a definition, [you said] that the slope was . . ., after which, since you had the phrase "the *xy* plane" there, you tried to place the line on a plane. When you saw "value," "the difference of the ordinates," "the difference of the abscissas," and "ratio," all of these made you think of the expression of the slope when we know two points that the line crosses, and then, of the slope of an increasing and decreasing oblique line, of a horizontal and vertical line.

Classroom transcript, March 9, 2006.

FIGURE 13.5. Feedback to writing (II).

dents to help them refine their wording of conceptualizations even further—again, without hurting their feelings. He or she can do this in such forms as written notes, conferences, or class mini-lessons, helping students clarify use of terms, explaining how usage varies by context, and supporting students as they learn in more detail about expectations for mathematical genres. In doing so, she issues invitations to the greater mathematicians' discourse community with her requests to make distinctions for "the reader who knows mathematics."

Invite Students to Use Official Mathematics Language in Formal Explanations

At the beginning of the third lesson in the unit, the students had the opportunity to incorporate some of the ideas contained in Ariadna's feedback in another written assignment. This time their task was to define the concept of slope and to construct a problem based on their definition. Figure 13.6 shows four samples of student writing.

What is remarkable about the definitions students produced for this assignment is that they are all accurate, even though, as the differences in wording and notation among them show, they have not been memorized. The students' ability to define the concept in their own words and to con-

Sample 1. The slope of a line is the tangent of the angle formed by the line and the x-axis, positive direction, $m = ([y_2 - y_1])/([x_2 - x_1])$. Problem: Given the points A(-4, 3) and B(2, 4), calculate the slope of the line that crosses the two points.

Sample 2. The slope of a line situated on a plane that has an xy system is equal to the tangent of the angle formed by the line and the x-axis in its positive direction. Problem: Points A and B belong to line d. Knowing that the coordinates of A(1, 3) and B(2, 4), find the slope of line d.

Sample 3. The slope of a line is the tangent of the angle formed by the line with the x-axis (positive direction). As a line is determined by two points, $P_1(x_1, y_1)$, $P_2(x_2, y_2)$, we can write the slope (m) as $(y_2 - y_1)/(x_2 - x_1)$ the difference of the ordinates/ the difference of the abscissas. Problem: Find the slope of a line knowing that the points A(2, 3) and B(5, 9) belong to this line.

Sample 4. The slope of a line is equal to the value of the tangent of the angle formed by the respective line and the x-axis, positive direction. The formula of the slope: $m = (y_2 - y_1)/(x_2 - x_1)$. Problem: A line intersects the y-axis in point A(0, 20). Find the area of the triangle formed by this line, the y-axis, and the line that forms an angle of 75 degrees with the x-axis. Find the slope of the line that divides the triangle into two similar triangles and intersects two of its sides in their middle.

Student artifacts, March 9, 2006.

FIGURE 13.6. Student definitions and problems.

struct problems based on their definitions suggests that they have understood the concept thoroughly.

If the first steps of this instructional sequence were meant to help students move from concrete examples and particular situations toward increasingly elaborate generalizations of the concept, the intent of the last step was to invite students to make the journey back, from the general concept to a particular problem situation. The principle here is to ask students to use all the teacher's explanations and feedback in applying their knowledge of the mathematics concept and genres to compose formal definitions and to generate new problems. Such a step serves to close the loop between the particular and the general, and in this case, the concrete and the abstract expressions of the key concept.

CONCLUSIONS

To help students learn the rules and norms of mathematics discourse, and to acquire the ability to produce and respond to such discourse, Ariadna asked students to attend to the structure of language from a variety of stances as they came to understand the key mathematics concept. First, she invited students to understand the key concept and to use everyday language to describe it. She helped them with their initial explanations by introducing bridging language to describe the construct with increased precision. Next, she invited students to use technical vocabulary in writing, and then, orally, to describe the concept, providing feedback to explain the conventions of the mathematical register and genres. Finally, she asked students to produce formal definitions and to draft problems of their own, applying knowledge of the two mathematical genres to develop abstract generalizations and concrete applications.

Ariadna's steps echo what we know about supporting processes of language acquisition more generally (Cambourne, 1995). Cambourne emphasized that students' willingness to engage is key—which brings us to another principle of Ariadna's teaching: Students are more likely to engage with the learning of subject-specific discourses when they feel safe about the risks they need to take. Even as Ariadna respected students' contributions, she shaped and refined them, explaining registers and genres of official mathematics language along the way, and helping everyone to communicate with the precision needed for "the reader who knows mathematics."

Research on subject-specific discourse acquisition suggests that best practice in mathematics literacy means finding ways to assist students in becoming members of the discourse community of mathematicians, that is, speakers of official mathematics language. In this view, simply asking students to read, write, speak, and listen as they engage in problem-based teaching, as is common in much current mathematics instruction, is not sufficient to develop needed mathematics discourse. Similarly, content-area literacy strategies that help students build on prior knowledge, draw inferences, attend to text structure, learn technical vocabulary, or write to learn offer necessary but not sufficient exposure for gaining entrée to this discourse community. A teacher must also demonstrate and explain discourse community expectations, as well as provide responsive support to students' attempts to participate in any subject-area community to which they aspire.

DISCUSSION AND ACTIVITIES

1. Recognizing that the key principle involves providing students with supported entrée into the mathematics discourse community, consider alternatives to Ariadna's instructional cycle. For instance, how could students work together to analyze various written explanations to discern features of official mathematics language descriptions of key concepts?

2. Work with other mathematics teachers to identify key concepts and plan instructional sequences that echo Ariadna's efforts to teach students official mathematics language to describe key concepts for "the reader who knows mathematics."

3. Consider the registers and genres required by the official languages of other disciplines and design instructional sequences that show students how to shape their language for use in these discourse communities.

4. Invite local mathematicians, engineers, biologists, chemists, historians, or other professionals to share primary source documents from their respective disciplines with students. Invite students to compare and contrast features of the language used in such documents, and to discuss connections between this language and their academic studies.

REFERENCES

Cambourne, B. (1995). Towards an educationally relevant theory of literacy learning: Twenty years of inquiry. *The Reading Teacher, 49*(3), 182–192.

Ernest, P. (1987). A model of the cognitive meaning of mathematical expressions. *Journal of Educational Psychology, 57*, 343–370.

Halliday, M. A. K., & Martin, J. R. (Eds.). (1993). *Writing science. Literacy and discursive power.* Pennsylvania: University of Pittsburgh Press.

Herbel-Eisenmann, B. A. (2002). Using student contributions and multiple representations to develop mathematical language. *Mathematics Teaching in the Middle School, 8*(2), 100–105.

Herber, H. (1970). *Teaching reading in content areas.* Englewood Cliffs, NJ: Prentice Hall.

Lemke, J. (1990). *Talking science: Language, learning, and values.* Norwood, NJ: Ablex.

National Council of Teachers of Mathematics. (1989). *Curriculum and evaluation standards for school mathematics.* Reston, VA: Author.

O'Brien, D. G., Stewart, R. A., & Moje, E. B. (1995). Why content literacy is difficult to infuse into the secondary school: Complexities of curriculum, pedagogy, and school culture. *Reading Research Quarterly, 30,* 442–463.

Pimm, D. (1987). *Speaking mathematically: Communication in mathematics classrooms.* London: Routledge.

Rittenhouse, P. S. (1998). The teacher's role in mathematical conversation: Stepping in and stepping out. In M. Lampert & M. L. Blunk (Eds.), *Talking mathematics in school: Studies of teaching and learning* (pp. 163–189). Cambridge, UK: Cambridge University Press.

Sfard, A. (2001). There is more to discourse than meets the ears: Looking at thinking as communicating to learn more about mathematical learning. *Educational Studies in Mathematics, 46,* 13–57.

Steinbring, H. (1998). From "Stoffdidaktik" to social interactionism: An evolution of approaches to the study of language and communication in German mathematics education research. In H. Steinbring, M. G. Bartolini Bussi, & A. Sierpinska (Eds.), *Language and communication in the mathematics classroom* (pp. 102–119). Reston, VA: National Council of Teachers of Mathematics.

Temple, C., Hinchman, K. A., Chandler-Olcott, K., Doerr, H. M., & Masingila, J. O. (2007, April). Mathematical communication in reform-based teaching: Understanding register in varied classroom tasks. In J. Masingila (Chair), *Supporting literacies in reform-based mathematics.* Symposium presented at the annual meeting of the American Educational Research Association, Chicago.

van Oers, B. (2002). Educational forms of initiation in mathematical culture. In C. Kieran, E. Forman, & A. Sfard (Eds.), *Learning discourse: Discursive approaches to research in mathematics education* (pp. 59–85). Dordrecht, The Netherlands: Kluwer Academic.

PART III

Adolescent Literacy Program Issues

CHAPTER 14

Intervening When Older Youth Struggle with Reading

Gay Ivey

This chapter:

- Considers the critical need for high-quality interventions for older inexperienced readers.
- Takes a critical look at existing popular interventions.
- Establishes criteria for designing interventions that make sense.

I recently met a young man who had quit school at age 16. Now at age 21, he needs to pass a skills test at work for a job promotion. Unfortunately, he does not read well enough to make sense of the test, but now, unlike in high school, he is motivated to learn. He recalls that he dropped out mentally in middle school and then officially when he got his driver's license in 10th grade. He remembers sitting quietly on the fringes of the classroom, and because he did not disrupt instruction, his teachers left him alone. My assessments of his literacy helped me to understand his indifference toward school. He was uncomfortable reading first-grade-level materials, and there were few words he could spell accurately. Participation in the activity of the classroom really was not an option for him.

There is no shortage of national reports indicating the large numbers of students in middle and high school classrooms who are still experiencing difficulty with reading and writing. These reports are easily corroborated by school visits and discussions with teachers who work closely with low-achieving students. When speaking to groups of secondary teachers in any given area, I often ask the question, "How many of you teach students who you believe read below a third-grade level?" Inevitably, hands shoot up all around the room, along with audible sighs. Teachers who work with older struggling readers feel deeply for their students. For those of us who learned to read early, it is difficult to imagine what it is like to have lived for 15 years or more without the richness that literacy brings to our lives.

We know that ultimately the entire school day must change radically in order for struggling adolescent readers to participate fully and make the most progress possible in literacy (Fisher & Ivey, 2006). But even in the best of contexts, the clock is ticking by middle school, and only high-quality interventions will accelerate the literacy development of students who did not experience productive reading and writing in the early grades. Also, given the demands to address a multitude of curriculum standards across the content areas, it is doubtful that students reading well below grade level would receive enough instruction in reading without a program focused on development.

Despite our best efforts to create literacy-rich schools for all adolescents, high-quality interventions for our students in most need are absolutely necessary now and in the foreseeable future. The purpose of this chapter is to examine the current state of interventions for older readers and to consider where our best efforts at designing interventions ought to begin.

TAKING A CRITICAL LOOK AT POPULAR INTERVENTIONS

Increased attention to adolescent literacy has given rise to a thriving marketplace for intervention programs. After so many years focused on early intervention and few options for older readers who struggle, some may see this recent availability of resources as a welcome relief. Ready-made programs may be particularly appealing to secondary educators who are thrust into the position of making curricular decisions without having the opportunity to develop strong theoretical knowledge about how older readers gain purposes and competence for literacy.

The majority of existing programs can be clustered into three categories. Here I describe these models and share a few words of caution about each one.

The Fix-It Model

Dustin struggles mightily with seventh-grade texts, and his reading difficulties are most noticeable when he is asked to read orally in class. He stumbles over every fifth or sixth word—what reading specialists would refer to as reading at his *frustration level*. In fact, an informal reading inventory indicated that he was comfortable reading the words only in passages written below the third-grade level. He says he hates to read, and that he would never voluntarily read outside of school.

Some teachers may see the solution to Dustin's problems as relatively simple: Teach him to decode. The fix-it model reflects a theory of intervention likened to a medical diagnosis. That is, target what you believe is the source of the difficulty and then repair it. The thinking behind this approach is that Dustin's failure to make progress in reading is due to his limited ability to read the words, and that if this particular problem were resolved, he would be a healthy, happy reader. It is relatively easy to find an intervention program that focuses on word-level skills for a student such as Dustin. Furthermore, it is not unusual to hear success stories of students who became skilled at reading words after involvement in intensive programs aimed at accomplishing just that. After all, it is not surprising that a program aimed at fixing decoding skills would help students get better at decoding.

But this approach and other fix-it model solutions miss the big picture. Although Dustin may learn to read more words correctly, there is no reason to believe that focusing on a singular aspect of the reading process would help him improve his overall reading comprehension, develop a more positive attitude toward reading, or heighten his inclination to read. Troubleshooting in one area sounds appealing, but it may result in progress isolated only to that area. In short, although Dustin might accomplish the instructional tasks required by a focused program, we might not see any changes in his real reading.

Students often exhibit specific characteristics of problematic reading; for example, weak decoding skills, a lack of fluency, trouble with vocabulary words, and difficulty getting the gist of what they read. A provocative question for teachers of older students to consider is this: *Are these observable "weaknesses" the root of the problem, or are they just symptoms of a lack of experience with reading?* It would not be surprising to discover that a lack of time spent reading might manifest itself in a myriad of ways across students, and that these symptoms might begin to subside as time spent reading increases. For instance, Dustin took part in a tutoring program that devoted 45 minutes twice a week to reading in manageable texts. When he read easier texts, he did not exhibit major decoding problems, and as he gained more experience with actual reading, he was able to read more difficult texts fluently. He even began to take books home to read on his own. It is doubtful that he would have made similar strides in a skill-focused program that left little instructional time for contextual reading.

The Reading-Problem-of-the-Month Model

Maureen, a high school reading specialist, takes advantage of professional development opportunities as often as possible. After all, she is the only reading expert in a school of 1,500 students located in a small industrial city. With nearly 60% of students reading two or more years below grade level, her school has failed year after year to meet the standards for state accreditation. Lately, she has noticed a rise of information on vocabulary instruction both in local teacher conferences and workshops and in advertisements for newly published books. Until this point, Maureen has not emphasized vocabulary development with students and teachers in her school. Now she is compelled to wonder if there is a link between low reading scores and limited vocabulary knowledge among her students. She even starts to fear that perhaps she has neglected this important aspect of her students' literacy development. Is the absence of a school-wide vocabulary focus to blame for persistent reading problems in her school?

What Maureen soon comes to realize, though, is that vocabulary has become the reading problem of the month. Like the fix-it model, though, this model wrongly assumes that focusing on one particular area of literacy will result in better reading. But it also suggests a widespread catastrophe: namely, that in classrooms everywhere students have missed the teaching of an essential skill associated with reading and that, furthermore, this oversight may be a large contributing factor to low reading achievement. Every so often a policy or a developing line of research popularizes a particular instructional practice or learning objective. Phonics, phonemic awareness, fluency, and comprehension have all been reading problems of the month. The precise origins of these perceived crises are hard to pin down, but they are typically perpetuated by a flood of commercially available materials that claim to solve the problem.

The Compliance Model

Lloyd is a middle school reading teacher, and he has been given the task of identifying several intervention programs to be considered by the school's literacy council. His search has been limited by instructions to include only options that are "researched-based." It is hard to find a group of elementary school teachers and administrators who are not deeply familiar with what the phrase "research-based" means in this context. It was popularized by No Child Left Behind legislation, and it is linked to the five big areas of reading studied by the National Reading Panel (2000): phonemic awareness, phonics, fluency, vocabulary, and comprehension. Schools who have been awarded certain government-based grants, such as Reading First, adopt this approach because their funding is tied to the use of programs that include instruction in each of these areas. Many companies have branded their products as "research-based" to appeal to this market.

But as Lloyd and other teachers of adolescents are learning, the popularity of branding instructional programs as "research-based" has spilled over into the secondary grades as well, even when there are no links to funding. But what does *research-based* mean? It is probably more important to consider what it does *not* mean. It does not mean, in most cases, that independent, rigorous experimental studies have been conducted on specific programs. It does not mean that there is evidence to support the notion that if instruction includes all five of these areas—phonemic awareness, phonics, fluency, vocabulary, and comprehension—readers will be magically created. It usually only means that the developers of the programs made sure to include categories of activities that match the five research areas studied by the National Reading Panel.

It is unlikely that older readers, even those who lack experience, would need regular, intensive instruction in all of the skills and concepts associated with proficient reading. Take phonemic awareness, for instance. There is no evidence that we have large numbers of adolescents who need instruction in noticing and manipulating sounds within words or that instruction in this area would lead to better reading (Ivey & Baker, 2004), yet the compliance model would have students wasting valuable instructional time developing this skill.

With so many instructional areas to cover in the compliance model, it is difficult to make room for time to read. To make matters worse, the National Reading Panel's report failed to make a strong case for the effects of wide reading, not because research does not support its efficacy, but because there were few studies of independent reading that met the criteria the panel established for studies to be included. A host of correlational studies indicating a strong connection between reading achievement and time spent reading were excluded from the review (Allington, 2006).

ESTABLISHING CRITERIA FOR SENSIBLE INTERVENTIONS

What the three aforementioned intervention models have in common is that fundamentally, they are all aimed at "fixing" students or "remediating" some skill that must have slipped past them. But with every passing year that students lag behind their peers in reading, the gap between what students need and the instruction they likely receive widens. So rather than focusing on what kids do not seem to know or do, the key to successful interventions is to change instruction dramatically. Students rarely benefit from more practice in what was too hard or irrelevant in every previous encounter.

The other problem with existing, widely available interventions is that they assume that the needs of older students still emerging as readers and writers are the same as those of younger emergent readers. Although it is essential to attend to students' developmental needs, adolescents have specific motivations for reading and writing, and these purposes must play a central role in instruction (Alvermann, 2002).

At the present time, our most promising interventions stem from the experiences and expertise of those who have worked with and studied older inexperienced readers and who are knowledgeable about both the developmental nature of literacy acquisition and the complex nature of what it means to be an adolescent learner. Although a program that takes into account the wide range of needs that exists for this population would be difficult to design and scale up for mass distribution and implementation, there are strong research-based principles for creating a workable framework for instruction. In this section, I describe four essential features of interventions that lay the groundwork for meeting individual needs: (1) personalized and ongoing assessments, (2) substantial opportunities to read and write, (3) extensive and varied collection of reading materials, and (4) expert teachers as instructors.

Personalized and Ongoing Assessments

Serena, Justin, and Kay are all seventh-grade students in the same school. All have been identified as needing extra help with reading following the schoolwide administration of a timed, computer-based reading assessment that required students to read passages that increased in difficulty as they proceeded through the test, and fill in missing words by selecting from lists of possible choices. All three students received approximately a fourth-grade-level reading score. What does this score indicate about these students as readers? How does it help teachers with instruction?

For sure, many scenarios would find all three students grouped together because of the similarity of their scores. But consider what happened when these same three students were given a range of informal assessments (e.g., informal reading inventory) and observed and interviewed over time to better understand their experiences. Let's begin with Serena. Inexperienced as a reader, she could recall only one time period when she read voluntarily outside of school. After seeing the movie *Titanic*, she visited the public library to check out a host of informational materials on the real-life disaster. When reading in school, she exhibited notable strengths in reading even fairly difficult words, and she had general understandings of most assigned texts. What presented a problem for Serena was the volume of unfamiliar vocabulary she encountered in subject-area reading.

Like Serena, Justin was hard-pressed to recount reading experiences outside of school. Also similar to Serena, he had strong word recognition skills in grade-level texts. But Justin appeared only to read words rather than think about what he was reading. After finishing assigned texts, he could rarely report the gist of what he had read. However, he consistently enjoyed and understood teacher read-alouds of high-interest young-adult fiction.

Kay differed remarkably from Serena and Justin. She struggled with reading the words even in second-grade-level texts, and her difficulty with decoding was further evident in the fact that she finger-pointed when reading at all levels. Although she was not interested in reading on her own, she also enjoyed teacher read-alouds. Quite surprisingly, Kay was in an honors language arts class, likely due to her strong ability to get the gist of what she read, even when it was extremely difficult to read the words.

Serena, Justin, and Kay exemplify the phenomenon Riddle Buly and Valencia (2002) identified when they created rich profiles of fourth graders who had failed state reading assessments. In a nutshell, a simple reading score from a formal test does not capture the complexity within students and the differences between students. Although some tests may give us a general idea of who might need extra help, only ongoing interactions and observations from an expert teacher can provide a more accurate picture of individual needs.

Relying on a single score may lead to instruction that is entirely inappropriate, setting up inexperienced readers to fall farther behind. Consider Kay as a prime example. Given a fourth-grade-level score, one might assume that she can read words fluently in an intermediate-level text, such as *Because of Winn-Dixie* (DiCamillo, 2000). But Kay only read without frustration in much easier texts, such as *Bats!* (Iorio, 2005) and other selections from the *Time for Kids* series. With many opportunities to read accessible texts written on a level much lower than her test score would have indicated, Kay began to read more difficult texts fluently. Comprehension was never a problem.

Substantial Opportunities to Read and Write

Considering how to conduct personalized and ongoing assessments of individuals may seem puzzling, particularly when formal tests seems so much more convenient. But this need not be the case. Of the many benefits of time spent reading and writing, the connections to assessment are possibly the most illuminating. I am bewildered by the fact that students who have never really read much are so often assessed and assigned labels that describe them as particular kinds of readers: *poor comprehender, weak decoder, nonfluent reader, resistant reader*. I have never played the piano, but I doubt that anyone would call me a poor pianist. With practice and technical knowledge, I may be brilliant at it. The point is that the label is irrelevant without the opportunity to try out the activity.

When inexperienced readers finally get the opportunity to read, and to do so when it is purposeful and manageable, we get a more accurate picture of their identities as readers and the instruction and support they need to explore the possibilities of a literate life. So when it comes to knowing students as readers in order to make instructional decisions, a good rule of thumb is to get students reading and writing as soon as possible. English language learners, in particular, provide excellent examples of this phenomenon. When my colleague Karen Broaddus and I studied a group of seventh- and eighth-grade Latino/a students in their language arts classroom (Ivey & Broaddus, 2007), we met José from the Dominican Republic, who had attended school in the United States for 3 years and learned to speak English quite fluently, but had not yet made much progress in reading. He appeared to be at a standstill in his literacy development until we found what engaged him. Among those activities was the reading and writing of rhyming texts and poems that resembled rap music. In the midst of his reading and writing, we became aware of basic confusions he had with the written language that were not evident in spoken English versus spoken Spanish (e.g., the sound linked to the letter *a*), which everyone assumed he had long ago understood. Moreover, because José was finally involved in reading and writing that mattered to him, he wanted to clear up these confusions in order to accomplish his own purposes.

But the benefits of actual reading and writing in an intervention extend far beyond just making our assessments more useful. Time spent in engaged reading is a crucial goal because it is explicitly linked to differences in reading achievement and in vocabulary development (Allington, 2006). Plus, although many students indicate limited enthusiasm for reading voluntarily in the middle grades, they report that in language arts classrooms, the opportunity to just read is actually their most preferred literacy-related activity and that they would be inclined to read under the condition that good reading materials are available (Ivey & Broaddus, 2001). Further, students who read more in school are more likely to read outside of school (Pilgreen & Krashen, 1993). This finding is particularly important, given that voluntary reading outside of school is closely tied to reading and writing competence (Anderson, Wilson, & Fielding, 1988). It is difficult to imagine inexperienced readers adopting the habit of voluntary reading without support, guidance, and opportunities to engage in it during school.

An essential caveat here is that when conceptualizing interventions, the time allocated for reading should be thought of as engaged reading rather than mandated, compliant reading (Guthrie, 1996). The latter brings to mind familiar classroom scenes: the teacher at the front of the class asking students to read aloud or telling students to read a selected passage silently, or perhaps a teacher with a small group of students at a table asking students to take turns reading. When students are engaged in reading, however, the classroom takes on a different look. Instead of seeing a teacher pulling students along from the front of the class or the head of the table, you see him or her supporting students from behind or side by side as they select and direct their own reading. Engaged reading involves students in reading because they are internally motivated—because the text contains information that matches what they want to know and when they want to know it.

Creating the context for engaged reading is the heart of a good intervention for older students. In the next section, I describe why text matters so much to this process.

Extensive and Varied Collection of Reading Materials

Ask adults what makes them want to read, and it is doubtful that they would respond with any reference to getting a higher score on the state reading test. But we do know that practice counts, and it counts a lot. However, to understand students' motivations to read, it helps to examine our own reasons. I have never been a big fan of fiction, so when I read, it is usually for information instead of for a story, but not just any information. I am often curious about important global matters, most recently the backgrounds and intentions of candidates for the upcoming presidential election. Sometimes I need specific information. When a family member was diagnosed with a particular kind of cancer, I searched the Internet to try to understand what the doctor had not explained adequately. I have to admit, though, that a lot of my reading would be viewed by much of the world as frivolous. For instance, I love shoes, and I am currently obsessed with a website (*www.zappos.com*) where I can not only buy shoes from a selection of thousands, but I can also read reviews of my favorite shoes posted by other shoe fanatics.

I suppose that other adults have specific purposes for reading, even though perhaps not everyone would so freely share their secret guilty pleasures. We can expect the same from older, inexperienced readers. Text matters tremendously to the individual, and successful interventions must consider reading materials in the broadest notions possible. There are certainly particular texts that interest a range of adolescents. For instance, *Life in Prison* (Williams, 2001), an autobiographical account of the horrors of incarceration as told by a gang founder on death row, has mass appeal. But more often than not, a crucial component of the intervention is identifying what engages individual students.

A start-up collection, at the very least, ought to include a variety of fiction and nonfiction on a range of topics, representing a wide variety of formats and difficult levels. Table 14.1 includes a sample of the types of materials necessary in addition to an assortment of high-interest fictional novels.

TABLE 14.1. Sample Range of Books for Intervention

High-interest books for older beginning readers

Morrison, T. (2004). *Remember: The journey to school integration*. Boston: Houghton-Mifflin.
Willems, M. (2003). *Don't let the pigeon drive the bus*. New York: Hyperion.

Wordless picture books

Billout, G. (2002). *Something's not quite right*. Boston: Godine.
Johnson, S. T. (2002). *As the city sleeps*. New York: Viking.

High-interest picture books with humor and sophisticated concepts

Fleischman, P. (1999). *Weslandia*. New York: Scholastic.
Cronin, D. (2004). *Duck for president*. New York: Simon & Schuster.

High-interest informational picture books

McCarthy, M. (2006). *Aliens are coming! The true account of the 1938 War of the Worlds radio broadcast*. New York: Knopf.
Hopkinson, D., & Ransome, J. E. (2006). *Sky boys: How they built the Empire State Building*. New York: Schwartz & Wade Books.

Bilingual books

Elya, S. M. (2003). *Oh no, gotta go!* New York: Putnam.
Paul, A. W. (2005). *Mañana iguana*. New York: Holiday House.

Transitional chapter books

Dahl, M. (2007). *Poison pages*. Minneapolis: Stone Arch Books.
Hansen, R. (2004). *Animal rescuers*. New York: Scholastic.

In attempting to create a context for engagement, the search for materials that matter to some students is ongoing. Often, adolescents' curiosities are not addressed in trade books, and so alternative materials such as magazines, newspapers, and the Internet are essential resources. Drew was uninterested in the topics of books available in his reading class, but he was eager to know about the recent rumor that his favorite baseball player was to be traded. A quick Google search on the Internet gave way to at least 30 late-breaking articles on the topic from newspapers across the United States. Drew read the first two articles in their entirety, then skimmed 10 or so others to look for additional information. In many ways, these alternative materials more closely approximately adult-level reading and purposes, and they represent the real-life reading adolescents will pursue beyond school.

But student engagement is not the only reason for diversifying reading materials. Different materials support different kinds of instruction about the reading process. For instance, we know a lot about what thoughtful reading entails, but not every text requires the same strategies for comprehension and evaluation. Certain texts lend themselves to particular instructional scenarios. One useful tip for inexperienced readers who might encounter unfamiliar vocabulary as they read is to know the different ways authors sometimes include definitions within the text. Consider this excerpt from *The U.S. Constitution and You* (Sobel, 2001): "England was a *monarchy*. A monarchy is a country in which one person—usually a king or queen—has complete control of the government, usually for life" (p. 12). In this case, the author provides an explicit definition. In other texts, a teacher may find an example of where an author implies definitions in the context surrounding the unfamiliar word. *Hoop Queens* (Smith, 2003) provides an excellent opportunity to examine how authors use imagery to craft their message to readers, as in this excerpt from a poem about female basketball player Nyksha Sales:

> Down by 2,
> 4 seconds on the clock,
> Weaving through traffic,
> Trying to lock
> In on target

Likewise, many graphic novels provide the context for helping students understand the concept of inferring. Without the benefit of extensive words and long descriptive narrative, the reader must infer what the artist intended by closely examining details in the drawings.

The bottom line is that there is no one set of materials that would sufficiently meet instructional needs or address individual needs for reading engagement. It may seem convenient to adopt a program that comes with what appear to be good reading materials, but packaged sets will rarely be comprehensive enough to meet the unforeseen needs and interests of adolescents. In the end, the teacher is in the best position to make the match between students and texts.

Expert Teachers as Instructors

In some ways, ill-fated interventions are easy to spot, even at the beginning stages of implementation. A telltale sign is the departure of the best teachers in the school. These are expert teachers who have been successfully meeting the needs of struggling readers without mandated programs. These teachers recognize the flaws of ineffective interventions, and if they have no choice but to deliver these programs with "fidelity" in their present situations, they elect to move on to other positions, other schools, or other districts.

An expert teacher does not deliver programs or follow teaching scripts. Expert teachers notice, teach, reflect, and adjust. Johnston and Costello (2005) characterize expert teachers as "resilient" (p. 257), that is, they never back down in the face of difficult teaching. I cannot think of a more promising situation for older struggling readers than to be placed in the care of a teacher who embodies a combination of strong theoretical and practical knowledge and resilience. However, when interventions bind teachers and students to a specific protocol, there is no room for flexibility.

The specific benefits of having a teacher make crucial decisions about instruction for older struggling readers are enormous. As mentioned previously, teachers are in the best position to make the match between students and text. For instance, even Troy, a new teacher, could view his student differently when he adjusted something as seemingly simple as what he provided him to read:

> "Changed books!!!! From Gary Paulsen to R. L. Stine and man-oh-man what a change! Changing books (subject matter combined with an easier reading level) has boosted my student's progress. Engagement and satisfaction come with ease."

One of the pitfalls of many interventions is limited materials or preselected materials that not only limit student engagement but also restrict the ability of the teacher to sufficiently explain important processes associated with reading. Matt, another new teacher, commented on how he solved this problem by selecting texts for teaching with his students' experiences in mind:

> "I chose a book where [my student] would have enough background knowledge to make inferences (a book on the Pittsburgh Steelers). This worked well."

Teachers are also in the position to notice what students need and to respond in efficient and meaningful ways. Tara explained one of these instances to me:

> "I noticed that [my student] had just been reading the words rather than sentences. Often she would get to the end of the page and not know what she had read. I showed her ways to check herself for comprehension."

Sometimes, the realizations are sobering but no less important because they beg for a response. Sara's experiences with one student highlight a major problem with interventions that do not involve the teacher in a significant way. She admitted, "I'm still having trouble engaging my student as she reads. She just seems very much like she wants to go through the motions and be done with it." Of all the patterns we can notice in students as they read, perhaps the trickiest and dangerous is compliance. If students look busy, we tend to move on to other, more noncompliant students. However, once we are aware that students are just "going through the motions," the problem is difficult to ignore. I suspect that a great deal of compliance exists in programs that involve no teacher or programs that require the teacher to set aside his or her expertise. In any case, the interventions we design ought to appeal to the sensibilities of our best teaches.

CONCLUSIONS

The four features of high-quality interventions for inexperienced adolescent readers I described in this chapter do not represent totally new ideas. Unfortunately, though, I have seen incredibly knowledgeable reading specialists succumb to the pressure of adopting programs that may do more harm than good for students who need the most help. For whatever reason, heavy marketing campaigns can make even an antitheoretical instructional program seem like the answer, even to successful teachers who know better. I hope this chapter serves as a reminder of what matters.

There is likely no one perfect intervention for inexperienced adolescent readers. Ultimately, the specifics of the intervention will depend on the needs of the students it is intended to serve. However, I believe that adherence to the four features described in this chapter will ensure a powerful foundation regardless of the details.

DISCUSSION AND ACTIVITIES

As you evaluate your existing intervention or conceptualize something new, the following guiding questions will be useful:

1. What role do assessments play, if any, in the intervention? Do the assessments truly uncover individual patterns of reading difficulties and engagement?

2. Do students get substantial opportunities to read? Is the environment conducive to engaged reading, or is student reading mainly compliant?

3. What is the status of reading materials in the intervention? Does the selection of materials limit or enhance reading engagement and instruction?

4. What role does the teacher play in the intervention? Does the intervention capitalize on teacher expertise or is the teacher merely a technician?

REFERENCES

Allington, R. L. (2006). *What really matters for struggling readers?: Designing research-based programs* (2nd ed.). Boston: Allyn & Bacon.

Alvermann, D. E. (2002). Effective literacy instruction for adolescents. *Journal of Literacy Research, 34,* 189–208.

Anderson, R. C., Wilson, P. T., & Fielding, L. G. (1988). Growth in reading and how children spend their time outside school. *Reading Research Quarterly, 23,* 285–303.

DiCamillo, K. (2000). *Because of Winn-Dixie.* Cambridge, MA: Candlewick.

Fisher, D., & Ivey, G. (2006). Evaluating the interventions for struggling adolescent readers. *Journal of Adolescent and Adult Literacy, 50,* 180–189.

Guthrie, J. T. (1996). Educational contexts for engagement in literacy. *The Reading Teacher, 49,* 432–445.

Iorio, N. (2005). *Bats!* New York: HarperCollins.

Ivey, G., & Baker, M. I. (2004). Phonics instruction for older students: Just say no. *Educational Leadership, 61,* 35–39.

Ivey, G., & Broaddus, K. (2001). "Just plain reading": A survey of what makes students want to read in middle school classrooms. *Reading Research Quarterly, 36,* 350–377.

Ivey, G., & Broaddus, K. (2007). A formative experiment investigating literacy engagement among adolescent Latina/o students just beginning to read, write, and speak English. *Reading Research Quarterly, 42,* 512–545.

Johnston, P., & Costello, P. (2005). Principles for literacy assessment. *Reading Research Quarterly, 40,* 256–267.

National Institute of Child Health and Human Development. (2000). *Teaching children to read: An evidence-based assessment of the scientific research literature on reading and its implications for reading instruction* (NIH Publication no. 44-4769). Washington, DC: U.S. Government Printing Office.

Pilgreen, J., & Krashen, S. (1993). Sustained silent reading with English as a second language high school students: Impact on comprehension, reading frequency, and reading enjoyment. *School Library Media Quarterly, 22,* 21–23.

Riddle Buly, M., & Valencia, S. W. (2002). Below the bar: Profiles of students who fail state reading assessments. *Education Evaluation and Policy Analysis, 24,* 219–239.

Smith, C. R. (2003). *Hoop queens.* Cambridge, MA: Candlewick.

Sobel, S. (2001). *The U. S. Constitution and you.* Hauppauge, NY: Barron's.

Williams, S. (2001). *Life in prison.* San Francisco: Chronicle.

CHAPTER 15

Instructional Moves That Support Adolescent Learners Who Have Histories of Failure

Douglas Fisher
Nancy Frey

This chapter focuses on how teachers can support the literacy development of students with disabilities or histories of school failure. It will look at how:

- Students with disabilities learn from whole school literacy efforts, provided they are in regular classrooms.

- Students with disabilities learn in classes with differentiated curriculum and instruction.

- Students with disabilities need access to accommodations and modifications.

The results are in: Magellan Middle School (a pseudonym) did not make *adequate yearly progress*. As such, the school is labeled a failure—a school in need of improvement. The principal schedules a number of faculty meetings to address this problem. Teachers and parents are upset by this distinction and want to get out of trouble as soon as possible. Upon closer examination, it is clear that Magellan did not make adequate yearly progress for one group of students—those identified as having a disability. Under state and federal regulations, however, failure to meet the accountability demands for any significant subgroup of students results in failure for the entire school. Although this can be seen as progress—for the first time accountability systems are focusing on groups of students that were often ignored—it is also difficult for school to respond.

A number of the faculty discussions at Magellan Middle School were healthy ones that focused on making progress with students who challenge the educational system. Other discussions were less healthy. Some of the less healthy recommendations included:

- Conducting residence checks to ensure that all students with disabilities live in the school's catchment area.
- Transferring a number of students with disabilities out of the school to reduce the number below what the state considers a "significant subgroup."
- Discontinuing special education services for a number of students to reduce the number below what the state considers a "significant subgroup."

Some of the healthier recommendations and decisions are the focus of the remainder of this chapter, which describes three "big ideas" for ensuring that adolescents with disabilities become successful, contributing members of school and society by participating in schoolwide literacy efforts.

STUDENTS WITH DISABILITIES LEARN FROM WHOLE-SCHOOL LITERACY EFFORTS, PROVIDED THEY ARE CONDUCTED IN REGULAR CLASSROOMS

Schoolwide literacy initiatives are becoming increasingly common. Just a few years ago, schoolwide initiatives at the middle and high school level were rare. Today, major organizations, such as the National Association of Secondary School Principals (NASSP), have published guidelines and technical support documents designed to help schools focus on the role that reading, writing, speaking, listening, and viewing play in content-area classrooms. More comprehensive reviews of schoolwide approaches to literacy instruction can be found in *Creating Literacy-Rich Schools for Adolescents* (Ivey & Fisher, 2006). In this chapter, we focus on the role that these schoolwide initiatives play in literacy learning for adolescents with disabilities.

Consider John Adams Middle School in Albuquerque, New Mexico. The faculty at John Adams developed their schoolwide literacy plan to address the needs of a diverse student population. Of the 872 students at John Adams, 78% qualify for free lunch, 82% are Latino/a, 10% are European American, 4% are Native American, 3% are African American, 1% are Asian Pacific Islander, and 18% qualify for special education.

The plan was designed to provide increased consistency for students such that they could develop habits for reading and writing. The plan included a focus on graphic organizers, teacher read-alouds, note-taking skills, writing to learn prompts, and social–behavioral expectations. Faculty members developed their literacy initiative as a part of their overall school vision, which was expressed as "Teach me respect, responsibility, and lifelong learning." Over several years, the faculty at John Adams engaged in professional development and peer coaching aligned with their schoolwide literacy plan. As a result, student achievement improved.

Importantly, improvements were not limited to students without disabilities. Evidence from John Adams suggests that students with disabilities benefit significantly from a schoolwide literacy focus. Of course, these benefits were accrued because students with disabilities attended regular classes with their peers without disabilities (e.g., McLeskey & Waldron, 2000). Access to the core curriculum and regular classroom, with supports and services, is the hallmark of inclusive education (Jorgensen, Schuh, & Nisbet, 2005).

Access to the core curriculum in a regular classroom is also consistent with the response-to-intervention (RTI) model outlined in federal policy and a number of research reviews (e.g., Fuchs & Fuchs, 2001). Essentially, the RTI model requires that supplemental supports are provided in regular classrooms and that educators assess the effectiveness of these interventions before considering alternative placements for students with disabilities. As Cortiella (2006) noted, "RTI is an individualized, comprehensive assessment and intervention process, utilizing a problem-solving framework to identify and address student academic difficulties using effective, efficient, research-based instruction" (n.p.). The RTI model assumes that students have access to quality instruction, such as that which is provided in a schoolwide literacy plan, before additional individualized interventions are developed.

A visit to the seventh-grade science class of John Adams Middle School highlights the role that schoolwide literacy plans play in improving achievement for students, including those with disabilities. Each day, the teacher starts the class with a writing prompt. On this particular day, students were asked to respond to the prompt "Think about a cell. What's it like? What is it not like? Please make your comparison and contrasts relate to things you know well."

As they entered the room, students took out paper and pen and began writing. Evidence for writing to learn suggests that these types of writing prompts focus students' thinking and allow teachers an opportunity to quickly assess student understanding (Kalman & Kalman, 1996; Klein, 1999). Students with disabilities benefit from this component of the schoolwide literacy plan as they clarify their understanding of the content. Students also benefit because their teachers gain a better understanding of the instruction each student needs to master the content standard.

Following a partner discussion about what they had written, students listened to their teacher read aloud from *Enjoy Your Cells* (Balkwill & Rolph, 2001) and explain his thinking about the text. Although this is an easier-to-read book, it contains information that helps students understand cell structure and function, which are one of the focus areas for seventh-grade science. Both the partner discussion and read-aloud help students with disabilities because they provide access to content information in ways that do not require independent reading of a text. Although we want students with disabilities to read at increasingly sophisticated levels, and to have structures and strategies to ensure that this happens, we cannot leave them behind by failing to ensure that they access grade-level content. In addition, the use of the think-aloud of the text is helpful as students begin to incorporate comprehension strategies, such as predicting, clarifying, summarizing, visualizing, and inferring, into their habits while reading (Wilhelm, 2001).

Later in the class, after a number of collaborative learning activities, the teacher provides an interactive lecture while students take notes. The lecture is brief, about 12 minutes, and reviews the content learned thus far, some new information about cellular structure, and opportunities for students to record, transform, and summarize information. Again, this helps students with and without disabilities develop a strong sense of the content. Students with disabilities are provided access to content knowledge while being taught note-taking skills. As part of the note taking, students summarize information—which helps them remember the content.

Whereas good teachers probably do these things on their own, the key to a schoolwide focus on literacy strategies is that they are used consistently across classrooms. This means that some of the same strategies used in this seventh-grade science classroom are also used in history, English, art, math, physical education, family and consumer sciences, and so on. This instructional consistency benefits most students, but it's critical for students with disabilities, who have not developed habits for reading, writing, and thinking. Over time, and with a great deal of practice, these thinking tools become routines for students, and they use them across their school day.

Strategies, however, even common strategies that build students habits of mind, are not enough. To learn the content while also developing literacy skills, students need classroom structures that facilitate learning. With this in mind, let's consider the second big idea.

STUDENTS WITH DISABILITIES LEARN IN CLASSES WITH DIFFERENTIATED CURRICULUM AND INSTRUCTION

It's very difficult for most students to learn in whole-class formats session after session. It's nearly impossible for students with disabilities to learn in situations where the entire class is expected to listen, read, or work independently hour after hour. It's also hard to ensure that students with disabilities receive the supports and services outlined in their individualized education plans (IEPs), especially services such as direct reading instruction, in a whole-class format. As a result, students with disabilities are often removed from regular classrooms to receive their individualized supports and services. This approach results in lost instructional time, as students walk hallways, as well as lost access to content information. The U.S. history teacher, for example, does not hold up the class for a student with a disability to return from one-to-one tutoring, speech therapy, or the like. In other words, when students are required to participate in whole-class instruction day after day, they don't achieve at levels expected of them.

Further, the exclusive use of whole-class instruction is inconsistent with the evidence that humans learn through a gradual release of responsibility (Pearson & Gallagher, 1983). The gradual release of responsibility model suggests that the teacher moves from assuming "all the responsibility for performing a task . . . to a situation in which the students assume all of the responsibility" (Duke & Pearson, 2002, p. 211).

In the secondary school classroom, the gradual release of responsibility can be implemented and achieved in a number of ways. Importantly, in every variation of the gradual release of responsibility, the teacher must model, guide, coach, and provide time for students to work together before assigning independent tasks. One framework for implementing a gradual-release-of-responsibility model contains four elements: focus lessons, guided instruction, collaborative learning, and independent practice (Frey & Fisher, 2006; Fisher & Frey, 2008).

Focus Lessons

Focus lessons typically involve whole-class instruction delivered the by the teacher. These lessons provide an opportunity for the teacher to model his or her thinking, to establish purpose, and to focus students on the task at hand. Interestingly, students who struggle with school often do not know to what they are supposed to pay attention. They experience school as a barrage of information and are not sure which is important and helpful and which is not. Establishing a purpose and modeling thinking are critical if students are to incorporate these habits into their practices (e.g., Hill & Flynn, 2006; Marzano, Pickering, & Pollock, 2001).

Importantly, it's very difficult to differentiate curriculum and instruction during the focus lesson. Focus lessons provide all students with general information about the skill, strategy, content, idea, or process under investigation. Real differentiation occurs during guided instruction and collaborative learning.

Guided Instruction

Guided instruction most often occurs when the teacher meets with small groups of students. During this time, the teacher can provide direct instruction, ask "just right" questions, use a variety of prompts and cues, and differentiate curriculum and instruction based on the needs of the particular group. In other words, this is where the real teaching occurs. The key to guided instruction lies in the alignment between the focus lesson and the guided instruction. When teachers establish a clear purpose and model the thinking required during the focus lesson *and* students have opportunities to practice these skills and strategies during guided instruction, learning occurs.

Consistent with the evidence on differentiating instruction (e.g., Tomlinson & McTighe, 2006) and RTI, the guided instruction phase of the gradual-release-of-responsibility model provides students with the systems of instructional support as well as the individualized instruction they need to be successful. Unlike tracking, where students with the same perceived abilities are grouped together for weeks and weeks (or even the entire year), guided instruction groups are based on identified needs. One day, the teacher may meet with a group of students who all need further instruction in understanding cause-and-effect relationships. Another day, the teacher may form groups that encourage conversations about the essential question. A specific student with a disability might be in both of these groups. Importantly, students with disabilities do not comprise a group for guided instruction.

Collaborative Learning

While the teacher meets with small groups of students to provide guided instruction, the rest of the class works in collaborative groups. These groups focus on tasks that require collaboration yet have an independent product—something each student completes based on the interactions of the groups. These are not simply groups of students working together on one project, which often results in one student doing all of the work and the others not learning anything.

Collaborative learning groups can be aligned with the focus lesson and guided instruction. Alternatively, they can allow students to practice areas already taught or can be used to introduce new ideas that will become part of the whole-class focus. Again, collaborative learning is a prime opportunity to differentiate instruction as groups of students work together to complete tasks.

Independent Practice

The final phase in a gradual release of responsibility is independent practice. This is the time when students incorporate what they have learned and complete tasks on their own. Again, in the most effective classrooms, the independent practice is directly linked with the focus lesson and guided instruction. In addition, before asking students to engage in independent practice, it is wise to give them ample opportunities to try out knowledge with peers in a collaborative learning situation.

The independent practice phase is also a perfect opportunity to differentiate instruction. As Carol Ann Tomlinson (2001) notes, teachers can differentiate on instruction content, process, or product. In the gradual release of responsibility model, teachers differentiate content in the guided and collaborative phases, process throughout instruction, and products during the collaborative and independent phases. In other words, when classrooms are structured in this way, teachers really *can* differentiate instruction for students. Let's take a quick look inside a classroom where this is occurring.

Ms. Cabrera knows her 10th-grade students well. She also knows the English language arts standards well. As she notes, "Our standards don't require that specific book titles be taught. Instead, they require that students develop the thinking skills to read any book." One of the things she knows about her students is that the connections they make between literature and their lives are superficial and not terribly helpful in understanding universal themes and big ideas. She also knows that these personal connections are critical to her students' understanding of literacy and are clearly evident in the state content standards.

On one particular day, Ms. Cabrera reads aloud several poems by Langston Hughes. As she reads these poems, students follow along. Ms. Cabrera uses a data projector to display the poems on the wall. She pauses several times as she reads to share her thinking. She makes a number of increasingly sophisticated connections between the poems and other writing and the poems in their historical context. For example, as she read "When Susanna Jones Wears Red," she noted the connection between the "ancient cameo" and the color of Susanna's skin. In her words, "He didn't have to tell me that she was black—I made the connection to understand what Mr. Hughes was trying to tell me."

Following the focus lesson, students began working in groups. One group was listening to poems being read to them. Ms. Cabrera recorded specific poems from *Poetry Speaks* (Paschen & Mosby, 2001) into an iPod and connected this to a headphone jack with six outlets. Their task was to listen to the author read his or her poem, talk with one another about the poem, and then identify a number of connections that would help them understand the author's purpose and point of view.

Another group was working on essays in which the students had to identify connections between the book that their teacher was reading aloud to them and the book they had selected to read independently. Ms. Cabrera and her students read literature to find out answers to big questions or ideas, such as "When a stranger comes to town . . . " or "What's worth fighting for?" For each of these questions, she reads a book aloud to the class, they discuss it in the class, and students select a book from a list of possible books to read on their own. This list contains books at a wide range of reading levels, topics, and genres—all of which could be used to answer the big question or theme.

A third group of students was engaged in study of words with multiple meanings. Ms. Cabrera believes that students should be able to work together to study the vocabulary words they need to know and that she does not need to take whole-class time to do so. The tasks required of students relative to vocabulary change weekly, from semantic feature analysis, to semantic mapping, to word sorting, to vocabulary cards (e.g., Brassell & Flood, 2004). Regardless of the specific task for the week, she knows that her students are getting time on task with vocabulary.

A fourth group is watching a DVD about poetry writing techniques, listening through headphones and taking notes. The film is excellent and provides students with information about different poets' use of words, symbolism, and their historical context as fodder for writing. Ms. Cabrera knows that showing the film to the whole class would be less effective because she could not meet with small groups to provide guided instruction if she did so. She also knows that providing students with a note-taking guide helps them attend to key points, focuses their postviewing conversations, and ensures that each student has a product as a result of the experience.

During this time, Ms. Cabrera meets with small groups of students for guided instruction. She purposefully selects the members of each group to ensure that she can tailor her instruction to their specific needs. As a group of students arrive at her table, she sets down *The Prince* (Machiavelli, 1963). She says to the group of students, one of whom has an identified disability, "We're not going to read this book today. I picked a book that you haven't seen before so that I could show you that you can make all kinds of connections. I want us to discuss connections with specific quotes from the book. Remember, I don't want just connections to your personal life. I want us to think about connections we can make between this book and other things we've read, connections with history, connections with the world. I'm really hoping that these connections will help us understand the book better. Let's start with this quote, it's a doozy. I picked it because you'll probably have a personal reaction, but remember that we're focused on connections beyond personal ones. Ready, here's the quote: 'He who causes another to become powerful ruins himself.' " The group discusses politics, other things they have read, and the world around them, including gangs and parents.

Just before the end of the period, Ms. Cabrera discussed some of the independent practice she expected of her students. She reminded them to read from their independent reading books and to make connections as they did so. She asked them to start summarizing their thinking about the connections they saw between the in-class book and their independent reading book. She also asked them to each read a newspaper article at home that evening and to bring it to class to talk about connections between current events and literature.

Like access to quality instruction in a schoolwide literacy plan, students with disabilities who participate in a classroom structured like Ms. Cabrera's receive purposeful and intentional instruction based on their needs and the standards at hand. It's important to note that this model is inconsistent with hour after hour of whole-class instruction. Students simply do not learn at high levels when they spend time in passive roles.

STUDENTS WITH DISABILITIES NEED ACCESS TO ACCOMMODATIONS AND MODIFICATIONS

In addition to access to quality instruction delivered in responsive ways, some students with disabilities require curriculum accommodations and modifications in order to be successful. Castagnera, Fisher, Rodifer, Sax, and Frey (2003, pp. 24–25) define accommodations and modifications in the following ways:

> An *accommodation* is a change made to the teaching or testing procedures in order to provide students with access to information and to create an equal opportunity to demonstrate knowledge and skills. Accommodations do not change the instructional level, content, or performance criteria for meeting the standards. Examples of accommodations include enlarging the print, providing oral versions of texts, and using calculators.
>
> A *modification* is a change in what a student is expected to learn and/or demonstrate. While a student may be working on modified course content, the subject area remains the same as the rest of the class. If the decision is made to modify the curriculum, it is done in a variety of ways, for a variety of reasons, with a variety of outcomes.

Again, modifications vary according to the situation. Listed below are four modification techniques:

- *Same–only less.* The assignment remains the same except the number of items is reduced. The items selected should represent areas of the curriculum. For example, a history test consisting of multiple-choice questions, each with five possible answers, was modified for a specific student by reducing the number of possible answers to two.
- *Streamline the curriculum.* The assignment is reduced in size, breadth, or focus to emphasize the key points. For example, in an English class, the students were required to produce a final essay on the theme "Man and Machine." This assignment was modified for a specific student by requiring the main points of the unit, one example from a book about the theme, and a list of books that address the theme.

- *Same activity with infused objective.* The assignment remains the same but additional components, such as IEP objectives or skills, are incorporated. This is often done in conjunction with other adaptations and/or modifications to ensure that all IEP objectives are addressed. For example, a specific student has an IEP objective to answer "yes–no" questions using his eyes to locate the words on a lap tray. In his world history class, the teacher and other students in the class remembered to phrase questions in a yes–no format so that this student could practice this skill in a natural setting.
- *Curriculum overlapping.* The assignment for one class may be completed in another class. Students may experience difficulty grasping the connections between the different classes. In addition, some students work slowly and need additional time to complete assignments. This strategy is especially helpful for both of these situations. For example, in a word-processing class, students can type assignments for other classes and submit them to the word-processing teacher for the typing grade and to the English teacher for the essay grade.

Deciding which technique to use depends on the type of assignment and the student. One assignment may need only to be reduced in size in order for the student to be successful, whereas another may incorporate infused objectives. All four techniques, as well as appropriate personal supports such as peers, paraprofessionals, and special educators in regular classrooms, should be considered for each situation. Additional examples of accommodations and modifications can be found in Figure 15.1.

These examples are organized into four areas: materials, projects and homework, instructional arrangements, and assessments. These are areas in which students typically require accommodations and modifications in order to be successful. Amanda Robinson, a social studies teacher, and David Porter, a special educator, at Central High School used these four areas to plan accommodations and modifications for students in the world geography class. As shown in Figure 15.2, specific accommodations and modifications can be implemented based on the structure of the classroom. You'll also note that the standards, or expectations, are not modified. What teachers can modify are the structures and evidence—the content, process, and product, in Tomlinson's words—used in the classroom. The standards remain the same, but how we get there and the evidence we accept that students are making progress can vary.

CONCLUSION

Students who have histories of failure in the educational system have too often been ignored or pitied. If we are to ensure that all students make

Materials, Books, Media, Worksheets, Software, Etc.
- Provide a calculator.
- Supply graph paper to assist in organizing and lining up math problems.
- Tape lectures.
- Allow film or videos as supplements to texts.
- Provide practice opportunities using games, computers, oral drills, and board work.
- Allow student to record thoughts and write while listening to audiotapes or videos.
- Provide visual aids or adapted study guides with picture cues to stimulate ideas.
- Allow use of computers for writing.
- Provide student with ink stamps for numbers, letters, date, and signature.
- Use print enlarger or light box to illuminate text.
- Use tactile materials.
- Find related reading materials on student's reading level.
- Use adapted computer hardware or software.

Projects, Supplemental Activities, and Homework
- Assign smaller quantities of work.
- Relate problems to real-life situations.
- Highlight problems to be completed.
- Read problems and equations aloud.
- Allow more time for completion.
- Provide study questions prior to an assignment.
- Encourage oral contributions.
- Assign concept maps or other visual tools.
- Provide sample sentences or sentence frames for the student to use as a model.
- Dictate report to a partner who writes it out or types it.
- Assign homework partners.
- Substitute projects for written assignments or reports.
- Organize pictures instead of words into categories.

Instructional Arrangements and In-Class Activities
- Break down new skills in small steps.
- Simplify instruction by demonstrating and guiding learning one step at a time.
- Role-play historical events.
- Underline or highlight important words and phrases.
- Group students into pairs, threes, fours, etc., for different assignments and activities.
- Pair students with different and complementary skill levels.
- Pick key words from text to read.
- Rewrite texts into easy-to-read books.
- Have the student complete sentences supplied by the teacher or peer.
- Engage students in read–write–pair–share activities to build background.
- Color-code important words or phrases.
- Use hands-on activities.

(continued)

FIGURE 15.1. More accommodations and modifications for diverse student needs. Adapted from Castagnera, Fisher, Rodifer, Sax, and Frey (2003). Copyright 2003 by PEAK Parent Center. Adapted by permission.

Assessment and Final Products

- Underline or highlight test directions.
- Read word problems aloud to the student.
- Reword problems using simpler language.
- Underline key words.
- Space problems farther apart on the page.
- Reduce the number of questions by selecting representative items.
- Permit oral responses to assignments and writing tasks.
- Allow oral responses to tests using a tape recorder.
- Use photographs in oral presentations.
- Assign final group projects with each student responsible for a specific role.
- Encourage the use of media for final projects (video, audio, photos, drawings, performances, etc.).

FIGURE 15.1. *(continued)*

progress and reach high standards, we must change the instructional routines and supports available to them (Hehir, 2007). Students with learning or reading disabilities benefit from schoolwide literacy plans, provided that they are conducted in regular classes. Students with disabilities also benefit when their teachers implement an instructional framework based on a gradual release of responsibility. This model requires that teachers plan lessons based on closing the gap between grade-level expectations and current student performance. It also requires that teachers understand student needs and hold high expectations for all their students. And finally, increased levels of achievement are predicated on the idea that general and special educators collaborate to ensure that students receive the accommodations and modifications necessary to ensure their participation and success.

DISCUSSION AND ACTIVITIES

1. Inventory the schoolwide literacy plan at a middle or high school. What structures are in place to ensure that all students are provided with opportunities to read and write in every class?

2. Develop or modify an instruction unit and base it on the gradual release of responsibility model. First decide on the focus and then determine the best guided, collaborative, and independent tasks students should do to learn the content.

3. Meet with a special educator to discuss accommodations and modifications and how these can be used to improve student achievement.

4. Attend an IEP meeting to learn more about the formal supports and services organized for students with disabilities. Compare these with the actual implementation. How is the formal plan implemented? Are there aspects of the IEP that aren't implemented?

Title of Course: World Geography

Major Unit Objectives
1. Students will describe the internal and external structure of the earth.
2. Students will explain how forces inside and outside the earth create and change land forms.
3. Students will summarize the main ideas of plate tectonic theory.
4. Students will identify and define the processes that break down the surface of the earth.

Materials	Items requiring accommodations or modifications
1. Book: *World Geography* 2. Software/CD, laser discs: *3D Atlas*, *Volcanoes* 3. Video: *Earthquakes* and *Volcanoes* 4. Worksheets (on plate tectonics, earthquakes, vocabulary, weather, and erosion) 5. Slides and overheads 6. Primary source: *National Geographic* magazine	1. Book chapters on audiotape 4. Modified worksheets to emphasize key concepts of units
Instructional Arrangements	**Items requiring accommodations or modifications**
1. Interactive lessons in centers using various media (computer, laser disc, slides) 2. Whole-class reading of Chapter 2; use of read–write–pair–share strategy 3. Student pairs complete vocabulary worksheets 4. Cooperative groups to complete topic worksheets (one topic per group)	1. Predetermined rotation schedule to ease transition from one center to next
Projects	**Items requiring accommodations or modifications**
1. Crossword puzzle of vocabulary words 2. Creating a visual guide to geography terms: includes term, definition, illustration 3. Culminating activity: multimedia presentation	1. Word bank and/or first letter can be provided 2. Limit the number of terms; use pictures and sentence strips

FIGURE 15.2. Social studies lesson with accommodations and modifications. Adapted from Castagnera, Fisher, Rodifer, Sax, and Frey (2003). Copyright 2003 by PEAK Parent Center. Adapted by permission.

REFERENCES

Balkwill, F. R., & Rolph, M. (2001). *Enjoy your cells.* Woodbury, NY: Cold Spring Harbor Laboratory Press.

Brassell, D., & Flood, J. (2004). *Vocabulary strategies every teacher needs to know.* San Diego: Academic Professional Development.

Castagnera, E., Fisher, D., Rodifer, K., Sax, C., & Frey, N. (2003). *Deciding what to teach and how to teach it: Connecting students through curriculum and instruction* (2nd ed.). Colorado Springs, CO: PEAK Parent Center.

Cortiella, C. (2006). *Responsiveness-to-intervention: An overview.* Retrieved February 11, 2006, from *www.schwablearning.org/articles.aspx?r=840.*

Duke, N. K., & Pearson, P. D. (2002). Effective practices for developing reading comprehension. In A. E. Farstup & S. J. Samuels (Eds.), *What research has to say about reading instruction* (pp. 205–242). Newark, DE: International Reading Association.

Fisher, D., & Frey, N. (2008). *Better learning through structured teaching.* Alexandria, VA: Association for Supervision and Curriculum Development.

Frey, N., & Fisher, D. (2006). *Language arts workshop: Purposeful reading and writing instruction.* Upper Saddle River, NJ: Merrill Prentice Hall.

Fuchs, D., & Fuchs, L. S. (2001). Responsiveness-to-intervention: A blueprint for practitioners, policymakers, and parents. *Teaching Exceptional Children, 38*(1), 57–61.

Hehir, T. (2007). Confronting ableism. *Educational Leadership, 64*(5), 8–14.

Hill, J. D., & Flynn, K. M. (2006). *Classroom instruction that works for English language learners.* Alexandria, VA: Association for Supervision and Curriculum Development.

Ivey, G., & Fisher, D. (2006). *Creating literacy-rich schools for adolescents.* Alexandria, VA: Association for Supervision and Curriculum Development.

Kalman, J., & Kalman, C. (1996). Writing to learn. *American Journal of Physics, 64,* 954–955.

Klein, P. D. (1999). Reopening inquiry into cognitive processes in writing-to-learn. *Educational Psychology Review, 11,* 203–270.

Jorgensen, C. M., Schuh, M. C., & Nisbet, J. (2005). *The inclusion facilitator's guide.* Baltimore: Brookes.

Machiavelli, N. (1963). *The prince.* Durham, NC: Duke University Press.

Marzano, R. J., Pickering, D. J., & Pollock, J. E. (2001). *Classroom instruction that works: Research-based strategies for increasing student achievement.* Alexandria, VA: Association for Supervision and Curriculum Development.

McLeskey, J., & Waldron, N. L. (2000). *Inclusive schools in action: Making differences ordinary.* Alexandria, VA: Association for Supervision and Curriculum Development.

Paschen, E., & Mosby, R. P. (2001). *Poetry speaks: Hear great poets read their work from Tennyson to Plath.* Naperville, IL: Sourcebooks MediaFusion.

Pearson, P. D., & Gallagher, M. C. (1983). The instruction of reading comprehension. *Contemporary Educational Psychology, 8,* 317–344.

Tomlinson, C. A. (2001). *How to differentiate instruction in mixed-ability classrooms* (2nd ed.). Alexandria, VA: Association for Supervision and Curriculum Development.

Tomlinson, C. A., & McTighe, J. (2006). *Integrating differentiated instruction and understanding by design: Connecting content and kids.* Alexandria, VA: Association for Supervision and Curriculum Development.

Wilhelm, J. (2001). *Improving comprehension with think-aloud strategies: Modeling what good readers do.* New York: Scholastic.

CHAPTER 16

Traveling Together over Difficult Ground

NEGOTIATING SUCCESS WITH A PROFOUNDLY INEXPERIENCED READER IN AN INTRODUCTION TO CHEMISTRY CLASS

Cindy Litman
Cynthia Greenleaf

ne·go·ti·ate *v.*
1. To bargain or attempt to reach an agreement through discussion.
2. To travel over difficult ground.

This chapter:

- Introduces Eduardo, an 11th-grade student, as he presented himself in the class at the beginning of the year.
- Describes the literacy learning routines that his teacher, Will Brown, established to support his students' learning of chemistry.
- Shows how Will sequenced instruction for his Introduction to Chemistry class to build academic dispositions and skills in his students.
- Follows Eduardo's progress from the beginning to the end of the year.

It is the first day of class. The computer monitor in front of Will Brown's class reads:

Welcome to Introduction to Chemistry

Please take your assigned seat. See seating chart on front table.
Preamble #1—Write 1/3 page and keep
- What do you know or think about mixtures and solutions?
- What do you want to learn about mixtures and solutions?

As students find their way to nine round tables labeled with team names—Carbon Cavaliers, Kinetic Kids, Solubility Stars, Periodic Pros—Will explains:

275

"We start every day with a preamble, about a third of the page each. We do a lot of things in the preambles that you won't want to miss. This is something you'll want to put back in your binder."

Will asks students to "be so kind as to share" paper with classmates who don't have any. As students begin to write, Will tells them, "Leave some space and when you hear good ideas from your peers, you can fill them in."

A few minutes later, Will invites volunteers to share their responses to the preamble questions. After receiving Will's confirmation that "It's just to tell what you write," Vicky volunteers. Will waits patiently for another "brave volunteer." A few seconds later, Raul raises his hand. While waiting for a third and final volunteer, Will tells the class: "What I'll want the volunteers to do when they tell us one of their ideas—and you don't have to tell the whole thing, whatever part you want—is just say your name first, introduce yourself, 'I am. . . . ' " Reassured by this additional support, Erika raises her hand.

Before hearing from Vicky, Will introduces norms for classroom discourse. "If you can't see the person who's ready to talk, you need to move your chair—you're not glued to this chair in this class (he demonstrates by reorienting a chair). *So let's all turn so we can see the person who's talking.* (to Vicky) *And I'm going to go to the other side of the room, to help train you to talk to the class. Everyone here needs to hear what you're saying to be part of that learning process. So I'll try to help you do that too."*

As the three students share what they know or think about mixtures and solutions, Will acknowledges, validates, paraphrases, frames, and elaborates students' contributions in ways that demonstrate his undivided attention to, and respect for, student thinking. No matter how seemingly meager the content, Will locates in each student's response a kernel of worthwhile scientific information and thought.

When it is her turn, Erika, an English learner, makes use of the template provided by Will. "My name is Erika Kanasani, and I think it's something that you can make or something like that. I don't really know."

"So we can make solutions? That's a good thing to know about," Will responds. "We can, and we will make them—very generally or very particularly."

Before moving on to what students want to learn about mixtures and solutions, Will acknowledges the usefulness of students' prior knowledge, "Those are good things, great." The preamble discussion leads to a hands-on investigation and observation of mixtures and solutions, where students are immediately immersed in active science inquiry and sense making.

When the period ends half an hour later, Will collects students' preamble responses and observations from the solutions lab they have started—"Not because I'm going to grade you, but in case you are absent tomorrow, your teammates will need it. Just in case you're sick." Before dismissing the class, Will observes, "Wow! What a nice start. I look forward to the other 170 days."

In this first class period, Will has set the course of the work students will do, together and with his help, over the year. Most of the students in this classroom did not initially see themselves as people who were capable of understanding science.

They were not particularly interested in learning science, in this case, chemistry. From day 1, however, Will puts these young people in the role of science learners, naming small groups with chemical terms, inviting them to become interested in mixtures and solutions and to bring their thinking and experiences into the room, and making them responsible for listening to, and learning from, each other. He builds routines that support their risk taking and set thoughtful expectations for classroom discourse, and he models and supports collaboration in a learning community. From the first day of class, he treats them as capable students, eager and able to "do science."

Eduardo alone is unmoved. Face and posture impassive, he discloses not a glimmer of interest, daring Will to penetrate his indifference.

This chapter is about Eduardo, an 11th-grade student enrolled in Will Brown's Introduction to Chemistry class at Skyline High School in Oakland, California. Eduardo's journey as reader and student in Introduction to Chemistry was gleaned from a multifaceted study of high school students who are profoundly inexperienced in academic literacy and who are enrolled in content-area classrooms where teachers required and supported high levels of disciplinary reading (Greenleaf, Litman, & Braunger, 2007). This study investigated how a diverse group of middle and high school teachers involved in an ongoing professional learning community integrated an instructional model, Reading Apprenticeship, into their ongoing subject-area teaching. As part of this study, we observed and recorded Will's class at least once a week, took field notes, collected lesson materials and samples of student work, administered reading assessments, conducted teacher and student interviews, and identified a few focal students for closer study to represent a range of the students in this class. Our intent was to document how literacy learning opportunities emerged in Will's Introduction to Chemistry class. Yet our observations moved us beyond literacy strategies to the interactions that fostered engagement and academic identity in Will's class. As Eduardo entered the unfamiliar landscape of rigorous academic work, we watched Will skillfully maneuver Eduardo away from his resistant stance toward a more powerful academic identity. Will's teaching illuminated a pathway toward academic engagement that we have come to regard as key to student literacy learning—an instructional stance we term "negotiating success."

By retracing Eduardo's and Will's steps on this journey, we hope to demonstrate that profoundly inexperienced and academically unprepared students can make considerable progress as readers and learners—even late in their academic careers—when classroom teachers provide routines and support for their learning. Our description of negotiating success moves the discussion of adolescent literacy development beyond the implementation of structures and instructional strategies, to consider the importance of the classroom climate as it is fostered by a teacher's stance toward students and their learning. We aim to describe the nature of classroom support necessary for disinvested or struggling students to build new identities as readers and students. Further, we hope to provide educators committed to the equitable participation of all students in the academic enterprise with a concrete instantiation of classroom practice that serves that goal.

MEET EDUARDO

When we first met Eduardo, he was an uncooperative and unmotivated student in Will Brown's Introduction to Chemistry class. Eduardo's participation during the first weeks of class took the form of passive resistance and frequent interruptions and disruptions. He was slow in responding to directions or chose not to follow them at all. When Will asked students to add to their notes what they had learned from their classmates, Eduardo sat with his binder closed (field notes, 9/9/02). During one lesson, Eduardo kept up a steady stream of negative patter, replying to Will's reminder to work quietly, for example, with, "We don't have to." He shunned collaboration, telling Will, "I like being alone" (field notes, 9/19/02). In a whole-class conversation about how to succeed in the class, Eduardo insisted that it didn't matter to him if he failed. Indeed, his behavior suggested that Eduardo had already failed. Even we wrote Eduardo off: He was not initially selected as a "focal student" in our study due to his frequent absences.

And there was little to suggest that things would change. Certainly, as an 11th grader, time was not on Eduardo's side. A former English language learner (he had been in English language development classes through ninth grade), Eduardo described his experience of reading in class as "frustrating" and claimed he "couldn't read, you know, that well." Furthermore, he was not a student who seemed likely to beat the odds. He seemed at first to have none of the personal qualities associated with resiliency—cooperativeness, a positive sense of self, a sense of self-efficacy, positive peer and adult interactions, social responsiveness and sensitivity, empathy, a sense of humor, low degrees of defensiveness, and critical problem-solving skills (Garmezy, 1983). He appeared to be a not-very-likeable student who seemed destined to contribute to the alarming dropout rate at Skyline High School. Even the most committed educator would be tempted to dismiss Eduardo as an unfortunate—albeit complicit—casualty of our educational system.

But Eduardo did beat the odds. After earning poor marks in the first grading period, largely due to incomplete assignments, Eduardo went on to earn an A in the second semester. Furthermore, Eduardo developed a preference for reading science texts over literature and expressed the desire to become an engineer. Although Eduardo's turnaround coincided with exposure to specific reading and science strategies and routines, our data suggest that the change was a result of his broader apprenticeship in the discipline-based literacies in Will's classroom, coupled with Will's constant promotion of the expectation that he could be successful. Frequent in-class "metacognitive conversations" throughout the fall semester—conversations that were wide ranging but focused on the *thinking processes* of reading and science—supported Eduardo in rethinking his own identity. He came to see himself as having the capability to succeed in class through working at it, and, consequently, experienced the "joy of figuring things out through science inquiry and through reading science" that Will described as the goal for his students.

Eduardo's surprising turnaround was largely the result of a process that we describe as "negotiating success." As you will see, much of this negotiation between Will and Eduardo took place in the context of ongoing classroom discussions, which gave Will a nuanced understanding of Eduardo's identity as a student, reader, and learner, as well as ongoing opportunities to engage and mentor Eduardo and his classmates in the thinking, language, and literacy practices of science. Thus Will's interactions with Eduardo occurred in the context of content-area instruction that benefited not only Eduardo but his classmates as well. Indeed, in this classroom where students had ongoing opportunities for teacher- and peer-supported science literacy learning, we witnessed, over time, shifts in many students' conceptions of reading and reading practices, and in their identities as readers and students. We have written about other Introduction to Chemistry students elsewhere (Greenleaf, Brown, & Litman, 2004). In order to situate Eduardo's story in its broader educational context, we now turn to a description of Will Brown's Introduction to Chemistry class.

READING APPRENTICESHIP
IN INTRODUCTION TO CHEMISTRY

Eduardo's teacher, Willard Brown, is a member of an ongoing professional learning community of teachers in the Bay Area of California, working to apprentice urban students to academic literacy practices by integrating reading apprenticeship into subject-area teaching (Schoenbach, Greenleaf, Cziko, & Hurwitz, 1999). Reading Apprenticeship is an instructional framework for adolescent literacy development based on an understanding of literacy as a social, cultural, and cognitive activity (e.g., Scribner & Cole, 1981; Smagorinsky, 2001; Street, 1995). According to this approach, if students are to become skilled readers of academic texts, the invisible processes involved in comprehending a text must be made visible and accessible to them as they engage in meaningful literacy activities (Freedman, Flower, Hull, & Hayes, 1995; Pearson, 1996). In Reading Apprenticeship classrooms, therefore, teachers reframe teaching as an apprenticeship into discipline-based ways of thinking, talking, reading, and writing, and instruction includes explicit attention to *how* we read and *why* we read in the ways we do, as well as *what* we read in content-area texts.

The Instructional Landscape

The Reading Apprenticeship framework directed our analysis of research classrooms to key features of the learning environment in Will's class, such as the frequency and nature of reading opportunities, explicit strategy instruction, collaboration and metacognitive support, as well as science inquiry.

Reading Opportunities

Increased reading opportunities in Will's classroom consisted of a more purposeful approach to reading traditional disciplinary materials such as the textbook, instructions and rubrics, handouts and reproducibles, as well as numerical and chemical equations and problems, and occasional journal or news articles. Reading often took place in class, and students, rather than Will, did the primary work of comprehending. In-class teacher- and peer-supported reading transformed a wide range of materials—tables and graphs, numerical equations, visual and physical models of atoms and molecules, mathematical and scientific notation, chemical equations, drawings of atomic structures, data arrays—into "texts," and materials such as lab protocols or the directions for textbook chemistry problems—often glossed over or ignored in traditional science classes—became sites of inquiry that explicated scientific thinking and reasoning. As a result, students developed the ability to access scientific and mathematical terminology, to interpret arrays of data, to comprehend scientific text, and to read and write scientific procedures and explanations—in contrast to traditional science classrooms which fall short in building student capacities in these areas.

Explicit Strategies Instruction

Reading comprehension strategies emerged inductively in the context of in-class-supported reading as students grappled with in-the-moment comprehension problems. Students often generated and shared their own authentic and resourceful strategies for solving comprehension problems. Will played a critical role by modeling his own strategy use, by creating ongoing opportunities for students to share reading difficulties and ways they solved problems, and by elaborating on student-generated strategies. In addition to capitalizing on such opportunities, Will sometimes taught high-leverage comprehension strategies. After engaging students in a shared inquiry into reading in the fall, Will introduced *team reads*, his adaptation of Reciprocal Teaching that used clarifying, questioning, and summarizing, in January. By this time, students were accustomed to identifying areas of confusion and sharing problem-solving strategies under Will's guidance, and team reads were a step toward greater independence.

Collaboration

Collaboration was a ubiquitous feature of Will's classroom. In addition to modeling his own interest in student thinking, Will created participation structures and discourse routines that supported student-to-student collaboration. During whole-class discussions, Will encouraged students to respond to one another by drawing their names at random and having students alternately share their own idea or build on a previous student's contribution. He also explicitly encouraged constructive criticism and provided the language to support the respectful challenging of ideas; for example, "If you thought differently, tell us, 'I thought differently.' Disagree with them. And a nice way to disagree with them is say, 'I thought differently from you.' "

Although Will occasionally assigned specific roles during team reads or cooperative labs, collaborative meaning making most often occurred in the context of ongoing reading and discourse routines, such as daily preambles or expert groups, where give-and-take occurred naturally in a joint effort to solve comprehension problems or practice disciplinary thinking. Reading and discourse routines that invited the sharing of confusion and questions as well as understandings increased participation by guaranteeing that every student's contribution would be regarded as worthwhile.

Will not only created participation structures that supported collaboration, he also participated actively in group work, serving as a mentor and model for both collaborative processes and disciplinary reading and thinking. He described this role as one of "itinerant mentor." Will was proactive in his interactions with groups, spending time with all teams rather than responding only to problems. He took up temporary residence during group work to model and guide students in disciplinary ways of reading, thinking, and talking—although his participation also involved substantial amounts of listening. Indeed, to promote students' thinking and confidence in their ability to do challenging work, Will avoided giving answers. Rather, he guided students to answer questions themselves: "I may leave them with a question that will just help them organize their information so they can go on and answer their own question. Or I may propose an idea to them and let them respond and let them talk for a while. I want to reinforce the idea that they're the learners and can learn. I want them to actually practice learning and practice figuring things out and know that they are the ones who are doing it."

Science Inquiry

To apprentice students to the inquiry-based thinking and reasoning at the heart of science, Will started the year focused on developing habits of observing and questioning. He helped students acquire a language for identifying common types of science questions (attention focusing, measuring and counting, comparing, action prompting, problem posing, values reasoning) and coached his students to see the connection between these question types and the types of inquiry that would be needed to investigate and answer them (an analogue of Raphael & McKinney's question–answer relationships, 1983).

Will offered his students a variety of science inquiry experiences, including team investigations of chemical problems and phenomena, prepared ("cookbook") labs, open-ended laboratory inquiries, and student-generated laboratory explorations designed to answer student-generated questions. He coached students to develop and carry out investigative plans, for both teacher- and student-designed questions. Finally, Will supported students in writing lab procedures to carry out the investigations they had designed. Through this inquiry cycle, teams shared their inquiry questions with the whole class, then later their research plans and their results.

These inquiry activities made visible the ordinarily invisible processes of students' conceptual change. Through ongoing reflection and collaborative inquiry, students shared their ideas, tests, data, and inferences with one another, and apprehended others' ways of thinking about the subject of inquiry or the inquiry process itself. These inquiry conversations also allowed Will the opportunity to coach students through the otherwise invisible thinking processes of science. Just as Will engaged students in ongoing metacognitive conversations about how, as well as what, they read, science investigations provided rich opportunities to engage students in ongoing conversations about science processes—how we do science—as well as science content.

Year-Long Literacy Routines

Introduction to Chemistry was the least demanding science class that could be taken toward admission to community or state college. It covered about half the content of Will's college-prep chemistry. In our research, we found that Introduction to Chemistry students faced considerable language and literacy challenges in science. Nearly 40% of the students scored below the 10th percentile on standardized reading tests, and only two scored above the 25th percentile.

The rigorous academic landscape of Will's classroom was alien to the majority of his students, who were accustomed to rote learning assignments that required little thought. As a Reading Apprenticeship teacher, Will focused explicitly on academic literacy throughout the year, emphasizing ways of reading, thinking, and talking that are particular to science. Rather than presenting a smorgasbord of activities, Will concentrated on a handful of reading and discourse routines that he used over and over again in different ways. Metacognitive literacy routines and tools such as talking to the text (TttT), in which students annotated the text with their reading and thinking processes, and double-entry I saw/I thought journals supported students in reading and discussing everything from laboratory equipment to lab procedures to Lewis dot structures to numerical equations, and increased opportunities for science and literacy learning from these texts. Table 16.1 describes these reading and discourse routines.

Metacognitive Conversation

Among the routines that supported students' growth as science readers and learners were the many opportunities Will offered his students to discuss the ideas and texts of chemistry. In Will's classroom, conversational routines included the preambles, expert groups, and team reads already described. These conversational routines generally began with individual reflection, then moved to small-group and whole-class discussion before returning to the individual, providing opportunities for students to revisit, revise, and deepen comprehension and content knowledge as well as to practice and refine discipline-based thinking and reading processes. Topics of these conversations were wide ranging—students might grapple with a difficult concept or operation, connect new ideas to prior knowledge or discuss real-life applications of chemistry in a preamble; synthesize and consolidate information and ideas from multiple sources in an expert group; or tackle a particularly challenging section of text in a team read—but they nearly always involved reading and text of some kind.

Instructional Sequencing over Time

Fall

Introduction to Chemistry students were often not invested in learning, and promoting genuine participation in these classroom routines required labor, patience, and tact. Students who were unaccustomed to

TABLE 16.1. Reading and Discourse Routines in Introduction to Chemistry

• *Preambles.*	Each day began with a "preamble," a daily warm-up that brought students' individual reading and thinking into the wider classroom community. Preambles were also the primary venue for reading instruction.
• *K-W-L.*	Students used the K-W-L strategy to monitor what they knew, wanted to know, and what they learned about a topic. K-W-L supported both reading and doing science. Each lab was accompanied by a K-W-L, and K-W-L was also embedded in every reading log.
• *Expert groups.*	Some preambles and assignments were done in "expert groups," where each team responded to a different prompt about a topic-related problem. These problems often involved synthesizing information from multiple sources. After working on the problem as a team, groups presented their solution to the class and solicited their peers' feedback and assistance.
• *Reading logs.*	The primary tool to support students' reading of the textbook was a two-column "I saw/I thought" reading log. In one column, students recorded what they "saw" in the text; in the other, they recorded their thoughts—patterns they saw, questions they had, connections they made to prior knowledge. The focus of the reading log changed depending on the content, the demands of the text, and students' increasing academic literacy skills. In addition to supporting textbook reading, students also used the double-entry I saw/I thought format to record and interpret observations during labs.
• *Bringing reading into the classroom.*	Reading happened in the classroom. Because the students were not yet independent readers of the complex science texts of chemistry, Will explained: "We have to bring the reading into class, as well as the comprehension." When reading and conversations about reading materials took place in class, students' comprehension problems and their thinking were in evidence, and the class could work collaboratively to both build dispositions for problem solving and solve comprehension problems with the text.
• *Team reads.*	Team reads were a modified version of Reciprocal Teaching (Palincsar & Brown, 1989) in which students alternately read a small section of text individually and discussed the section with three teammates. In both the individual reading and small-group conversations, students monitored their reading and thinking processes and practiced three cognitive strategies: clarifying, questioning, and summarizing. Through this cycle of reading and talk, students practiced discipline-based reading skills and gained stamina for challenging reading as well as knowledge of the chemistry content.
• *Cooperative labs.*	Lab roles (facilitator, reader, editor, and resource person) involved facilitating, rather than doing, each task. The "reader," for example, coached teammates' close reading of procedural and informational texts associated with the lab investigation and facilitated discussion—but team members shared responsibility for reading and making sense of the material.
• *Inquiry.*	The spirit of inquiry was a common thread binding literacy and science in the classroom.

thinking about their reading initially saw little value in reading science materials or keeping a reflective reading log. Often, doubt and discomfort surfaced in the form of complaints—about having to write a log, about the length or difficulty of the reading, or about the dullness of the material. To help these students participate more skillfully in the literacy and science activities expected and valued in his class, Will began the year by establishing routines and structures that supported students in rethinking their conceptions of reading and learning and of themselves as readers and learners. In daily preamble prompts and accompanying metacognitive conversations, Will created ongoing opportunities to negotiate with his students more successful ways of being in the classroom, encouraging them to take on new, more powerful identities as readers and learners.

Winter

To support students' development as science readers, Will provided ongoing opportunities, and conveyed their responsibility, to reflect on their own thinking and learning through a small number of metacognitive literacy routines such as double-entry (I saw/I thought) reading logs, K-W-L activities, and team reads. As new reading opportunities arose in the classroom, Will modeled his own sense-making processes by thinking aloud as he worked to make sense of a reading or chemistry problem. By making his own reading and reasoning processes—the confusion, clarifications, and connections—visible, Will demonstrated mental engagement and problem solving as the hidden work of comprehension. His willingness to show his students how he actually *worked* to comprehend texts, helped students realize that it is strategic effort, not magic, that is involved in comprehension. As students read multiple types of science texts and carried out laboratory experiments and explorations using these complex literacy practices, they demonstrated emerging independence and internalization of science literacy competencies.

Spring

By spring, the focus in Will's classroom had clearly shifted to science content. The now-familiar metacognitive routines and structures became the backdrop against which learning science content happened. Will noted that as his students worked together on increasing their understanding of their reading and the chemistry, they developed not only a greater understanding of chemistry but also a sense of responsibility for their own and each others' learning. Although Will continued to play an active role as itinerant mentor, we also witnessed students mentoring one another, and their interactions were often distinguished by scientific thinking and discourse.

EDUARDO'S JOURNEY

Will designed his classroom routines and structures to move students toward more powerful academic identities, but students were sometimes reluctant traveling companions. During their first weeks together, Will guided an unwilling Eduardo to find his footing in an unfamiliar and forbidding landscape. As they traveled together over this difficult ground, with Will's support, Eduardo gained traction and enthusiasm and, eventually, the knowledge, skill, and will to move forward more confidently toward a new identity.

Fall: Finding Common Ground

Eduardo's turnaround began with Will's observation that, despite Eduardo's refusal to participate in most classroom activities, he seemed to enjoy being part of class discussions. At first, Eduardo's participation in classroom discussions was largely tangential—telling a classmate that he couldn't hear what she said, for example (field notes, 9/19/02), or piggybacking on another's idea with an off-handed, "Sounds good" (field notes, 9/9/02). However, Will consistently demonstrated that he valued students' thinking and participation, including Eduardo's, however negligible his contributions appeared to the classroom researcher! During a preamble discussion of summaries, for example, when Eduardo declined to share, saying his idea was similar to what a classmate had already said, Will asked him to share his thinking anyway, explaining, "It's important to hear different voices." By mid-October, under Will's mentoring, Eduardo was making more substantive contributions to classroom discussions and even volunteered to be the spokesperson for his team's expert group report.

Likewise, during group work, Will was careful to focus on Eduardo's potential contribution to his team, rather than on his misconduct. Will coupled his expectations for Eduardo's participation with the support necessary to ensure Eduardo's success as a group member. During an expert group activity in mid-October, Will asked an idle Eduardo, "How are you contributing to the group?" When Eduardo explained that he didn't have a book because of a library fine, Will talked with him about coming in at lunch until he could get a book of his own (field notes, 10/15/02). Will's focus on solving the problem that impeded Eduardo's participation, rather than laying blame, softened Eduardo's resistance. The following day, Eduardo came to class on time, took his assigned seat, and announced to Will that he took off his hat—signaling a new willingness to be part of the class. When his team made their expert group report to the class, Eduardo assumed the role of spokesperson (field notes, 10/16/02).

In the ensuing weeks, frequent metacognitive conversations provided ongoing opportunities for the class to explore social, personal, and cognitive aspects of reading and doing science. During these conversations, Eduardo expressed concern that the material was too hard, and Will expressed confidence in Eduardo's capabilities. Will shared strategies he used to make science reading more interesting and comprehensible, and he had students discuss what was easy, hard, interesting, and confusing for them (field notes, 10/23/02). Eduardo's confidence was increased both by the realization that reading science requires effort of everyone, including expert readers such as Will, and by the metacognitive reading routines that helped him identify his areas of confusion and provided support for solving problems.

In addition to providing support for solving reading problems, metacognitive conversations surfaced Eduardo's conceptions of schooling and what it meant to be a good student—conceptions that worked against his success—and put them on the table for negotiation. At the beginning of the year, when Eduardo learned that students could use their reading logs during tests, he snapped, "That's cheating." Metacognitive conversations challenged Eduardo's conception of reading proficiency as a fixed trait and helped him see that even good readers improve with practice and opportunities for collaboration. Gradually, Eduardo came to see reading as a tool for learning, rather than as an exam for separating good students from bad. Rather than shunning his fellow students, he came to value collaboration—both benefiting from, and contributing to, his classmates' thinking and learning.

As a result, Eduardo became increasingly willing to take risks as a reader and learner. In late October, despite complaining that an upcoming lab was "too hard," Eduardo participated and found the lab doable—as Will had predicted (field notes, 10/29/02). When Eduardo completed his lab report early, Will, leveraging Eduardo's increasing confidence, gave him a related reading assignment from the textbook, modeling how to use the "I saw/I thought" metacognitive reading log. Although the double-entry reading log was a well-established classroom routine, Eduardo had neglected his reading and reading log assignments and was not yet proficient in its use. Eduardo read his textbook for the duration of the class, making notes in his log (field notes, 11/12/02). The following week, during expert group reports on the lab, Eduardo was conspicuous for his engagement, serving as spokesperson for his group. He expressed interest in others' reports, asking one group a sophisticated question about measurement. When Will polled the class about who had their reading logs for a class discussion of the textbook, only Eduardo had his (field notes, 11/14/02). As he was leaving class, Eduardo asked Will for permission to take home his reading log, despite the fact that there was no assigned reading. He insisted, "I want to read tonight."

In addition to Will's mentoring, Will's grading policy, which awarded up to 80% credit for late assignments, was also instrumental in Eduardo's transformation. By allowing students to make up for late work, the policy held students to high standards but did not undermine the motivation of students such as Eduardo, who got off to a bad start.

Winter: Gaining Momentum

Seeing his efforts pay off was a crucial factor in Eduardo's turnaround. In late November, this young man, who claimed a few months earlier not to care whether he failed, sang aloud after getting back a corrected test: *"I got a B, and I'm so happy!"* The following week, when Will consulted his grade book about Eduardo's grade, Will told Eduardo, "You're right on the border." In fact, despite making considerable progress, Eduardo ended up with a D during the first marking period due to missing assignments.

Despite his low grade, Eduardo's new identity as a student had taken root. During the first semester, Eduardo's progress appeared primarily in the form of increased engagement—a willingness to participate in classroom routines—with little corresponding progress in completing assignments, including reading logs. He showed signs of a new resolve, but this resolve was still fragile and erratic. Eduardo continued to complain that the material was too difficult throughout the first semester (field notes, 12/5/02). However, following the winter break, Eduardo emerged as an agent of his own learning with his focus clearly on chemistry. He was frequently the first student in the room and was often finished with his preamble before his classmates settled down. In January, when Eduardo was confused about what had happened in a lab, rather than dismissing the lab as "too hard," he concluded that he needed to learn more about acids (field notes, 1/3/03). With the introduction of team reads in January, Eduardo was in fact able to work through an article on acids and bases, puzzling out the meaning of such technical words as *calorimetric* by examining its component parts.

With Will's guidance and encouragement, Eduardo practiced a variety of cognitive strategies, from questioning to clarifying. Reading in the article that "any acid will react with any base," he wondered, "Is that true?" He accurately explained the concept "driving force," to Will's apparent surprise. Although Eduardo and his teammates sometimes failed to notice what they didn't understand, and their summaries tended to identify the topic, rather than capture the gist of the passage, team reads helped Eduardo gain access to text that would have prompted passive resistance—or outright defiance—just months before.

As Eduardo gained confidence and expertise as a reader, Will also pushed him to use disciplinary language to describe his own thinking more precisely. During a lesson on summarizing, Will asked the class, "What is the important idea that keeps coming up [in this passage]?" When Eduardo responded, "The things about acids and bases,"

Will prompted, "[Can you use] another word?" Eduardo amended his response: "*Properties.*" The following day, Will highlighted the importance of Eduardo's contribution of "finding the word *properties*" during a recap of the previous day's lesson (field notes, 1/8/03, 1/9/03).

About this time, Eduardo also showed increasing interest in chemistry for its own sake. He chatted informally with Will, asking questions about chemistry—even when they weren't on the exam—and did extra reading for homework.

Spring: Traveling Companions

Will continued to mentor Eduardo in negotiating the demands of school. When Eduardo confided one day that he was tired, Will advised him, "Just work slowly and steadily when you're tired." Later in the period, Eduardo expressed surprise when he solved a problem about molecules and smells correctly. Will responded confidently, "Of course!" (field notes, 4/3/03).

In addition to providing support and encouragement, Will increasingly challenged Eduardo to think in discipline-based ways. During a preamble about smells, Will probed for the rationale behind Eduardo's prediction that two molecules with similar molecular formulas would smell similarly, and encouraged Eduardo to evaluate differences between the molecules systematically. Will also invited a teammate, Samuel, into the discussion and noted, "We have two different ideas that are both good ones."

Overcoming his initial resistance to working with others, Eduardo's collaboration with his teammate Samuel deepened over the year. Whereas Samuel served as Eduardo's tutor initially (e.g., coaching him on how to study for quizzes and do his reading log), by the end of the year, Eduardo and Samuel interacted as equals. In May, during an exploration of the relationship between molecular characteristics and smell, Will, pausing in his rounds as itinerant mentor, pointed out to Eduardo's group, "These molecules have almost the same formula, so that doesn't help. So there's something about the structure." Samuel suggested, "Hexagons." Will pointed to something that violated Samuel's theory that the hexagonal shape of the molecules accounted for their smell, saying, "These are hexagons, too, but they have what?" Eduardo noted, "Carbons on the inside." Will repeated (with enthusiasm), "Carbons on the inside!" According to the teacher's guide, students rarely apprehend the pattern of carbons on the inside. Eduardo was the first student in Will's class to notice this.

During the second semester, Eduardo also emerged as a leader among his peers: He admonished others for their tardiness, was intolerant of frivolity (except when he himself enjoyed an occasional lapse!), and encouraged classmates' participation in class discussion. In assuming this role, Eduardo frequently appropriated Will's supportive language, show-ing a special affection for Will's characterization of the class as "bright young students" (field notes, 5/27/03). During a preamble discussion on Lewis dot structure, for example, Eduardo took a lead role, volunteering to put his solution on the board and encouraging a classmate—whom he inveigled with the designation "bright young thing"—to do the same. In addition to getting his own problem right, Eduardo suggested corrections to his classmate's solution.

In April, as students worked on incomplete assignments, Will asked Eduardo to tutor Seth, who had been absent. He explained to Eduardo, "You'll become a super expert." Indeed, in the course of tutoring Seth, Eduardo used the periodic table, his reading log, and other handouts and papers to explain how to figure out the number of bonds. Eduardo's efforts were successful. At end of the period, Eduardo told Will proudly, "Seth's got it," and Seth told another classmate, "I thought that was hard [before Eduardo taught me how]." Eduardo suggested to Seth that he ask Will for a periodic table so that he could finish the assignment at home, and, duplicating the encouragement and support he received from Will, Eduardo also offered Seth, "Come tomorrow and I'll help you" (field notes, 4/24/03).

Eduardo Looks Back

In the collaborative learning environment nurtured in this classroom, Will's actions and, through Will's influence, the actions of classmates car-ried individual students through the many challenges of negotiating the unfamiliar language and literacy practices of science. In an end-of-year interview, Eduardo articulated how Will's ongoing support and the collab-orative learning environment he created, turned him around academi-cally.

> "I went to Dr. Brown, you know, and I seen that he cared for my grades and helping me out. When he told me I can get my grades up, I tried it and I seen it go up, so then I thought, from there on I said, you know, 'If I can do that, I might as well try harder.' And I started try-ing harder in school, in all my classes. . . . He just told me, 'Come, second lunch,' you know, 'and we'll talk it out.' Then we did labs I missed and it got my grade up. Dr. Brown made me realize you can [catch up]. So I thank him a lot.
>
> "Then Samuel [a teammate] helped me. I seen him, you know, working on this in class, on the labs. And since he was my partner for the whole year, he helped me out. We had some quiz, and the day before, he gave me a little sheet and he told me, you know, 'Just study this and you should get a good grade, just study.' And I started doing

the preambles, and he helped me out when I didn't understand it. . . . When I got my quiz back, I seen I got an A, I thanked him, and from there on, just started working hard.

When asked if there had been particular things Dr. Brown had done that year to support his reading of chemistry, Eduardo responded:

"Yeah. He picks me a lot in class. . . . I talked to him, and I told him, you know, if we could do more reading logs, and if he could pick me a lot.
    "When I had my first [reading log] and I tried it, you know, I did it with [my teammate] Samuel in class, you know. And he helped me realize it wasn't hard, you know. And one day, I came during lunch, and Dr. Brown helped me with what you're supposed to do, so from there, from both of their help, you know, I tried it at home and it came out. I got an A on it, you know."

In addition, Eduardo expressed his preference for reading in science:

"You know, I rather read this [chemistry textbook] than the English book. See, science seems interesting to me, so, you know, so I like to read."

Afterword: Traveling Solo

Eduardo repeated the first semester of Introduction to Chemistry as a senior to make up for the D he had received the first semester in Will's class and continued his success from the spring. His new chemistry teacher had him tutor his classmates. Eduardo graduated on schedule and planned to attend community college the following fall, en route toward his goal of becoming an engineer.

NEGOTIATING SUCCESS

The reading apprenticeship framework provided a starting point for our investigation into how teachers such as Will Brown might support underprepared and underachieving students to see themselves as readers, thinkers, and students. At the same time, our detailed analysis of classroom events and interactions alerted us to additional important aspects of the instruction (Thomas, 2003). Negotiating success emerged from this inductive analysis as a construct with the potential to explain the growth we witnessed in some classrooms in students' identities as readers and learners.

Like many teachers in our study, Will was fiercely committed to educational equity and worked with administrators and colleagues to implement structural and curricular reforms that promoted this goal. Will, who chaired the science department at his school, developed open enrollment requirements for Honors Chemistry designed to usher more African American and Latino/a students into rigorous academic classes, and worked concertedly with a fellow science teacher to create an enrollment pipeline from biology to chemistry and to design successful learning experiences for groups of students at Skyline who were underrepresented in the higher sciences nationwide. Yet in our research, it was classroom pedagogy rather than commitment to equity per se that determined whether such structural and curricular reforms were successful.

Perhaps because commitment to equity is a value rather than a practice, we found no direct correlation between commitment to equity and particular educational policies or classroom practices. Teachers in our study translated their commitment to underprepared students into a wide range of sometimes conflicting classroom practices. For example, teachers implemented very different classroom rules and policies based on a common desire to build students' academic knowledge and skills, differing in the extent to which they held students accountable to grading policies or modified policies in response to student need. In a move to hold all students to high standards, some teachers enforced a strict policy for late work. Other teachers, also motivated by concern for equity, prioritized learning opportunities over accountability and had more generous policies for accepting late work. Will explicitly encouraged students to make up missing assignments and implemented policies that rewarded students for doing so. Indeed, it was never too late to complete assignments in Will's class, and one student who had virtually dropped out of school continued to attend Introduction to Chemistry, working hard through the very last day of class to complete missing assignments and pass the course. Policies and practices that valued learning over accountability were a salient feature of classrooms where seemingly intransigent students made unexpected progress—and a core element of negotiating success. Table 16.2 summarizes key features of "negotiating success" with underprepared students.

Key elements of the Reading Apprenticeship framework—ongoing literacy learning opportunities, explicit strategy instruction, collaborative learning structures, and metacognitive inquiry into reading and learning—set the stage for instruction that fosters academic achievement. Yet without classroom interactions that emphasize student capabilities and reward effort toward learning, students may make little progress over the difficult terrain of high academic challenge. In order to benefit from high-quality curriculum and instruction, students must avail themselves of these learning opportunities. Will supported students to invest themselves in the rich

TABLE 16.2. Key Features of Classroom Practices That Negotiate Success with Adolescents

---

- *Classroom policies, norms, and assessments value learning rather than accountability.*
  The heart of negotiating success is ongoing formative assessment as embodied by the Latin *ad sedere*, meaning "to sit down beside." As its etymology implies, assessment is primarily used as a tool for providing guidance and feedback to students and to inform instructional decision making. For teachers who engage students in negotiating success, instructional decision making is guided by the question: "Will this encourage or discourage this student from investing him- or herself in the learning process?"

- *Teachers interpret student behavior generously, assuming all students want to learn.*
  Teachers assume that all students can and want to achieve at high standards and seize on any glimmer of student interest or disciplinary thinking—no matter how small or awkwardly expressed—as an opportunity to increase engagement and learning. This approach to elaborating on students' nascent instructionally focused thinking is akin to the powerful language facilitation strategy of responding to the intent rather than the form of children's speech with slightly more information or in a more sophisticated way (e.g., Whitehurst et al., 1988).

- *Teachers establish positive relationships with students strategically to leverage learning.*
  Caring teacher–student relationships are used as a lever for raising student achievement. Although teachers often make themselves available to students at lunch and after school, positive teacher–student relationships develop in the context of the classroom, rather than through extracurricular contact, and are inclusive of all students in the class. Knowledge of individual student interests and acknowledgment of individual student contributions are used to foster academic engagement.

- *Teachers establish metacognitive conversation to bring students' resources, knowledge, and even misconceptions into the classroom.* Classroom discourse routines and structures provide opportunities for students to bring conceptions of reading, learning, and school that do and do not serve them well into the classroom, where they can be acknowledged and influenced by the teacher and classmates. Ongoing conversations about problem-solving processes allow teachers to access, mentor, and guide student thinking and reading processes.

- *Teachers provide frequent opportunities and support for in-class reading, writing and talk.*
  The *success* in negotiating success is measured by students taking on more powerful identities as readers and students and, ultimately, achieving high levels of academic literacy. Frequent opportunities for in-class teacher- and peer-supported reading, writing, and talk help students negotiate academic language and texts. Literacy routines engage students in complex discipline-based activities and support them in gaining proficiency and capacity in academic reading and discourse.

---

literacy and science learning opportunities in Introduction to Chemistry by filtering his interactions, classroom policies, instructional moves, and decisions though a single criterion: "*Will this encourage or discourage this student from investing him- or herself in the learning process?*"

Negotiating success thus encompasses a broad range of classroom practices that position the teacher as a partner in a negotiation on behalf of students, who may neither appreciate nor desire such advocacy. In negotiating success, teachers must navigate a course between support and challenge, and making headway requires insight, patience, flexibility, and generosity.

CONCLUSIONS

Many students who have reached middle or high school with little experience of academic success have established identities as nonstudents or nonreaders. These negative reader identities coexist with multiple other identities in students' in-school and out-of-school lives. Most adolescents need support to develop key dispositions for approaching and engaging themselves in challenging academic tasks. These include general dispositions to be interested and critical learners—such as curiosity, tolerance for ambiguity, and the habit of mind to construct understanding—or the expectation that one should construct understanding of a topic—rather than passively carry out the prescribed procedures (Yore, 2004). Such dispositions also include ways in which students can themselves maintain confidence in the value of persistence and in their own abilities, even while struggling through challenging academic text.

A critical and often unacknowledged part of some adolescents' literacy development therefore involves helping them transform the identities of nonreader and nonlearner they construct in response to negative experiences in school into new identities as capable readers and learners (Gee, 1996; Mahiri & Godley, 1998). As adolescents explore, or try on, possible selves, teachers can encourage them to try on new reader identities, to explore and expand their visions of who they are and who they can become (Davidson & Koppenhaver, 1993). This shift in identity is critical if students are to embrace literacy, reengage as readers, and improve their academic performance. Feldman (2004) reminds us that "learning not only changes what we know and do, but it changes who we are" (p. 144). When we ask students to learn something new, we are asking them to become someone new. When teachers are able to provide consistent support for students to try on new ways of acting, thinking, and interacting, we see significant shifts in academic identity over the course of an academic year.

In this chapter we described how one teacher's willingness and ability (1) to provide learning opportunities that illuminated students' conceptions of reading, reading practices, and identities as reader and student; (2) to investigate and interpret students' thinking processes and learning experiences; and (3) to design and modify instruction and support based on this assessment of student need—a stance that we have labeled "negotiating success"—was a key factor in supporting one underprepared student to shift his identity as a reader and student. By offering the construct of "negotiating success," we hope to contribute to efforts to better understand and describe how teachers might translate their *commitment to equity* into *classroom practices* that help all students achieve high levels of academic literacy. Moreover, we hope to move the discussion of adolescent literacy development beyond a focus on school structures and instructional strategies to the quality of interactions in classrooms that support and foster new and more resilient learner identities.

DISCUSSION AND ACTIVITIES

1. Observe in a secondary classroom. Analyze teacher–student interactions using the key features of classroom practices that negotiate success with adolescents. Identify opportunities—both taken and missed—for the teacher to negotiate success with students. For each missed opportunity, generate an alternative response that sets the stage for negotiating success.

2. Interview a teacher about classroom policies, norms, and assessments. What are the underlying assumptions about students behind these policies, norms, and assessments? Analyze ways in which these policies support or undermine opportunities to negotiate success with adolescents.

3. Develop a grading policy that rewards learning rather than compliance. Consider what such a grading policy will demand of the classroom teacher.

4. Look back through Eduardo's development as a reader and learner in this class. What do the metacognitive conversations, documented through field notes, reveal about his capacities and resources? Consider how to structure classroom conversation to create ongoing opportunities for assessment of student motivations, interests, stamina, *and* knowledge and skill. Create a set of sentence stems for a teacher to use to support a stance of inquiry and negotiate success with learners in the classroom.

5. Interview one or more adolescents about their conceptions of reading, learning and school (if possible, choose students who are not faring well in class). (1) Probe students' early reading experiences, current in- and outside of school reading habits and preferences; (2) ask students for their self-assessment and goals as a reader; and (3) solicit students' advice about what teachers could do for them to help them become better readers by making reading assignments better. Analyze responses to identify students' conceptions of reading, learning, and school and of themselves as readers and students.

6. The policy or stance of negotiating success has profound implications for teacher–student interactions. What implications does negotiating success have for curriculum and instruction (e.g., pacing, participation structures, teacher's role)?

REFERENCES

Davidson, J., & Koppenhaver, D. (1993). *Adolescent literacy: What works and why* (2nd ed.). New York: Garland.

Feldman, A. (2004). Knowing and being in science: Expanding the possibilities. In E. W. Saul (Ed.), *Crossing borders in literacy and science instruction: Perspectives on theory and practice* (pp. 140–157). Newark, DE: International Reading Association.

Freedman, S. W., Flower, L., Hull, G., & Hayes, J. R. (1995). *Ten years of research: Achievements of the National Center for the Study of Writing and Literacy (Technical Report No. 1-C).* Berkeley, CA: National Center for the Study of Writing.

Garmezy, N. (1983). Stressors of childhood. In N. Garmezy & M. Rutter (Eds.), *Stress, coping, and development in children* (pp. 43–84). New York: McGraw-Hill.

Gee, J. (1996). *Social linguistics and literacies: Ideology in discourses* (2nd ed.). London: Falmer Press.

Greenleaf, C., Brown, W., & Litman, C. (2004). Apprenticing urban youth to science literacy. In D. Strickland & D. Alvermann (Eds.), *Bridging the gap: Improving literacy learning for preadolescent and adolescent learners in grades 4–12* (pp. 200–226). New York: Teachers College Press.

Greenleaf, C., Litman, C., & Braunger, J. (2007). *Academic literacy in the eleventh hour: Possibilities and imperatives for profoundly inexperienced high school students.* Manuscript in preparation.

Mahiri, J., & Godley, A. (1998). Rewriting identity: Social meanings of literacy and "revisions" of self. *Reading Research Quarterly, 33*(4), 416–433.

Pearson, P. D. (1996). Reclaiming the center. In M. Graves, P. van den Broek, & B. M. Taylor (Eds.), *The first R: Every child's right to read* (pp. 259–274). New York: Teacher's College Press.

Raphael, T. E., & McKinney, J. (1983). An examination of fifth and eighth grade children's question answering behavior: An instructional study in metacognition. *Journal of Reading Behavior, 15*, 67–86.

Schoenbach, R., Greenleaf, C., Cziko, C., & Hurwitz, L. (1999). *Reading for understanding: A guide to improving reading in middle and high school classrooms.* San Francisco: Jossey-Bass.

Scribner, S., & Cole, M. (1981). *The psychology of literacy.* Cambridge, MA: Harvard University Press.

Smagorinsky, P. (2001). If meaning is constructed, what's it made from? Toward a cultural theory of reading. *Review of Educational Research, 71*(1), 133–169.

Street, B. (1995). *Social literacies: Critical approaches to literacy in development, ethnography and education.* London: Longman.

Thomas, D. R. (2003). A general inductive approach for qualitative data analysis. Retrieved august 2003, from *www.health.aukland.ac.nz/thomas/resources/inductive 2003*

Yore, L. D. (2004). Why do future scientists need to study the language arts? In E. W. Saul (Ed.), *Crossing borders in literacy and science instruction: Perspectives on theory and practice* (pp. 71–94). Newark, DE: International Reading Association.

CHAPTER 17

Literacy Assessment for Adolescents
WHAT'S FAIR ABOUT IT?

Mark W. Conley

This chapter:

- Introduces principles of fair literacy assessment for adolescents.
- Demonstrates these principles in classroom practice.
- Suggests action research to evaluate our own assessment practices.

PRINCIPLES OF FAIR LITERACY ASSESSMENT FOR ADOLESCENTS

A good way to start this conversation is to consider what it is about our assessment practices that are not particularly fair. It is popular to argue that state and national assessments are not fair, especially those focused specifically on literacy. The same criticisms can be leveled against state and national assessments in the content areas (mathematics, science, social studies, and English) that are so heavily dependent now on solid literacy understandings and skill, rather than on discipline-specific knowledge and processes (Conley, 2005). But what is it about these assessments that seems so unfair?

James Popham, a long-time proponent of responsible assessment, captures succinctly many concerns about fairness of large-scale state assessments:

> Standards-based tests supposedly measure students' mastery of a state's officially approved content standards, that is, the skills and knowledge constituting the state's curricular aims. Yet because most states have adopted too

many content standards and stated them too vaguely, most states' standards-based tests just don't do a decent job determining a student's mastery of those standards. (2003, p. 50)

The problem, Popham writes, is that the hodge-podge of state standards and benchmarks underlying the tests say little, if anything, about what all would agree are desirable curriculum or assessment practices at the classroom level. This omission is an interesting irony in that not only is it difficult to claim accountability, because the standards are so numerous and ambiguous, but it can be nearly impossible to consider performance data generated by state tests to make specific changes in classroom practice.

The problems are compounded by ways in which large-scale assessment data are often reported—as percents (e.g., 60 or 70% successful), as categories (e.g., proficient or struggling), as statistical representations (e.g., below the third stanine), or even as coded language based on standards (e.g., proficient on standard VII, benchmark 3A)—none of which tells us much about our students' day-to-day literacy strengths and needs. Often, the center of our concerns about large-scale state and national assessments can be located in these incomprehensible ways that the tests and their results are communicated to us, our schools, the media, and communities. Add to that our "results-oriented" assessment culture in which results are frequently accepted at face value, with little, if any, questioning of the validity or value of the tests in the first place. Schools are deemed failures and students are marginalized despite the possibility that the tests are seriously flawed. No wonder we feel that these kinds of assessments are unfair!

What kinds of assessments are fair? Rick Stiggins, another assessment expert, provides several important guidelines (Stiggins, 2004). To be fair, assessments need to be based on clear targets or goals. They have to be accurate, assessing what has been taught and learned. They also have to provide feedback that adolescents can use to make good decisions about directing their attention and effort. And, finally, good assessments communicate information not only about performance but about growth. When all of these conditions are met, Stiggins says, we can say that an assessment is "fair." Put another way, when teachers place assessment information in the hands of their students, when their students understand the goals and what they need to do to achieve them, and when results are communicated with learning as the central concern, *then* assessment is fair.

To this, Popham adds the notion that assessments should be instructionally useful in order to be fair. Instructionally useful tests clearly articulate targets and desired student performance in ways that are consistent with Stiggins's ideas about placing assessment directly in the hands of the users. Not many large-scale assessments meet the criteria for being instructionally useful, but many classroom tests do. Tests that are instructionally useful share these characteristics:

- *Significance.* The test measures a worthwhile curricular aim. Instructionally useful tests can be related to curricular standards that are recognized as important.
- *Teachability.* The test measures a concept or strategy that is actually teachable. Constructs such as intelligence are not particularly useful for teaching. However, assessments of knowledge and strategies can be instructionally essential.
- *Describability.* The test makes use of clear and explicit language to describe concepts or strategies that are assessed. Tests that are esoteric or ambiguous are not as useful as tests that clearly represent what is being tested and how students are performing.
- *Reportability.* The test facilitates clear communication about how students are doing and how instruction needs to be changed to promote students' learning.

When we consider fair assessment and, particularly, instructionally useful assessment in the context of adolescent literacy, this picture becomes much more complex. The reasons are grounded in adolescents themselves as well as all of the complicated contexts in which adolescents live and learn. On the one hand, research in the past 10 years has resulted in a very rich picture of adolescents, including the formation and influence of identity, development, motivation, gender-related affiliations, racial and ethnic backgrounds, and multiple literacies (Alvermann, Hinchman, Moore, Phelps, & Waff, 2006). The notion of multiple literacies has opened up recognition that adolescents can be literate or struggle with literacy in a variety of ways. In a landmark study, Elizabeth Moje and her colleagues (Moje et al., 2004) documented how adolescents routinely engaged in discourse about problems in their community, such as water pollution, and yet a science teacher was unable to include their experiences in a unit about activism on behalf of the environment. Even when the teacher invited students to volunteer related experiences, the students still held back on offering what they knew because they felt it would not be valuable to the in-school discussion. In light of this complex view of students, assessment needs to take into account the many different ways that students come to, and participate in, classroom learning events.

For years, advocates of content-area literacy have tended to treat the content-area disciplines as monolithic (Conley, 2008). What this means is that, for example, science has been viewed as a single entity, not a discipline characterized by subdisciplines such as biology, chemistry, and physics. There can be many different philosophies about the goals and best ways to teach science. Similarly, mathematics has been characterized single domain, rather than one subdivided into algebra, geometry, and calculus. Within each discipline, there are often heated debates about purposes, whether to increase content knowledge, develop more strategic ability, or empower adolescents toward greater questioning, participation, and discourse. Rather than recognizing and responding to the complexity of teaching and learning in the disciplines, we in literacy have offered generic prescriptions for instruction and assessment, such as encouraging wide reading or the use of general teaching activities such as concept mapping, the know–want to know–learn (K-W-L) strategy, and reading/study guides (Fisher & Ivey, 2006). Viewed from an assessment standpoint, this generic approach eases the task of assessment. All that is needed is to assess general literacy strengths, using informal reading inventories, spelling inventories, writing samples, interviews, and observations, while keeping track of students' purposes for reading and writing.

The problem with this generic view is that it does not get even close to the complexity of adolescents, their literacies, and the changing purposes, expectations, and opportunities for learning that characterize an individual adolescent's movement throughout his or her day. Put in conventional assessment terms, what we have been prescribing for assessment from a literacy perspective is simply not valid. To be sure, information from general surveys, interviews, and observations can provide general information about an adolescent's literacy. But these techniques do so little to shed light on the issues that Moje and her colleagues (2004) reported: the complexities of adolescents' literacies and their willingness and opportunities to gain conceptual and strategic knowledge and expertise in and through subject-matter discourse. In order for literacy assessment to rise to meet this more complex view—of adolescents, their literacies and discourses, and subject matter—a much more explicit and targeted approach to assessment is required.

A system of fair literacy assessment for adolescents is presented in Figure 17.1. Consider what this system might look like through assessment in your own classroom.

PRINCIPLES OF FAIR LITERACY ASSESSMENT IN CLASSROOM PRACTICE

Recognizing and Building on Adolescents' Multiple Literacies

Carol Santa (2006) writes about her fears that current assessment policies narrow our vision of adolescents and the literacy curriculum that serves them. Adolescents and their experiences with literacy are highly diverse. A now common refrain is that adolescents can be incredibly literate in out-of-school experiences, such as those related to the media, games, and popular culture (Alvermann, Moon, & Hagood, 1999; Morrell, 2004). However, as complex as those out-of-school literacies can be, adolescents

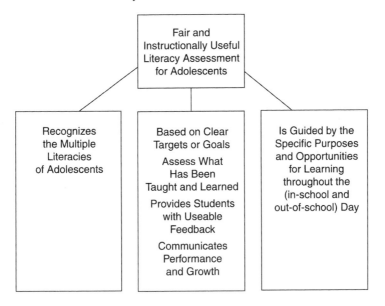

FIGURE 17.1. A model for fair, instructionally useful assessments for adolescents.

need guidance in acquiring the literacies and the discourses valued in the disciplines and the world of work. Assessment that focuses narrowly on one kind of literacy, such as print literacy, or one area of the curriculum, such as reading, misses the larger goal of helping adolescents build new literacies from their already richly literate experiences. As a result, fair literacy assessment for adolescents *must recognize the multiple and changing literacies of adolescents* both in the here-and-now and for their future. So what does assessment grounded in a vision of adolescents' multiple literacies look like?

I have a vision of a learner that guides my thinking about this question. Although I have been an educator for 30 years now, I have often taken side roads into other occupations, including aviation and lutherie (the ancient art of guitar building). Each time I do this, I place myself back in the position of a beginner, learning new things but relating them to what I already know. I have experienced passion for the new learnings, especially when I am able to compare what I already know as a learner with the new experiences. It has been especially motivating when my teachers acknowledge what I know while helping me understand connections to new concepts. My teachers have been extraordinarily literate in multiple ways, modeling what they know and are able to do, observing me as I try out the new ideas, providing me with useful feedback, and even assessing my performance with respect to clearly stated standards. Not too surprisingly, these principles of effective teaching and assessment have been a constant whether the activity involved landing an airplane or bracing a guitar top. In each case, I found myself clearly apprised of the goals for learning, keenly aware of what literacies I brought to the experience, in the hands of a knowledgeable and observant teacher, and continually updated on my progress toward the eventual goals.

Assessment that contributes to this vision starts with adolescents. What do they *know*, what do they know *how to do*, and what do they *care about doing* that could be a foundation for further learning? Where do they want to go in their lives? And how do they see themselves getting there? We are sometimes reluctant to ask these questions because the answers could seem uninformed, immature, or just plain silly. On the other hand, research has documented the aimlessness of adolescents and individuals into their 20s precisely because we are not asking these questions (Arnett, 2004; Schneider & Stevenson, 2000). It is also mighty difficult to build new knowledge and help adolescents move into other disciplinary and career worlds unless we and they clearly understand what they bring to the enterprise.

We can find out about adolescents' multiple literacies and create opportunities to build on them by asking them what they know and providing occasions for them to demonstrate what they can do. For example:

• Ask students to write a literacy autobiography, which can be tailored for use in the various content areas (e.g., "When have you been particularly literate with numbers? Where have you used your environmental literacy?").

• Have students keep a technology and media literacy journal and ask them to record, for a day or more, all of the instances of their interactions with technology (e.g., e-mail, instant messaging, web pages, word processing) and the media (e.g., television, movies, iPod, DVDs, CDs, newspapers, magazines, fanzines). Compare journals for evidence of learning something new, communicating with others, different topics, and so forth. Discuss with the class how these resources can be used with class topics and assignments.

• Ask students, "What will *your* future bring?" Have them interview a few people in an occupation that they would like to learn and ask them what kinds of preparation and education were needed. Students should also ask how reading, writing, and communicating are involved in the occupation they are investigating. Ask them: "What do you know now that will help you in your future occupation? What will you need to learn?"

The real advantage of designing assessments like this is that you will learn more about your students' multiple literacies while they showcase and explore what they know. This process will provide you with opportunities to incorporate your adolescents' multiple literacies into your teaching as well as find ways to build on their talents and experiences.

Grounding Instruction in Clear Targets and Goals

When I started my teaching career, goals for assessment were an after-thought. After all, the hard work was in the planning and execution of my lessons. As a beginning English teacher, I often surprised myself with the mountain of paperwork that would accrue, followed by puzzling over what sort of evaluation approach might make sense. But this isn't the worst part of this story. I learned that, without considering targets or goals ahead of time, I missed the opportunity to let students in on key purposes for learning. As a result, the students did not have the opportunity to focus their efforts effectively. Bottom line: It helps teachers plan and teach better, but also to engage students in their own assessment, if *instruction is grounded in clear targets and goals.*

With the movement toward greater educational accountability, it is not too difficult to establish targets or goals. National, state, district, and even school standards specify overly numerous choices for what to teach. The difficulty comes in selecting and communicating standards in ways that guide instruction and assessment. Standards written in "edu-speak" can be decipherable to experienced educators but can also be incomprehensible to others, especially students. Consider how you might rephrase the following curriculum standards, from Michigan's content standards, in ways that your students and/or their parents might understand as goals for teaching and assessment:

- The ability to use knowledge of social patterns on earth to understand processes that shape the human environment to make decisions about society (social studies).
- The ability to represent quantitative situations with algebraic symbolism, numerical operations, and algebraic thinking is essential to solving problems in significant contexts and applications (mathematics).
- In the physical sciences, explaining how real-world contexts include phenomena such as motion, electromagnetic interactions, or physical, chemical, and nuclear changes in matter (science).
- All students will explore and use the characteristics of different types of texts, aesthetic elements, and mechanics—including text structure, figurative and descriptive language, spelling, punctuation, and grammar—to construct and convey meaning (English).

Some goals and targets are embedded in state assessments. As much as we may dislike teaching to a test, sometimes there are valuable goals and targets within state tests, including the following (Conley, 2005):

- Analyzing questions.
- Taking a stand on content.

- Providing evidence for a stand or position.
- Thinking about what you know.
- Organizing your thinking.

"Backwards mapping" is a technique teachers can use to uncover the tested skills hidden within published tests (Conley & Gritter, 2007). To do backwards mapping, teachers can take the tests just like their students, while keeping a think-aloud journal of the cognitive or mental steps required for each type of item. Often, this leads to a list of skills, such as the ones above, that reflects the actual thinking required for students to do well on the test—as opposed to what the test makers thought they were embedding as a foundation for the test. A teacher may discover important life skills underlying the tests, such as being able to take an informed stand on an issue and defending it.

Finally, goals and targets do not have to come from standards or assessments at all. Teachers still make determinations about what is important for students to know, and know how to do, based on the students, the texts and tasks at hand, desired performances, content that comes before and after a lesson, as well as numerous other factors. The point here is that for responsible assessment, try to be as clear as possible with yourself and your students about goals and targets. That way, you will be in the best position to make effective teaching and assessment decisions, and students will be in a better position to learn.

Assessing What Has Been Taught and Learned

In the mid-1990s, Michigan experimented with a broader vision for assessment in English and language arts. The idea was to encourage students to make thematic comparisons across multiple genres—poetry, magazine articles, short stories, and plays. The assessment committee responsible for construction of the new state test envisioned questions that encouraged higher-order thinking along with responses that required extended constructions of meaning. This, the committee reasoned, was the perfect way to encourage teachers to teach literature using multiple genres and a great deal of meaningful writing. The assumption was that good assessment drives instruction in desirable directions and *is best when it focuses on what has been taught and learned.*

And so, for teachers, it is important to consider carefully what is going to be taught and learned and then figure out how to assess appropriately. Perhaps it would be useful to consider how things could go wrong before discussing how to make assessment congruent with teaching and learning. Michigan's broad vision for assessment was curtailed by a nervous assessment company. The company's lawyers worried that such a broad assessment would be expensive, suffer from reliability problems, and invite lawsuits. The political solution was to change from lengthy extended response items to multiple choice. As a result, the instructional model remained the same—thinking about broad, thematic statements across diverse texts—an English teacher's dream. However, the assessment format forced students to make a decision among four thematic statements, all of which appeared plausible in light of the content of the texts. This fairly clear case of incongruence between the instruction implied by the testing framework and the assessment format persists to this day.

How can teachers recognize and correct mismatches between teaching and assessment in their own classrooms? One way is to learn from assessments over time. Teachers design and administer assessments with the best of intentions every day. But it is also important to watch for cases of a collective "Huh!?" voiced by students when they take our tests. Massive rates of failure are often the first clue that an assessment is not measuring what has been taught or learned. Obvious problems are mismatches between content and tasks students have practiced during instruction combined with content and tasks on tests that are purely foreign to them. Other problems can come from overestimating students' ability to transfer their learning to more sophisticated content and tasks. Matching instruction to assessment means considering carefully what has been taught and what students likely have learned and then designing tests that reflect that vision.

Providing Students with Useable Feedback

There are times when just getting a B, a 90, or a "pass" is sufficient, especially if the score is a form of gatekeeping—such as just passing a difficult class or getting a score that is sufficient to earn a driver's license. But these kinds of scores do not provide information that could help us change our teaching, or help students learn more. For that to happen, *assessment must provide students with useable feedback.*

Providing effective feedback starts with a good understanding of students and clear targets by which to assess their learning. What do students know now? What are they able to do now? What big ideas do students need to learn? What tasks do they need to perform? Once you are able to answer these questions, it is time to think about the kinds of assessment that will provide useable feedback. Consider the case of teaching students the mathematical concept of area. Students are often exposed to the concept and formula for area at a very young age. When they get to middle school, many students can recite the area formula: length times width. And yet, few students may know that the concept of area actually stands for physical space. Students could complete a worksheet about area and take a paper-and-pencil test containing questions requiring computations of area—and still not understand that area is about physical space. So, what sorts of questions or tasks might help students understand what *area* means and also provide students with useable feedback about their under-standing?

One approach is to have students wrestle with a real-world, authentic task. In the case of area, real-world tasks are represented by the need to carpet or paint a house, for example. One mathematics teacher asked students to design their dream house. Using chart paper, students designed their house to scale, measuring the area of each room, including the floors and walls, and ultimately, the entire house. Next, students researched how much surface area a typical gallon of paint covers (about 400 square feet) and how much per square foot a typical carpet costs, and they calculated the costs of painting and carpeting the house, using their area computations and cost figures for paint and carpet. To assess their work, students were organized in pairs to cross-check their calculations and conduct a house inspection. The teacher circulated to observe the conversations, check students' work, and answer questions. The result? The teacher and her students gained useable feedback about their under-standing of area as it applies to carpeting and painting a house. Together, they located areas of understanding that still required work, and they were able to celebrate their successes. Not coincidentally, the focus of instruction—designing the dream house—was consistent with the assess-ment: checking calculations and reviewing the decorating scheme. Far more than receiving a simple numerical or letter grade, students received feedback that helped them understand what they had learned.

Communicating Performance *and* Growth

So many of the large-scale, high-stakes assessments such as state tests only assess performance. That is, these tests only provide snapshots of what students may have achieved, rather than a fuller picture of what students have actually learned over time. Performance-oriented measures are con-venient for policymakers and local school board members who concern themselves with broad questions about how school systems are improving. State tests, for example, can yield information about how many more stu-dents are reading well, compared with previous years. Because most state tests are not standardized, however, it is impossible—and, some would argue, unethical—to compare an individual student's scores on a reading test from year to year. Furthermore, performance-oriented tests often do not shed any light on a student's growth in specific areas, such as reading in social studies or mathematics, reading graphical representations in sci-ence, or improvements in composing, revising, or editing. A more com-plete approach requires assessment that *communicates performance and growth*.

So what do assessments devoted to growth look like? First, they are intimately connected with targets or goals. Growth-oriented assessments are targeted to provide very specific information about how and what students are learning. Secondly, growth-oriented assessments often take many forms, from observation of students while they are working to analysis of student work. Yet another feature of these assessments is that they can be given multiple times. Frequent assessment affords teachers many opportunities to see how students are doing and make instructional changes where necessary.

Consider this classroom example. A science teacher is working toward helping students understand how carbon is the basis of all life. The topical area is plants. She plans her early lessons to assess what her students believe about plants, their nutrition, and growth. Her assessment consists of pairing students to discuss a set of interview questions:

- How do plants get their nutrition (eat)?
- How do plants breathe?
- How do plants grow?

As students discuss the questions and record their responses, the teacher circulates, listening for their ideas. Not surprisingly, she hears little evidence that students implicate carbon in the life processes of a plant. She also hears many ideas that come from students' experiences with gardening and indoor plants. Some of these ideas represent misconceptions, including the idea that plants grow by taking up nutrients from the soil.

Throughout the lessons and labs that followed, this teacher observed changes in her students' thinking. A lab lesson demonstrated plant nutrition through hydroponics. A related experiment documented the uptake of carbon into plants. As the lessons progressed, the teacher observed changes in how her students were talking about plants and the role carbon plays in their nutrition and growth. The lessons culminated in a unit test using questions comparable to those found on the state test. But students were also paired again to review and change their original interview questions and responses. Based on these assessments, this teacher was able to track her students' performances (on the unit test) and their growth in understanding (via the paired interviews).

Creating Purposeful Learning Opportunities

Assessments should never be administered for their own sake. Assessments afford teachers and students *occasions for creating purposeful learning opportunities*. Here are some examples.

- A teacher discusses with her students issues and events in the local community that are connected to the current topic of study. For example, local churches have banded together to fight poverty and homelessness.

Several of the students' families have participated in the local campaign to build awareness and contribute to a special emergency fund for homeless families. The topic of study is immigration and cycles of poverty in the United States.

• Students take a pretest consisting of the culminating activity for a lesson or unit. In this classroom, the big idea concerns conversions from English to decimal units and where and why that information might be important. Through the pretest, students learn both about the targets for instruction and assessment. They also learn what they need to do to focus their attention on the new learnings. Finally, they gain an understanding of what they already know and are able to do with respect to the new learnings (e.g., some students have traveled overseas, where decimal units are more common).

• A teacher observes her students while they are engaged in persuasive writing. She discovers areas in which students require further instruction, such as providing evidence for their assertions. She is also able to discern the different kinds of help required by different students (e.g., some students have trouble writing introductions, others are stuck on the task of developing reasons). Through her informal assessment, she is also able to provide students with corrective feedback.

• Students complete a science unit project requiring Internet searches in response to important questions about global warming. As students complete the questions, they learn more about their topic of study, leading to more questions and additional areas of study (e.g., saving endangered species, preserving the rainforests).

ACTION RESEARCH TO ASSESS OUR OWN ASSESSMENT PRACTICES

Each year I teach a course called "Classroom Literacy Assessment." In this course my students, all experienced teachers, research their own systems of assessment in order to create improvements. Their choices of what to improve fall into the following categories:

Devising an Assessment for a New Curriculum or Program

Though publishers often provide assessments that go along with a new curriculum or program, these assessments may not work well with your students. Moreover, there are frequently other kinds of assessment, such as observations, checklists, or surveys, that are important as part of an ongoing focus on classroom assessment. Teachers research these alternatives and then devise an assessment appropriate for the new curriculum or program.

Improving upon or Revising an Existing Assessment

Some curricula or programs are portrayed as assessment systems. There are many assessment approaches for writing, including 6-traits (Spandel, 2004) and the Collins Writing Assessment program (Chadwell, 1999; Collins, 1992). Although these programs can be very effective in general terms, such as providing an assessment framework, there are often important pieces that are left out or not completely addressed. For example, the notion of a writer's voice can be very difficult to teach or assess. Teachers research these assessment programs and then devise options to improve them.

Developing a Better Understanding of State and/or District Assessments

Whereas some state or district assessments can be valuable from a performance perspective, it is often not clear how these assessments relate to classroom assessments. And so, some teachers take up the challenge of better understanding state or district assessments and then making connections to their classroom assessments. In one very interesting case, a teacher questioned the persistence of a district assessment, despite the fact that she could not discern its value for her students. Her project consisted of asking school and district personnel about the purpose for the test. Surprisingly, no one could answer her questions until she happened upon a retired reading specialist, who told her the original purpose and then expressed dismay herself that the test was still in practice. The district test was soon replaced. In short, gaining a better understanding of state and district assessments can lead to some fundamental changes in the entire assessment system.

Improving Communication about Assessment

When I first started teaching the assessment class nearly 15 years ago, teachers often complained about their required report cards. The chief complaint was that report cards did little to portray students' actual accomplishments and areas of need. They were either too detailed about the wrong concepts or skills, or they were not detailed enough. Since the early years, there has been a renaissance of changes in report cards, many of which now provide opportunities to portray growth.

Perhaps a bigger change, however, is the recognition that communication about assessment extends well beyond the report card. It starts with effective communication about goals and targets, which can take the form of brochures, information sheets, and letters home specifying upcoming topics of study and activities, and ways for parents to get involved. This practice raises awareness of both students and their parents regarding how to focus their attention and efforts.

Parent conferences are also a productive occasion for communicating about assessment. As a parent, the best parent conferences for me have been those wherein teachers layed out goals, explained their purpose, offered some information about how the goals were pursued, and shared before-and-after samples of my children's work. Combined with information sent home, these activities gave me a complete picture of what the teacher and my child were trying to accomplish, how my child was doing, and what the teacher was doing to help (Conley, 2005).

Sometimes I encounter resistance to these ideas from weary teachers who say, "Why should I send out brochures or letters when none of the parents read them?" Or, "I only have 10 minutes for each parent during parent conferences and there just isn't time." Some teachers wonder if conflicts with parents will continue if they follow these steps. My response is that the struggles to communicate won't evaporate, but that these steps reflect professionally responsible communication about assessment. Some parents may not read the brochures or letters. There may only be 10 minutes in the gym, especially for middle and high school teachers. And some parents may disagree with your goals or approaches to instruction and assessment. On the other hand, by following such steps, one can at least demonstrate one's own commitment to fairness through assessment.

CONCLUSION

And so, for adolescent literacy assessment, what is fair about it? As I have described in this chapter, there are several current practices that can make assessment unfair. Narrowly prescribed or overly ambiguous standards and assessments can make state assessments and the practices that result from them unfair. Assessments that obscure rather than communicate performance are unfair.

Fair assessment starts and ends with clear targets or goals. Knowing what is being assessed helps teachers make consistent instructional and assessment decisions, and it helps—and even motivates—students to learn more effectively. Useful targets are specific, avoiding the abstractness or edu-speak characteristic of many state standards or assessment frameworks. Identifying clear targets can be challenging, especially when one considers all of the ways in which literacy manifests itself in the content areas: through reading, writing, speaking, and listening embedded in all kinds of content-area assignments and activities. However, clear targets can also focus teachers' inquiry into what a diverse group of adolescents might bring to a set of topics and related instructional and assessment activities.

Another important principle concerns grounding instruction in clear targets or goals. In other words, once targets and goals are identified, teachers need to ensure that instruction and assessment are congruent. A related idea is that assessment should focus particularly on what has been taught and learned. Often, the best way to ensure that targets, instruction, and assessment match up is to study and compare instruction and assessment over time, paying particular attention to students' performances and thinking.

Assessments should provide students with useable feedback so that they can direct their efforts and improve. Many state assessments provide only snapshots of performance, which are important for policymakers but usually not sufficient for teachers and their students. Performance assessments should be balanced with growth-oriented assessments, or assessments used on multiple occasions over time to track students' growth toward desired learnings. Good and fair assessments also create purposeful learning opportunities in which teachers can learn about what students already know or have experienced, determine where students need extra help, and assist students in extending their learning into other areas of interest. Taken together, these principles represent a vision for adolescent literacy assessment and the commitments we can all make to ensure that it is both fair and effective.

DISCUSSION AND ACTIVITIES

1. One of the most shocking situations is the lack of consistency in how we as teachers come to understand assessment. Picture this: a school full of teachers who were all taught about assessment in different, almost random ways. A message from this chapter is that for assessment to succeed, there must be clear targets or goals. Discuss your approaches to assessment with a colleague or your grade-level or subject-matter team. What differences do you detect in your assessments? What similarities? What are some ways that you can make your targets or goals more consistent with one another?

2. Few, if any, of us are left untouched by state standards or assessments. Try these activities:

   • Reword a state standard in such a way that you could explain it to your students and/or their parents.
   • Compare state standards in literacy or your content area with your classroom curriculum and assessments. How congruent are you with the state standards? How do you know that what you are teaching is worthwhile?
   • Using sample items from a state test in your content area, take the test. On a separate piece of paper, keep track of the steps you need to take for each of the test items (e.g., take a stand, support your decision, think about what you know). Consider ways that you are teaching these assessed skills in your curriculum.

3. Create a pre-assessment for a topic you will teach in which you explore:

   • What students already know or have experienced about the topic.
   • The multiple literacies your students have available to explore the topic.
   • The literacies your students will need to learn about the topic.

4. Using ideas presented earlier about researching your own assessment practices, make a change in your approach to assessment.

5. Design a culminating assessment activity that extends your students' learning.

REFERENCES

Alvermann, D., Hinchman, K., Moore, D., Phelps, S., & Waff, D. (2006). *Reconceptualizing the literacies in adolescents' lives.* Mahwah, NJ: Erlbaum.

Alvermann, D., Moon, J., & Hagood, M. (1999). *Popular culture in the classroom: Teaching and researching critical media literacy.* Newark, DE: International Reading Association.

Arnett, J. (2004). *Emerging adulthood: The winding road from late teens through the 20's.* New York: Oxford University Press.

Chadwell, G. (1999). *Developing an effective writing program for the elementary grades.* West Newbury, MA: Collins Education Associates.

Collins, J. (1992). *Developing writing and thinking skills across the curriculum.* West Newbury, MA: Collins Education Associates.

Conley, M. (2005). *Connecting standards and assessment through literacy.* Boston: Allyn & Bacon.

Conley, M. (2008). Improving adolescent comprehension: Developing comprehension strategies in the content areas. In S. Israel & G. Duffy (Eds.), *Handbook of research on reading comprehension.* Mahwah, NJ: Erlbaum.

Conley, M., & Gritter, K. (2007). A pathway for connecting standards with assessment: Backward mapping of assessment tasks. In J. Paratore & McCormack (Eds.), *Classroom literacy assessment: Making sense of what students know and do* (pp. 21–33). New York: Guilford Press.

Fisher, D., & Ivey, G. (2006). Evaluating the interventions for struggling adolescent readers. *Journal of Adolescent and Adult Literacy, 50*(3), 180–189.

Moje, E., Ciechanowski, K., Kramer, K., Ellis, L., Carrillo, R., & Collazo, T. (2004). Working toward third space in content area literacy: An examination of everyday funds of knowledge. *Reading Research Quarterly, 39*(1), 38–70.

Morrell, E. (2004). *Linking literacy and popular culture: Finding connections for lifelong learning.* Norwood, MA: Gordon.

Popham, J. (2003). The seductive allure of data. *Educational Leadership, 60*(5), 48–51.

Santa, C. (2006). A vision for adolescent literacy: Ours or theirs? *Journal of Adolescent and Adult Literacy, 49*(6), 488–478.

Schneider, B., & Stevenson, D. (2000). *The ambitious generation: America's teenagers, motivated but directionless.* New Haven, CT: Yale University Press.

Spandel, V. (2004). *Creating writers through 6-trait writing assessment and instruction.* Boston: Allyn & Bacon.

Stiggins, R. (2004). *Student-involved assessment for learning.* Upper Saddle River, NJ: Prentice Hall.

CHAPTER 18

Program Development

David W. Moore

This chapter on secondary school literacy program development:

- Begins with background information.
- Presents leadership structures.
- Describes instructional sites.
- Analyzes characteristics of effective programs.

With U.S. youths' reading test scores remaining stationary and achievement gaps among groups persisting (Grigg, Donahue, & Dion, 2007), with high school graduation rates hovering about 50% in urban schools (Graduation profiles, 2007), and with high-stakes tests expanding (Callahan, 2007), adolescent literacy programs have been mushrooming. Although reading educators have advocated secondary school reading programs since at least the 1930s (Moore, Readence, & Rickelman, 1983), the current attention to them is unprecedented.

Developing quality programs that enable students to move beyond basic reading and writing to the more complex academic literacies of adolescence is challenging yet crucial.

KEY TERMINOLOGY
AND INFLUENTIAL RECOMMENDATIONS

Terminology

In the late 1990s about half of the high schools in a large U.S. survey reported having reading programs (Barry, 1997). However, analyses of many of these programs revealed that they offered intervention services only to special needs students or English learners, virtually ignoring the reading development needs of others. Additional programs offered only

313

minor services, such as creative lesson planning, cooperative learning, and extra study time. Because educational terms such as *reading program* often have multiple meanings, some clarification of terminology is appropriate here.

This chapter concentrates on secondary school reading programs that address academic literacy. Here *program* means a comprehensive schoolwide curricular agenda. Such agendas concentrate on what is taught throughout the entire school; they go beyond special classes as well as products and services that might be purchased or adopted.

Secondary school refers to precollegiate institutions where students attend mostly separate subject-matter classes. Subject-matter separation can begin as early as fourth grade, although it typically is found first in middle schools that start at sixth, seventh, or eighth grade; secondary schooling ends at twelfth grade. To be sure, adolescents develop literate lives in ways not governed by school structures. But adolescents' literacy proficiencies in schools deserve attention in part because they shape youths' occupational and academic futures. Moreover, this chapter focuses on *academic literacy*, the reading and writing used in school contexts. Academic literacy programs might connect with youths' lives beyond school, but emphases are placed on the language encountered inside school across scholastic domains.

Influential Recommendations

Several documents currently available provide an informative backdrop for developing secondary school programs in academic literacy. Their main points are presented here to suggest the intellectual milieu encompassing secondary school literacy program development.

In 1999 the International Reading Association Board of Directors endorsed *Adolescent Literacy: A Position Statement*, which members of its Commission on Adolescent Literacy composed (Moore, Bean, Birdyshaw, & Rycik, 1999). As Figure 18.1 shows, this statement contains seven research-based principles for supporting adolescents' literacy growth. The first three items address materials, instruction, and assessment—three major components of curricular programs. The second set of three items concentrates on teachers—vital influences in any literacy program. The final item calls attention to the contexts of adolescent literacy that permeate schools.

In 2004 the Alliance for Excellent Education, in partnership with the Carnegie Corporation of New York, published *Reading Next: A Vision for Action and Research in Middle and High School Literacy* (Biancarosa & Snow, 2004). This document recommends research-based ways to meet struggling readers' needs while moving the adolescent literacy field forward. The right-hand column of Figure 18.2 contains the *Reading Next* elements aimed at improving secondary schools' infrastructure. As can be seen, items 10 and 12 point to major components of a literacy program, time

1. Adolescents deserve access to a wide variety of reading materials that they can and want to read.
2. Adolescents deserve instruction that builds both the skill and desire to read increasingly complex materials.
3. Adolescents deserve assessment that shows them their strengths as well as their needs and that guides teachers to design instruction that will best help them grow as readers.
4. Adolescents deserve expert teachers who model and provide explicit instruction in reading comprehension and study strategies across the curriculum.
5. Adolescents deserve reading specialists who assist individual students having difficulty learning how to read.
6. Adolescents deserve teachers who understand the complexities of individual adolescent readers, respect their differences, and respond to their characteristics.
7. Adolescents deserve homes, communities, and a nation that will support their efforts to achieve advanced levels of literacy and provide the support necessary for them to succeed.

FIGURE 18.1. *Adolescent Literacy.* From Moore, Bean, Birdyshaw, and Rycik (1999). Copyright 1999 by the International Reading Association. Reprinted by permission.

and assessment. Items 11, 13, and 14 sensibly emphasize human resource support for teachers. Item 15 identifies two key characteristics of effective literacy programs: comprehensiveness and coordination.

To assist educators involved with adolescent literacy policy and practice, the Center on Instruction published *Academic Literacy Instruction for Adolescents* (Torgesen et al., 2007). This report begins with well-researched recommendations for literacy instruction in the content areas, then describes literacy interventions for struggling readers and English language learners. Next, this report discloses the advice a group of senior adolescent literacy researchers offered middle and high school literacy leaders. Figure 18.3 contains this advice. The points in Figure 18.3 present a valid, systemic perspective on secondary school literacy programs.

Instructional Improvements	Infrastructure Improvements
1. Direct, explicit comprehension instruction	10. Extended time for literacy
2. Effective instructional principles embedded in content	11. Professional development
3. Motivation and self-directed learning	12. Ongoing summative assessment of students and programs
4. Text-based collaborative learning	13. Teacher teams
5. Strategic tutoring	14. Leadership
6. Diverse texts	15. A comprehensive and coordinated literacy program
7. Intensive writing	
8. A technology component	
9. Ongoing formative assessment of students	

FIGURE 18.2. *Reading Next.* From Biancarosa and Snow (2004). Copyright 2004 by Alliance for Excellent Education. Reprinted with permission from Carnegie Corporation of New York.

Advice to a Middle or High School Literacy Leader

1. Provide a clear message about the importance of literacy.
2. Curriculum, assessments, and school structure must focus on improved literacy outcomes.
3. Instruction that builds reading comprehension should occur in content areas and in interventions designed to meet the needs of struggling readers.
4. Staff development is critical to help teachers design and implement instruction that will improve student reading comprehension.
5. Additional and/or redesigned resources will be needed to address improvement in students' reading comprehension.

FIGURE 18.3. *Academic Literacy Instruction for Adolescents.* From Torgesen et al. (2007). Copyright 2007 by Center on Instruction. Reprinted by permission.

The remainder of this chapter builds on the documents just presented in three sections on adolescent literacy program development: leadership structures, instructional sites, and characteristics of effective programs.

LEADERSHIP STRUCTURES

Leadership is essential for literacy program success. Literacy leadership plays a major role in supporting school populations' commitments to building a culture of literacy (Davidson & Koppenhaver, 1993). Commitments to literacy are seen in the norms of behavior that circulate throughout schools. Visitors to a secondary school that is committed to literacy might observe unusual numbers of students carrying library books or paperbacks; they might hear teachers, staff, and administrators talking about lessons that embed reading and writing; and they might notice conspicuous displays of students' literacy performances along with posters promoting new books and literacy-related events. Students, teachers, staff members, and administrators in such schools would be demonstrating their dedication to reading and writing.

Figure 18.4 shows leadership structures commonly distributed across secondary school sites. The nomenclature used in this figure presents common titles, but, as noted earlier, educational terms are slippery. Literacy *coaches* might be called *specialists, facilitators, consultants,* or *implementers* (Roller, 2006). Charter schools and small school districts might not even have district-level literacy leaders and committees. Countless variations are possible. The relevant point here is that leadership structures typically are distributed across *administrators, literacy leaders,* and *committees.*

School site	Administrator	Literacy leader	Literacy committee
District	Superintendent, assistant superintendent	Literacy curriculum coordinator	Advisory council
School	Principal, assistant principal	Literacy coach	Literacy improvement team
Core/ department	Core leader/ department chair	Literacy cadre	N/A

FIGURE 18.4. Literacy leadership.

Administrators play absolutely crucial roles in developing literacy programs (Wepner, Stickland, & Feeley, 2002). Their primary role is to recognize and support reading professionals as they plan, implement, and develop effective reading instruction (Professional Standards and Ethics Committee of the International Reading Association, 2004). Administrators sponsor literacy programs by stating their support explicitly and frequently. They allocate needed time, space, and materials; staff the program and sustain professional development; and reward faculty who embrace and help accomplish literacy goals.

District

At the district level of a comprehensive secondary school literacy program, leadership structures might include a superintendent or assistant superintendent, literacy curriculum coordinator, and literacy advisory council.

Literacy Curriculum Coordinators

Literacy curriculum coordinators at the district level work mainly with administrators and teachers in areas of staff development and curriculum design. They guide the adoption and purchase of commercial materials, then supplement the materials according to program requirements. They might produce newsletters and develop professional libraries, procure grants, and support school media specialists in acquiring print and digital reading materials. They typically help support literacy-related initiatives, such as those involved in immigrant assistance and school-to-work transitions. Especially in today's era of standards-based accountability, literacy coordinators often take the lead in conducting summative literacy assessments and reporting the results to state-level authorities, school board members, parents, and other constituents.

Literacy Advisory Councils

Literacy curriculum coordinators generally form and chair advisory councils consisting of stakeholders such as community members, parents, students, teachers, and administrators to help prioritize efforts. For instance, a council might (1) recommend focusing a program on struggling readers who are not served well in separate intervention classes; (2) concentrate on developing partnerships with the business community; and (3) suggest a range of special literacy services for English language learners who are newcomers.

School

At the school level, literacy program leadership positions might be distributed among a principal or assistant principal, literacy coach, and literacy improvement team. These school-based positions are parallel to school district ones.

Literacy Coaches

Literacy coaches have become highly visible literacy leaders at the school-building level (International Reading Association, 2006). To illustrate, U.S. Senator Patty Murray (D –WA) considers them so important that since 2003 she has introduced the Pathways for All Students to Succeed (PASS) Act, a $1 billion plan for hiring literacy and mathematics coaches for grades 6–12 at a ratio of at least 1 for every 20 teachers (Pathways for All Students to Succeed Act, n.d.).

The Literacy Coaching Clearinghouse (*www.literacycoachingonline.org*) is a fresh venture of the International Reading Association and National Council of Teachers of English. Its mission is to build teachers' capacities to offer quality literacy instruction, thereby increasing students' literacy achievement. The National Council of Teachers of English, acting alone, offers a gateway website (*www.ncte.org/collections/literacycoach*) with links to many valuable resources on literacy coaching.

Coaches work primarily with teachers, providing literacy-based professional development (Roller, 2006). At present, more literacy coaches work in middle schools than in high schools. They support the development and implementation of classroom literacy services, spending much of their time with assessments and planning instruction. For instance, literacy coaches' duties range from conversing with colleagues about students' reading needs, to holding core/departmental meetings and coplanning lessons, to modeling lessons and debriefing teachers' videotaped lessons.

Figure 18.5 presents six qualities that define the work of effective literacy coaches (Shanklin, 2006). In line with the general role of a literacy

1. Facilitates collaborative dialogue for teachers at all levels of knowledge and experience in a building.
2. Facilitates development of a school vision about literacy that is site-based and linked to district goals.
3. Demonstrates both evidence-based student and teacher learning.
4. Provides ongoing, job-embedded professional learning.
5. Provides classroom observations that are cyclical and knowledge building over time.
6. Supports rather than evaluates.

FIGURE 18.5. Characteristics of effective literacy coaching.

coach, the qualities point to ways in which coaches can support teachers' classroom literacy instruction.

Literacy Improvement Teams

Literacy improvement teams at the school level function in a manner similar to advisory councils at the district level. Team members study literacy assessment data, state-level criteria, and the professional literature to determine their school's standing. They help develop school literacy goals and corresponding action plans.

Electing representatives of the various academic cores or departments to school-level literacy improvement teams leads to balanced viewpoints and connections among all faculty members with literacy goals. Subject-area teachers can address the reading and writing demands specific to their disciplines. Additionally, guidance counselors or social workers can lead efforts for emotional and health supports that shape literacy, and students can represent their points of view on what is needed. Administrators are also important members of such a team. Literacy improvement teams meet regularly, on a long-term basis, to analyze results and refine goals and plans. As one teacher put it, these teams serve as the "conscience of literacy leadership" (Fisher, 2007, p. 98).

Core/Department

Typical secondary school organizational structures include cores (sometimes called *families*, *pods*, or *teams*) in middle schools and departments in high schools. Core leaders and department chairs play important roles of recognizing and supporting literacy initiatives in their domains. Literacy committees rarely exist at sites as small as cores or departments.

Literacy cadres are central groups of teachers who commit to 1- to 3-year professional development efforts in literacy instruction. Cadre participants can be drawn from teachers of the same discipline or from multiple disciplines. They might be compensated through federal or state funds, or they might earn professional growth credits to advance on the salary schedule. Literacy cadres usually begin by collaborating with a literacy coach and one another to explore and expand effective practices.

Literacy cadre training typically is intensive, meeting a few times each month. Participants consult the professional literature and training materials to examine research-based teaching practices. They apply selected practices in their classrooms, conducting action research on their effects and writing and talking about their critical reflections on the practices. They observe the practices in one another's classes, then debrief their observations. Many participate in ongoing lesson study.

Over time cadre members become literacy leaders. After focusing on their own teaching and their students' literacy achievement, literacy cadre members pass their new-found expertise on to networks of colleagues during staff development sessions. Mandating all teachers' participation with a literacy cadre might be tempting, but working with volunteers is best (Anders, Hoffman, & Duffy, 2000). The volunteer pool tends to build as teachers see literacy instruction making a difference in colleagues' classrooms.

In summary, academic literacy programs require leadership for direction and support. Effective programs distribute such leadership across school sites (Langer, 2002). Additionally, these programs deliver instruction in more than one location.

INSTRUCTIONAL SITES

Secondary school literacy programs address students' abilities in places that fit secondary schools' organization. Such instruction occurs mainly in literacy classes devoted to reading and writing as well as in content-area classes devoted to subject matter. Many programs also provide literacy services through sites outside of conventional classrooms.

Literacy Classes

Literacy classes can stand alone or supplement what is taught in English/ Language Arts. Programs that offer literacy classes usually have students take them in addition to their core English/Language Arts classes. A difference typically is made between inclusive literacy classes (i.e., courses designed for all students) and intervention classes (i.e., courses designed for students who struggle with reading). Depending on school populations, literacy classes intended only for special needs students or English Language Learners also might be offered.

Inclusive Classes

Inclusive reading classes, which are more common in middle schools than high schools, are designed for all students. Teachers in these classes generally concentrate on vocabulary and comprehension strategies that apply to more than literary texts. They might teach students how to use word parts to determine unfamiliar word meanings, assess one's own understandings, and repair misunderstandings. They might also teach students to recognize how texts are organized and use that organization as a tool for learning. In addition, teachers might help youth learn to locate reliable information online and take tests strategically. Teachers in these classes typically make it known that all readers encounter challenging passages, so they present strategies that apply to all levels of challenge.

In this era of standards-based accountability, teachers in inclusive classes often devote special attention to the state reading and writing standards that students find especially challenging. Moreover, effective teachers prepare students for the state exams without focusing only on them; they discount intensive test-preparation drills (Langer, 2002).

Intervention Classes

Many secondary school programs offer intervention classes intended to accelerate youths' literacy development. These classes usually admit students whose reading test scores are at least 2 years below grade level or whose teachers recommend enrollment. Students might be required to enroll in these classes, or they may enter voluntarily. They might take the course as an elective or an English/Language Arts credit. A common goal of these classes is for participants to make 1½–2 years reading growth in 1 year of instruction.

Intervention classes normally provide extra help by using materials created for struggling readers and keeping student–teacher ratios smaller than regular classes. Many adolescents of poverty have experienced checkered academic literacy instruction, so their reading and writing struggles are due more to missed learning opportunities than to difficulties in learning per se. These youth often have well-developed funds of general knowledge and strategic thinking abilities, so effective interventions link these resources to the academic tasks at hand. Students who think that reading involves pronouncing words steadily and understanding their messages automatically benefit from interventions that show how to strategically access the meanings of unfamiliar words and work through the demands of disciplinary texts. Because many youth who have experienced setbacks with academic literacy come to identify themselves as nonreaders, interventions are designed to promote literate identities and reconnect these students with academic literacy. For a small segment of students with reading difficulties—perhaps 10%—that has trouble with basic word processing (Kamil, 2003), interventions are designed to remove this roadblock to more sophisticated literacies.

As secondary school literacy interventions have increased, commercial interests have followed. Figure 18.6 lists selected materials currently on the market that are designed as comprehensive, core offerings. Among other things, the *many dimensions* in the figure caption refers to student anthologies, corresponding teachers' editions, and resources for multiple strands of literacy instruction aligned with scope and sequence plans. These materials also include components such as technological supports, leveled libraries, and assessments.

Figure 18.7 lists selected commercial materials that are limited to a specific service (i.e., *few dimensions*, as noted in the caption). For instance, Accelerated Reader provides multiple age-appropriate books along with a computerized system that monitors and rewards student test performance with the books. Saxon Phonics provides systematic intensive phonics instruction with words largely presented in isolation. Teachers are expected to weave students' uses of these materials into more comprehensive webs of instruction.

Several recent resources have reviewed secondary school literacy intervention materials (Alvermann & Rush, 2004; Deshler, Palincsar, Biancarosa, & Nair, 2007; Shanahan, 2005). These reviews contain information about the materials' goals (e.g., fluency, comprehension), theoretical premises (e.g., individualized, discussion-based), components (e.g., assessments, technology), and data-based evidence of effectiveness (e.g., control group, independent evaluator). In addition, Chapter 14 of this text, an article by Greenleaf, Jiménez, and Roller (2002), and textbooks by Beers (2003), Curtis and Longo (1999), and Schoenbach, Greenleaf, Cziko, and Hurwitz (1999) give especially valuable information about secondary school literacy intervention classes.

School Success Classes

Many high schools provide school success classes—sometimes called *academic boot camps*—to instruct incoming ninth-grade students in what is needed to succeed in their new, potentially more demanding situations. These courses have titles such as Success Seminar, Bridge to High School, and Freshman Experience. Literacy coaches often affiliate with school counselors and others in preparing and presenting these classes.

School success classes focus on teaching students how to learn, how to take charge of their learning, and how to develop habits of effective learners. Along with reading and writing proficiencies, these classes address general school success skills such as managing time productively,

Title	Publisher	Website
Achieving Maximum Potential (AMP)	Pearson/AGS Globe	agsglobe.com
Caught Reading Plus	Pearson/AGS Globe	agsglobe.com
Corrective Reading	Science Research Associates	sraonline.com/index.php/home/curriculumsolutions/di/corrective reading/102
Hampton–Brown Edge	Hampton–Brown/National Geographic School Publishing Group	hbedge.net/
High Point	Hampton–Brown/National Geographic School Publishing Group	hbhighpoint.com
Jamestown Reading Navigator	McGraw-Hill/Glencoe	www.glencoe.com/
LANGUAGE!	Sopris West	language-usa.net
Merit Software	Merit Software	meritsoftware.com
Passport Reading Journeys	Voyager Expanded Learning	voyagerlearning.com
Ramp-Up Literacy	America's Choice	americaschoice.org
Read 180	Scholastic	teacher.scholastic.com/products/read180/
Read Now with Power Up!	Renaissance Learning and Steck Vaughn	renlearn.com
Reading with Purpose	McGraw-Hill/Glencoe	glencoe.com/catalog/index.php/subject?c=1668&s=7645
Soar to Success	Houghton Mifflin	eduplace.com/intervention/soar/
Wilson Reading System	Wilson Language	wilsonlanguage.com

FIGURE 18.6. Secondary school literacy intervention materials: Many dimensions.

Title	Publisher	Website
Academy of Reading, Academy of Reading 2000	Autoskill International	autoskill.com
Accelerated Reader	Renaissance Learning, Inc.	renlearn.com/reading.htm
Be a Better Reader	Globe Fearon	agsglobe.com
Comprehension Upgrade		
Reading Upgrade	Learning Upgrade	learningupgrade.com
Failure Free Reading	Failure Free Reading	failurefree.com
IndiVisual	IndiVisual Learning	indivisuallearning.com/
Jamestown Education	Jamestown Education/ Glenco Online	glencoe.com/gln/ jamestown/index.php4
Junior Great Books	The Great Books	greatbooks.org
Lindamood–Bell	Gander Publications	blp.com/index.html
My Reading Coach	Mindplay	mindplay.com
Phono-graphix	Read America	readamerica.net
PLATO Reading Strategies	PLATO Learning, Inc.	plato.com
READ RIGHT	READ RIGHT Systems	readright.com
REWARDS	Sopris West	rewardsreading.com
Rosetta Stone	Rosetta Stone Language Learning Success	rosettastone.com/en/ education/k12-edu
Saxon Phonics Intervention	Harcourt Achieve	saxonpublishers.harcourtachieve.com
Strategies for Older Students (SOS)	Lexia Learning	lexialearning.com/ products/reading/sos.cfm
TeenBiz 3000	Achieve3000	achieve3000.com
Thinking Reader	Tom Snyder Productions	tomsnyder.com/products/ product.asp?SKU=THITHI

FIGURE 18.7. Secondary school literacy intervention materials: Few dimensions.

setting and meeting goals, resolving conflicts productively, and attributing learning to individual effort rather than luck. Incoming students might meet school alumni and community leaders who describe the mission, history, and traditions of the school and who serve as role models for academic success. Emphasis is on self-actualization—becoming all that someone can become.

Content-Area Classes

In addition to literacy classes, schoolwide secondary school literacy programs provide reading and writing instruction in content-area subjects. For instance, English/Language Arts teachers explain the connections they make while interpreting "But soft, what light through yonder window breaks?" Mathematics teachers demonstrate how to make sense of terse sentences such as "Describe the graph of the inequality $|x - 3| < 2$." Science teachers show how to use Greek and Latin word-part knowledge to determine the meanings of terms such as *heterozygous*. And social studies teachers have students use timelines as tools for reading and recalling historical eras.

For a secondary school literacy program to be schoolwide, reading and writing instruction needs to be connected with the school's content-area classes. The literacy cadres noted earlier are one way to instill academic literacy instruction across the curriculum. In a similar approach, the faculty of a particular school, core, or department identifies their students' literacy needs, then arranges for training sessions in addressing those needs. The teachers examine a set of general literacy strategies, such as graphic organizing or self-questioning (Barry, 2002), then determine how these strategies best fit their particular classes. They also identify strategies that are specific to their disciplines (e.g., interpreting literary characters' traits through dialogue, completing multistep mathematical operations, determining biases in public documents reporting scientific lab experiments) and determine how to teach them.

Instructional frameworks, which state the specific teaching practices that a program recommends, offer especially good direction when infusing literacy goals and practices across the content areas. Frameworks provide program participants with a common focus, language, and perspective toward literacy improvement. District-level advisory councils or school-level literacy improvement teams typically produce or adopt a framework, including only defensible instructional elements supported by research.

Figure 18.8 lists the elements of three representative literacy frameworks. Ash (2004) offers her framework for middle schools, basing it on "classroom experience, work with middle-school teachers, and a synthesis of successful tutoring programs and critical literacy theories" (p. 1). The Carnegie Corporation of New York funded development of the far-reaching Biancarosa and Snow (2004) report, and the profession has been granting it considerable stature. Figure 18.8 lists this report's recommendations for instructional improvements—that is, those items that are appropriate for an instructional framework. Fisher (2001) credits his framework as the key instrument in turning around reading performance in a large urban high school.

No matter what framework is put into place, effective program leaders and participants work for deep understandings of its contents. Frameworks are not meant to comprise a grab bag of rainy-day activities; they are meant to serve as a principled approach toward validated instructional practices.

Some secondary school program leaders work on their own to connect literacy instruction with the content areas. They might begin by consulting relevant textbooks such as those by Alvermann, Phelps, and Ridgeway (2006), Braunger, Donahue, Evans, and Galguera (2005), Buehl (2001), and Vacca and Vacca (2008). Other program developers bring in external, technical assistance. They might turn to college or university fac-

Ash (2004)	Biancarosa and Snow (2004)	Fisher (2001)
Guided reading of text	Direct, explicit comprehension instruction	Anticipatory activities
Direct instruction of comprehension strategies	Effective instructional principles embedded in content	Read-alouds
Peer-led discussions of text	Motivation and self-directed learning	Graphic organizers
Word study	Text-based collaborative learning	Vocabulary instruction
Purposeful oral reading and text production	Strategic tutoring	Writing to learn
Inquiry that involves self-selected reading and writing	Diverse texts	Structured notetaking
	Intensive writing	Reciprocal teaching
	A technology component	
	Ongoing formative assessment of students	

FIGURE 18.8. Literacy instruction frameworks.

ulty members with expertise and experience in literacy across the curriculum. Or they might sign up agencies such as those listed in Figure 18.9 to promote literacy instruction in content-area classes.

Service providers such as Project CRISS provide consultants along with explicit plans and materials for staff development. Other providers, such as America's Choice, Success for All, and Talent Development High School, go even further, providing comprehensive school reform models that address such matters as personnel to hire, literacy classes to offer, and technical assistance to obtain (cf., CSRQ Center Report on Middle and High School CSR Models, 2006). The reviews of instructional materials presented earlier (Alvermann & Rush, 2004; Deshler et al., 2007; Shanahan, 2005) also assess many of the service providers listed in Figure 18.9.

Additional Sites

Secondary school program developers who enact schoolwide approaches often create reading and writing situations for adolescents that go beyond literacy and content-area classes (Moore & Hinchman, 2006). Their goal is to embed literacy development opportunities throughout the school. Additional sites for adolescent literacy development include libraries and media centers; extended opportunities; and cross-age, home–school, and community–school partnerships.

America's Choice	americaschoice.org
Advancement via Individual Determination (AVID)	avidonline.org
Creating Independence through Student-Owned Strategies (Project CRISS)	projectcriss.com
Disciplinary Literacy	instituteforlearning.org
STEPS	stepspd.org
Strategic Instruction Model (SIM)	ku-crl.org/sim/index.html
Strategic Literacy Initiative (SLI)	wested.org/stratlit
Strategic Teaching and Reading Project (STRP)	ncrel.org/sdrs/areas/issues/educatrs/profdevl/pd2lk199.htm
Success for All (SFA)	successforall.com
Talent Development High School (TDHS) Talent Development Middle School (TDMS)	csos.jhu.edu

FIGURE 18.9. Adolescent literacy professional development service providers.

Libraries and Media Centers

Youth can obtain materials for their personal or class-required independent reading or inquiry projects at libraries and media centers. Additionally, librarians and media specialists often go far in providing literacy-
rich school settings. They offer safe havens for adolescents to meet before
and after school and refine their academic learning. They are instrumental in identifying and providing books for schoolwide independent and
summer reading requirements. Still more, they offer individualized computer software that fits individuals' learning styles and protects them
from embarrassment. For instance, reading fluency software with voice
recognition capabilities can monitor readers' rate and accuracy, dispas-
sionately prompting readers with correct pronunciations as needed.

Especially in middle schools, librarians and media specialists often
engage youth in promotional efforts to encourage reading and writing.
Along with reading contests, read-a-thons, book fairs, storytelling events,
and such, they promote touchstone texts. Working with the school literacy
team, they select an accessible yet substantive book, perhaps *The Skin I'm
In* (Flake, 1998), *Whale Talk* (Crutcher, 2002), or *Speak* (Anderson, 2006),
for everyone in a school to read. They promote the book through posters,
announcements, class visits, assemblies, and teachers' meetings. Administrators, athletic coaches, and others chime in on the wonder and power of
the touchstone text. Students read and respond to the book during desig-
nated times. When possible, the author visits the school to talk about the
book, in particular, and literacy, in general.

The book is called a *touchstone text* because it is meant to inform the
lives of those who read it; it is meant to serve as a common experience to
which everyone in the school can refer when enacting and talking about
their own lives. As Nielsen (2006) puts it, touchstone texts "inhabit the
reader, and the reader, in turn, writes the texts into his or her life" (p. 5).

Extended Opportunities

Extended opportunities give youth additional chances to improve their
reading and writing. For example, extending the school day or year provides more time to learn, and different instructional settings sometimes
offer added benefits. Extended literacy learning opportunities typically
occur before and after the regular school schedule: for example, early
morning tutoring sessions, late afternoon book clubs, Saturday acade-
mies, and summer school interventions. Online programs that serve students across school district lines are pioneering new models of teaching
and learning literacy. Many follow performance-based models that per-
sonalize reading and writing for each individual. Extended opportunities
are focused on improving test performance, facilitating the transition to
high school (i.e., school success classes), and enriching current knowledge

and proficiencies. Class titles such as Books for Boys, Read to Achieve, and Start Up! are common. Another type of extended opportunity occurs when English/Language Arts teachers team with social studies teachers. Here two teachers combine their classes into a 90- or 120-minute block and integrate their subject matter and literacy instruction.

Cross-Age Partnerships

Older students work with younger ones in cross-age partnerships. Older students might tutor younger ones in the same schools, although middle and high school youth usually visit elementary schools in these arrangements. Youth might produce children's picture books according to particular genre-based guidelines, then share the books with their primary grade buddies and deposit them in the children's classroom libraries. Youth also might coauthor books with their partners; support children's efforts with their literacy-based schoolwork; write back and forth online and in print as pen pals or book club members; read aloud, reread, and share books to promote interest as well as fluency; and tutor children in specific literacy strategies.

Home–School Partnerships

Home–school partnerships usually emphasize communication, updating family members about their youths' status through meetings, telephone calls, newsletters, progress reports, and face-to-face conferences. Instructional partnerships that seek to connect homes and schools through literacy include compacts and family book discussions.

Literacy compacts are agreements youth, family members, and teachers sign, indicating their promise to perform certain actions. Some actions typically included in a literacy compact are:

- Student will read a self-selected book for at least 1 hour each week outside of school.
- Student will talk with a family member at least once a week about what he or she is reading or writing in school.
- Student will complete homework prior to the day it is due.

Family book discussions involve youth and at least one family member in discussing a book they have both read. Teachers typically introduce to a class a list of no more than 15 books suggested for family book talks. Students consult with their family member, rank their top choices, then receive a book for themselves and their family partner.

The youth and family member might record their thoughts about the reading any time or at the ends of chapters, then have the partner react to what he or she wrote. The reactions can be done in writing, too. Conversely, the family partners might talk about what he or she read, with or without written prompts. After finishing the book, students share their assessments of the experience with their partners, one another in class, and the teacher. Students also might write a report of the experience, perhaps including some audio or visual record of their discussions.

Community–School Partnerships

Community–school partnerships connect youth with retirees, local business personnel, governmental leaders, postsecondary institutions, and service group members such as Rotarians and Optimists. *Community members*, acting on their own or as representatives of local groups, might promote literacy by coming to schools and participating in book discussions, describing career or general life experiences for students' reports, or serving as an external audience or evaluator for students' exhibitions.

Service learning is a widespread community–school partnership with a literacy component. Youth volunteer their time in child- or senior-care centers, food banks, or health and recreational facilities, where they inquire into issues related to their service, then report what they learn.

Workplace partnerships involve youth in hosting guest speakers, job shadowing, internships, and mentoring arrangements. Again, students normally document and report their workplace experiences.

Business and community groups sometimes grant money for educational purposes. Educators fund technological resources as well as books through these partnerships. And postsecondary schools have bridge programs with their secondary partner schools to help youth transition to the new, often intimidating, college or university settings.

In brief, secondary school programs offer literacy instruction mainly in classes devoted to reading and writing and through professional development efforts to connect it with content-area classes. Other sites for literacy development include libraries and media centers, extended opportunities, and partnerships. When determining expectations and guidelines for these sites, literacy leaders do well to adhere to the characteristics of effective programs, discussed next.

CHARACTERISTICS OF EFFECTIVE PROGRAMS

Effective secondary school literacy programs share certain characteristics that appear in various forms, befitting the various settings. Educators can use such characteristics as guidelines when planning and assessing programs. The characteristics presented here—direction, resources, professional development communities, responsiveness to students, and monitoring for continuous improvement—were synthesized from the recommendations presented earlier in this chapter (Moore et al., 1999; Biancarosa & Snow, 2004; Torgesen et al., 2007).

Direction

Practically every study of instructional improvement notes the importance of clear direction (Fullan, 2001). To be effective, program participants require clear understandings of where a program is meant to go as well as the means to get there.

Mission and Goals

Missions are what people aspire to achieve. Clear missions create the glue that unites a program's participants and directs decision making. Mission statements are lofty and far-reaching signposts that aim in a certain direction, rather than blueprints of specific actions. The stated mission of literacy programs may focus on concerns mainly inside schools, such as in programs that seek

- To ensure the academic success of students at all levels of achievement and in all content areas.
- To develop in each student the necessary proficiencies to acquire and apply knowledge.

Other missions may address actions inside as well as outside schools, such as in programs that intend

- To empower youth to become self-directed lifelong learners inspired by their personal quests for understanding.
- To enable adolescents to develop the communication skills they need for succeeding in, and improving, the changing world.

Goals are subordinate, intermediate statements that support mission statements. They direct programs more explicitly and narrowly than mission statements by focusing participants on doing what is needed to accomplish the mission. Literacy-related goals often are stated in terms of student outcomes, such as the following:

- To enable students to read actively and strategically.
- To increase learners' academic vocabularies in every discipline.
- To develop avid readers.
- To build youths' academically literate identities.

To be practical, student-outcome goals take into account what is tested on local and state assessments (Langer, 2002). Teachers address the format of such assessments while promoting meaningful goal-directed learning.

Standards of Practice

Standards of practice define what effective teachers know and are able to do. For instance, effective secondary school literacy teachers are known to use multiple texts, teach comprehension strategies, and engage students in substantial amounts of reading (Allington, 2007). Standards of practice for literacy across the content areas are named in the instructional frameworks presented in Figure 18.8. To clarify these standards, teachers read and listen to descriptions of them, view actual demonstrations as well as video recordings of them in action, and use rubrics to assess how effectively the practices are implemented. Linking standards of practice to goals and clarifying them is a good way to provide direction in a program.

Development Cycles

Development cycles provide direction by clarifying the overall, ongoing process of initiating and implementing a program. They are long-range multistep tools for knowingly and systematically directing programs. Development cycles contain steps such as the following (Irvin, Meltzer, & Dukes, 2007; National Association of Secondary School Principals, 2005):

1. Assess needs.
   - National, state, and local tests
   - Business, community, and educational stakeholders
2. Decide directions.
   - Mission
   - Student outcome goals
3. Design an action plan.
   - Objectives
   - Steps
   - Person(s) responsible
   - Resources
   - Timeline
   - Evaluation
4. Implement the plan.
   - Course development
   - Professional development
   - Culture of literacy

5. Monitor and adjust.
   - Student learning
   - Faculty and administrator capacity

Resources

The term *resources* refers mainly to the materials, people, and time needed to create and sustain a program. For instance, classroom space and furnishings are needed for literacy classes. Print and digital reading materials that are meaningful to youth, that matter and are of interest to them, and that are at multiple levels of difficulty, are needed for effective instruction. Highly qualified teachers and support staff are needed. Time is needed for instruction as well as for professional and program development.

The use of various resources is closely connected, so planning needs to be judicious (Deshler et al., 2007). For instance, if a program decides to reduce its literacy intervention class sizes, then more classrooms and teachers or other services probably are needed. If multilevel reading materials are prized, then contingencies are needed for obtaining them and arranging classes to work with them.

Notably, during a recent statewide secondary school literacy initiative, the programs that identified limited resources as a deterrent to success tended to be the ones with less sense of professional community (Bacevich & Salinger, 2006). Schools with a stronger sense of professional community found ways to overcome their lack of resources and be successful.

Professional Development Communities

Infusing reading and writing instruction across the content areas is a big part of a comprehensive schoolwide program. However, such infusion can be challenging because the structure and culture of secondary schools often work against it (O'Brien, Stewart, & Moje, 1995). Subject-matter teachers tend to focus instruction entirely on the subjects, disregarding explicit attention to reading and writing. Professional development communities devoted to literacy instruction address this situation directly.

Small groups of teachers working in professional communities to develop their day-to-day instruction characterize effective programs (Dufour & Eaker, 1998). A program's mission, goals, and standards of practice are highlighted as teachers collaboratively support the problem solving and risk taking needed to accomplish them.

Professional community meetings might begin with open-ended sharing, move to a focused consideration of a selected issue, and end with action plans. Community members share knowledge in an open, collegial manner, reviewing standards and the professional literature and consulting with knowledgeable others. Colleagues support one another's teaching by exchanging resources, observing and coaching one another, and assessing what students produce. Professional development communities are key to enabling secondary school teachers to improve their students' literacies.

Responsiveness to Students

Adolescent growth in literacy requires a continual stretching from students, sometimes uncomfortably so. Because of this challenging aspect, effective secondary school literacy programs respond to students' social–emotional interests along with their intellectual ones (Hinchman, Alvermann, Boyd, Brozo, & Vacca, 2003/2004).

Teachers are responsive when they tap into youths' backgrounds and abilities as foundations for school-based learning. For instance, literature teachers show how literary strategies for inferring fictional characters' motivations are like everyday strategies for figuring out peer and family members' motivations. They select texts that speak to youths' concerns and keep pace with their developing sensibilities. They embrace today's new literacies, or 21st-century skills, that include digital, multigenre representations.

Adolescents' gender, peer group, socioeconomic class, and a host of other social–cultural factors influence how they participate in academic literacy practices. Teachers respond to this complexity in part by emphasizing positive relationships in class. They treat everyone as insiders, as members of the literacy club. They demonstrate how academic literacy and learning can fit everyone's life, and they select texts that acknowledge the varied social composition of high school students. Teachers accommodate students who are learning English in part by routinely providing comprehensible texts, introducing key vocabulary, and supporting their comprehension strategies.

Effective literacy programs have plans for responding to individuals at risk of failing. Tiered procedures are in place, such as schoolwide screening, individual progress monitoring, diagnostic testing, parental conferencing, inclusive reading class placement, mentoring, weekly progress reports, intervention class placement, and special tutoring. Demonstrating high expectations and caring attitudes while moving through these procedures allow teachers to respond effectively to students.

Monitoring for Continuous Improvement

A common finding among highly effective literacy programs is their regular use of assessments to guide decision making (Langer, 2002). Programs that beat the odds examine a range of information sources and act on the data as soon as possible.

At the school level, assessments inform program emphases. Administrators and literacy leaders examine national and state assessments of their schools, along with district or school benchmarks. They draw on rating scales, such as those Ivey and Fisher (2006) provide, to assess the literacy instruction in English/Language Arts and content-area classes, the prevalence of self-selected reading, the quality of interventions being provided, and the schoolwide support for literacy. They conduct regular literacy walkthroughs in their schools to evaluate the implementation of literacy practices, and they observe classroom lessons, perhaps using the Learning Point Associates forms (*www.learningpt.org/literacy/adolescent/observation.php*) for detailed analyses. Such school-level assessment data are used to guide decisions about school actions in general as well as about groups and individuals in particular. Program members use the data openly to determine the next steps, not to assign blame or shame.

At the classroom level, teachers and students use assessments to inform instructional decisions. They might complete monthly or quarterly reviews of their progress toward stated goals, such as ones addressing the amount of self-selected reading or the quality of each student's responses to reading. Informal assessments such as fluency checks, vocabulary appraisals, strategy trials, and self-assessments of writing provide ongoing monitoring. When conducted during and immediately after units of instruction, assessments show teachers what needs to be retaught, and students, what still needs to be learned. Constant observations enable teachers to monitor students' performance and provide just-in-time recognition and support.

A CLOSING WORD

Secondary school programs that effectively develop students' academic literacies share certain features. Their leadership structures cut across the school district and school to provide needed direction and support. These programs promote reading and writing in multiple locations and provide multiple services. They are characterized by schoolwide cultures that enhance the literacies of all youth.

DISCUSSION AND ACTIVITIES

1. Outline a schoolwide literacy program for your school, attending to features listed in this chapter. Consider how this program will meet the literacy needs of all the students in your school.

2. Describe the steps you would take to organize a schoolwide literacy program planning team in your school, bringing various ideas for such a program together into a comprehensive whole.

3. Discuss the resources you would need to implement your vision of a schoolwide program. What human and material resources do you need to make your program work? What are the essential elements, and what are those features that would be nice but are not required?

4. Discuss the similarities and differences in program goals and design for a secondary school literacy program at the middle school level and at the high school level.

REFERENCES

Allington, R. L. (2007). Effective teachers, effective instruction. In K. Beers, R. E. Probst, & L. Rief (Eds.), *Adolescent literacy: Turning promise into practice* (pp. 273–288). Portsmouth, NH: Heinemann.

Alvermann, D. E., Phelps, S., & Ridgeway, V. G. (2006). *Content reading and literacy: Succeeding in today's diverse classrooms* (5th ed.). Boston: Allyn & Bacon.

Alvermann, D. E., & Rush, L. S. (2004). Literacy intervention programs at the middle and high school levels. In T. L. Jetton & J. A. Dole (Eds.), *Adolescent literacy research and practice* (pp. 210–227). New York: Guilford Press.

Anders, P. L., Hoffman, J. V., & Duffy, G. G. (2000). Teaching teachers to teach reading: Paradigm shifts, persistent problems, and challenges. In M. L. Kamil, P. B. Mosenthal, P. D. Pearson, & R. Barr (Eds.), *Handbook of reading research* (Vol. 3, pp. 719–742). Mahwah, NJ: Erlbaum.

Anderson, L. H. (2006). *Speak*. New York: Penguin.

Ash, G. E. (2004). *Everything secondary administrators need to know, but are afraid to ask: Understanding pragmatic adolescent literacy planning*. Naperville, IL: Learning Point Associates. Retrieved October 17, 2006, from *www.learningpt.org/pdfs/literacy/adolescent.pdf*

Bacevich, A., & Salinger, T. (2006). *Lessons and recommendations from the Alabama Reading Initiative: Sustaining focus on secondary reading*. Washington, DC: American Institutes for Research. Retrieved November 22, 2006, from *www.air.org/publications/documents/ARI%20Popular%20Report_final.pdf*

Barry, A. (1997). High school reading programs revisited. *Journal of Adolescent and Adult Literacy, 40*, 525–531.

Barry, A. (2002). Reading strategies teachers say they use. *Journal of Adolescent and Adult Literacy, 46*, 132–141.

Beers, K. (2003). *When kids can't read: What teachers can do–a guide for teachers 6–12*. Portsmouth, NJ: Heinemann.

Biancarosa, F., & Snow, C. E. (2004). *Reading next: A vision for action and research in middle and high school literacy–a report to Carnegie Corporation of New York*. Washington, DC: Alliance for Excellent Education. Retrieved August 18, 2005, from *www.all4ed.org/adolescent_literacy/index.html*

Braunger, J., Donahue, D. M., Evans, K., & Galguera, T. (2005). *Rethinking preparation for content area teaching: The reading apprenticeship approach*. San Francisco: Jossey-Bass.

Buehl, D. (2001). *Classroom strategies for interactive learning* (2nd ed.). Newark, DE: International Reading Association.

Callahan, J. (2007). High school assessments 2006–07. *Diplomas count: Ready for what?* Retrieved June 12, 2007, from *www.edweek.org/ew/articles/2007/06/07/40policy 3.h26.html*

Crutcher, C. (2002). *Whale talk*. New York: Dell Laurel-Leaf.

CSRQ Center Report on Middle and High School CSR Models. (2006, October). *Comprehensive School Reform Quality Center*. Retrieved January 12, 2007, from *www. csrq.org/MSHSreport.asp*

Curtis, M. B., & Longo, A. M. (1999). *When adolescents can't read: Methods and materials that work*. Cambridge, MA: Brookline Books.

Davidson, J., & Koppenhaver, D. (1993). *Adolescent literacy: What works and why* (2nd ed.). New York: Garland.

Deshler, D. D., Palincsar, A. S., Biancarosa, G., & Nair, M. (2007). *Informed choices for struggling adolescent readers: A research-based guide for instructional programs and practices* (commissioned by Carnegie Corporation of New York). Newark, DE: International Reading Association.

Dufour, R., & Eaker, R. (1998). *Professional learning communities at work*. Bloomington, IN: National Educational Service.

Fisher, D. (2001). "We're moving on up": Creating a schoolwide literacy effort in an urban high school. *Journal of Adolescent and Adult Literacy, 45*, 92–101.

Fisher, D. (2007). Creating a schoolwide literacy initiative. In J. Lewis & G. Moorman (Eds.), *Adolescent literacy instruction: Policies and promising practices* (pp. 95–109). Newark, DE: International Reading Association.

Flake, S. G. (1998). *The skin I'm in*. New York: HyperionBooks.

Fullan, M. (2001). *The new meaning of educational change* (3rd ed.). New York: Teachers College Press.

Graduation profiles. (2007, June). *Diplomas count: Ready for what?* Retrieved June 12, 2007, from *www.edweek.org/ew/articles/2007/06/12/40gradprofiles.h26.html?print=1*

Greenleaf, C. L., Jiménez, R. T., & Roller, C. M. (2002). Reclaiming secondary reading interventions: From limited to rich conceptions, from narrow to broad conversations. *Reading Research Quarterly, 37*, 484–496.

Grigg, W., Donahue, P. L., & Dion, G. (2007, February). *The nation's report card: 12th-grade reading and mathematics 2005*. U.S. Department of Education, Institute of Education Sciences, National Center for Education Statistics. Washington, DC: U.S. Government Printing Office. Retrieved March 8, 2007, from *www.nces.ed.gov/ pubsearch/pubsinfo.asp?pubid=2007468*

Hinchman, K., Alvermann, D., Boyd, F., Brozo, W. G., & Vacca, R. (2003/04). Supporting older students' in- and out-of-school literacies. *Journal of Adolescent and Adult Literacy, 47*, 304–310.

International Reading Association. (2006). *Standards for middle and high school literacy coaches*. Newark, DE: Author.

Irvin, J., Meltzer, J., & Dukes, M. (2007). *A leadership model for improving adolescent literacy*. Alexandria, VA: Association of Supervision and Curriculum Development.

Ivey, G., & Fisher, D. (2006). *Creating literacy rich schools for adolescents*. Alexandria, VA: Association for Supervision and Curriculum Development.

Kamil, M. L. (2003). *Adolescents and literacy: Reading for the 21st century*. Washington, DC: Alliance for Excellent Education.

Langer, J. A. (2002). *Effective literacy instruction: Building successful reading and writing programs*. Urbana, IL: National Council of Teachers of English.

Moore, D. W., Bean, T. W., Birdyshaw, D., & Rycik, J. A. for the Commission on Adolescent Literacy of the International Reading Association. (1999). *Adolescent literacy: A position statement.* Newark, DE: International Reading Association. Retrieved March 18, 2006, from *www.reading.org/resources/issues/positions_adolescent.html*

Moore, D. W., & Hinchman, K. (2006). *Teaching adolescents who struggle with reading: Practical strategies* (2nd ed.). Boston: Allyn & Bacon.

Moore, D. W., Readence, J. E., & Rickelman, R. (1983). An historical exploration of content area reading instruction. *Reading Research Quarterly, 18,* 419–438.

National Association of Secondary School Principals. (2005). *Creating a culture of literacy: A guide for middle and high school principals.* Reston, VA: Author.

Nielsen, L. (2006). Playing for real: Texts and the performance of identity. In D. E. Alvermann, K. A. Hinchman, D. W. Moore, S. F. Phelps, & D. R. Waff (Eds.), *Reconceptualizing the literacies in adolescents' lives* (2nd ed.; pp. 5–27). Mahwah, NJ: Erlbaum.

O'Brien, D., Stewart, R., & Moje, E. (1995). Why content literacy is difficult to infuse into the secondary school: Complexities of curriculum, pedagogy, and school culture. *Reading Research Quarterly, 30,* 442–463.

Pathways for All Students to Succeed Act. (n.d.). Retrieved June 2, 2007, from *www.murray.senate.gov/pass*

Professional Standards and Ethics Committee of the International Reading Association. (2004). *Standards for reading professionals: Revised 2003.* Newark, DE: International Reading Association.

Roller, C. (2006). *Reading and literacy coaches report on hiring requirements and duties survey.* Newark, DE: International Reading Association. Retrieved June 2, 2007, from *www.literacycoachingonline.org/library/resources/reading-3.html*

Schoenbach, R., Greenleaf, C., Cziko, C., & Hurwitz, L. (1999). *Reading for understanding: A guide to improving reading in middle and high school classrooms.* San Francisco: Jossey-Bass.

Shanahan, C. (2005). *Adolescent literacy intervention programs: Chart and program review guide.* Naperville, IL: Learning Point Associates. Retrieved May 11, 2007, from *www.learningpoint.org*

Shanklin, N. (2006, September). *What is effective literacy coaching?* Literacy Coaching Clearinghouse. Retrieved June 2, 2007, from *www.literacycoachingonline.org/briefs.html*

Torgesen, J. K., Houston, D. D., Rissman, L. M., Decker, S. M., Roberts, G., Vaughn, S., et al. (2007). *Academic literacy instruction for adolescents: A guidance document from the Center on Instruction.* Portsmouth, NH: RMC Research Corporation, Center on Instruction. Retrieved May 3, 2007, from *www.centeroninstruction.org*

Vacca, R. T., & Vacca, J. L. (2008). *Content area reading: Literacy and learning across the curriculum* (9th ed.). Boston: Allyn & Bacon.

Wepner, S. B., Strickland, D. S., & Feeley, J. T. (2002). *The administration and supervision of reading programs* (3rd ed.). Newark, DE: International Reading Association.

CHAPTER 19

Multiple Dimensions of Adolescent Literacy Teacher Education

Patricia L. Anders

This chapter:

- Describes the teacher education research base, providing a summary of both the preservice and inservice literatures.

- Highlights three challenges described by the literature (the increased demographic diversity of students who enter secondary classrooms; the expanding definition of literacy and text; and the language and culture of the disciplines, which are of particular importance in the secondary school).

- Concludes with a discussion of best practices, which earn that name because of the quality and quantity of research that support them.

This chapter explores theoretical and practical dimensions of teaching secondary teachers about adolescent literacy. Too many times, literacy is conceived as one-dimensional—do such-and-such and achieve a specific result. Practicing teachers are bombarded with this message, and teacher educators are receiving the same message, although to a lesser extent (Anders, Hoffman, & Duffy, 2000). In this chapter I hope to dispel this conceptualization. I intend this chapter to offer teacher educators principles and possibilities that acknowledge, celebrate, and honor the complexities of teaching teachers about theories and practices that contribute to young peoples' literacy development.

Professional development begins during teacher preparation and continues through the induction years and throughout the career. Teachers preparing to teach adolescents take classes that may or may not cohere and are likely to be of varying quality and perceived usefulness. Upon certification and employment, a teacher's career is launched. The first 3 years, the induction years, may or may not be enhanced with a program of mentoring and other forms of support. Throughout one's career, a teacher participates in hours of professional development, sometimes sponsored by the school district or school, and other times through graduate work, both of which may be of greater or lesser meaningfulness. The editors of this volume have asked me to write about what teacher educators and professional developers need to consider when teaching teachers about adolescent literacy.

As I approach this task, I recall my own story, and I wonder the extent to which my experiences are similar to those of my imagined audience. I had two preservice experiences as I prepared to be a secondary teacher, one at a small liberal arts college and the other at a research-one university. I married between my junior and senior years of college and transferred from the college to a university. My first program emphasized a model of teaching that I now realize would be categorized as a "technical model" (Schön, 1983). We evaluated textbooks and developed lesson plans to teach those textbooks. In contrast, the model of teaching emphasized at the university would likely be categorized as critical and constructivist, serving me in deeper, more generative ways (Richardson, 1997). Professors challenged me to create curriculum, emphasized critical thinking and meaningful, authentic, relevant activities for students, whom I was admonished to know well (see Goodlad, Soder, & Sirotnik, 1990, for an in-depth discussion of the differences between these teacher education programs).

Student teaching, which was a semester-long internship, and my induction years were filled with professional development activities. The district in which I taught was transitioning from a junior high model to a middle school model. The district provided intensive professional development for teachers as the "middle school idea" was adopted, and the faculty members of each school created its own particular brand of middle school. Also, I was teaching in the district's most demographically diverse school. In that school we white middle-class, mostly female teachers were challenged by kids who were ethnically and linguistically different from us. Because of our concern, the principal organized a professional development program based on Glasser's (1969) book, *Schools without Failure*. In addition to the district- and school-sponsored professional development, I was earning my master's degree in curriculum and instruction with a concentration on the courses required for the state's reading specialist endorsement. My particular master's degree program was especially designed to provide course work in what was called "secondary reading." The program was federally funded and was meant to help its participants become better classroom teachers. Twelve teachers forming a cohort group and representing different content areas participated. This period of my professional development was profoundly dynamic. I recall exciting sessions with ideas argued thoughtfully, applied, and refined. I remember caring and supportive instructors, professors and colleagues with whom I learned, studied, and evaluated ideas that I accepted and applied or considered and rejected.

After finishing my master's degree, I spent 5 years as a high school reading specialist. Instead of receiving professional development, I became one who led professional development. I enjoyed this position and its responsibilities greatly, but now that I think about it, I remember noticing that some colleagues who were close to my age and career stage appeared bored and frustrated with teaching.[1] I began my doctoral program while serving as a reading specialist, and was involved in research projects and writing for both presentation and publication. This intense professional development early in my career may have served to keep me in the field, whereas most of the teachers with whom I began my career left teaching.

Recently, as I prepared for a talk I was to give at a professional development meeting, I Googled *content-area literacy* and found a blog on which teachers were complaining about the professional development they were receiving. The teachers described their professional development experiences as redundant and irrelevant; as a teacher educator and professional developer, I worry continuously that I may be contributing to teachers' dissatisfaction and frustration! I imagine that most readers of this chapter, whether teacher educators, professional developers,[2] or those concerned with planning teacher education, have the same concern. What follows are principles, practices, and considerations that deserve our attention and may provide pathways for teacher educators to consider.

PRINCIPLES, PRACTICES, AND CONSIDERATIONS

A Snapshot of Literacy Teacher Education and Professional Development Research

Teacher educators usually have a lifelong commitment to teaching and learning—they are in for the long haul. Although this seems like a commonsense assumption, evidence for this claim is not easy to find. There is a dearth of research about teacher education programs, as pointed out by Zeichner (2006), who describes teacher education research as dominated by descriptions of the structure of programs and who

---

[1] It occurs to me that my induction years were extremely challenging. I was working with people whom I respected and liked, enjoying both the relationships and the ideas. I wonder if others were bored or frustrated because they were considerably more isolated than I was.

[2] For ease of reading and writing, I use the term *teacher educator* to designate both undergraduate and graduate teacher educators and those who provide professional development. If I present an idea that is of particular note to one of the subgroups, I make a distinction as to which group I am addressing.

decries the lack of well-done in-depth studies of educators, programs, practices, and outcomes. Not surprisingly, then, we know very little about those who practice teacher education, and what is known is mainly from self-report studies (see Hamilton & Pinnegar, 1998), which are valuable but not sufficient for drawing conclusions about the people who assume the role of "teacher educator" or the preservice and/or inservice programs they implement.

Some would argue that a tension exists as to whether the goal of teacher education is to maintain the status quo or to direct teachers toward some sort of change (Griffin, 1983). Richardson (1994), however, reminds us that change happens continuously, and so the real issue is whether we, as teacher educators, are directing some sort of change, whether the teachers themselves are agents of their own change, or whether change is happenstance.

For sure, there are instances when particular changes that are desired become the target for professional development. A technical inservice program, with the objective of transmitting information, is appropriate. For example, if the school is installing a new computer system, it makes sense that time would be devoted to teaching the teachers and staff about the system. It is also common for elementary schools to use top-down, direct-instruction-type professional development when a new reading or math program is adopted. Likewise, preservice teacher education meets various objectives—some of which are technical and easily transmitted, such as laws related to the placement of students in special programs, the various types of formal evaluation measures, and reviews of practices implicated by various theories. Technical transmission of knowledge, as a form of teacher education, is not the focus of this chapter. Although teachers are likely to appreciate the information, it is not likely that this sort of instruction contributes to developing a teacher's theories or practical understanding of teaching and learning. Rather this chapter focuses on teacher education that is intimately related to, and influential on, a teacher's developing identity as a teacher. This sort of teacher education is sometimes identified as being reflective.

Schön (1983), along with Zeichner and Liston (1996), provide more insights as to the differences between the "technical practitioner" and the "reflective practitioner." Both use the term *reflection* in a Deweyian sense, "to convey the sense of a teacher who is comfortable gazing upon and evaluating her practice, a teacher who is open to seeing differently and anew, and a teacher who has agency over her own practice" (Zeichner & Liston, p. 6). In this day of nationally imposed policy, state-level high-stakes tests, and calls for standardized national assessments, this may seem like a pipe dream. Nonetheless, experience and research tells us that working with young people on a day-to-day basis, "in the trenches," requires thinking teachers who make decisions based on empirical evidence on-the-fly as they engage and interact with adolescents. From where I sit, these are the sorts of teachers that America's students need.

Preservice Teacher Education

The state of literacy teacher education research is bleak. Recently, the International Reading Association sponsored a study (Risko et al., 2007) to review teacher education research and found only 75 studies that met trustworthiness criteria for investigations related to the preparation of reading teachers. In that corpus of work, 11 studies focused on content-area reading, with no set of studies that could be identified as "adolescent literacy" teacher preparation. Of those 11 studies, the researchers conducted the studies with their preservice teachers as research participants. None of the studies emphasized issues of diversity or made any apparent attempt to help transition the future teachers to the classroom, confirming the oft-made criticism that there is little coherence between teacher preparation and induction (Wideen, Mayer-Smith, & Moon, 1998).

Anders et al. (2000) began their review of teacher education research by claiming that

> [reading teacher education] . . . has received little attention from the reading research community. Reading researchers have attended to the reading process, drawing inferences and conducting studies to test their theories. Relatively few researchers have asked questions about the processes that teacher go through as they learn and continue to learn to teach reading. (p. 719)

This situation, albeit dismal, is not surprising when understood in the context provided by Bransford, Darling-Hammond, and LePage (2005), who explain that teacher education is informed by four categories of research: (1) basic research on learning, development, language acquisition, and social contexts; (2) research on how learning conditions and teaching practices influence learning; (3) research on how teacher learning affects teaching practices and student outcomes; and finally, (4) research on how teachers learn successful practices. Research on reading and literacy is considerably advanced in the first of these four categories, and as a field we are on the brink of becoming far more sophisticated in the second, third, and fourth. For example, the International Reading Association (2003) sponsored a study to investigate the characteristics of the most successful elementary reading teacher education programs and discovered features that were common across outstanding programs:

- A cohesive curriculum that addresses how students learn to read as well as effective teaching strategies.
- A variety of course-related field experiences in which excellent models for the teaching of reading are available.

- A clear vision of literacy, quality teaching, and quality preparation informing the program design.
- Responsive teaching that is adaptive to the needs of diverse candidates.
- An active learning community among faculty, mentor teachers, and students that supports shared norms of practice and continual learning and improvement.
- Continual assessment of candidates and the program to guide decisions.
- Adequate resources tied to the mission of the program.

No such study informs teacher educators for the preparation of secondary teachers. This is not surprising. Many of us who have long been associated with adolescent literacy, which historically has been variously labeled as secondary reading, content-area reading, and content-area literacy, often feel like stepchildren in the field of reading and/or literacy. This is likely to change in the near future, however. As discussed in previous chapters, attention to the importance of adolescent literacy is increasing for numerous reasons, including the achievement gap, the demands for students to achieve ever increasingly sophisticated literacy skills, and the incredible explosion of multiple literacies available to learners of all ages.

In most secondary teacher education programs, preservice teachers take one course with a title such as "content-area literacy/reading," "secondary reading," or "adolescent literacy." In these courses, professors are likely to emphasize principles and practices related to curriculum and instruction, the psychology of learning, and adolescent development (see, e.g., Anders & Guzzetti, 2005)—topics that have a substantial research base. Typically, little attention is paid to struggling readers at the secondary level because reading specialists—those who have completed graduate work in reading—customarily work with those students. The language research base, which should be incorporated into these courses, is not nearly as well developed as it is for emergent and beginning language learners (Anders & Pritchard, 1993; Valdés, Bunch, Snow, Lee, & Matos, 2005). There is a corpus of texts, articles, and syllabi, easily accessed on the Internet, for the teacher educator preparing to teach an adolescent-oriented course (see also Anders & Hinchman, 2008).

One challenge facing adolescent literacy educators is that the students in teacher preparation classes are diverse, representing a wide range of content areas and backgrounds. Some evidence suggests that these students hold several misconceptions that the teacher educator needs to challenge. For example, Gunstone and Slattery (1993) found that their students' beliefs and understandings about the teaching and learning of science changed only with long-term teacher education that incorporated preservice teachers participating in an "apprenticeship of observation" as a springboard to begin a reconstruction of their beliefs and understandings.

In addition to language and conceptual challenges, teacher educators and future teachers are confronted with ever increasingly broadened definitions of literacy and text—few modern classrooms rely on a single textbook as a resource; rather, teachers and students alike are experiencing and experimenting with a range of modalities for finding and negotiating information. A small but growing body of literature is describing these multiple literacies, particularly those used by adolescents outside of school (Alvermann, 2002; Xu, Chapter 3, this volume; Wilber, Chapter 4, this volume), but very little research describes the use of multiple literacies in the classroom.

Adolescent literacy teacher preparation is clearly in its infancy, although there is a historical legacy on which to build (Alvermann & Moore, 1991). The general sense seems to be that preservice teachers are not given adequate opportunities to develop much needed linguistic and language development understandings; that multiple literacies are ripe for use and investigation; and that psychological, pedagogical, and curriculum principles may be the central focus of instruction in most teacher education programs. As language and literacy teacher educators engage their colleagues in associated curricular areas—professors who specialize in educational foundations, adolescent development, and content-area methods—to create or revise their teacher education programs, they need to aim their discussions toward program coherence.

That's not to say that all professors need to have the same message or think alike. It means that "coherence should abide in the common ground among faculty around professional norms and expectations, as well as in the way that learning experiences are organized and conceptualized" (Shepherd, Hammerness, Darling-Hammond, & Rust, 2005, p. 294). Teacher education for secondary teachers will improve when priorities are realigned by educators, researchers, and policymakers to converge in ways that inform understandings of how teachers learn to employ best practices on the basis of linguistic and psychological developmental principles across multiple content areas and contexts. Further, teachers leaving their teacher education program should have the sense that they are at the beginning of a journey of lifelong learning that will be nurtured by what they gain from professional development and their reflection on their experiences.

Professional Development

The quantity of teacher education research in the area of professional development is somewhat more extensive than it is in preservice teacher education, due partly to the considerable literature on teacher beliefs and investigations related to teacher change. It is also the case that generalizations from professional development in settings other than the secondary school are often applicable. Richardson and Anders (2005) summarize these principles in the following list:

- Schoolwide purview: The professional development should involve everyone in the school in developing a school culture of improvement and be adapted to fit the particular school context.
- Long-term course: The professional development should be perceived as having impact over time and for the long term, and follow-up should be planned for and implemented.
- Consensus and commitment: Participants and administrators should agree as to the goals and vision of the professional development program.
- Adequate support: Funds should be made available for materials, outside speakers, and substitute teachers.
- Collegiality: Learning communities and group dialogue should be an integral part of the program.
- Subject matter: Focus should be placed on subject-matter content rather than generic teaching methods.
- Beliefs: Participants' existing beliefs should be acknowledged.
- Facilitators: An outside facilitator/staff developer should be involved.

The studies that contribute to the preceding list include small-scale investigations that focus on the nature of the teacher change process and on the development of an understanding of the elements of professional development processes, and large-scale studies that attempt to determine, describe, and/or test the factors/elements/aspects/characteristics of effective professional development programs. The first six characteristics from the above list are well known; the last four characteristics are the product of more current research and are likely to be overlooked or ignored in large-scale professional development programs because of the difficulty in implementing them and the possible sense of loss of control by those administering and directing the program. Nonetheless, they may be the make-or-break components of a successful secondary-level professional development program and, as such, are briefly discussed below.

Collegiality

The secondary school context has long been described as one of isolation for teachers (Lortie, 1975). In a typical drive-by, short-term, one-shot type of professional development, teachers can remain isolated from one another—never having to come to terms with their beliefs and practices, never having to share them in a public forum, and thereby not contributing to a community of learners or developing a shared sense of norms among colleagues. This sort of professional development may have the effect of reinforcing existing practices rather than challenging practices and providing a context for reexamining and critiquing oneself. Wilson and Berne (1999) report that teachers need opportunities to talk about subject matter, students, learning, and teaching in general. Courtney Cazden (2001) summarizes the importance of using intensive discourse in professional development. She points out that social interaction allows skilled teachers to demonstrate expert strategies to less skilled teachers and makes hidden thought processes public and shared. These communal interactions allow teachers to share and distribute information and cognitive burdens, providing for a richer context for learning. The resulting dialogue requires both language comprehension and language production, which results in demanding cognition and deeper processing of information. The social settings in which dialogue takes place provide spaces and opportunities for the development and establishment of community norms that honor thinking and intelligence. Little (2002) affirms Cazden's points by noting that a sense of community and healthy dialogue in a department or school provides space and opportunity for the establishment of a collegial norm of question asking and reflection about practices, programs, and theories.

Subject Matter

The good news is that teachers learn what they are taught. According to Hammerness, Darling-Hammond, Grossman, Rust, and Shulman (2005), past teacher education was often limited to a bit about classroom management and some "tricks of the trade" (p. 396). In some school districts, professional development continues to be characterized in this way with one-shot, sporadic in-service programs. The consensual recommendation among teacher education scholars, however, is for long-term professional development that targets subject matter and the transformation of that content knowledge by integrating it with pedagogical knowledge to construct practice (Richardson, 1997). Consider the broad influence of the National Writing Project.[3] In this program of professional development, teachers participate in the writing process and then carry that experience to their classroom as they work with their students and to their colleagues as they serve as teacher-leaders in their school and community. The success of the National Writing Project is replicated in other studies. For example, Lieberman and Wood (2003, as cited in Hammerness et al., 2005) found that when "teachers have opportunities to interact with their

---

[3]The website for the National Writing Project is *www.writingproject.org/contact.csp*; its address is National Writing Project, University of California, 2105 Bancroft Way, #1042, Berkeley, CA 94720-1042. Their many publications are listed at the website.

subject matter in ways that they aim for their own students to do (such as engaging in writing workshops, getting feedback on their own writing, giving critiques), they are more likely to engage in those practices in their classrooms" (p. 396).

Beliefs

Preservice teachers are influenced by the beliefs they bring to teacher education, as are inservice teachers. In many instances, inservice teachers are represented in the literature as recalcitrant and resistant to change. Richardson and Anders (Richardson, 1994) concluded from their study that when professional development takes teachers' beliefs into account, teachers are more likely to be willing participants in the professional development program. Peck (2002) reports on a professional development program that ignored teachers' beliefs and experiences and resulted in teachers feeling discouraged, devalued, and misunderstood.

Facilitators

A facilitator often works full- or part-time in a school and consults closely with teachers, often observing in classes, modeling practices by working with students, videotaping lessons and conducting extensive dialogue with the teachers. This is a very different role than that of a "staff developer" who visits, delivers, and leaves. A facilitator has a relationship with the teachers and partners with them to accomplish a shared vision. The research on the role of a facilitator is scanty; nonetheless, it is difficult to conceive of a professional development program that honors collaboration, dialogue, and the development of community norms without such a person.

Professional Development Programs

Examples of professional development programs that incorporate these principles are evident in the literature. Cooper and Jackson (2005) describe the programs of professional development provided by the National Urban Alliance—programs that provide many success stories about dramatic achievement for children of color. Their programs are tightly structured but are also responsive to the individual needs of the teachers and students in the school and district.

Two commercially available professional development programs that focus on adolescent literacy and that meet these requirements include CRISS (creating independence in student-owned strategies; Santa & Hayes, 2007) and the Reading Apprenticeship (Schoenbach, Greenleaf, Cziko, & Hurwitz, 1999). Both emphasize cognitive strategies, but do so with a focus on the secondary school.

Other models aimed at facilitating teacher change and growth through professional development include study groups, book clubs, and teacher research efforts. Kathy Short (Matlin & Short, 1996) facilitates study groups with teachers and principals to address their issues, questions, and needs. The study groups are organized around a particular theme or topic selected by the teachers or principals. Short provides resources that the participants read or view and then facilitates conversations based on the participants' response to those resources, particularly in relationship to their experiences. Flood, Lapp, Ranck-Buhr, and Moore (1995) create book clubs wherein teachers and their principal read multicultural literature as a means of discovering beliefs, attitudes, and practices related to students of diverse backgrounds. The books serve as a mediating tool for discovering these powerful insights, which also lead to changes in practice.

Simon Hole and Grace McEntee Hall (2003) use the professional development program, "Critical Friends" (Tripp, 1993), as a framework for inspiring teachers toward reflective practice. In this particular practice each teacher composes a story from practice; teachers then choose a story to discuss by answering questions such as "What happened?", "Why did it happen?", "What might it mean?", "What are the implications for practice?", and "What new insights have been learned?" Hole and McEntee Hall promote the storytelling accompanied by critical analysis as a terrific pathway of reflection for teachers.

The notion of the "Critical Friends" groups for professional development is well accepted by secondary teachers who participate in the National School Reform Faculty (NSRF). Silva reports on one such group that meets monthly as a community of learners, offering themselves to each other as consultants. One outcome of this particular group is that members have conducted research to address a question that is not addressed by the known literature or the experience of colleagues. In support of this group's professional development practice, which provides the group members with extensive learning opportunities, Silva quotes Linda Darling-Hammond (2000):

> [we formed our group] so that the complex practices envisioned by ambitious standards have a chance to be studied, debated, tried out, analyzed, retried and refined until they are well-understood and incorporated into the repertoire of those who teach and make decisions in schools. These opportunities must be collaborative rather than individualistic. (p. 223)

Other teacher groups and university/school partnerships engage in "teacher inquiry" or teacher research. Some use student work as a pathway to reflection, others use a schoolwide question or issue about which to conduct research. For example, one school with which I worked wondered if their students were learning the core conceptual vocabulary they were intentionally and conscientiously being taught across the curriculum. We designed a multiple-choice vocabulary test and gave it to all the students. Indeed, freshmen did far less well on the test than did seniors, and those few seniors who did not do well received special help before graduation.

This sampling of literature suggests that professional development that is likely to make a difference is constructed in such a way as to allow for teacher reflection and teacher research. The ideal program is one in which teachers are in charge of their careers and responsible for their development. Such programs provide opportunities for teachers to be critical literacy users themselves. Dozier, Johnston, and Rogers (2006) are teacher educators who practice this principle. In their book, *Critical Literacy, Critical Teaching*, they quote bell hooks, explaining that "most of us were taught in classrooms where styles of teaching reflected the notion of a single norm of thought and experience, which we were encouraged to believe, was universal" (p. 10), and then they describe the obstacles that are created from such a perspective:

- A narrow technical, hierarchical, and monological view of literacy that includes a systemic concern for conventions over meaning and personal involvement.
- Separation of in-school and out-of-school literacies.
- A view of teaching as telling.
- Unproductive representations of students couched in a language of deficit, standards, and normative frameworks that force attention to difficulties rather than assets.
- A goal of avoiding the display of incompetence. (p. 10)

My call for teacher educators to provide space and opportunity for teachers to develop critical perspectives and reflexivity relies on teachers having sound content and pedagogical knowledge, as is described in this volume. Other reliable sources include the content knowledge described in the International Reading Association/National Council of Teachers of English Standards for Reading Professionals, the references cited in this volume, publications such as the *Journal of Adolescent and Adult Literacy*, and other peer-reviewed journals. Educators can draw on foundational knowledge about content and pedagogy as they reflect upon critical and compelling issues.

A SAMPLING OF CHALLENGES AND ISSUES FACING ADOLESCENT LITERACY

The current issues discussed and described below are a sampling of what is compelling in the field of adolescent literacy as this chapter is being written: diverse student demographics, technology and multiple literacies, and the language and culture of the secondary school core curriculum. Although presented below as three separate subheadings, the contents of these sections overlap considerably.

Diverse Student Demographics

A reader might be tempted to skip this section—we all know about the sea change that is taking place in current U.S. education—states (e.g., California) where the "minority is the majority," classrooms with many students whose mother tongue is not English, and increasing numbers of students who live in poverty. It would be a mistake, however, to skip this section, because the situation described herein is about more than those headlines. Youth in our classrooms and around the world are members of an evolving culture that has never before been seen in history.

I recently read a Marge Piercy novel (*Sex Wars*, 2005) that described the lives of young people who immigrated to the U.S. from England in 1868. In the streets of New York, these young immigrants mingled with others from many parts of the world. On the pages of that novel, I read about the shifting boundaries of personal beliefs and behaviors as young people made their way in a society very different from the one in which they were born. They created new identities for themselves, identities that were barely recognizable by their relatives and acquaintances who arrived later. Now in the beginning years of the 21st century, an analogous situation is occurring, but the global contacts are not only face-to-face, they are also digitally virtual. Young people, especially, are in contact with one another on a global basis rather than only on the streets of a particular city.

The consequences of this global virtual migration are tremendous. George Lipsitz (2005) captures the dawning of this age in his inspirational foreword to a book, *Youthscapes*, in which he writes: " . . . the category of youth . . . as a social achievement, [is] not so much a given category based on biological age but a social position structured by the simultaneous powers of consumption, creativity, schooling, citizenship, surveillance, and social membership" (p. xiv). I share this source because, as educators, we need to recognize the ramifications of globalization on the youth in our classrooms—an injunction that is truer today than ever before. This is a day and age that calls upon us to know our students in ways that we have never before attempted.

As a college student, I recall being in the student union during the Vietnam War protests. I overheard students on the phone talking with peers at other universities around the country; they were coordinating protests and informing each other of the activities at their individual institutions. My generation had the telephone; today's generation has the Internet, which is a hundred times more empowering. National borders and different languages are no longer barriers to a youthful global community. These considerations, which I can only hint at here, are well documented in the literature and suggest that as educators we need to open our eyes and pay attention to the youth who populate our classrooms.

In classrooms around the country are students who have risked their lives to cross borders to attend our schools; their backgrounds of experiences need to be linked to our curriculum and to our practices. There are students whose backgrounds are closely wedded to the cultures of parents and grandparents that are far different from the backgrounds of those who are doing the teaching. Schooling works well when the teachers know their students intimately. Best practices need to be transformed in ways that are culturally sensitive and that are sensible to the students who are being asked to engage them.

We have good knowledge about the psychology of learning, but we know little about the interaction of culture and learning. There are some studies, however, to guide us. The recent award-winning book by Gonzalez, Moll, and Amanti (2005) is one such source. In that book, teachers are encouraged to become intimately involved in the communities of their students to learn of the possible connections that can be made from the community's "funds of knowledge" and the school curriculum. A tried-and-true axiom of teacher education is that teachers need to know their students. Cognitive psychology, especially the assumptions related to prior knowledge, is well known and accepted. What is less well understood are the dynamics of youth culture and learning—a serious area that is undertheorized and demands research.

An artifact of culture is language. Just as the cultures in classrooms are diverse, so is the language that students bring to the classroom. Valdés et al. (2005) summarize the language-related "big ideas" that all teachers should understand:

- Speakers of every language in the world use many different varieties or dialects depending on regional and class origins. . . . Such differences are a natural result of human language development and not a "problem" to be rectified.
- Children come to school as competent speakers of the varieties of language spoken in their homes and communities. All children are not necessarily literate in the language they speak, but they can learn to be literate in that language.
- All speakers use many different registers and styles of English, which vary by context. The classroom is a context for academic English and teachers need to instruct students in the conventions of school language such as acquiring the ways to discuss ideas, to understand texts, and to demonstrate learning through modeling, practice, and feedback. (pp. 59–60)

These principles are particularly relevant to secondary teachers who need to deal not only with the languages students bring to the classroom, but are also responsible for helping students to become literate in the particular content areas.

Technology and Multiple Literacies

This is an exciting but daunting time for young people and their teachers in the secondary school. They are offered challenging content to engage and learn through multiple modes of communication. Students are able to join NASA scientists as they explore Mars simply by uploading a website. Virtual interviews are available with authors, and students can interact with other students anywhere in the world. The exciting potential of multiple literacies was powerfully brought home at a conference sponsored by the National Council of Teachers of English Assembly for Research in February 2007. At that conference, researchers from around the world acquainted participants with the multiple literacies that students were using to engage their universe. One of the keynoter speakers, Jay Lemke (2007), elaborated on several of the daunting realities of current schooling practices and multiple literacies:

- Our curricula exclude domains of interest to students, including popular culture and social networking.
- Our schooling structures enforce superficiality, with time frames too short for in-depth learning.
- Students are finding better ways to support their own literacy interests in online peer networking communities.
- Commercial media are winning their hearts and minds.

These concerns challenge secondary educators to rethink the nature of curriculum and instruction in the secondary school. If teachers were to embrace a multiple literacies perspective, they would enthusiastically adopt a stance that invites students to make connections across texts and media. They would assist students in developing peer networks and becoming critical thinkers and users of all sorts of media, helping them to resist commercial interests for the academic.

That's not to say that we all understand how to do this. Much research is needed; Lemke (2007) provides three particular topics to which literacy education researchers need to attend:

1. We need to understand what is and is not workable in bringing pop culture and online new media literacies into close connection within school learning and traditionally valued literature works in all media.
2. We need to re-imagine literacy education as an experiential trajectory for students that crosses between in-school and after-school

contexts, home-based and community-based settings, and online and peer-network-supported sites of literature practice. When we enforce boundaries, students learn in more fragmented ways and do not apply critical skills across the board.

3. We need to add to our view of literacy as a generic individual competence a broader notion of literature communities and literate social networks where members contribute on the basis of their unique and diverse literacy profiles.[4]

Lemke's arguments are compelling, but they are not an easy sell due to current policymakers devoted to the values of teacher accountability and standardization of curriculum and instruction. Maira and Soep (2005) describe another reason for the hard sell: As young people leap nationalistic boundaries by exploring virtual spaces around the globe, those with an investment in the status quo are likely to promote nationalism. In Arizona alone the current headlines reflect this stance: A wall is being built across the desert between Arizona and Mexico (dividing families and limiting commercial and educational opportunities); 4 hours of daily English language learning is mandated for students who are speakers of other languages (an edict from the Arizona State Department of Education); and a law is passed by the Arizona legislature that a U.S. flag be hung in each Arizona classroom receiving state funding.

These local examples portend a crisis in secondary literacy teacher education, a clash between the ways in which teachers need to respond to issues of language and culture that are radically different from the status quo and those legislators and policymakers who strive to maintain the status quo.

Language and Culture of the Secondary Core Curriculum

As compelling and interesting as the foregoing discussion might be, it is likely to be peripheral and far reaching next to the local concerns of most secondary teachers and their teacher educators. That is, each secondary school is immediately faced by two issues: students who are poorly handling the literacy demands of the existing secondary curriculum, and teachers who need to improve their capacity to invite and engage students in the language and culture of the disciplines.

Discussion of these two issues appropriately begins by thinking about adolescent development. Although variability in normal development is generally understood by teachers in the early grades, it is as least as great—but often less appreciated—in the adolescent years, offering special

---

[4]Lemke concluded his talk with the point that obviously the current high-stakes tests to which adolescents are subjected are completely inadequate to measure the reality of their literate lives.

challenges to those teaching in middle and high schools. Wide variability in physical development and in the development of sexual characteristics is most obvious, but there are also major differences in cognitive, linguistic, and social development among 12- to 16-year-olds. Differences in height and physical maturation, along with the cultural meanings attached to these characteristics, have consequences for self-concept, self-esteem, and self-confidence. Differences in the development of cognitive, linguistic and social skills have consequences for academic progress, especially true when students are confronted with departmentalized, impersonal school environments with more rigid expectations for what is learned and how it is to be mastered and displayed. Eccles et al. (1993) note:

> These different developmental trajectories intersect with the developmental tasks of adolescents in American society—expectations with respect to independence, competence, and identity construction in relation to gender, sexuality, race, and culture, among other factors. The mix of these developmental trajectories in a class of adolescents means that the teachers in middle school and high school classrooms will necessarily be confronted with dealing with a large range of developmental needs. (p. 99)

If teachers don't understand these huge ranges in developmental norms, they can easily categorize students by race and language differences—a practice that often serves to segregate students from their developmentally different peers and limit their opportunities for engaging and interesting curriculum and instruction (Eckert, 1989), thereby further limiting their developmental potential.

These developmental pathways must govern whatever programs of instruction are offered to secondary struggling readers. At present, eight federally funded research projects are exploring issues related to struggling readers. These programs of instructional research will provide further insights as to the interventions that are appropriate and helpful. Hopefully their insights will suggest ways for secondary readers who are viewed as unsuccessful to come to revalue themselves and to appreciate the benefits of literacy. Too many times youth become pathologically depressed by their status as poor readers and are beaten down by those who try to get them to read on grade level (Dozier et al., 2006).

Whatever programs of instruction are offered, they must be presented in the context of a developmental program in which all students are given literacy instruction across the curriculum. If the above description of adolescent development is taken seriously, it is easy to recognize that *all* adolescents are in need of instruction related to the language of the disciplines. That is to say, each discipline has a language that is peculiar to that discipline. Think of the different meanings even simple words have in different disciplines. An example is the word *root*. In math class this term refers to finding the square root; in social studies, students might be asked to "discover their roots"; in English, students might study the roots of words; and in biology, students might be studying the structure of plant and tree roots.

Likewise, each discipline has a particular culture—artifacts, tools, and ways of doing. Consider, for example, how the discipline of history takes advantage of timelines and maps and, in contrast, how science relies on experimentation and uses tools such as microscopes, beakers, and slides. These examples are just the tip of the iceberg—each discipline *is* a discipline because of the structure of the knowledge represented. Bruner (1960/2003) suggests that "grasping a structure of a subject is understanding it in a way that permits many other things to be related to it meaningfully. To learn structure, in short, is to learn how things are related" (p. 7).

In a recently completed dissertation, McArthur (2007) explored the ways that content-area teachers in preparation transformed the literacy practices being taught in a content-area literacy class to fit with the structure of their disciplines, their ways of knowing. She found that although principles of good literacy instruction remained intact, future teachers adopted the practices to fit their conceptions of the ways things are done in different disciplines. She explained her observation by citing King and Brownell (1966), who proposed that characteristics of the disciplines provide a framework for the creation of curriculum and instruction. This notion is supported by Darling-Hammond and Bransford (2005), who write:

> The discussion of expertise in the earlier part of this chapter emphasized the importance of well-connected knowledge that is organized around "big ideas of the disciplines." For example, we noted that the concept of life cycles can be learned as a set of isolated facts (for example, students memorize the life cycle of some organism) or as an organizing principle that provides a basis for thinking about a variety of issues, including ways to prevent species from becoming endangered, ways to intervene to control pests, and so forth. (p. 86)

Students who have the opportunity to learn the "big ideas of the disciplines" are more likely to be able to remember the information for a lifetime and also use those big ideas as organizing features to learn new information.

These three current challenges facing preservice and inservice teachers are merely exemplars of the sorts of issues to which teacher educators need to respond in innovative and creative ways. The term *best practices* might suggest to some that there are quick-and-easy recipes for teaching and learning. I hope this chapter has helped to dispel this myth. There might well be "good ideas" with varying degrees of related research or theory to justify their use, but what we have to help ourselves and teachers understand is that practices are not without context. Professional development needs to be a curriculum that makes space for teachers to exert agency over the construction of their own professionalism.

CONCLUSION

Throughout this book, best practices related to adolescent literacy programs, curriculum, and instruction are described. A teacher, reading specialist, or literacy coach becomes facile with these strategies and practices over time and through a process of awareness, experimentation, and reflection. The job of teacher educators is to provide a context for those critical aspects of teacher learning and development. But it is also our responsibility to provide spaces and opportunities for reflection—for teachers to take control of their own development, to make it a norm in the profession that teachers are self-aware, critical, and reflective. At present, this meta-level is not the norm. Fostering it is a challenge for all of us and can only be addressed by our own reflection, inquiry, and conceptualization of literacy teacher education.

Several questions that are ripe for research come to mind. For example, it would be fascinating to engage teachers and the adolescents with whom they work in questions and inquiry projects related to the social nature of literacy and its relationship to issues of local and global social justice. Further, the field desperately needs much more complicated and nuanced assessment measures of both teachers and students. The particulars of content-area literacy need further investigations. Teachers and teacher educators would benefit from close studies of literacy in action in each of the content areas. And, as this chapter has demonstrated, intense in-depth research is needed on teacher education at both the preservice and inservice levels.

Clearly, the messages of this volume are not the norm. Those of us in the field of adolescent literacy have a long row to hoe with regard to promoting our ideas and practices. We who contributed to this volume are committed to acknowledging the complexities of adolescent literacy development. We recognize that practice cannot be essentialized and reduced to "best," but instead must be contextualized and transformed to meet the needs of diverse and dynamic and young people.

DISCUSSION AND ACTIVITIES

1. What would you expect new teachers of adolescents to know about teaching litereracy across the curriculum when they come to your school? What kind of support would they need, and how could you help them?

2. Imagine yourself charged with planning professional development in literacy instruction for secondary teachers in your school. How would you begin to orchestrate such activities, and what would the activities be?

3. Imagine yourself participating in professional development that did not seem to be satisfying your needs. How could you address this dissatisfaction in a positive way? How could you become involved in further planning efforts to shape professional development in your school?

REFERENCES

Alvermann, D. E. (Ed.). (2002). *Adolescents and literacies in a digital world.* New York: Lang.

Alvermann, D. E., & Moore, D. W. (1991). Secondary schools. In R. Barr, M. L. Kamil, P. B. Mosenthal, & P. D. Pearson (Eds.), *Handbook of reading research* (Vol. 2, pp. 951–983). New York: Longman.

Anders, P. L., & Guzzetti, B. (2005). *Content area literacy instruction.* Mahwah, NJ: Erlbaum.

Anders, P. L., & Hinchman, K. (2008). Content area literacy. In L Wilkinson, L. Morrow, & V. Chou (Eds.), *Improving the preparation of teachers of reading in urban settings: Policy, practice, and pedagogy* (pp. 111–115). Newark, DE: International Reading Association.

Anders, P. L., Hoffman, J. V., & Duffy, G. G. (2000). Teaching teachers to teach reading: Paradigm shifts, persistent problems, and challenges. In M. L. Kamil, P. B. Mosenthal, P. D. Pearson, & R. Barr (Eds.), *Handbook of reading research* (Vol. 3, pp. 719–742). Mahwah, NJ: Erlbaum.

Anders, P. L., & Pritchard, T. G. (1993). Integrated language curriculum and instruction for the middle grades. *Elementary School Journal, 93*(5) 611–624.

Bransford, J., Darling-Hammond, L., & LePage, P. (2005). Introduction. In L. Darling-Hammond & J. Bransford (Eds.), *Preparing teachers for a changing world: What teachers should learn and be able to do* (pp. 1–39). San Francisco: Jossey-Bass.

Bruner, J. S. (2003). *The process of education: A landmark in educational theory.* Cambridge, MA: Harvard University Press. (Original work published 1960)

Cazden, C. (2001). *Classroom discourse: The language of teaching and learning* (2nd ed.). Portsmouth, NH: Heinemann.

Cooper, E. J., & Jackson, Y. (2005). In response to Richardson and Anders: Professional preparation and development of teachers in literacy instruction for urban settings. In J. Flood & P. Anders (Eds.), *The literacy development of students in urban schools: Research and policy* (pp. 231–240). Newark, DE: International Reading Association.

Darling-Hammond, L. (2000). *The right to learn: A blueprint for creating schools that work.* San Francisco: Jossey-Bass.

Darling-Hammond, L., & Bransford, J. (Eds.). (2005). *Preparing teachers for a changing world: What teachers should learn and be able to do.* San Francisco: Jossey-Bass.

Dozier, C., Johnston, P., & Rogers, R. (2006). *Critical literacy, critical teaching: Tools for preparing responsive teachers.* New York: Teachers College Press.

Eccles, J. S., Midgley, C., Wigfield, A., Buchanan, C. M., Reuman, D., & Maclver, D. (1993). Development during adolescence: The impact of stage/environment fit on young adolescents' experiences in schools and in families. *American Psychologist, 48*(2), 90–101.

Eckert, P. (1989). *Jocks and burnouts: Social categories and identity in the high school.* New York: Teachers College Press.

Flood, J., Lapp, D., Ranck-Buhr, W., & Moore, J. (1995). What happens when teachers get together to talk about books? Gaining a multicultural perspective from literature. *Reading Teacher, 48,* 720–723.

Glasser, W. (1969). *Schools without failure.* New York: Harper & Row.

Gonzalez, N., Moll, L. C., & Amanti, C. (2005). *Funds of knowledge: Theorizing practices in households, communities, and classrooms.* Mahwah, NJ: Erlbaum.

Goodlad, J. I., Soder, R., & Sirotnik, K. A. (Eds.). (1990). *Places where teachers are taught.* San Francisco: Jossey-Bass.

Griffin, G. (1983). The work of staff development. In G. Griffin (Ed.), *Staff development* (pp. 1–12). Chicago: University of Chicago Press.

Gunstone, R. G., & Slattery, M. (1993). A case study of development in pre-service science teachers. *Science Education, 77*(1), 47–73.

Hamilton, M. L., & Pinnegar, S. (1998). The value and promise of self-study. In M. L. Hamilton (Ed.), *Reconceptualizing teaching practice* (pp. 235–246). London: Falmer Press.

Hammerness, K., Darling-Hammond, L., Grossman, P., Rust, F., & Shulman, L. (2005). The design of teacher education programs. In L. Darling-Hammond & J. Bransford (Eds.), *Preparing teachers for a changing world: What teachers should learn and be able to do* (pp. 390–441). San Francisco: Jossey-Bass.

Hole, S., & McEntee Hall, G. (2003). Reflection is at the heart of practice. In G. McEntee Hall et al. (Eds.), *At the heart of teaching: A guide to reflective practice* (pp. 50–59). New York: Teachers College Press.

International Reading Association. (2003). *Prepared to make a difference: Research evidence on how some of America's best college programs prepare teachers of reading.* Newark, DE: Author.

King, A. R., & Brownell, J. A. (1966). *The curriculum and the disciplines of knowledge: A theory of curriculum practice.* New York: Wiley.

Lemke, J. (2007, February). *New media and new learning communities.* Paper presented at the annual meeting of the National Council of Teachers of English assembly for research, Nashville, TN.

Lipsitz, G. (2005). Foreword: Midnight's children: Youth culture in the age of globalization. In S. Maira & E. Soep (Eds.), *Youthscapes* (pp. vii–xiv). Philadelphia: University of Pennsylvania Press.

Little, J. W. (2002). Locating learning in teachers' communities of practice: Opening up problems of analysis in records of everyday work. *Teaching and Teacher Education, 18*(8), 917–946.

Lortie, D. (1975). *Schoolteacher: A sociological study.* Chicago: University of Chicago Press.

Maira, S., & Soep, E. (2005). *Youthscapes: The popular, the national, the global.* Philadelphia: University of Pennsylvania Press.

Matlin, M. L., & Short, K. G. (1996). Study groups: Inviting teachers to learn together. In K. Whitmore & Y. Goodman (Eds.), *Whole language voices in teacher education* (pp. 85–92). York, ME: Stenhouse.

McArthur, K. G. (2007). *"What more is literacy?" The language of secondary preservice teachers about reading and content.* Unpublished doctoral dissertation. University of Arizona, Tucson, AZ.

Peck, S. (2002). "I do have this right. You can't strip that from me": Valuing teachers' knowledge during literacy instructional change. In D. L. Schallert, C. M. Fairbanks, J. Worthy, B. Maloch, & J. V. Hoffman (Eds.), *51st yearbook of the National Reading Conference* (pp. 344–356). Oak Creek, WI: National Reading Conference.

Piercy, M. (2005). *Sex wars.* New York: Penguin Books.

Richardson, V. (Ed.). (1994). *Teacher change and the staff development process: A case in reading instruction.* New York: Teachers College Press.

Richardson, V. (1997). Constructivist teaching and teacher education: Theory and practice. In V. Richardson (Ed.), *Constructivist teacher education: Building a world of new understandings* (pp. 3–14). Washington, DC: Falmer Press.

Richardson, V., & Anders, P. (2005). Professional development of teachers. In J. Flood & P. Anders (Eds.), *The literacy development of students in urban schools: Research and policy* (pp. 205–230). Newark, DE: International Reading Association.

Risko, V. J., Roller, Cummins, C., Bean, R., Block, C., Anders, P., et al. (2007). *A critical review of the research on teacher preparation for reading instruction.* Newark, DE: International Reading Association.

Santa, C. M., & Hayes, R. (2007). *Is CRISS based on solid research? You bet!* Retrieved July 18, 2007, from *www.projectcriss.com/prc/pages/training/articles*

Schoenbach, R., Greenleaf, C., Cziko, C., & Hurwitz, L. (1999). *Reading for understanding: A guide to improving reading in middle and high school classrooms.* San Francisco: Jossey-Bass.

Schön, D. (1983). *The reflective practitioner.* New York: Basic Books.

Shepherd, L., Hammerness, K., Darling-Hammond, L., & Rust, F. (2005). Assessment. In L. Darling-Hammond & J. Bransford (Eds.), *Preparing teachers for a changing world: What teachers should learn and be able to do* (pp. 275–326). San Francisco: Jossey-Bass.

Silva, P. (2003). Linking student learning to teacher practice through critical friends groups. In G. McEntee Hall et al. (Eds.), *At the heart of teaching: A guide to reflective practice* (pp. 34–40). New York: Teachers College Press.

Tripp, D. (1993). *Critical incidents in teaching: Developing professional judgment.* New York: Routledge.

Valdés, G., Bunch, G., Snow, C., Lee, C., & Matos, L. (2005). Enhancing the development of students' languages(s). In L. Darling-Hammond & J. Bransford (Eds.), *Preparing teachers for a changing world: What teachers should learn and be able to do* (pp. 126–168). San Francisco: Jossey-Bass.

Wideen, M., Mayer-Smith, J., & Moon, B. (1998). A critical analysis of the research on learning to teach: Making the case for an ecological perspective on inquiry. *Review of Educational Research, 68*(2), 130–178.

Wilson, S., & Berne, J. (1999). Teacher learning and the acquisition of professional knowledge: An examination of research on contemporary professional development. In A. Iran Nejad & P. D. Pearson (Eds.), *Review of research in education* (Vol. 24, pp. 173–209). Washington, DC: American Educational Research Association.

Zeichner, K. (2006). Studying teacher education programs: Enriching and enlarging the inquiry. In C. F. Conrad & R. C. Serlin (Eds.). *The Sage handbook for research in education: Engaging ideas and enriching inquiry* (pp. 79–94). Thousand Oaks, CA: Sage.

Zeichner, K., & Liston, D. (1996). *Reflective teaching: An introduction.* Mahwah, NJ: Erlbaum.

Index

Page numbers followed by an *f* or a *t* indicate figures or tables.

361